Don't Miss the Miracles

A Memoir

CHUCK JOHNSTON

*Sometimes you're having a great
time with Chuck, and you realize—this will probably
make it into tomorrow's journal entry. For decades, Chuck
has risen early each morning to pray and reflect on the previous day.
The last paragraph or two in each entry has always lived under the same
heading—Don't Miss the Miracles. Rather than a listing of his personal exploits
or heroics, Chuck's "miracles" have almost always manifested in the form of
friendship, with family first, but also with anyone else who ventured into his
path. The events and interactions he recorded were at times painful, other times
hilarious, and most often just ordinary. But Chuck has always held to this
truth— it was all sacred. This memoir, pieced together from memories,
pictures and journals, chronicles the last eighty years (give or take)
of the miracles he witnessed along the way—from Buckhead
to Bankhead. — Terrell Gilbert, friend,
co-worker and son-in-law*

ISBN: 9780578683867   Paperback
        9781087943114   Hardcover
        9780578839349   Digital

        Library of Congress number: 2021902222

Published by Grove Park Books, Atlanta, Georgia

Website: www.chuckjohnstonmemoir.com

Cover photo: The author at Chamrousse, French Alps – 1965

Editing and design: Emily Carmain, Noteworthy Editing

DEDICATION

Many have poured into my life, but none to the extent of my mother,
Jane Dillon Johnston (JDJ), and my wife, JoElyn Jones Johnston
(JJJ). Each has given up part of herself for me. How do I ever repay
that? (I don't.) They play leading roles in the story that follows. To
them I dedicate this memoir.

ACKNOWLEDGMENTS

Too many have taken a hand in this memoir to mention here, but I will take
a stab at it. While Karen Cone labored to transcribe years of my handwritten
journals, daughter Evelyn Anne Clausen encouraged me to test my memory of
episodes in my past life, and then she provided prompts and assignments along
the way.

Emily Carmain, a highly regarded professional editor, humbled herself to take
up my cause—I being much more naïve than some of her other clients about what
goes into putting a book together. She has made something amateurish appear
professional, and for that I'm grateful.

My wife, JoElyn, daughter Jane, son-in-law Terrell, son-in-law Jonathan,
brothers Dick, Dillon, and Warren have edited or cheer-led or both. Their stamp
is on this book one way or another.

I am truly a part of all whom I have met. Yet many of you who have been a
big part of my life will not find your names in this book. God has abundantly
lavished me with friends who have impacted me significantly. Just know that you
will appear in Memoir II, should I live long enough and should my memory hold.

TABLE OF CONTENTS

LOOKING AT LIFE AND TIME AT AGE TWENTY-TWO

There seems to be within me at the close of certain days the urge to write down the happenings of those days. There is no need for anyone to read what I write. As a matter of fact, I can't imagine anyone having the interest or the patience to read more than a page or so. It is so hard for one human to share an experience or a feeling with another.

The events which I am most compelled to write about at present are those which lie behind. It seems that a lot of profound things have happened to me in my twenty-two and a half years. Writing about the past might be an indication that I am past the peak of youth and am now headed down the road towards slow but steady decay. At the close of certain days I will enter in my Journal a section of recollection.

I, too, look forward to the future. I will make no prediction. I have no ambition to be great; I have not the least fiber of greatness within me. I will be content if I can live each day as though it were my last—drinking in the simple wonder of the flashing minutes. I hope I can become less dependent on "things" for my happiness and can turn more and more to those things on which no monetary value can be placed. I have only begun to form myself as a completed person. This must be my task.

Signed:

Chuck Johnston
August 10, 1963

PREFACE

Why I Want to Write Memoir

I was first nudged as to how I would spend much of my retirement by realizing that I had fifty-some years of journals that extend back to my early twenties. I wanted to go back in time and see what I said. While I waited to have some of the early handwritten journals transcribed, I experimented with what I might be able to remember. I began reading noted writers of memoir (e.g., Vladimir Nabokov), and several of them counseled that memory was as valid an account of an event as an at-the-time written account. So I moved from "history" via the journals to "memory." I used the phrase from Nabokov's memoir title to trigger my writing: "Memory, speak about Grandpa," and I was off and running.

To Understand a Span of Life

I am willing to use my story to shed some light on how we cover our given span of years, but to do so I must be honest and open. Do I really want to expose my true self to others or even to myself? Here is a first truth you should know: I have for the better part of seventy-something years tried to ignore what is deep, deep down inside where I don't even know it—a phrase found in a children's book, *I'll Fix Anthony* (one of JoElyn's favorites that she often read to our daughters). I haven't wanted to see it or know it.

"Some men see things as they are and ask why. I dream of things that never were and ask why not." — *Robert Kennedy*

I have stifled emotions, thinking for the most part that these are the bad/evil side of myself. Whether it was sexual desires that haunted my youth and beyond or my desire to put a football tackle on my mom when she was obnoxiously drunk, I suppressed my emotions. *Suppressed* is not a strong enough word. *Abolish* or *annihilate* might come closer to describing my quickly developed skill at burying emotion so deeply, quickly, and thoroughly that these emotions became hidden from me.

Part of what I want to accomplish in this memoir is to deconstruct myself so that at the end I can say, "Oh, that's who I *really* am." From early on, I have constructed myself to be "one of the Johnston boys" and, on top of that, to manage life through a moral template borrowed whole from Peachtree Road

Presbyterian's youth program and from North Fulton's Student Christian Fellowship. I have wanted to be a successful boy, a good boy, a fun boy—all of that within strict bounds, of course.

I want to understand my own span of years. We can talk until we are blue in the face and not reveal ourselves as effectively as we can do in writing. With a written account, I can go back over it, trying to make sense of what I have said in writing. I will never profess to know all of human nature, but let me embark on the equally impossible undertaking of understanding my own life and the part others have played in that life. Let me take a vow of honesty, something that was missing in how I lived a good bit of my life.

My sense (my memory) is that up to the point of this writing I have lived a remarkably happy life. Why?

I think that my Biblical perspective must be largely responsible for the overarching grade of "happy," because I've certainly had my share of pain with people, and I haven't run away from that pain. In fact, in some ways I have walked into it. My ability to function within the upside possibilities via the power of positive thinking has sometimes put me into positions for which I wasn't well suited. But I had to try to find out whether or not these were doable career choices. Would I have been so noble if I had known the outcomes in California or at the Atlanta Ballet, to use two examples? Herein lies the beauty of not knowing what the future holds.

"The emphasis [among Africans] on life as a continuum reminded each family member of their connection to those who preceded them and those who will follow. ... Our practices pointed beyond us toward ancestors and progeny." —Barbara Holmes, Joy Unspeakable

I wouldn't erase a single incident or major undertaking in my life. By engaging in this writing, I'm seeing that each day there is something that contributes to the next day or the next year. So maybe that's how I can say in good conscience that "I have lived a remarkably happy life." I believe that every aspect of my life is ordained. I will not here debate whether the aspects are pre-ordained or just made to fit together after the fact.

My simple faith has operated somewhat on slogans of the faith: "I can do all things through Christ Who strengthens me," or "all things work together for good." While my Biblical understanding has certainly grown in spurts throughout my life, I now realize that it's been a childlike faith that has carried me through. It's only now that I need a more mature faith, now that I near the point at which this life as I know it will draw to a close. But let me begin in a somewhat chronological order.

PART ONE

The Early Years (Birth to 21)

Chapter 1: Grandpa

Maternal grandfather Walter Solomon Dillon was born December 13, 1874, and died in 1953 at age 78. He and Big Gram are buried at Westview Cemetery. Grandpa was the third oldest of seven children. Grandpa's parents, my great-grandparents, were Evangeline Arford (1855-1937) and Wesley Taylor Dillon (1847-1885) of Elnora, Indiana.

Grandpa, the Scholar

On Piedmont Road, just north of Peachtree Road in Buckhead, there were two driveways and a grass strip with a big clump of bushes separating our home growing up from that of Walter and Agnes Dillon, my maternal grandparents. In fact, the site of our home, with plenty of front and back yard, was for decades their side yard. We started building at the end of WWII, so I'm guessing the work began late in the fall of '45 and was completed just before Warren's birth, June 23, 1946. Our house was brick painted white, with a front porch running to the right of the living room plate-glass window, and a same-size porch running above it.

Often, when as a single-digit kid I would get up in the middle of the night to go to the bathroom, I would look out our upstairs bathroom window and see a little desk lamp shining out of the darkness on Big Gram and Grandpa's glass porch. It was Grandpa studying or writing. It was probably more like 5 a.m. than the middle of the night, and this was the way Grandpa started his day.

It was on the glass porch in this early hour that Grandpa wrote his weekly editorial for the Lions Club *News*. He was a founding member of the Atlanta Lions Club (est. 1920) and served two terms as its president starting in 1928. He obviously was strongly associated as a Lion because the first lion cub obtained by the Atlanta Zoo was named "Walter."

I remember his writing favorably about Dwight Eisenhower's candidacy for president. This took a little bit of courage since the South was overwhelmingly in the Democratic Party camp and Eisenhower was running as a Republican. I learned to love Abraham Lincoln more from one of Grandpa's columns. Most of Grandpa's columns were not about politics, but more about values that were imbued in an Indiana farm boy who went on to be included in *Great Men of the South*, a thick tome about men who made a difference, whether in Jackson, Memphis, Charleston, Birmingham, or Atlanta.

He went to the University of Illinois Law School. He finished law school in 1900, practiced law for eight years with a Chicago law firm, and married Agnes Nelson of Hazlehurst, Mississippi, in the middle of those eight years, in 1904. Just after his marriage, the Chicago law firm sent him for a stint to work with a mining company in Mexico, and his young bride, Agnes, went with him. Grandpa came to Atlanta in 1909, the same year in which Jane (aka Mom), the older of his two daughters, was born (September 23).

Of his practice of law in Atlanta, the 1922 edition of *Men of the South* had the following to say:

> "Among the men of learning and ability who are contributing to the prestige of the Atlanta bar is Walter S. Dillon, senior member of the well-known law firm of Dillon, Calhoun & Dillon [Commercial law]. Mr. Dillon ... is one of the city's most successful attorneys.... Mr. Dillon manifests a deep interest in municipal affairs and for one term represented the fourth ward in the common council.... Mr. Dillon represents the highest type of citizenship and among his fellow practitioners is recognized as a lawyer of high attainments who respects the unwritten ethics of the profession."

Grandpa's practice of law ended prematurely when he had a stroke about 1943. In the 1940s when I can first remember him, he was slightly stooped and walked with a cane, but he had no other ill effects of the stroke that I picked up on.

Grandpa, the Teacher

Here on the glass porch Grandpa would read poems to me and my brothers from *One Hundred and One Famous Poems.* He may have had another book of poems or two because it seems that we got an extra dose of Frost, Sandburg, and Vachel Lindsay, but this could have come from Mom. I was easily stirred by heroism. "The Charge of the Light Brigade" and "O Captain! My Captain!" were ones we heard often from *One Hundred and One Famous Poem*s.

It was on this glass porch that we prepared for summer meetings of the Noah Webster Club. Grandpa created this idea as a way to hook in his rambunctious grandsons, and he named the club after Webster, an English-language spelling reformer. We bought into the whole idea enthusiastically, drawing heavily on our set of Compton Encyclopedias. The meetings themselves more likely were held in the living room adjacent to this porch to give them the weight that Grandpa desired us to experience. His theory was that the younger we began having to get up and speak in front of an audience, the more likely we were to avoid the stage fright that hampers so many adults. We would meet on one Sunday afternoon in each of the three summer months. Everyone who attended had to prepare a written report that would then be presented. (Only Big Gram was exempt; she said it was because she prepared the refreshments, which I primarily remember as Coke Floats or Root Beer Floats.) Grandpa would assign the broad topic (e.g., birds, Indian tribes, states); then each of us would choose a topic within that category, with no two people choosing the same topics. I think I probably did robins and Cherokees and Georgia because I was the youngest when we were doing this. Interestingly, all four of Grandpa's Atlanta grandsons went on to use public speaking to advantage in their careers.

Grandpa took us fishing to pass on to us the love of that hobby. I pause on the word *hobby.* Stemming from his childhood on an Indiana farm, as a boy he may have viewed fishing as man bringing home good food for the family to eat. On one occasion Grandpa took us to Lake Blackshear in south Georgia. I got painfully sunburned sitting still and quiet (not my nature), and never catching a fish. We stayed in a "cabin" that only had a partial wall between us and people next door. The group on one side of us had come to drink and stay up past 9 p.m.; and Grandpa embarrassed me by telling these neighbors to be quiet because we had young children that needed their sleep.

The more positive memory is of going fishing with a guide in the St. Simons Island streams and marshes. When we were with the guide, we were with a member of the Sullivan family, descendants of African royalty. Ben Sullivan had been Grandpa's guide when both were younger men. Now, as Grandpa took his grandsons, it was Qu-zee Sullivan, Ben's son, who took us. Qu-zee spoke with a beautiful accent, particular to the Geechees on the Georgia coast and Gullah on the South Carolina coast—African people who settled on these islands and also in the Bahamas. There was a lot more action in the salt water than there had been in the still and hot waters of Lake Blackshear.

Frank Gordy, our neighbor from down the street, and founder of The Varsity, would invite Grandpa to go with him fishing on his farm lake—such a thoughtful gesture by a busy young man for an older neighbor. At least once, if not several times, Mr. Gordy would take along his daughter Nancy, and Grandpa would bring his grandson Binkie (aka Warren). Both children were around five. We've always thought of Nancy as Warren's first girlfriend.

Grandpa, the Farmer

At first light, he would turn off his lamp, gather up his buckets and baskets, and head down the hill to the chicken yard. Here he would gather the eggs, and feed and water his beautiful white laying hens. The two chicken houses with a feed and garden-tool shed connecting the two, were beautiful in the sheen of their unpainted wood, and in such features as the roosts that you could pull up by pulley to scrape out the chicken manure that would accumulate under the roosts. This manure went into the wheelbarrow and out to be spread over the fields of vegetable gardens.

Then as the sun shone bright (and hot in summer), Grandpa would go to his terraces of vegetables and gather in all that were ripe and ready for eating. There were other chores involved with keeping the chicken yard in apple-pie order such as swing-blading grass and burning the trash. (Grandpa collected the trash in a tall funnel-shaped basket and lugged it down each morning to the chicken yard.) There were cans and bottles in the trash, and they were thrown into a pile that was over a bank behind the chicken houses. When the ashes of the trash fire had cooled, we would sometimes find treasures that had been thrown out and now resided in the ashes. It could have been old cigarette lighters or spare pieces of costume jewelry or marbles or the like.

The back part of the chicken yard, below the chicken houses, consisted of four terraces cascading down to the creek. While Grandpa's health was strong, he planted all of these terraces in vegetables. In the chill of March a black man in a mule-drawn wagon would come down Piedmont Road, going to plow up the gardens of many between Peachtree and Roswell Roads. Grandpa would hire this man with the mule to plow, to dig up his garden, all four terraces of it. Once it was tilled, Grandpa spread a stored stock of chicken manure over the plowed-up dark soil. It would look for several days as if it had snowed because of the little chicken feathers embedded in the manure. Now Grandpa was ready for spring planting. For the finer tilling of the soil, such as digging a furrow in which to plant seeds (e.g., lettuce seeds), Grandpa had a "plow" with a wheel in the place where the mule would go on a bigger rig. He or my strong brother Dick would push this smaller plow as the final preparation for planting.

We brothers learned something about a good work ethic by working alongside Grandpa. We might push the wheelbarrow full of chicken manure into position where Grandpa could then spread it. Or, as he would place cabbage slips into the rich tilled soil, we would come along behind with buckets of water, sloshing against our legs and into our shoes, as we further lightened the heavy bucket by pouring about a cup full on each plant.

As Grandpa trudged back up the hill from the chicken yard late in the morning, near lunch time, he would bring two baskets of vegetables and eggs; one he would leave on our back stoop, and the other he would take to his home where Missouri (the cook, pronounced Ma-sur-rah) and Big Gram would turn the raw materials into midday dinner. This was their big meal of the day, whereas we, next door, a more modern family, had sandwiches for midday lunch. I will say that on those summer occasions when we would be invited next door for "dinner," maybe when Aunt Virginia (Grandpa's younger daughter, Mom's sister) and her husband, Uncle Wally, were here for their summer visit, it was a grand reenactment of Thanksgiving dinner. Missouri the cook became Missouri the server who would bring us at the table bowls of steaming vegetables and platters of chicken. On the best days we would end with warm Apple Brown Betty, with maybe a scoop of ice cream on top—the Brown Betty made from Grandpa's apples.

Remember, Grandpa grew up on a farm, so the rural life was in his blood. I love that he was passionate about pouring into the lives of his grandsons, and a big part of that was to give us some of the "farming" experience. Even before we

Grandpa with grandsons (L-R) Dick, cousin Wally, Chuck, and Dillon

lived next door (that commenced in 1946), he called us together with the following farm/business proposition:

"Boys, I want you to help me with my egg route. Fresh eggs are delicious and better for your health, and they are scarce during these war times. So, there are people that want some of my eggs. I just have to get the eggs to them. Dick, I'll pay you ten cents a dozen to deliver the eggs; Dillon, I'll pay you five cents a dozen to help your big brother deliver. And, Chuckie, I'll pay you a penny per egg carton to collect the cardboard cartons and bring them back to me. And your mom has agreed to drive you boys on the delivery route."

We boys filled a need that Grandpa had, but it was also for him an opportunity to pass wisdom down to his grandsons. I felt grown up at ages four and five being a part of a delivery team. Mom, the driver and delivery team boss, helped us each open a saving account at the Citizens & Southern Bank, so our learning experience was complete. Oh, by the way, our egg earnings had to go into those savings accounts. Even then I think those were called our "college savings accounts."

When Grandpa grew older and less able to tend all the terraces of vegetable gardens, he planted some of the fields with alfalfa grass and bought a steer (or, rather, he bought a young male cow, and I watched with some pain of my own as a veterinarian came and castrated the animal). This (now) steer we named Ferdinand. Grandpa taught me about feeding it, including hay, and about when to let Ferdinand in and out of the barn for grazing in Grandpa's beautiful terraced fields.

He might have wondered why Ferdinand wasn't putting on more weight until he learned that we had taken up the sport of bull riding. I one time stayed on for three bucks, though two bucks usually threw me sprawling out into the grass. Great fun! Dillon came down to try the sport a time or two. This type of activity that we found growing up on our little in-the-city farm now reminds me of part of one of the poems Grandpa would read us:

I should prefer to have some boy bend them [the birch trees]
As he went in and out to fetch the cows –
Some boy too far from town to learn baseball,
Whose only play was what he found himself,
Summer and winter, and could play alone. (From Robert Frost's "Birches")

Ferdinand eventually went to the butcher and came back in pieces wrapped in white butcher paper. A new freezer was bought to hold Ferdinand, along with the figs and tomatoes and okra and squash frozen for winter's eating.

Grandpa put some of his money alongside the lesser amount from my savings account, and he went with me to buy a steer of my own—as an investment. I picked out a young Black Angus male who immediately let me hug him around the neck. I named him Blackie. I was probably in the sixth or seventh grade (age eleven or twelve). Friends of mine would come over after school to play with Blackie—which mainly consisted of watching him come to me when I gave my cow call and then petting him. They had heard tales of my riding Ferdinand, and some friends wanted to try the same with Blackie. Maybe on separate occasions Tom Garden and Bobby Stephenson might have tried it once, but with Blackie it was mostly a matter of just sitting up on his back.

Ms. Paschal, the principal of R.L. Hope School, invited me to bring Blackie up to the school's lush front yard (next door to our house) to graze. Her well-intentioned gesture was, as they say, "too much of a good thing." The grass was so green—damp with chlorophyll—that Blackie caught diarrhea within an hour and soon made a mess of the area right by the flagpole where he was tethered.

Blackie was a bookend to a season of my life. When you have two brothers that you want to be just like, you don't mind when you begin to move into sports and have to leave behind the freer form of play. Grandpa had taught me a lesson about working hard and making money. Blackie became a good three times bigger than when I had bought him two years earlier, and I sold him. Just as I saw Chad at age thirteen hugging the much-loved family dog Cocoa's neck with such affection, I hugged Blackie's neck for a last time. They loaded him into the back of a truck, and that provided a painful closure to a beautiful part of my life. I wouldn't sob that much again until Grandpa's death a year or so later.

Grandpa's Love Overrides My Shortcomings

It was my job to use a basket shaped like a cone to carry trash from the back of Grandpa and Big Gram's house to the chicken yard where Grandpa would separate it into the burnables, which would go up in flames every day, and the tin cans and such that would be thrown on a big pile towards the edge of the property. I grew tired of my job and I decided that I could dump some of this trash to the side of the aluminum garage, over towards the school playground. This cut my trek to the chicken yard in half. Grandpa was soon on to what I was doing.

"Chuck, I thought I could count on you to do this job for me. I'm not well, and I need help. What entered your mind that you would do such a sneaky thing? You've let me down. How many times have I told you, 'If a job is worth doing, it's worth doing well.'"

I'm so embarrassed, even now, that I can't imagine what I might have said. I expect I said, "I'm sorry, Grandpa. I guess I might have been just being lazy."

To which he might have said, "Well, we'll get over it, but get every smidgen of trash away from the garage and carry it where it needs to go. I expect more from you. I'm disappointed." Even to this day it pains me to remember letting him down.

The End of a Life Well Lived

It's interesting how much language floats around you as a child that has little meaning to you. Being "retired" just meant to me another term for being a granddad. Grandpa was a retired lawyer. I understood that he had been important, and then he had had a stroke. The only vestige of the stroke was that he walked with a cane. Even so, he was as strong as an ox.

Then the season came when he announced that he had an important message to deliver at that year's Christmas dinner. He spoke about the importance of health. The adults at the table, especially Mom, had tears in their eyes; and I was the clumsy kid who asked after he had spoken, "What's the important announcement?" The adults knew what I didn't—that Grandpa had been diagnosed with cancer of the intestines. He had three painful months until death came in March of my seventh-grade year.

Late in his illness I was sitting by his bed in the evening to give Big Gram a reprieve. He woke up strange and a little wild, as if in a nightmare, saying, "Who is this?" and acting scared of me. Gram scurried into the room, and in a scolding manner said to him, "You know who this is. This is your grandson Chuckie. You've scared him."

"In John Bunyan's The Pilgrim's Progress, the main character, Christian, makes dozens of key friendships on his journey …. But no single person goes with him the whole way." — Walter Henegar, 12/22/19 sermon, "Your Family"

And then his bad spell left him and he said in a soft and gentle tone, "I am so sorry, Chuckie. If ever a grandfather has loved his grandson, I love you." I was shaken by seeing him in a delirious state, but I have never forgotten his sweet, sweet words. He would have said the exact same thing had it been Dick, Dillon, or Warren at his sickbed that night. He loved us each and all with a stern, deep, deep love. Though we were blessed with love all around us throughout our youthful days, it could be argued that next to Mom and Dad, Grandpa's love had the most lasting impact on all of us.

Not many days after this bedside episode, he died in his sleep. I had my first experience with grief that hurts in your lungs, during the flow of hot tears and still when the tears stop. Now when I think back, I can't imagine this loss for Mom. She and Grandpa were so very close, being lovers of poetry and literature together. He softened the relationship between Mom and Big Gram. Now the buffer was gone. I remember Westview Cemetery. It had for me a feeling that only the elite were buried in these hallowed grounds. Riding in a police-escorted convoy and being looked upon with pity was heady stuff for this twelve-year-old boy.

Q&A Conversation That Never Happened

- Grandpa, growing up on an Indiana farm, what was that like?
- Did you have chores to do before you went to school? Did you have chores to do when you got home from school?
- How did you get to school? Was it a rural school or was it a town school? What was a school day like?
- How old were you when you learned to love poetry? How did that happen?
- You wake up early in the morning, when it's still dark, to read and write. Is it fun? Did you do that when you were a boy?
- Who had the biggest influence on you growing up?
- We met Aunt Aida when we went with you to her farm in Elnora, Indiana. What other brothers and sisters did you have? Tell me about your mother and father.

These are all questions I wish I had asked Grandpa. It's almost to me as if he didn't have a past, just the five or six years of his life when I was old enough to be aware. He was just what I saw and lived next door to on a day-to-day basis. He walked with a cane, and it was said that he had had a stroke and had to retire. What was that like? He didn't drive. Did he drive before his stroke or did he walk up to the corner, as did our neighbor, Mr. Ralph McGill, and catch the bus to work? I could also have asked him:

- Grandpa, did you like being a lawyer? What does a lawyer do? Would I like being a lawyer?
- What is it like to grow old? Do you like being a grandpa?

(See **Appendix 1** for more about Grandpa's life.)

Early 1920s — Big Gram and Grandpa with Virginia (left) and Jane

Chapter 2: Big Gram

Maternal grandmother Agnes Nelson Dillon, born in 1881, died in 1980, at age 99. She and Grandpa, married for forty-nine years, are buried at Westview Cemetery. Big Gram's parents, my great-grandparents, were Martha Jane Flowers (dates unknown) and George B. Nelson (born August 11, 1846; died 1920). Big Gram was the oldest of six children. Aunt Maggie Belle was the youngest.

Overdeen—the Home

Gram and Grandpa's home had been built before the early 1920s when they bought it and moved out from their home on Fourth Street. The house must have been considered important because it had a name—Overdeen. (Big Gram thought it was funny that the beaus of her two daughters, Jane and Virginia, dubbed the house "Overdone.") The massive two-story house, resting on a very visible granite foundation, was white stucco with midnight-green trim. Until the mid '40s, the house had a big living room and dining room with heavy mahogany pocket doors on either side of a central hallway. The wide hallway, with a carpet runner down the middle, led from the front door to a grand stairway; the landing, halfway up to the second floor, had a window seat under an enormous story-tall window opening onto the gigantic back yard oak trees. The second floor had the bedrooms for this nuclear family of Big Gram, Grandpa, Mom, and Aunt Virginia.

Basements are made for little boys like me, especially the one in this house. I could stay down in theirs playing for hours. It was cool in the summer days before air conditioning. And it held treasures in items no longer of use upstairs or in the yard, but perfect for play. It had an outside entrance with eight-foot reclining doors such as one would picture on the storm cellar in *The Wizard of Oz*. Then, a stone's throw down the hill, Mr. and Mrs. Bishop lived in a little house, once servants' quarters, that one passed alongside when taking the path to the chicken yard. She was our second-grade teacher at R.L. Hope, and he was with the FBI.

From Peachtree Road north to their driveway—1955 Piedmont Road—and beyond, Piedmont was a dirt road when the Dillon family of four first moved there. Mom, then a twelve-year-old, rode her horse out from their 4th Street home as a part of the move. R.L. Hope, a Fulton County System elementary school, was located next door to them. When the school needed to increase its capacity, in the mid-to-late 1920s, Big Gram and Grandpa sold or gave the back end of their side yard to the school so the school would have adequate playground. I learned when looking into R.L. Hope School at the Atlanta History Center that the school built on this site in 1909 had two classrooms plus a room for teaching domestic science (e.g., cooking).

Decades later Big Gram and Grandpa sold the rest of that side yard to us for our home. I always understood that they owned five acres after slicing off part for the school and part for our home, but I never heard what it was when they first bought it—maybe as much as eight acres. (It is now the site of Tower Place.)

This impressive granite and stucco home had a substantial porch going around two of its sides. A granite wall, two feet wide across the top, provided the outside skirt to the porch, and it provided a place for Big Gram's huge cement planters and a place for a boy like me to sit and to play. The planters held a profusion of colorful petunias cascading over the side with numerous red geraniums shooting up from the centers of the planters. Every late spring and summer morning, Gram came out in the cool of the morning with a bucket of water from which she would pour goodly amounts of water on each of the half-dozen growing bouquets. She was not afraid of work, as this daily chore required multiple trips.

After Grandpa's retirement, they divided the big house into seven apartments. With the little house in the back yard, that gave Gram eight "rental properties." Big Gram and Grandpa's attractive quarters took half of the first floor. Big Gram's widowed sister, Aunt Maggie Belle, lived in one apartment. A lovely older widow, Mrs. Harvey, lived in another.

At some point well before I turned six, we lived in the largest of the apartments.

One fateful day, we were awaiting the return from their road trip to Cherokee, North Carolina, of Big Gram, Grandpa, Aunt Virginia, Little Wally, Dick, and

Overdeen, Grandpa and Big Gram's house

Dillon. When they pulled in at the back of the house in their wood-paneled station wagon, Mom, who was frying chicken on the stove, rushed down to greet her boys and all of the returning family members. With greetings, the lifting out of suitcases, and the conferring of souvenir Indian gifts for "Little Chuckie," who wasn't invited on the trip, someone looked up and saw smoke pouring out of the upstairs kitchen window of our apartment. The hot grease on the stove with the chicken had caught fire and then ignited the curtains at the window behind the stove.

Fire trucks came. The fire was extinguished, but not before burning up most of the kitchen and spreading heat and smoke damage to the halls and apartments on the second level and to the floor above that. Mom had responded with excitement at the honking of the horn signaling the return of the travelers. Until now I hadn't stopped to think of the impact of this mistake on Mom's sense of shame, not to mention her relationship with her parents.

We moved back to Little Gram's at Garden Hills; yet I can remember, while the house was being restored, my sneaking up and into Mom and Dad's charred bedroom and discovering partially melted weight-loss caramels that became my secret. At each opportunity I would cram a couple in my mouth until one day they were all gone. I now recognize "weight-loss caramels" as the oxymoron that it is—another hoax on American's downtrodden moms of the 1940s.

Mr. and Mrs. Thompson were Big Gram and Grandpa's next-door neighbors. Theirs was a large log home, and, once again, the basement was the boy's wonder spot. They also had a garage-type building full of gadgets and a trap door. There is little wonder why I grew up with a vivid imagination.

Big Gram, Maggie Belle, and Mrs. Harvey

Around 5 o'clock or so every afternoon, weather permitting, Big Gram, Maggie Belle, and Mrs. Harvey would gather in the shade of the front yard, under the sprawling dogwood tree. Even on the hottest summer days there always seemed to be a light breeze there, stirring the leaves of the dogwood. I would climb up in the tree, both for the fun of climbing and for the pleasure of hearing what they were talking and laughing about. I learned that they were mostly talking about memories, some going back to childhood. I wish I had listened more closely since Big Gram was born on a plantation in 1881 in Hazlehurst, Mississippi. Her father, George Nelson, was, according to Warren's research, the largest slave-holder in his county.

I do remember that as a young lady, Big Gram had ridden in a Confederate Memorial Day parade in New Orleans. I do remember that one man, named Benjamin, who had been a house slave before The War, chose to stay on and serve the Nelson family. Gram saw this as evidence of the close bond that existed between slave and slave owner. I wonder if it were more like Brooks, the lifetime prisoner in *The Shawshank Redemption*, who was so used to institutional life that he couldn't exist as a free man on the outside.

The Harder Side of Big Gram

Even as a young child—maybe especially as a young child—I wasn't comfortable with how Big Gram treated Negroes (the polite term in the '40s and '50s for African-Americans). The earliest "yard man" I can remember was "One-eyed Jim," a man strong as an ox, who said very little. He could take down a tree and chop it into firewood or polish a floor. He mowed the grass, raked the leaves, and trimmed the shrubs. Big Gram pushed Jim mercilessly, it seemed to me. The way she would talk to him, no human being should talk to another. She was bossy with "the help," and I guess I never was comfortable with bossiness.

He worked HARD, but it was never quick enough to suit Big Gram. In the first year of Big Gram's life as a bride, she had lived with Grandpa in Mexico where he served as a lawyer for a mining company. Years later, when I was a little boy, she loved to tell that the only Spanish expression she learned was *anda le*, which meant "to hurry." "The Mexican servants were so pokey. I was forever telling them, *anda le, anda le.*" So said Gram.

In time Jim passed on, felled either by old age or just being beaten down. He gave way to Cleve, who drove a car and was better educated than Jim. Yet Big Gram treated him like a young child, except that she never told Cleve he was doing a good job.

In my early years, Gram rented Admiral Vardaman's house at Sea Island. (It's now interesting to discover that Vardaman was from a line of Mississippi segregationists, this not necessarily known to Big Gram. His father, a senator, is reported to have said near the beginning of the 1900s, "If it is necessary, every Negro in the state will be lynched; it will be to maintain white supremacy."

There was a small servants' quarters house behind, where Clara, our maid, would stay. Clara was there for the month but would have Saturdays off—sometimes going to the black night club on St. Simons and once or twice driving all the way to Atlanta and back. We would follow Big Gram's tradition,

Big Gram circa 1900

and Clara would prepare a big meal for noon time. We boys would talk with Clara about the music groups she would hear in St. Simons or when back in Atlanta. We would have these conversations when Gram wasn't around; otherwise, she would have chastised us for being too *familiar.*

As has been said, our Sea Island lunches were the main meal of the day, eaten together in the dining room. On one such occasion, Uncle Wally and Little Wally (aka Snick), Aunt Virginia's husband and son, came to the lavish noon meal with nothing on from the waist down except a towel, just to get a rise out of Gram.

When Big Gram and Grandpa would pull into the Standard Oil station at the corner of Piedmont and Peachtree, a black man would pump the gas, check under the hood to make sure the car had enough oil and check the air pressure in all four tires. I, being a talkative child, would chat a few sentences with this man, who worked for tips. Gram would give him some loose change instead of a dollar bill, and off we'd go. After one of those times, maybe a day or two after, Grandpa summoned me to come talk with him. I remember where he sat and I sat (on their glass porch) as he lectured me gently about *not being so familiar with servants.* "They don't like it. They're not used to it. They are there to serve us, not to be our friends."

I immediately knew that Big Gram had put Grandpa up to giving me this little lecture. She was sometimes bossy with him. This was not Grandpa's heart, he having grown up on an Indiana farm working hard on the land. Interestingly, Grandpa only rarely engaged "hired help" in the chicken yard or in the gardens. He did the hard work himself, in time teaching us boys how to help him.

Thirty-Some Years of Vigor Before the Decline of Her 90s

Grandpa died in March 1953, four months shy of their forty-ninth wedding anniversary. Gram was given purpose in life to make her want to live on past her husband's death. Yes, she certainly grieved, but she had the apartments to run, and she was tough. She had some good relationships with the tenants, but I mostly heard her being bossy. If a tenant fell behind on rent without any explanation, Gram would have the locksmith come and change the lock so they would have to come to her if they wanted to recover their belongings. When she had a vacancy, she would advertise the apartment with a "want ad" in the *Constitution* or the *Journal,* or both. The ad would always feature "near a car line," meaning the Oglethorpe-to-downtown trolley that ran up and down Peachtree. This was the same one that our neighbor Ralph McGill would take to work and back, walking in front of our house each way. The stress of the apartments, I contend, is what extended Gram's life.

Her self-appointed role as the overseer of our house and the lives therein was probably another life-giving stress for her. It was a death-inducing stress for my mom. Gram always seemed to know what was going on next door at our house. She knew when people came and went. When we were little, if she heard crying coming out of our house, she would quickly appear at our place, to see what was the matter. If Mom was spanking one of us, then Gram would interfere by showing pity for the rightly disciplined child or by asking all about the infraction, as if to say, "Could this angelic child possibly deserve discipline?" Worse than that, she would criticize Mom sometimes for how she looked or what she was wearing. The only person who seemingly wasn't rattled by Gram was Dad. I loved the way he would call her Aggie (for Agnes) and would graciously call her out if she were overstepping her bounds—bounds that were nonexistent except when Dad was in the house. He would always begin, "Now, Aggie ..."

Shortly before 1960, having rented Admiral Vardaman's beach house for several years, Gram decided she would build her own Sea Island beach house. The Vardaman place was at 35 Sea Island Drive at what was then the residential tip-end of the island. The lot Gram bought, also facing the drive, was at 28th Street and Sea Island Drive. She engaged Uncle Charlie as her architect. He came up with a modern design that fitted into the beach setting and that made us all boastful of his imaginative mind and the range of his architectural styles. If not boastful, Gram was at least satisfied. She especially liked the fountain in the front.

At some point in Dick and Mary Anne's relatively short courtship, they went to stay at Gram's almost-finished beach house, with Gram as their chaperone. Gram took her assignment seriously. At one point Dick was sleeping late so Mary Anne tiptoed into his room to bring him a cup of coffee. To this day Mary Anne bears emotional scars from the "dressing down" she got from Gram for entering Dick's room when he was asleep and in what she would have called his bedclothes—totally unacceptable by Gram's standards.

A humorous-in-hindsight incident on that same trip was Mary Anne, in the pitch-black dark of the night, going into what was, unbeknownst to her, an unfinished bathroom to brush her teeth. She borrowed some of the "toothpaste" on the sink and proceeded to brush her teeth. There were only three problems with this unfinished bathroom. There was no electricity or water, and what Mary Anne took to be toothpaste was really caulking, there for the workmen to finish the sink the next day. I honestly don't know the details of how Mary Anne got the caulking out before it hardened. I just know she did because I've seen her since and she has beautiful teeth. I wonder how much persuasion it took Dick to get Mary Anne to return to this house for their honeymoon, but return they did. Maybe it was the knowledge that Big Gram would not be going with them this time.

As a family, we enjoyed the house several summers while I was still in high school. Gram finally decided to sell because, with her and our limited use of it, she could not justify the upkeep charges from the Sea Island Corporation.

Entering into Old Age

While Warren was in the real estate business, he negotiated the sale of Gram's home and property for the building of Tower Place. The care of the place and the renting of the apartments became too much for her. She would have been around ninety. She first moved to an apartment near Toco Hills and then to Colony Square, where she lived the longest before going to Fountain View Assisted Living. It was at the Toco Hills apartment where great-grandson Richard put Coke bottles in the trash compactor and exploded them, causing an elderly Gram to politely question what was going on.

At some point Bessie was hired to give Gram some assistance. It was sad that from time to time Gram would contend that her "lingerie" or her "linens" had been pilfered, of course suspecting Bessie. The sad thing is that her "fine linens" were a mishmash of stained cloth placemats and ill-matching sets of cloth napkins—no longer really "sets." Her "lingerie" was now just tired old undergarments. When one lives into one's nineties, there is the tendency to live in a fantasy world, maybe all the more if one grew up on a Mississippi plantation.

After Mom's death, when Gram had moved to Colony Square and we were living in Rome (Georgia), Dad would come every Wednesday to take care of Gram's laundry needs and her grocery list. He was the son-in-law she may not have esteemed or loved, but he was the son-in-law who was her faithful servant during the six years that Dad outlived Mom. When Dad, a widower, married Harriett Wilcox, a widow, Gram famously said, "Well, now that Dick is no longer in the family, what are we going to do?" I responded in astonishment, "Gram, what do you mean that Dad is no longer in the family? He's my dad!"

In the family or not in Gram's eyes, Dad continued faithfully showing up at Gram's every Wednesday to see after her, right up to the time he dropped dead of a heart attack. She now was alone with all family in hers and in the generation below her gone: first, Virginia's husband Wally (1960 or '61), then Virginia ('62), then Mom ('71), and, finally, Dad ('76).

Bessie continued to serve Gram. At Berry Academy, we were geographically the closest of Gram's grandsons. I took over the check writing and bill paying. JoElyn, baby Jane, and I would come down from Berry Academy once a week when we could. Our routine would be to take Gram out for what was now her favorite meal—an Arby's roast beef sandwich and a Jamoca shake. Colony Square and her apartment there were an upbeat place to visit. Gram had become sweeter in what was to be the last decade of her life. Maybe she finally realized that she was not self-sufficient and needed the help of others. Even though, in all honesty, Gram took on some of the appearance of a witch, she and baby Jane got along famously.

As Gram became less able to do for herself, Mrs. White was added to work with Bessie in caring for Gram. Finally, she needed the care of a nursing home, and somehow we selected Fountain View, either on or near Briarcliff Road. It was nice, though not without the scent of disinfectant and the elderly sitting in their doorways—some with no sound or change from a blank face as we passed by; some who would "oooh and aaah" over baby Jane; others who would mutter something unintelligible. Bessie and Mrs. White continued to serve Gram right up to the end.

Her Last Days

In July of 1980, not long after we had moved to Atlanta and Cross Creek, Gram fell and broke her hip. She was admitted to Piedmont Hospital. As I was about to depart from my daily late-afternoon visit with her, she said, "Don't leave me. Stay with me through the night. Don't leave me alone through the night."

"Gram, I love you, but I have a wife and child who need me. I can't leave them. You'll be all right."

"Well, then, I won't be here when you come back tomorrow," she said pitifully.

"Gram, you will be all right. I will see you tomorrow," I responded. Gram was the master of emotional blackmail. Dad was the only one in the past to defy such manipulation, and I was of a mind to follow his example.

She was there in the morning, but she wasn't. When I visited her, she didn't utter a word and seemed as if she were now closed to the outside world. Either she had had further mental deterioration in the intervening twenty-four hours, or she was determined to punish me for not doing her bidding the evening before. She was capable of that. There was a sister back in Mississippi who Gram treated as if she, the sister, were dead. They had had a falling out over the settlement of the parents' will, and Gram resolved not to speak to or of her sister from that time on. The sister had laid claim to the family piano that Gram had wanted.

"But, Sister, you already have a piano," Gram said.

To which Sister reportedly replied, "But I don't have a piano like this one."

(Note: This Nelson Family lore passed down to us four boys was so scandalous, that siblings would have a lifetime falling out over a piano, that when it came time to claim some pieces from our childhood home, we were exceedingly deferential to one another. Gram had taught us, by negative example, not to put too much value into stuff.)

Back to Gram's broken hip: The doctor said that she would not survive surgery so we moved her back to Fountain View where Bessie and Ms. White could care for her.

The end came for Gram in August of her one-hundredth year as all of her grandsons, except Little Wally, were together at Pawley's Island. Mrs. White and Bessie called to tell me that the end was near. I felt that they were calling me to come back, which I might have done—more for the sake of Bessie and Mrs. White, than for Gram, who probably wouldn't know I was there. However, I easily acquiesced when I was discouraged by the group from leaving.

She was born sixteen years after the end of the Civil War, February 3, 1881. She passed on Thursday, August 7, 1980. We held the graveside service of burial that Saturday at the Westview Cemetery plot alongside Grandpa, who had predeceased her by twenty-eight years. She had outlived her younger daughter by eighteen years and her older daughter by ten years. Since Gram lived to be ninety-nine, there are many more stories about her, including Warren's story of "The Blue Angel."

Chapter 3: Little Gram

Paternal grandmother Helen Rose Boles Johnston—born 1880; died 1958, at age 78. Her father, my great-grandfather, was Louis Rend Boles, a Pittsburgh riverboat captain; her mother, my great-grandmother, had the maiden name of McKinney. My paternal grandfather, Clarence Marcellus Johnston, was born in 1880 and died in 1935, at age 55. Both are buried at Westview Cemetery. His parents were Lucy M. Slack Johnston (1855-1918) and Marcellus D. Johnston (1851-1924) of Springfield, Ohio.

Little Gram's Departed Husband Whom I Never Knew

I borrow this information about Grandpa Johnston from brother Dick's memories, and I quote him. After all, he had a five-year head start on me in family membership:

"Dad told me that his father was an outstanding catcher, was offered a contract by the Pittsburgh Pirates when he was sixteen, but declined the offer because professional baseball players at that time (around 1900) were a ruthless, disreputable bunch.... For Mom, he [her father-in-law] had a wonderful personality—warm, outgoing, sensitive, caring—the personality of a good salesman and a model for his oldest son."

While Dad Was Away in the Army

As if by size, Little Gram was gentle and soft-spoken, Big Gram forceful and opinionated. I saw less of Little Gram because we didn't live next door to her.

Perhaps that made her special—someone whose company I would relish. She would be the grandmother with the soft, fragrant skin. Her husband, my paternal grandfather, died of heart disease during brother Dick's early months of life, in 1935; so he is the one grandparent I never knew. For a while, from before my vivid memory, we lived in Little Gram's home. This was while Dad was serving his Army stint in Amarillo, Texas.

Things I would hear secondhand about Little Gram, things more a part of her adult world, intrigued me and gave her greater dimension. She made her own hats, hats with feathers and veils such as women wore in those days. She had no car and didn't drive, so it would be Mom who would take her grocery shopping at Colonial Stores or the A&P. These were big outings for Little Gram. With Little Gram dressed for the occasion, they sometimes made an event out of an outing by stopping at Abraham's Delicatessen (aka Abe's) and having a sandwich together.

Little Gram shopping in downtown Atlanta in the late 1930s.

(The two or maybe three times in my young life I had the opportunity to have one of Abe's sandwiches, I thought they were the most wonderful sandwiches I'd ever eaten. Abe's characteristic sandwich had plenty of mayonnaise and was piled high with layers of thin-sliced meat and delicious coleslaw.) This was a treat for both Mom and Little Gram. These two unsung souls loved each other and had loved each other since Mom, as a young bride, joined the three brothers and their parents for Sunday night supper.

A House Built with Character

Little Gram's house was two stories and a basement. It had one bathroom. Little Gram's room and the shared bathroom were on the right as you went up the stairs leading from the front door. To the left of those stairs was another big room with a small paneled room off of it to the side. This paneled room sat squarely atop the screened porch below. The screened porch opened off of the living room on the main level. As you faced the house from North Hills Drive, the porch and the paneled room atop sat on the left side, between Little Gram's house and the next-door neighbor. Situated to the rear of the upward-ascending stairs, between the big living room and the kitchen, was a dark and dusky little room with the house's one telephone. In front of the kitchen, to the right as you came in the front door, was the dining room. Its corner cabinets gave this room its character. The kitchen was tiny by today's standards, what we would now call a galley kitchen.

Under the ascending steps, with access through the "telephone room," were the stairs down into the basement. I could and did spend exploratory moments in the two chambers of the basement, one filled with tools of all sorts, the use of some I could only imagine. The other chamber, which opened to the back yard, housed Uncle Charlie's old Army Jeep; the walls were lined with car-related items such as pumps, tire repair kits, mostly empty cans, some of wax and such and some of motor oil and radiator "stop leak." This lowest level, that opened onto the back yard, had about it a wonderful mustiness and oiliness. I would always return to the upstairs with smudges on my clothes and grime on my hands. There was no doubt where I had been. At times like that, Little Gram would pull out a canister of Twenty-Mule Team Borax, a soap powder that would take your hide off if you scrubbed with it too hard. It had granules like sand to give it a sandpaper quality.

As if the house alone weren't "classy old" enough, it was enhanced even more when annually Uncle Charlie would put up his Christmas tree. As one might guess from his vocation of architecture, Uncle Charlie was artistic and a builder, and he took those gifts into placing each ornament on the tree—these ornaments from his rich treasure chest of childhood Christmas memorabilia. The final touch was the red metal toy fire truck that he placed just so, under the tree.

I remember that, while I was living at Little Gram's, I had scarlet fever, which was then considered a serious childhood disease. A nurse from the Public Health Department came out and tacked up a sign at the front door that read QUARANTEENED. My most precious toys were stacked in the back yard and torched for fear that others would catch the germs from my things. I must have had high fever. Bright colors would swirl around in my head, much worse than nightmares that at least had a story line.

Whether from this illness or others more in general, I remember listening to the radio while lying in bed sick: *The Breakfast Club*, *Queen for a Day*, and the *Buster Brown Hour* were among my favorites. I also got comic books. If I seemed well read as a child it was because these were not just ordinary comic books; these were "Classic Comics." I remember *Swiss Family Robinson*, *Robinson Crusoe* and *The Three Musketeers* among the titles.

Song of the South

Little Gram and I had our own special outing when Dad, Mom, Dick, and Dillon headed over to Athens for a college football game, maybe even the Tech vs. Georgia game. My parents, being both wise and compassionate in the raising of their boys, never were unfair when it came to meting out special experiences. I was thrilled to be going downtown with Little Gram to see a movie. I definitely thought I was the lucky one.

We rode the Oglethorpe trolley down to the Fox Theatre and saw a big blockbuster movie: *Song of the South*. It was November 1946, and I was still five years old. (An aside about transportation: Little Gram had no car and was adept at getting downtown for shopping by bus. What I am here calling a bus was in the 1940s a *trackless trolley*, a trolley that had tires but had its power by cables that extended from the back of the trolley up to overhead power lines.)

What a glorious afternoon being in this somewhat spooky Moorish temple of a theater and of hearing Uncle Remus tell story after story of animal characters like Br'er Rabbit, Br'er Bear, and Br'er Fox. The Tar Baby wasn't an animal; but it wouldn't be Uncle Remus without the story of the Tar Baby. I can hear Uncle Remus chuckle now when I think about his delight in telling his funny animal stories. I'm sure that surround sound didn't exist in 1946, but I sure do remember glorious sounds filling the Fox that sunny fall Saturday:

Zip-a-dee-doo-dah, Zip-a-dee-ay.
My, oh my, what a wonderful day.
Plenty of sunshine headin' my way,
Zip-a-dee-doo-dah, Zip-a-dee-ay.

There's a bluebird on my shoulder—

It's the truth, it's actual—
Everything is satisfactual.
Zip-a-dee-doo-dah, Zip-a-dee-ay.
Wonderful feelin', Wonderful day!

To this day I sing "Zip-a-Dee-Do-Dah" because I haven't gotten it out of my head after having "rolled" myself to sleep singing that song after my glorious day with Little Gram. (Up until age seven or eight, to fall asleep I would lie on my back and, holding my blanket near my face, roll my shoulders from side to side.)

It has for me been a hiking song, with my young daughters or even in these later days with fellow adult hiking buddies when energy would begin to lag.

As glorious as it all was, the movie hardwired into my psyche that this is what the "Old South" for Negroes was like. Uncle Remus was obviously being treated well. He was happy; he made the children happy. As a prototype of a black man, he was carefree and had lots of leisure. In my naive five-year-old soul, why wouldn't I want the South to "rise again?"

Two Additional Memories from North Hills Drive

I fell on my head off the top of our bunk beds when I was somewhere below age five. That's a terrifying fall for a little guy. I can remember a pronounced goose egg on my forehead. That probably counts as a concussion when I'm justifying my missing brain cells.

Uncle Charlie came home from WWII with a cinder in his eye from his journey on the troop train. (Uncle Charlie ranked #3 among that generation of Johnston boys. Dad and Uncle Bill were numbers one and two, with Dad being the oldest.) With Charlie moving in with his mother, we moved to an apartment in Big Gram's big house until construction of our 3349 Piedmont Road home was completed.

Relating to Little Gram from Two Miles Away

After we had moved from Little Gram's to Big Gram and Grandpa's, a great treat for me would be to spend the night with Little Gram. On the hottest summer day, it would be cool in the morning on her screened porch. Little Gram would set a fancy place for me at the table with flowers on the table and a glass of orange juice waiting for me at my place. I imagined it to be like breakfast at a fancy hotel. Then she would ask if I wanted waffles, pancakes, or French toast. As I would retell this exquisite breakfast experience to whomever would listen, I would pronounce the offerings as "wassils, pantates, and fence toast."

Little Gram made dolls for her grandsons. We loved to play imaginary games with our dolls. She made me an exquisitely detailed World War II soldier that I named "Soldier Boy." He even had authentic battle ribbons on his chest. I would love to have that doll today. The truth be told, he was totally destroyed in the more robust imaginary play of our older childhood. Living next door to the school playground, we had collected a healthy arsenal of hard rubber softballs. These were our missiles in our hearty game of War. It was my troop of dolls lined up on my bed against Dillon's troop of dolls on his bed. As brother #2, Dillon, gained his own room, and brother #4, Warren, moved in with me, he and I continued this raucous game until the dolls were in tatters. Soldier Boy may have even been missing limbs. This is a long way off from talking about Little Gram's artistic skills with needle and thread, but it does show that boys love "battle" and have to be taught later in life to value craftsmanship. It's only now that I wish I had "Soldier Boy" in pristine condition.

A walk to Little Gram's on Sunday afternoons was a great treat for me at my single-digit age and beyond. Even though I would frequently have to run to catch up with Dad and Mom, it was fun. But Little Gram's house at 2848 North Hills Drive (Garden Hills) had a charm for me, almost like something in fairytales. I associate the smell of gardenias with this house and these visits. There would be a lady's magazine or two—*Ladies' Home Journal* or *Better Homes & Gardens* (with its fascinating "before and after" spread on an architectural home makeover)—for me to thumb through while the adults would talk. Little Gram would have some sort of special beverage and a cookie to offer me; that was nice, but that's not what drew me. It was Little Gram herself and the sweet interplay between my Dad and his mother.

I remember another memory of family solidarity, this one occurring annually on Christmas afternoon: After Mom and Dad had exhausted themselves creating a sparkling Christmas for the four of us, they would meet Uncle Bill, Aunt Marianne, Uncle Charlie, and Little Gram at Little Gram's to see Uncle Charlie's tree decorated with antique ornaments. Along with seeing the tree, they drank milk punch. This was the only occasion for this group to drink mid-afternoon together, and, as far as I know, the only time all year to drink milk punch.

Little Gram went into declining health. She was so confined to her bed and perhaps losing some awareness that as nurses came into the house to take care of her, Uncle Charlie moved to the Darlington Apartments to gain some independence. Little Gram never knew that he wasn't still living there. When she passed away, it was in the fall of my freshman year at Vanderbilt ('58). The funeral at Westview Cemetery was on a Saturday. Dick couldn't get away from med school, and Dillon had to dress for a football game; so it fell to me to meet Warren (then in seventh grade) and have the two of us represent the brothers. Tom Garden let me borrow his gray Dodge, cautioning me not to let his parents see me as he was not supposed to lend out his car.

I met the family near the gates at Westview. Dr. Wilson was waiting in his car; I went over and sat with him to give him some background on Little Gram (Helen Boles Johnston), whom he had never met. He was there to support us four boys who had been central figures at Peachtree Road Presbyterian Church. Little Gram may have had Anglican Church roots, but I don't ever remember her going to church, unless it was something like a baccalaureate service for one of us. The burial was fairly impersonal, save for the presence of Dad, Uncle Bill, and Uncle Charlie—lost in their memories but stoic in any show of emotion.

Chapter 4: Dad

I can believe that Mom and Dad were affectionate with each other. Just by their natural affectionate temperament, I can imagine that they hugged and kissed in courtship and in marriage. I have never imagined their intimacy beyond hugging and kissing. My father—Richard Boles Johnston, who went by "Dick"—came to Atlanta as an employee in sales at American Airlines in the early days of aviation. Mom was here, finishing her college career at Sweet Briar and University of Illinois and her debut. This would have been in the late 1920s, early 1930s.

He from Ohio, she from Georgia. He two years older than she. He tall, dark, and handsome, and she a blonde Southern beauty. They were meant for each other, as they used to say.

I loved to hear about their wedding (June 6, 1933) in the front yard of Mom's childhood home at 3355 Piedmont Road. The altar was between two massive fir trees. A wide white runner formed the pathway for the bride to follow from the wide steps of her home to the altar. Her bouquet was of lilies of the valley. The reception was on the porches with orchestra and dancing on the lawn. Someone confused the two punch bowls. Children and old people drank from the spiked bowl while the young people, seeking a little buzz, drank from the non-alcoholic bowl. Since it was later reported to be one of the most fun parties ever, I assume the mistake was discovered and rectified. Mom and Dad flew to Niagara Falls for their honeymoon, courtesy of American Airlines, Dad's employer.

Dad as Debonair: His Dress, His Routines, Control of Temper

All the years that I lived life alongside Dad, I observed a very disciplined man who lived on routines. He was particular about his clothes. The laundry folded his dress shirts "just so" and with no starch. He had multiple suits, mostly blues and grays, with maybe one lightweight khaki suit and one of seersucker. His shoes were professionally polished, as were his fingernails. He was always clean-shaven. It was fun to watch him pack for one of his weekly trips. He could do it in ten minutes. Because "he had a place for everything and everything had its place," he rarely if ever forgot anything. His chest of drawers had a similar high level of organization.

He took care of his clothes. The first thing he would do when he got home was to take off all of his business clothes and put them away neatly, even putting shoe trees in his shoes before putting them away. In his white boxers and keeping on his white dress shirt, he would put on the khaki pants that were waiting limp in his closet, his slippers, and then he would come and join us at the dinner table.

I never saw Dad lose his temper. He and Mom would have fights, but his emotions never got out from under him. He would get upset with one of his sons, but he never lost his temper.

More than a few times he would say to us four boys at the dinner table, "Boys, control your tempers. Remember, when you lose your temper, you are momentarily out of your mind, and nothing good can come of that. When you lose control of your temper, you lose."

Dad spoke with pride that he had always kissed his father on the cheek upon greeting him, so clearly Dad wanted the four of us to do the same with him. It was a pleasant expectation. There was an amiable bear-hug quality about Dad that made me want to be near him.

When I was very little and I fell asleep in the car on a late-night return to the house, Dad would carry me in and up the stairs to my bed. There was absolutely no more loved and secure feeling than to be in Dad's strong arms, snug up against his neck. There was an Old Spice / tobacco smell when close up to Dad that would be still sweet to me if I could take it in today.

Dad — debonair and disciplined

Sticking My Head into the Trunk and Getting Smashed

I must have been five, I could have been six. The trunk of our old Packard was open as the Christmas tree man put in our joyously selected tree. I stuck my head into the trunk just in time to be struck by the descending trunk lid. They tell me I was an overly curious child. A deep and long gash opened across my forehead and into the hairline; it bled profusely and throbbed. The tree stand was at the corner of Piedmont and Peachtree, and our house was only three doors down Piedmont. I was whisked home where Dad went to work wrapping my head from my eyes up with pads and gauze and surgical tape. When I arrived at the emergency room for multiple stitches, I was certain that the doctors there were impressed by the bandaging I had gotten not far from the scene of the crime. For you see, shortly before this episode, Dad had returned from his relatively brief stint in the WWII Army serving as a male nurse. Thereafter, Dad was the medical expert in our family, especially when it came to wounds that needed bandaging.

Sunday Afternoon Walks

How Dad prepared for a Sunday afternoon walk speaks of him as both debonair and keeper of routines. He would clean up and dress for the occasion—pressed khakis, a sports jacket (corduroy in the winter), a tie, and one of his brimmed fedora hats. He would announce that any who wanted to join him were welcome for the customary Sunday afternoon walk to Little Gram's in Garden Hills. Mom would almost always join Dad, and I would often tag along. I was proud of how Dad would speak to everyone we passed. To the ladies he would tip his hat, which meant he took the front brim of his hat between his thumb and index finger, held it just long enough to make a very slight bow. (The knights of old would open their visors to show themselves friendly to a passerby, he told me, and this was the modern-day version of that courtly gesture.) Mom and Dad walked briskly, so every third or fourth step I would run to catch back up. On the way we walked through Johnson Town, an unpaved street inhabited by black families in weathered clapboard houses. Dad's friendliness here was unchanged. He spoke to all he passed. He was good to his mother, who was alone much of the time. Though he never mentioned it, I got the idea that he was bringing some money to her as well as just enjoying being with his mom.

Time at the St. Simons Beach

This was the one time in the year when we had Dad's undivided attention for a week or two. That meant that we passed the football with him on the beach. He taught us how to ride the waves. At just the right point in the tide, you might find all five of us—the male Johnstons—riding waves for an hour at a time. (In more modern times it became known as "body surfing.") We tried to go further on the waves than Dad, but we'd be better off trying to better him in something else. While building sandcastles may have been primarily the interest of youngest brother Warren, Dad showed us that creating fun sandcastles was very much an adult undertaking. He pitched in, and we joined him. We were forever trying to outwit the rising tide by creating intricate systems of moats to save beautiful castles. We never succeeded. First the moats would concede their space to the tide, then a corner of the castle would topple, then a little bit more would go, and finally there would be nothing but a smooth mound of sand where once stood a magnificent castle.

During our beach stay we went to one movie at the theater near the lighthouse, something we never did as a family when we were back in Atlanta. It was pleasant in the village in the cooler evening time. After the movie we would get milkshakes. I can't think of any in the family who didn't choose chocolate. Dad was the leader in that.

At least one day during our beach stay, we would ride the ferry from the enchanting village pier out to Jekyll Island. We would always walk around the Millionaires' Village to see the vacation homes of Rockefeller, Vanderbilt, Gould, Macey, Crane and others. The ride out and back on the ferry was probably the most fun part.

Dad also throughout our youth would provide occasional fine-dining experiences. I particularly remember Dad teaching us the proper use of finger bowls, which were always a part of a meal at the Cloister. He said that if we didn't know about finger bowls we might think it was soup and dip in with a spoon. (Back in Atlanta that fine-dining experience might be at Hart's or at Ansley Golf Club, but neither of those establishments had finger bowls.)

Teenagers at the St. Simons beach, from left, Dick, Dillon, Chuck, and Warren.

Love of Sports: Punting and Passing, a Thanksgiving Day Game

Athletics was a huge part of what Dad passed on to us. I was not initially a hard worker about chores or homework, but Dad told us so many legends of great athletes who had devoted themselves to be better in their respective sport that there was no way I wasn't going to train hard and obey training rules. Boxing was big in the '40s, as were football, basketball, and baseball. While having dinner with Mom and business clients out at Aunt Fannie's Cabin one night, Dad met and got the autograph of one of his boxing heroes, Jack Dempsey. He could hardly sleep for thinking about how excited his sports-minded sons would be in the morning when he showed us the autograph. He was sorely disappointed when our enthusiasm didn't match his. We recognized the name of the boxer, but that was about it.

Track was seen mainly in connection with the Olympics, hence stirring tales of Jesse Owens. At Columbus Academy (Ohio), Dad lettered in football, basketball, swimming, track and baseball. At Lehigh, he played collegiate football. Post-college his sport was golf, and he rarely missed his Saturday golf game.

Should we have our Thanksgiving Feast before the Tech/Georgia Freshman Football game or after? This was a big decision. When we ate after the game, Dad was tired of his stomach growling while those sitting around us at the game would talk about how full they were from their delicious meals. When we ate before the game, what were the negatives of that? Well, one year the temperature was in the low 20s for the game. I was six or younger. We rushed to that game after a bountiful meal. ("My eyes were bigger than my stomach," most especially when sitting before a feast or in a cafeteria line.) We took our seats and nearly froze to death. At some point in the game I began to turn green, and with no advance warning my meal started up my throat and spewed out my mouth, most on the man's wool navy overcoat on the row beneath us, and as it instantly cooled it froze to his coat. Dad tried desperately to apologize to the poor recipient of my eruption and to clean off his overcoat as best he could. After that, we always waited and had our meal after the Tech/Georgia Shriners' Bowl Game.

Even more than sports in general, Dad wanted "to be there for his sons." I remember frosty mornings, maybe 8 a.m., we would be playing Gray-Y football on the field at E. Rivers School, chilly fog rolling off of Peachtree Creek that ran alongside the football field. There would be usually just two fathers standing on the sidelines; one of them was always Dad, in his long black overcoat. The other was usually Bob Schell's father. When we were at North Fulton, Dad supported us by attending practices when he was in town. He would watch unseen standing behind the old concrete stadium, but then he would speak with the coaches as we all ambled off the field and into the locker room. Years later, when I was thirty-five years old and married with a child, I ran in my first Peachtree Road Race

(1976), and there was Dad, along with Uncle Bill, standing at about 10th Street cheering me on. I finished 1,672nd out of 2,300 runners. I kidded with Dad about whether he ever imagined that one of his sons would let him down by finishing in 1,672nd place in a sporting event. (Now, with 60,000 running, he and I both would be proud of that finish.)

His Favorite TV Shows: Highway Patrol, Gunsmoke

The first family in the neighborhood with a TV was the McGill family. We would go three houses down and join "Little Ralph" in first watching the test pattern, and then watching *The Woody Willow Show* when the day's programming began at 4 o'clock in the afternoon. Woody Willow and his friends were puppets in WSB's first locally created show—this one for kids.

I think I was in the seventh or eighth grade before we had a television. Nobody loved our TV more than Dad. One of his favorite shows was *Gunsmoke*, starring James Arness as Marshal Matt Dillon. It started in the 1950s and lasted until 1975, so there must have been other loyal fans, as well as my dad. *The Jackie Gleason Show* started in 1952. Gleason played a variety of characters including Joe the Bartender; the most talked-about sketch was "The Honeymooners" in which Gleason played a blowhard Brooklyn bus driver, Ralph Kramden, with Art Carney as his upstairs neighbor, Norton, and Audrey Meadows as Ralph's wife, Alice. We watched that together as a family along with *The Colgate Comedy Hour* and *The Ed Sullivan Show*. After we became too busy to watch much television, Dad watched and loved *Highway Patrol* with Broderick Crawford. We kidded Dad about his fondness for Crawford, who to us was not cool; he was so overweight that he seemed slow getting in and out of his Highway Patrol car.

Saturday Night Dinner Conversations: Golf, Business, and Future Careers

Occasionally Dad and Mom had someone over for dinner (most often Uncle Bill and Aunt Marianne), but usually we boys had Dad all to ourselves Saturday after he had returned from his eighteen holes of golf at Ansley Golf Club. This time was particularly meaningful to us since many work weeks Dad was away traveling as a sales executive for Fleischman's Distilling.

"How did you shoot today, Dad?" was a question truly interested in an answer. We loved Dad's hole-by-hole account of eagles, birdies, pars, and bogeys. Dad, who usually shot in the high seventies or low eighties, would recount in make-you-want-to-listen fashion his longest drives, his most memorable putts, and gallant escapes from sand traps. We also talked about the greats of the past— Bobby Jones, Byron Nelson—as well as those of the '50s and '60s like Ben Hogan, Sam Snead, Gary Player, and the up-and-coming Arnold Palmer. I knew more about the great female golfers of the '40s and '50s—Babe Zaharias, Patty Berg, Louise Suggs—than I know of today's great female players.

While sports topics dominated, we did talk about other things. We were interested in his business travels and the people he worked with: the Grabenheimers in New Orleans, Walt Lake in Miami, Smittie from Columbia, South Carolina, and the Hertz family, father and son, in Atlanta. There were others that I don't recall. Occasionally Dad would take a business call at home; that was the only time we ever heard him utter cuss words, and they were limited to "hell" and "damn." He taught us at the dinner table that cussing was a sign of a weak vocabulary. We heard with pride of his high regard for Warren Oaks, Dad's boss both at American Airlines and Fleischman's Distilling, for whom our little brother Warren was named.

We also heard a bit of oft-repeated advice that clearly impacted the lives of his four sons: "Boys, I don't care what you ultimately pick as your life's work; just make sure it's something you really enjoy doing. There are too many people who hate their jobs and just live all week for the weekends. That's no way to live."

Ansley Golf Club was a nice gift from Dad to all of us. It was the smallest and least prestigious of the three or four country clubs that our friends' families belonged to. It was mainly an athletic club for golf, and that fit Dad's needs. But they had a nice pool and what seemed to us an elegant dining room. It was a special treat when we went to the Sunday buffet at Ansley. As hungry boys able to consume unbelievable amounts of food, our eyes would "bug out" at the buffet tables laden with all the foods we liked.

A mainstay of the summer was the Ansley swimming. Often we would time our swim to come at a little before that time in the afternoon when Dad would sink his last putt of the day on the eighteenth green, which lay at the bottom of the bank that separated the pool from the golf course. Often we would watch him chip and putt for the last time of that day; and then he would come and join us in the pool. (Dad had been a fine competitive swimmer at Columbus Academy, Ohio. He told us that he had once raced against Johnny Weissmuller—who went on to win three gold medals in the 1924 Paris Olympics in swimming and became a movie superstar by playing Tarzan.

Thirty years or so later, when serving as the Executive Director of the Atlanta Ballet, I met Al Davis when, with Lynda Courts, we were asking him for money. When I realized that he was a liquor wholesaler, his name rang a bell as one of the cast of business characters about whom Dad would weave his dinner table stories. When it was established that this was the same Al Davis with whom Dad had worked, now in his eighties, he motioned me aside to say in low tone and confidential manner, "I just want you to know, your dad was a straight-shooter." I took his remark to mean that Dad was loyal to Mom. Even though I had no reason to think that Dad was anything but true to his wife, it made me feel proud that Mr. Davis thought highly of Dad's character.

Teaching Us About Alcohol

Responsible consumption of alcohol was a dinner table topic from time to time. "Consume a moderate amount of alcohol slowly, and you won't get in trouble." When Dad spoke of alcohol, we took him to mean the array of beverages sold by his employer, Fleischman's Distilling: bourbon, gin, vodka, and Black & White Scotch. He would say, "Whiskey is concentrated food derived from wheat. Just as eating a big meal can leave you relaxed and even sleepy, so it is with alcohol. Over-eating is no more virtuous than over-drinking."

I inferred by Dad's example that two drinks consumed in pleasant social settings was "responsible drinking." In a sense having drinks with owners of large bars and restaurants (e.g., Antoine's and Arnaud's in New Orleans) was a major part of his job. Those were for him "pleasant social settings," as was sitting at the dinner table with Mom and their four sons.

The Johnston brothers at Sea Island, early 1950s—from left, Dillon, Dick, Warren, and Chuck

Chapter 5: My Brothers

Dick

In our prime childhood years, there were six places at our kitchen table. While Dad had his place at Mom's right hand, he was often missing because of his business travels. Mom sat at the head of the table with her back to the kitchen; Dick sat at the other end with his back to the wall but with a full view of the rest of us. He was clearly the one to back up Mom if our hilarity got out of bounds, which it had a tendency to do. When we didn't acknowledge that Mom was serious when saying "rein it in," Dick would step in and immediately sober us up.

From the time I can remember, Dick was always to me a Greek god. I know that was a blessing because I always admired him as someone to emulate. He appeared to me, five and a half years younger, to be handsome, built, and serious. We, his younger brothers, respected him—partly because we did and partly because he made us. We were not to go into his room without permission, and, for the most part, we didn't. The threat for any form of misbehaving on our parts was that he would "frog" us; that is, he would hit us hard on the muscle at the side of our shoulder with his knuckles, with the knuckle of the middle finger raised. It would create a very temporary whelp on the muscle that would quickly disappear. The whelp was the "frog."

Maybe this was Dick's leadership training that prompted so many achievements as he aged into high school and beyond. Sure, Dick was bigger and stronger, but his hold over us was more our adherence to a Johnston Boys code of conduct, coming initially from Dad and Mom, but which Dick modeled. And he was The Enforcer.

I didn't want to disappoint Dick; I feared that more than letting our parents down. My earliest memories of Dick begin from the time we moved into our house at 3349 Piedmont Road, in June of '46. His room was the control center for the upstairs. As I mounted the stairs to the second floor, I turned to my left facing the street, and Dick's room was to my left, with one window overlooking the upstairs front porch and the front yard, and two windows on the side looking out over R.L. Hope School. He was a benevolent leader, yet we adhered to the rules. His was the only room upstairs that we didn't enter without permission.

I don't know what so inspired Dick about sports that he at a very young age placed high priority on conditioning and training rules. It could well have been Dad's stories of his own exploits and love of sports. Dad filled the dinner table of our youth with stories of his favorite sports heroes: Joe Louis, Red Grange, Jim

Thorpe, and Jesse Owens, to name a few. Dick picked up Dad's heroes and added his own: Mel Ott, Jackie Robinson, Joe DiMaggio, and the New York Giants of the 1950s (e.g., Bobby Thompson, Eddie Stanky, Al Dark). I learned a lot from Dick about character as exemplified by admirable sports figures. I'm surprised that I so lauded Ted Williams, since he was known to be a bit of a rapscallion; generally I went for humble and clean-cut heroes.

Dick set the example for the three of us who followed behind him of being modest about his athleticism and achievements; and he placed a high priority on sportsmanship. Our childhood was sprinkled through and through with stories of great acts of sportsmanship, stories both from Dad and then from Dick. Sportsmanship was more important to Dick than winning, and he was a fierce competitor when it came to winning. Even before he knew he would be going to Vanderbilt, he would quote to us the words of the great *Nashville Banner* sports writer, Grantland Rice: "It's not whether you won or lost but how you played the game." That quote today is much maligned; but the three of us younger brothers believed it then because of Dick, and I suspect we are still a part of that minority of sports fans who believe it to this day.

A poem Dick would recite to us and to himself was the backdrop of our zest for manliness:

Do you fear the force of the wind, the slash of the rain,
Go face them and fight them, be savage again.
Go hungry like the wolf, go wade like the crane.
You'll grow ragged and weary and swarthy, but you'll walk like a man.

There is nothing in this capsule of masculinity that precludes crying over issues of the heart (Crying over being physically hurt, however, was discouraged.), and I saw Dick cry openly at Grandpa's death and other such times.

Not only were classical music, opera, and art permitted in Dick's canon of manliness, those rich cultural perks were encouraged by him. He bought classical music records and played them often when he was in his room. One album title I remember he owned was "Classical Music for People Who Hate Classical Music." Dick did not qualify for the record's title, but the selections on the recording were very tuneful (e.g., Wagner, Grieg, Copeland). Mozart was a little sedate for me; Beethoven I liked better.

He loved operatic arias, so I learned from him the names of several of the major sopranos of the time. I learned not to like Maria Callas because she was a *prima donna* in the negative use of the title. I liked Joan Sutherland, but my favorite was Leontyne Price, because of her voice and because of her back story of having been discovered while a maid in Mississippi. Dick was inspired by his fifth-grade teacher, Mrs. Gates, who would weekly play and teach the best-known classical music on her wind-up Victrola (with the logo of the dog listening to "His Master's Voice").

Dick was eclectic in his love of music. My early introduction to Robert Shaw (later longtime Atlanta Symphony director and Trinity School parent) and to choral music was via Dick's record of the Robert Shaw Chorale. Even more different was Jimmy Rodgers, a railroad man who sang the lonesome blues country style (e.g., "I'd rather drink muddy water and sleep in a hollow log, than be in Atlanta, treated like a dirty dog."—"Blue Yodel #1, T for Texas"). Hank Williams and Bill Monroe were really good, but Lester Flatt, Earl Scruggs, and the Smoky Mountain Boys were the gold standard. I learned from Dillon in my college years at Vanderbilt (I'm sure passed down from Dick) that one could enter the Ryman Auditorium (original home of the Grand Ole Opry) free during the 11 to midnight hour. We did that from time to time and heard some of the greats. Some would go from their stint on the Ryman stage to Ernest Tubb's Record Shop down the street and perform again on a little stage there. Often we followed them.

Dick was our leader when it came to summer jobs. He was hired by a contractor to dig out of solid red clay a basement for an addition to a house somewhere in the vicinity of Chastain Park. Dick recruited Dillon and me to work with him, and we would be paid so much per hour by the contractor. It was definitely a pick-and-shovel job—use huge swings of the pick to break loose the clay, then, when there was a shovel full, pitch it up out of the hole. This was done in June or July in the baking sun. Dillon and I didn't complain because Dick wasn't complaining. This was all a part of our unwritten code of toughness.

We may have worked as much as ten days before Dick noticed that the contractor wasn't coming around. At this point we were owed a tidy sum for our stoicism and productivity. Perhaps it was the nice owners of the house who advised Dick that we should stop working because it looked as if the contractor had absconded with the advanced money paid him and without any intent to pay us, his laborers. Sometime later we three each received a court summons. All I can remember of the court proceedings was one of the lawyers asking how we would define "normal." It seems that the defense was pleading insanity on behalf of the contractor. The homeowners got no recovery of funds, so they were stuck with liens for unpaid building supply bills. The homeowner offered to pay the three of us, but Dick told him that since he, the owner, was stuck with such a loss, we laborers would not ask him to pay us for what was the contractor's obligation. Dick—always the gracious one, and on our behalf, as well.

Probably the next summer he led us into the most lucrative summer work of our youth—working as counselors and, in my case, junior counselor, at the YMCA Day Camp and then teaching swimming lessons in the Chastain swimming pool. Dick taught us how to teach little kids to swim and our YMCA counselor training taught us this, as well. The Y had different skill levels to which the campers could aspire: tadpole, minnow, fish, shark, barracuda (something like that). Dick was known by the moms as an excellent teacher, so he had a waiting list for his services. Often he would pass to Dillon or me new prospective students that he couldn't accommodate. I was proud of him at the day camp because he rose in the leadership ranks to where he was in line to move from aquatics director to camp director. He had to miss a summer to take biochemistry. So, he missed his hard-earned opportunity, and that summer Lloyd Chapin, who was behind Dick in seniority, was named camp director. The next year, maybe his last at Day Camp, he served under Lloyd—Lloyd as director and Dick as aquatics director.

In his senior high school year, Dick was captain of the football team and president of the North Fulton student body. In his senior year at Vanderbilt, he was elected to the highest honor for a senior male—Bachelor of Ugliness. I don't know why I was not intimidated by the level of Dick's achievements— his top-level Honor Society academics as well as his athletic prowess. And, as a little brother, I was keenly aware of his self-discipline, only some of which he passed on to me. For instance, he had "training rules"—things that serious athletes did and didn't do. Getting enough sleep was an important part of this. Also, Dick didn't eat candy bars or potato chips, and he didn't drink carbonated soft drinks. Some of these sorts of things were a part of our "brothers' code."

Dick, North Fulton captain

Dick dated in high school. I remember viewing that from afar and wondering if I would ever have the courage to ask a girl out. Even at the beach he made friends with some attractive girl each summer. I had crushes on girls as far back as sixth grade, and I could relate as a friend, especially with the tomboys, but I was terrified at the idea of telling a girl that I liked her.

The beach was a good place to show off one's tan, and Dick was always "the best in class" in this category. He also had a Charles Atlas build, which I would have striven for if it didn't require so much pain and discipline. (Charles Atlas was a fitness guru of the era who ran a large ad in the funny papers or in comic books.

There would be a skinny kid lying down on the beach. A bully would come by and kick sand in the kid's face. Muscular Charles Atlas would come to the kid's rescue and send the assailant packing. Charles Atlas would then show the kid some simple workout equipment he could buy to achieve his own Charles Atlas build.) We spent a lot of time passing the football on the beach.

Dick was in Vanderbilt med school while Dillon and I were Vanderbilt undergraduates. Dillon coached me in how to approach exams. Part of it was getting organized and part of it was learning the art of cramming. Part of cramming, especially if it were to include an all-nighter, was to take a pill that Dick could provide from the hospital. Whatever it was, it came under the category of Speed or Dex. For both Dillon and me, it was cool to have a brother in med school. I never took this brain-quickening drug outside of the context of Vanderbilt exams. It was advised to save it for your last exam or two because too many back-to-back nights of little sleep and Speed could spell trouble.

There were multiple stories of students who might fall asleep while following this drug/sleep-deprived routine on the last night, miss their exam, and not wake up until two or three days later. Or one student who was so brilliant as his exam began that his hand could hardly keep up with his brain that was full of brilliant information exactly applicable to the exam. Two hours later he finished in exaltation, only to discover later that his exam paper was one huge black dot. He had poured out his brilliance in wonderfully formed sentences all on one page of the exam booklet, words tumbling on top of words.

Early in my Vanderbilt life, we established Thursday night supper when the three Johnston boys came and sat together and lingered, often until they were closing up Rand Hall. I remember finishing those meals with vanilla ice cream topped with chocolate pudding. Dillon would deliver treats from the athletic training table in the back where he got his meals.

In the second semester of our Thursday night suppers (spring '59), instead of a trio we became a quartet. Dick brought to join us someone in whom he had developed a great interest, Mary Anne Claiborne. We knew Mary Anne somewhat since she was in Dillon's Vanderbilt class ('60) and was from Buckhead. That auspicious supper together was the beginning of new health being brought to a male-centric set of four brothers who desperately needed another point of view. Mary Anne led the way in helping the four of us grow beyond our boyhood status.

It was a year and a half later that Dick and Mary Anne were married—August 13, 1960. They stayed their first year of marriage, if not two, at the Davidson County Hospital, a hospital for the mentally handicapped. Dick hereby was furnished room and board, if not more, in exchange for medical services to the patients. It was a testimony to his nature that he was able to execute this internship at the mental hospital while succeeding in his grueling medical training. Mary Anne was teaching at Ensworth School at this same time. I thought it spoke well of both of them that they were able to share their newly married lives with folks who were so far gone mentally that they scared me. I spent the night with them occasionally in their little-bitty miniature apartment and ate meals with Dick and Mary Anne in the "mess hall." The hospital residents reminded me of the indigent elderly that were housed in the "old folks' homes" at Chastain Park. We would pass them near the golf course when I was a kid in YMCA Day Camp. They scared me then, especially when an old woman who resembled my impression of a witch would blurt out something I couldn't understand as we would pass by with our counselor.

In his senior year of high school, at the zenith of his sports career thus far, captain of a football team laden with talent (e.g., Wade Mitchell was a future all-American), primed to go to Vanderbilt on a full athletic scholarship, Dick re-hurt a knee that had been injured in his junior year and was out for the season. I am only just now seeing this as the Greek tragedy that it was. The oldest brother who has achieved every possible accomplishment that he has undertaken, was slapped down hard at age seventeen. It is not intended to be humiliating, but it has to feel that way to sit out the season on the sidelines in street clothes.

A lesser person might well have "thrown in the towel," but not my big brother Dick. He set his determined self to rehabilitation of that painful knee. I can picture him sitting on the edge of his bed doing knee lifts with a weight dangling by a string attached to his ankle, sweat drenching his t-shirt. One more lift, so slow it was painful to watch, one more lift after that. Dick was determined to make a comeback. Having lost the initial opportunity for a football scholarship, he went early to Vanderbilt and entered the demanding summer football practices as a "walk-on," hoping to gain a scholarship that his canceled senior year had denied him. He felt encouraged in his first practice; he was doing it. Then he put together a string of good practices. His muscles and confidence were growing stronger.

Midway through week two on an especially hot August afternoon, the sounds of helmets hitting pads and the barking of coaches and the banter of players high on adrenalin were drowned out by an eerie hush. Dick lay on the ground, soon to be tended to by training room personnel, as coaches and players moved down the field and resumed practice; soon the sounds of barking and banter again filled the practice field. His was a bloodless injury, at least on the outside of his body. Unable to walk, he was carried off the field with so much facial contortion that one could not detect whether it was sweat or tears causing white channels down through the grime of a warrior's face.

The sports career of a truly admirable athlete was over. Lou Gehrig had his farewell speech when disease ended his sports career prematurely and Ted Williams hit a home run on his last at-bat. Dick had to settle for hobbling out of the Vanderbilt football locker room on crutches, never to enter again, never to follow in the shoes of Dad or Jim Thorpe or Jesse Owens in terms of fulfilling the fullest extent of his amazing sports potential.

At age twelve, I felt dejected, I'm sure, over the death of Dick's competitive sports career, though I may not have recognized it as such at the time. But looking back, I know how profound for Dick was this day in the summer of '53. It's only now that I see in Dick a loneliness that must have been there in spades as he went back to his dorm room with pain pills in his hind pocket, hunching over crutches that soon would begin to cut bruises under his arms. I now weep for a glory denied Dick at this young age. I now grieve for my own loneliness in not being able to connect my soul to his, at not being able to appropriate some of his drive, at not "living life together" and sharing his highs and his lows—not even knowing if he has lows. Maybe this is what holds sacred this concept of a birth brother, the longing for something that will forever be elusive.

(See **Appendix 10** for more about Dick's career.)

Dillon

When we lived at Little Gram's, we three brothers (Warren wasn't born yet.) shared the room over the screened porch. It was paneled with rougher wood in a way that gave it character. We slept on bunk beds. Dillon was good at making friends.

I remember Dillon more vividly after we moved to our Piedmont Road house. I would have been five and a half, and Dillon two years older. Our play was all centered in the woods in those early years. Today Ellie, Chad, and Martha Jane have a trampoline. Then we had the creek. Dillon taught me everything I needed to know about play. We built dams on the creek. It was fun to see how much of a lake we could form, a lake on which to play with floating things. Eventually we would break the dam just

Dillon in the late 1950s

to see how swift was the destruction once a crack began in the dam. In no time multiple hours of work were washed away. We built little villages using sticks as the framing and sheets of green moss as the sheetrock. Sometimes these little villages were swept away by the torrent of the broken dam.

Frank Albert from across the street was called "Bub." He was Dillon's age and Dillon's friend. But a high moment for me in my single-digit years was to join a neighborhood gang. This was not the Crips or the Bloods; it was the Coyote Kids.

It was Dillon, Bub, and me. We built a secret hideout in the woods. We spent a lot of time in it, and it was well concealed. We had rituals of which Memory has not revealed to me. Dillon was the brains behind this Western-type gang. Our prototype was the James Brothers Gang (i.e., Jesse James). They were idolized by Dad—maybe "idolized" as a clever way to instill in us four boys an unbreakable loyalty to each other.

Dillon and Bub challenged each other to a boxing match. They set it far enough ahead in the summer so that both boxers would have plenty of time to train. Remember, Dillon and Dick were both big on training. Bub was a bit heavier than Dillon, maybe even a little fat. It was hot, and Bub wasn't quite as rigorous in his training, of which Dillon was critical and maybe even saw an advantage for "his team." The day of the big fight came. Four posts and ropes formed the ring in the corner of the Alberts' front yard, and chairs were brought in for the spectators. Neighbor John Newman was the impartial referee. The Alberts, a five-kid Catholic family, took their seats, and the Johnstons, a four-kid Presbyterian family, took their seats, and the fight began. I believe Big Gram and Grandpa were in attendance. I can't give you a blow-by-blow description of the fight, but I do know that Dillon won. The gate receipts went to the winner. In a show of magnanimity, Dillon announced that he would donate the prize money to Peachtree Road Presbyterian Church. After we got home, someone suggested that giving the prize money to the Presbyterians could have felt to the good Catholic family as if salt were being rubbed into the wounds. In a fairly close-knit neighborhood, we passed on from the fight with feelings intact. (It's easy for me to conclude that because I was on the winning side.)

I wish I had been as good a big brother to Warren as Dillon was to me. I'm sure it must have existed, but I don't remember discord between Dillon and me. Just as his being glad to include me in the Coyote Kids, he always seemed glad to have me tag along. When his friends would come over from school in my early double-digit youth, he was always glad to include me in touch football games or whatever they might be up to. (Our front yard was the neighborhood's most level and open yard for touch football.) When he decided he wanted to be a pitcher, I was his catcher. I can still remember the sting of his fastball in the palm of my hand. When Dillon was training for Golden Gloves boxing competition—he together with Teddy Keen—I was his sparring partner in our basement boxing ring.

Maybe the pinnacle of this inclusion of his little brother was when he had just met Anne. He took me with him downtown to Davison's Department Store to meet Anne Coggan, a new girl-of-interest to Dillon. Anne served on the College Board, a group of girls selected from different colleges helping Davison's sell clothes to college-aged girls. Shortly after this meeting, Dillon invited me to join him and Anne in a game of Monopoly at Anne's parents' apartment on Scott

Boulevard. I don't remember the back and forth of the game—certainly not winners and losers—but I've never forgotten Dillon and Anne's generosity of including me in that evening.

Dillon must have been in the ninth grade and I in the seventh grade when Buddy Fowlkes had heard that Dillon was fast; Buddy invited Dillon to join him on the track at Grant Field for a Sunday afternoon workout. Buddy was training to run in a national AAU meet, Adult Division. He wanted some company in his workouts; Buddy also worked with younger youth at Camp Fritz Orr, and he liked helping youth. Once again, Dillon invited me to come along. Buddy got into helping us to the extent that he made an early version of starting blocks for each of us—a block of wood for each foot with a tin facing, slanted for the foot in a starting position, and attached to the ground via a spike down the middle of the block. Then Buddy coached us to get high up on our fingers with the fingers lined up just behind the starting line. Buddy ran a 9.5 100-yard-dash in the National AAU Championships, which was close to the best ever, if not the best, for a 35-year-old man.

Advance a couple of years and Dillon is towards the end of his junior year at North Fulton, I nearing the end of my freshman year. Dillon is running for student body president. One of his campaign parties was at the gym behind Ivan and Louise Allen's home. Word came to Dillon that some boys were drinking beer at their cars on the Allen property. He had made commitments to Ivan III's parents that there would be no alcohol, so he set out to quash the drinking, and I and one or two others with him. I am embarrassed to this day that I acted overly excited, said something about us being a posse, and Dillon had to tamp me down. The boys with the beer easily complied with Dillon's request to put the beer away since he had made the commitment he had to the Allens. Dillon went on to make the best presidential speech of the morning, only to lose the race to Bobby Cruikshank. Dillon's campaign speech was based on the Beatitudes, and Bobby's was a series of promises, tailored to different age groups, most of which were promises over matters wherein the Student Council had no say. Bobby delivered a crushing election defeat to Dillon. Dillon was content to be the senior class president.

I will not here let Dillon's humbleness keep me from stating the truth, that as a high school sophomore and beyond, he was a once-in-a-decade halfback and sprinter. In those days the Atlanta newspapers covered high school sports with their own prep school sports editor, Gene Asher. Each football season especially, Dillon had numerous pictures and headlines in the paper. One game he ran for 248 yards, and another game he scored five touchdowns—both headline-grabbing feats. He went to Vanderbilt on a full football scholarship, and in his college senior year, for part of the season, he led the SEC in punt returns, just ahead of All-American back Billy Cannon of LSU.

I followed Dick and Dillon to Vanderbilt. There Dillon guided me through the fraternity rush process which went on all fall semester of my freshman year, as I remember. The Vanderbilt football players who were Phi's participated fully in fraternity life, Dillon being one of them. When it came time for me to be initiated, Dillon, knowing my interest in teaching, arranged for Jimmy McCallie to be my Big Brother. That initiative on Dillon's part set me up for "the success track" throughout my career in independent schools. It was the co-head of the McCallie School in Chattanooga, Dr. Bob McCallie—Jim's dad—who hired me into my first job in education. And henceforth Jim always stood ready to provide a strong recommendation for me for future jobs.

Dillon and I ran Vanderbilt track together for the two years we overlapped as Vanderbilt students. Lamar Alexander was a teammate in my class. Dillon was a sprinter; I ran middle distance. In one meet—against Kentucky that had a smaller squad—the opponents had no mile-relay team. So, to keep everybody sharp, we ran a freshman team against the varsity team, and probably gave the freshmen about a half-lap lead. Dillon and I were both running the anchor legs. As Dillon prepared to pull up alongside me to pass, his team having overcome the huge deficit, I gradually began to pull out in my lane, thinking I was being funny and also thinking this was the sort of borderline tactic that Buddy Fowlkes would applaud. Dillon started hitting me on the shoulder with his relay baton to get me to move back to the inside lane, and I held my ground. Dillon was furious with me; and I immediately knew I had done the wrong thing. This is another of those things that embarrasses me to think about some sixty years later.

Upon my 1962 Vanderbilt graduation, I headed to NYC—my first time there—to stay a few days with Dillon in his apartment at the Choir School of St. Thomas Church, 57th and Avenue of the Americas, near Carnegie Hall. While Dillon was working on his master's degree at Columbia University, he taught classes and lived in the dorm at this boarding school that recruited boys to sing the female parts in this Anglican church choir. One of the many people that Dillon introduced me to was a more senior Choir School teacher, Gordon Clem, who handled the math while Dillon taught English.

Everything was an eye-opener for me. Dillon took me to delicatessens with their exotic treasures: Dannon yogurt with the fruit to be stirred up from the bottom and bagels—two edibles I had never had before. They had not yet come to the South. Even after stirring up the fruit from the bottom, the yogurt was still more tart than ice cream, the product against which I measured all midnight snacks. But it was like my early reaction to beer; I didn't like it, but I knew I needed to cultivate a taste as I took on the coolness and freedom of being an adult.

On one of the midnight excursions to the neighborhood deli, he told me to be subtle and notice the woman with the head scarf and sunglasses. Once outside he told me it was actress Lauren Bacall. I was star-struck: "This world that Dillon lives in is really something."

After seeing *The Fantasticks* off Broadway (with its haunting song, "Try to Remember") we went to an Episcopal worship service in the theater community that started at 11:30 p.m. Saturday night and might have lasted as late as 1 a.m. Sunday morning. This service, led by the Reverend Sidney Lanier, who would later officiate Dillon and Anne's wedding, was designed for the theater people who only had one day off a week, and that was Sunday. This late night / early morning service gave them the opportunity to spend Sunday in their pajamas, should they wish.

In addition to *The Fantasticks*, Dillon had gotten us tickets to *A Strange Interlude*, a Eugene O'Neill play in nine acts, with a break for supper after the first five acts; I thought that was super-cool. Dillon also introduced me to the Museum of Modern Art (MOMA), located close to the Choir School. There I met for the first time Picasso and the Impressionists. This was my first experience of art museums as an alluring place.

A couple of details of Dillon's life in NYC are telling of his character. Dad was alone in his NYC apartment while Mom remained in Atlanta to see Warren through his last year or two of North Fulton. Maybe once a week Dillon and Dad would meet for dinner. They would draw dinner out as long as they could, and then Dad would say, "I'll walk you partway back to the Choir School (53rd Street)." The two of them would get engrossed in conversation, and next thing they knew, they were at the Choir School. So, Dillon would say, "Let me walk you back halfway to your apartment (85th Street)." Again, in fun and free conversation, they found themselves at Dad's apartment. This time they established the halfway point; and there reluctantly turned, and with back to each other, headed off to the less nurturing environs of their respective apartments.

The second detail confirms Dillon's love of games and the physical side. He found a rugby team with Sunday-afternoon-in-Central-Park matches in which to throw himself, and throw himself in he did, up to the point when he tore his shoulder up and had to have reconstructive surgery.

New York was the place of Dillon's wedding to Anne Coggan. After dating for six years, Dillon and Anne were married August 23, 1963, at a friend's estate north of NYC. Dillon graduated from Columbia University a year later. New York was now a chapter closed. Paris and Charlottesville were up ahead.

(See **Appendix 11** for more about Dillon's career.)

Warren

Mr. Bradshaw was the builder of our new house in Big Gram and Grandpa's side yard. When it was being planned, it had an upstairs bedroom for Dick alone and then the whole back of the upstairs was set aside for Dillon and me to share. The fourth space, a bedroom like Dick's at the front of the house, was set aside as a guest room, and, as such, it was wallpapered in pink roses. We were moving into this house just as Warren was coming home from Emory Hospital as a newborn (June '46). He and his nurse-for-a-week stayed in that "guest room," which was his for the first year of his life.

Warren, age 20

Then, giving credence to pecking order, Dillon moved into the pink-rose room, and Warren became my roommate in the space that had a lot more room for play. It had cubbyholes where, should you want, you could climb from the back of one closet to the other; there were little doors all along the way should one wish to abort the trek from one closet to the other. The room had solid windows all across the back that opened and closed with a crank. Even in the hottest part of the summer, it got so chilly with the attic fan pulling the cool night air through all those windows that we had to cover with a light blanket. At each end of the room was a dormer window with the perfect space for a desk. Warren and I shared that room from 1947 until 1958 when I went off to college, and, of course, on my returns home.

There is the oft-repeated story of my adjustment to no longer being the baby of the family. This episode occurred on a leisurely Saturday morning, with Dad lingering over the newspaper and coffee, with Big Gram stopping by to visit, and with Warren (aka Binkie) in the kitchen demonstrating just how cute and precious he was.

As a six-year-old, I had gone into the back yard, picked a long stem of privet hedge, stripped the leaves and bark off, and made myself a supple switch that made a swish sound when I quickly moved it through the air. I often did this and played with it as if it were a sword. As I was entering through our back door and passing the kitchen table and hearing Big Gram going on and on about how cute and adorable Warren was, I pulled back the supple end of my privet-hedge switch and let it fly across the small of Baby Warren's back. He jumped as high as a nine-month-old toddler could (Yes, Warren was a precocious child, standing and taking steps at nine months and putting words together months before any baby previously born up and down Piedmont Road.) With the jump he let out a baby's version of a blood-curdling scream. Big Gram's jaw dropped and she scrambled to swoop the precious baby into her arms. Dad, meanwhile, was encamped behind the sports section, having seen it all but not saying a word. I said in my most innocent tone, "Oh, excuse me," as I passed quickly out of the room. As Dad would later tell the story, he never reproached me for my dastardly deed because he knew exactly what I was experiencing in being replaced as the cutest one.

We honestly couldn't tell any stronger love from Mom or Dad for any one of us over the others. There was great comfort for us brothers in that fact, and that may have contributed to why we never fought. Big Gram, however, had her favorite, and she wasn't hiding it. It was Warren. To be fair to Big Gram, she may have been being protective of the youngest, the baby in the family; and maybe I had my season to be that preferred child. That Big Gram and Warren shared a name—Gram's maiden name and Warren's middle name were both Nelson—may have contributed to the partiality. Big Gram surprised Warren with the gift of a car, having deduced that he had to have one to get back and forth from Athens. Note: Living in a slightly earlier time, we older three didn't own a car until we had graduated from college.

Warren became a terrific little brother. We played together hour upon hour, much as I see Chad and Martha Jane doing. We shared the big room across the back of the house, playing endless games of battle with our dolls, his against mine. Hard rubber softballs, captured when being lost over the playground fence into our back yard, were our ammunition. I envied Warren for having a June (the 23rd) birthday, with mine falling two weeks before Christmas. He would get the buckets and shovel and other beach toys we would then use together during our two weeks at St. Simons. Dad introduced us to the art of sandcastle building, but we could never have enjoyed it so much without the resources from Warren's annual June birthday.

While in college and beyond, Warren and I shared life together even though we missed sharing any North Fulton High School years. Warren went into the eighth grade the same year I went off to Vanderbilt. As was true of his three older brothers, he played football and ran track. While I was the odd brother out in athletic prowess, Warren was in the league with Dick and Dillon in being an outstanding running back. Warren, Tim Woodall, Bob Wheeler, and Warren's other teammates went to the City Championship football game, the Ira Jarrell Milk Bowl. I came down from McCallie School where I was teaching for that big Friday night game, only to miss it because President Kennedy was assassinated that afternoon (November 22, 1963), and the championship game was moved to the next night, a night when I had to be back in Chattanooga for the McCallie ninth grade football team's banquet at the Signal Mountain Country Club. Warren, by the way, was an excellent running back and an accomplished runner of track. He held his own in any comparisons to his two oldest star-brothers. I was always proud of Warren and glad to have him as one of the "college boys."

Warren and I each had our own shotguns and would go hunting together some in the winters. We went a few times to a forested area running alongside the Chattahoochee, called Morgan Falls. Then, once if not twice, Warren joined Tom Garden and me in a hunt with Lam Hardman at the Indian Mounds in Nacoochee Valley. That adventure, that ended with boiled squirrel for dinner, began with a lavish lunch in the Hardman home in Commerce, complete with servants tending to service of the meal.

Years later, Warren wrote a column titled "Southern Lite," which included this vivid description:

"As was his daily practice, [Mr. Hardman] walked home from the [mill] where he was president and joined his wife and the other family members around the dining room table, just as the scene was set by the arrival of platters of fried chicken and sliced ham, bowls of collard and turnip greens, fried okra and potato salad, accompanied by plates of sliced tomatoes and buttermilk biscuits. Iced tea was the only beverage offered, poured unsweetened from a round clear glass pitcher into tall ice-filled glasses sporting sprigs of freshly-picked mint and adorned with a slice of lemon." (From a June 2015 *Valley News* column)

(See **Appendix 12** for more about Warren's career.)

Chapter 6: My Youth (from 1945 Thereabouts to 1962 Graduation)

Thanksgiving with Champ

I don't remember all the building blocks of my walk as a Believer. But my earliest "outreach" memory is of sharing Thanksgiving dinner and afternoon with an orphan named Champ, who came to us through Second Ponce de Leon Baptist Church. When I was ages three to five, we lived not far from there in Garden Hills, so maybe we attended that church. Champ lived at the Baptist Children's Home which was way far away, out near the airport. I know, because we would drive Champ back there after we had milked every moment with him that we could. I'm guessing we did this for about three years while we were living with Little Gram and maybe for a year after we moved to Piedmont Road. Champ was around Dick's age. This would have put them at around eight, nine, ten.

We had presented Champ with his own new football as a welcome-to-our-home gift, so there was a lot of football passing as part of the afternoon. What can be more bonding than boys moving around together passing a football? It's good for brothers, for dads and sons, and for boys and near-strangers. Without necessarily intending to, you draw closer. The drive back was a mixture of hilarity and sadness. There are key times when saying "goodbye" hurts in the throat and chest, and this was one of them. Unbeknownst at the time, one of these painful goodbyes was the last one. Why is it that we have in life these soulmates that we never see again? Where is Champ now?

My Best Friend in My Early Years: Bobby Stephenson

Bobby Stephenson and I grew up around the corner from each other—he on Ivy Road that is now the Buckhead Loop, and I on Piedmont Road where now sits part of Tom Cousins' Phoenix Building. Probably around second grade we became playmates, he the only sibling of a much older sister and I one of a pack of four brothers. There was more going on at my house than there was at Bobby's. His quiet felt good to me occasionally; our chaos felt good to Bobby at times. We were "at home" in each other's houses.

As I'm sure has already been stated, I grew up next door to our elementary school, R.L. Hope School. Its principal, Ms. Paschal, appeared to be the stereotypical 1950s school principal during the school week, glasses, bun on the back of her head (convenient place to stick a pencil for quick retrieval), and large enough to intimidate little kids. Living next door, we had seen her in her weekend and holiday disguise—in blue jeans and driving a weathered-looking pickup truck, looking every bit as if she had been doing farm labor. A defining episode with Ms. Paschal included Bobby.

Class Prophecy read at R.L. Hope graduation, June 1953: Chucky Johnston's admitted to the bar—student, lawyer, he'll go far.

In the middle of an afternoon PTA meeting, some mother who should have been minding her own business, came in to the meeting all a fluster:

"Ms. Paschal, come quick. There are two boys so high up in the giant oak tree in the back that you can barely see them. They are going to fall to their deaths." Ms. Paschal gave the appearance of being in earnest pursuit of bad boys, when she got to the back of the school, to the massive oak whose girth would take three adults hand-to-hand to reach around it. How many stories tall? Maybe four or five or possibly six. And Bobby and I were way up in it. In no uncertain terms Ms. Paschal told us to come down, which we most assuredly and quickly did. When she got us close to her, she said in a soft and pleasant voice, "Boys, if it were a Saturday and I had on my blue jeans instead of this dress, I might be up there with you. But do me this favor—when you know I'm having a PTA meeting, don't choose that day to climb to the top of this monster tree. There are a lot of grown people who don't know what you and I know about climbing trees."

Where his family greatly impacted me was in the trips Mr. Stephenson, Bobby, and I would take to the Stephenson 350-acre farm in Covington, south and east of Atlanta. Back then, with only two-lane roads to take us there, it felt like a long trip. Mrs. Stephenson would pack a picnic basket full of good things for our long ride and for our lunch.

How did I know in my bones from an early age that the way African-Americans were treated in the Jim Crow South was wrong? On the negative side, my sensitivity may have come from a reaction to Big Gram who would school us on how we were to treat "the Darkies" and who was mean to One-eyed Jim and Cleve, black men who did her yard chores and heavy housework. Big Gram also referred to blacks as "the help" or as "Niggras," thought by her and others as more refined than "Nigger." On the positive side, my early awareness of just how disenfranchised the blacks were may have come from Mr. Stephenson who treated the sharecropping black families on his family farm as fellow human beings and tried to bring to them advantages that we in the well-off white world took for granted—as an entitlement because we, after all, were white.

We read that Roosevelt brought electricity to the rural South back in the '30s; these lovely sharecropping people were behind the times. Yet, until they had it, they didn't know what they were missing. Over the span of a year or more, Mr. Stephenson worked long hours on Saturdays to bring electricity into the home of the family matriarch Betty Sims, who lived with three of her adult children (Ed, Leroy, and Florida) near the entrance to the farm. (At my single-digit age, Betty seemed to be in her eighties. There's a good chance she wasn't that old.)

After Betty's house was electrified, Mr. Stephenson went through the same hard labor at the home of the next generation of the family, Maud and his wife, Willie, who lived deeper into the farm at the end of a road that was bordered on each side by good-sized cotton fields. One of their thirteen children was named Polly, after Bobby's mother, Mrs. Stephenson.

Bobby and I managed to be a little help to Mr. Stephenson—maybe holding the ladder, maybe handing him tools and supplies when he was up in the attic. (But, in truth, we spent a lot of our time playing and exploring. We loved watching Maud working on his anvil in his blacksmith shop.) Can you imagine Mr. Stephenson's delight when, after weeks and months of doing this work, he turned on the switch that finally ignited the lights of the house? Bobby, now Bob, reminded me recently that, when Betty and Maud and Willie first had electric lights, they didn't use them much, preferring the kerosene lamps that they were used to. (Think about how many generations before them depended on kerosene for light. And, in its time, kerosene was a step up from candles.)

Here are some things that I experienced on The Farm in the '40s and '50s that were really from an earlier era:

- ✓ All the water supply for the household was drawn from a deep well. One turned the hand crank in one direction to lower the bucket to beneath the water, making sure not to splash and stir up mud, and then putting muscle behind raising the bucket full of water to the surface. The water was cold and clear, and it tasted mighty good on a hot summer day.

- ✓ Since there was no running water in the house, so neither was there a toilet. There was an outhouse, and we learned to use it. (An outhouse is a bit like a Jiffy Johnny; both can have overpowering odor.)

- ✓ The yard was hard-packed red clay. They used some type of dried branch to sweep the yard rather than the mowing that I was accustomed to from back in our Buckhead neighborhood.

- ✓ When in the beginning cold of October the hog was butchered, no part was wasted. The intestines were washed exceedingly and then boiled in oil to produce something, as I remember, that tasted like fried onion rings, and were just as good; this was chitlins. Sausage was another by-product that I took home to my family. It was a bit spicy for me, as best I can remember.

- ✓ We occasionally shared a meal at her table with Betty, and the entire meal was prepared on a potbellied stove that had burners over the wood-burning fire similar to the burners on our electric or gas stoves.

- ✓ In the winter, this same potbellied stove provided all the heat for the house. Air conditioning in the hot seasons came from the breezes that blew through the screened doors and screened windows. (Screens were essential because flies were a big problem for these farmhouses.)

- ✓ We picked cotton, but not for long. By the time we wrestled a few clumps of white cotton from the tenacious bolls, we had little cotton in the bottom of our long and dragging bag to show for our exertion. We didn't last long at that labor.

Maud plowed the fields with a mule and plow. He let Bobby and me try it, but we didn't last long. I couldn't pull down hard enough for the plow to dig down deep into the soil. With me, the blade of the plow just skimmed along the top. Plowing with a mule was hard work. And I saw at a different season of the year how back-breaking was the picking by hand of the cotton. Early in my life, seeing the rigor of manual labor made me henceforth understand what was meant by "earning your living by the sweat of your brow."

Bob Stephenson, both of us now in our late seventies, shared with me these remembrances of Maud:

"The mules were named Ike and Mamie. Maud took very good care of them. I remember hearing of him going out in the middle of the night during a lightning storm to check on them and reassure them. Most days, Maud would wake up well before dawn, get a fire going in the fireplaces to warm up the home, and then would get to work on the farm. What used to impress me so much about Maud, besides his low-key, gentle and friendly manner, was how he would turn certain items into essentially brand-new ones. He would find an old rusting hammer head out in the woods or somewhere, take it to his blacksmith shop, sharpen and shine it up, make a handle for it and then paint the handle red, white and blue or some other bright colors and take pride in showing it to others."

Sharecropping has a bad name as a form of colonialism or of economic dominance. "[It is] estimated that only a quarter to a third of sharecroppers got an honest settlement, which did not in itself mean they got any money," author Isabel Wilkerson wrote in *The Warmth of Other Suns: The Epic Story of America's Great Migration.* "The Negro farm hand … gets for his compensation hardly more than the mule he plows, that is, his board and shelter. Some mules fared better than Negros."

However, I did see a positive side of a practice that was in widespread use. The multiple generations of this family that lived on the Stephenson farm liked Mr. Stephenson—that was clear to me as a boy. I know he was fair with them. I suspect that when the cotton was sold, Mr. Stephenson covered the cost of taxes and supplies (seed, fertilizer, tools, feed for the mules) and the rest he turned over to those who had toiled all year to make a crop happen. Their take of the sales income had to cover all their household expenses, including those of raising children.

What an amazing experience the Stephensons gave to me, in the '40s and early '50s, of going back in time.

Aunt Virginia

We would go together to Brookwood Station on a still-cool summer morning. Down by the tracks we would wait (and wait) until the first sign that the train was coming—a bright beam of a light that I knew was "The Southerner's" headlight. At first there was no sound, and then would begin the sound of airbrakes and steam. It was a behemoth that moved towards you and then would pull alongside you without hurting anybody. "Now, don't stand too close or the air current will pull you under the wheels," we were told.

Aunt Virginia would emerge, stepping onto a little stool, and then onto the platform, being escorted gallantly by the porter. Uncle Wally wouldn't let Virginia fly because his father had barely escaped years earlier from a plane that crashed into the Boston Bay upon takeoff.

Without knowing a thing about women's fashion, I knew Aunt Virginia, coming down from New England, was the most stylish woman on the East Coast. We would all embrace. She may have had gifts for us, but that would come later.

Did I mention her travel companion, Little Wally? Oh, yes, he would emerge a bit after her. It would seem that he always had a problem—a cinder in his eye, a boil, a medical test to last the duration of the summer for which he was to eat all the sugar that he could. That's when I learned about banana splits, though I was probably only allowed to have one all summer. Being an only child, he lacked the give and take, the toughness of boys growing up in a pack of brothers.

A few years later, when we older boys were in high school, we would occasionally be talking with friends about Little Wally, and they would be incredulous when we told them about some of our summer play:

"You really tied him up and left him?"

"Yes, we were playing a normal game of the Jesse James gang versus the lawmen. This is how you play it. Little Wally was either the bad guy or the good guy, I don't remember. But if you got caught and overpowered, you either got put in some place you couldn't get out of or you were tied up. This day it was 'tie him up.'"

"But why did you go off and leave him?"

"Why wouldn't we? You have to willingly submit to being tied up, because part of the fun was untying yourself. We had never experienced someone who couldn't get untied. I guess we may have gotten a little slow in getting back to check on him. Come on! Don't blame us! Was Little Wally a sissy? No, he really wasn't. He was built like a second-string athlete. Maybe it was that he was disadvantaged when it came to rough-and-tumble play. No brothers, you know."

Seeing Aunt Virginia off at the end of her month's stay was another one of those stick-in-the throat tear-inducing moments. Again, it occurred at Brookwood Station, with the train pulling in from the south with all its bells and whistles, so to speak. This time she was stepping up into the train instead of stepping off. Then it was her face at the window, and then she was gone. And on came the pain.

It was June 3, 1962. I was in line outside of Neely Auditorium on the Vanderbilt campus waiting to file in for our baccalaureate service, when I was approached by an official-looking person.

"Are you Chuck Johnston? [nod yes] There's a phone call for you in the alumni office, if you will follow me."

It was Uncle Bill on the other end of the line. "Chuck, I hate to give you this news on the day of your graduation, but the plane on which Virginia was flying back from France crashed... Yep, upon takeoff! Paris, Orly Field—and all 122 Atlantans on board were killed—including Aunt Virginia."

Here was another "goodbye," but much more severe than the tight chest and tears I had experienced in earlier years at the Brookwood Station.

"Why, why does something like this happen? My sweet Aunt Virginia."

Uncle Wally had died of a heart attack, and for a year or so Aunt Virginia had been in deep grief, as would be expected. She'd decided she would come to Atlanta and try life here as a change. She grew up in Atlanta, went to Washington Seminary, and made her debut here. So she had a lot of friends. It was some of these friends from the past who invited Aunt Virginia to go with them on a chartered-flight art tour of Europe sponsored by the High Museum of Art. Her recovery was beginning.

Standing in line that graduation day were classmates who lost both parents in that crash, but I could only focus on my own grief. And how about Big Gram and Mom? Poor Mom, even at the death of her only and beloved little sister, she could not grieve. Mom and Dad decided to keep it from Big Gram—who, after Grandpa died nine years earlier, had "taken to her bed" for a couple of months in total collapse. They were afraid the same would happen here in Nashville, away from home and Tully, her doctor. Remembrance of this collapse influenced the decision not to tell Big Gram about the Air France plane crash until the car transporting Big Gram back from my Vanderbilt graduation arrived at her home on Piedmont Road.

Even in this crushing time in Mom's life, she had to hold it in and "soldier on" until they got Big Gram back to Atlanta the next day. And then she had to contain her grief to tend to her mother. How might life have been different for Mom if her sister had lived?

The Bachelor Uncle for Whom I Was Named

First of all, here is a piece of writing that Uncle Charlie must have done as a grammar school assignment:

The Story of My Life, by Charles Johnston
I was born on May 11, 1916. The early part of my life was not filled
with any exciting experiences. The only exciting thing that ever
happened was the storm in Miami, Florida in 1926. I had a lot of fun
after the storm, and I found a lot of good things. Outside of the
storm I haven't had much more happen to me, but I expect
something will happen at least I hope.
The End

(This school assignment, in exquisite handwriting, appeared among my things on a nearly deteriorated piece of notebook paper.)

Uncle Charlie was a radio man in a Boeing B-24 bomber during WWII. He would have been in his mid-twenties. (He left for the war before he graduated from Georgia Tech, I know, because I think I attended his Tech graduation at the Fox Theater in '46 or '47.) For an account of his capture by the Germans, I turn to my brother Dick's account:

"His plane was shot down over Austria or southern Germany on Christmas Eve. He walked to a farmhouse, which happened to be occupied by a Nazi officer who offered him a place at Christmas Eve dinner, then drove him to the authorities."

Thus Uncle Charlie became a prisoner of war, the only POW that I have ever known, much less had as an uncle. He wouldn't talk much about the war experience, but because Dad and Uncle Bill were with him sometimes when he was tipsy with alcohol, they learned in bits and pieces that he had escaped from prison and was hiding out in a barn when the Germans entered and threated to riddle the haystack with machine gun bullets if the escapees didn't come out. He and his companions came out and went back into captivity, the cruelty of which Uncle Charlie never spoke. The only visible injuries were his feet, misshapen by frostbite. Again from Dick: "He was freed by Patton's advance."

Uncle Charlie had a WWII Army Jeep that he kept for trips up to his lot at Lake Burton, one of Georgia's beautiful Georgia Power mountain lakes. At the marina there, Laprades, he kept a simple outboard motor boat. I remember thinking I was going to freeze to death one time when riding up to the lake with Uncle Charlie and Dillon in the woefully drafty Jeep. Dillon and I found a pot of warm chili buried under some equipment. Uncle Charlie said we could take spoons and eat out of the pot; I'm convinced that warm chili spared me from death by freezing. We stopped at the pharmacy in Clarkston, the last town before the lake, and got our customary chocolate milkshake from the soda fountain.

Uncle Charlie in WWII

There were little boyish indulgences like the milkshakes that endeared Uncle Charlie to us.

On another occasion, during a spring break, I spent a week at Lake Burton with Uncle Charlie. We installed the foundational posts, put the connecting two-by-eights around the periphery and one down the middle, and then laid the floor boards across the open expanse. This accomplishment took us all week. Why? Primarily because Uncle Charlie had a severely inexperienced assistant, but also because each board had to be put across the bow of Uncle Charlie's modest boat, maybe as many as six at a time, and slowly driven across the lake from Laprades to the base of Charlie Mountain, where sat Uncle Charlie's lot, with Dad's untouched lot to one side, and Uncle Bill's to the other. Again, call it an indulgence if you will; I call it a recognition of my ten-year-old maturity—Uncle Charlie let me drive the boat alone back to Laprades to pick up the needed bags of cement. The "cabin" never advanced beyond having one of the best constructed floors and foundations conceivable. For years after it was up, this floor was where we would hold our family picnics.

Maybe it was the difference in our ages, or maybe I was obnoxious in my younger years; but I never reached the closeness to Uncle Charlie that I would have liked. Towards the end of his life he was at Piedmont Hospital fighting cancer, and I went to see him on his May 11th birthday. I don't know what possessed me, some sort of newfound reality check, I guess, but I must have said something like, "It stinks for you to have to be in here on your birthday." Jon Whirlow, Uncle Charlie's close companion, contacted me shortly thereafter and said Charlie had requested that I not visit him in the hospital.

This could bring on a discussion of how we Johnston males, Dad's generation and ours, have a confounding way of not seeing the bad in people or situations. Maybe I was trying my hand at being more real. I clearly chose the wrong time and place to try out something that was not my real nature. Jon and I were not estranged after Uncle Charlie died. In fact, we spent many Saturday mornings over at what had been both Jon and Charlie's Cross Creek three-level condominium, cataloging more than a hundred sets of house plans that Charlie had drawn over his lifetime as a quality home architect. Jon gifted the plans, in neatly labeled packing tubes, to the Atlanta History Center. Jon was particularly fond of JoElyn, and for some years after we stayed in touch, occasionally sharing a meal together.

Uncle Bill—Generator of Fun and Humor

Uncle Bill, the older of Dad's younger brothers, was the tallest (six-foot-two) and played basketball at Princeton. I was given his middle name, Louis, as my middle name. To my memory he was the master of puns and fun. His puns were

5

too silly to remember, but they sure did make us laugh. It must have been his genes that infected his nephews—my brothers—Dillon and Warren. They are the comedians in our generation.

Fun with Uncle Bill came in the form of hiking and eating. A couple of memorable hikes were to Blackberry Hill, a wooded property he owned off of Stratford Road with a beautiful stream. There I had my first experience of picking and eating blackberries.

Fun was just going over to Uncle Bill's house. Aunt Marianne, his beautiful redheaded wife (nicknamed "Torchie"), added to the fun by her efforts to hold Uncle Bill in check. One Saturday morning, when home from college, Dillon and I invited ourselves over for breakfast with them. Their home was inviting with its entire side devoted to a glass porch that overlooked woods and Uncle Bill's carefully attended bird feeders.

Uncle Bill was the ringmaster of what turned into a gala breakfast. (Aunt Marianne was at first out of the picture, still in the back waking up and "making herself presentable.") We began with bowls of Cheerios and fruit. We then progressed to bacon and eggs and toast. From there we progressed to French toast and syrup. Aunt Marianne entered the room while this third course was being prepared and was flummoxed: "What? I can't believe you guys! Bill, have you lost your mind? What all have you had for this little breakfast?"

I think as much to confound Aunt Marianne as to keep pace with his younger nephews, Uncle Bill then offered ice cream with blueberry syrup and whipped cream. And, of course, Dillon and I, though replete, were not about to drop out of the competition. At which point Aunt Marianne threw up her hands and left the banquet hall to us crazies. I learned from Uncle Bill that, though old, one need not give up all boyish delights.

Chewing the Johnson Grass Weed

The "front yard" to Grandpa's chicken yard was a smaller vegetable garden, and, nearer the gate to the chicken yard, fruit trees—apple and fig.

In my early double-digit youth, I was standing on the edge of that garden. And I indulged in one of my many summer treats. I pulled from out of its tougher outer casing a long stalk of Johnson grass. The first few inches of this inner stem were pale green and tender. It tasted sweet, not as sweet as honeysuckle, but it lasted longer because you could chew up the stem a ways, not unlike eating sugarcane. So as I indulged, I thought to myself (or maybe I even said it out loud):

"When I become famous and become president of the United States, I am not going to lose my feel for or love of the 'down home' treasures of life. I'm going to be humble, down-to-earth, and of the people. All summer I'll have stalks of Johnson grass delivered to the White House in floral boxes so that I can chew on

Johnson grass when I'm thinking alone or when I am in honest-to-goodness, heart-to-heart conversations with senators and ambassadors and such. I want to have the charm and humility of Abraham Lincoln, Grandpa's favorite."

Early Interest in Politics

Since age eleven, watching the two political conventions of 1952, the first ever to be televised, I have loved politics. In the '52 Republican convention I remember being sympathetic to Robert (Bob) Taft, son of a former president, as one who had faithfully served and waited his turn to be the candidate. Along comes a war hero, General Dwight Eisenhower, and edges him out.

Politically the South was called "the solid South"—solid for whoever ran as a Democrat. So presidential candidates didn't waste time campaigning in the Southern states. Yet Eisenhower came that same summer and spoke at Hurt Park, this as a favor to his longtime Republican friend, golfer Bobby Jones. Bobby Jones, one of the few Republicans in Georgia, rose from his wheelchair and introduced Eisenhower. Bobby Stephenson and I rode the bus downtown by ourselves and were in the crowd that heard both men speak.

All I remember of Eisenhower's speech was his reference to passing the statue of Henry Grady, which I thought was pretty clever since it gave Eisenhower Henry Grady's theme of "The New South" to pump up this the-South-shall-rise-again audience. (Somewhere among my things I have an "I Like Ike" button.)

When the speaking was over, Bobby and I got close to the open convertible into which Eisenhower climbed for the return motorcade to the airport. We heard him sigh as he took his seat; and I was surprised how big he was and that his thin hair was red. But, if you think about it, television was black and white, movies and newsreels were black and white, as were newspapers and magazines. It's little wonder that I didn't expect to see red hair.

On the Democratic side in that same summer of '52, I was pleased that Senator Richard Russell of Georgia was so highly regarded. He ran for president and came in fourth to Adlai Stevenson, who became the Democratic nominee in '52 and '56. In '56 the drama of the Democratic Convention was on the vice presidential choice. Young John Kennedy was soaking his ailing back in the tub in his hotel room, when it looked like momentum was swinging towards him as the vice presidential candidate. I was pleased that Georgia had cast all its votes for Kennedy. It took gumption and conviction for a Southern state to vote for a Massachusetts politician. Kennedy was out of the tub and quickly dressing to enter the hall when the momentum shifted towards Tennessee Senator Estes Kefauver, who ended up on the Stevenson/Kefauver ticket that was defeated roundly by Eisenhower and Nixon.

In the fall of '60 I was a junior at Vanderbilt, and both Kennedy and Nixon, the two presidential candidates to succeed Eisenhower, came to Nashville. They showed their personalities even by the path they took to the podium. Kennedy entered from the back of the crowd, allowing himself to be touched and having his cuff links taken off of him as souvenirs. Nixon entered from the back of the stage. (In fairness he was the sitting vice president so had to be more guarded, but it put him at a crowd-appeal disadvantage.) I was in a position behind the podium for a better spot to see Nixon speak; he and Pat Nixon passed right by me in a dense and almost jostling crowd. I said to Pat, "I'm sorry, Mrs. Nixon, for the press of the crowd." If she responded, I didn't hear it. It wasn't as if we had a conversation.

In the winter of '60, when Kennedy was just being talked about as a possible candidate for president, being smitten by him and his near miss on the VP position in '56, I wrote him and offered my services on his campaign team. I got a nice letter back from him and signed by him declining my offer. I still have that letter. (See **Appendix 3** for scanned letter from JFK.)

Kennedy's White House was dubbed "Camelot" because it was so youthful and regal. There was King Arthur and Lady Guinevere, Lancelot, and all the rest. The great literary and artistic luminaries of the country were invited to state dinners so tastefully put on by Jackie. You have to know this to feel the impact that his death had on all of us in this country and abroad.

I was with Dillon in the Loire Valley of France after one of his rugby matches (spring '65). The host team feted Dillon's team from the Paris Racing Club at a wine cave. The young son of the winery's owner, when he identified Dillon as an American, came up to him when we were together and asked Dillon, "*Avez-vous pleurer quand vous entendu dire que le Président Kennedy avait été tué?*" (Did you cry when you heard that President Kennedy was shot?) Dillon said with a hand of connection on the boy's arm, "*Oui, j'ai pleuré.*" (Yes, I cried.) To which the earnest French lad replied, "*Moi, aussi.*" (Me, too.) Before we left to make the drive back to Paris, the host of the party, the boy's father, presented Dillon with two bottles of his wine.

North Fulton Politics

At sixteen years of age I ran for president of the North Fulton High School student body. The year before, as a rising junior, I had won the office of treasurer on the slogan "Let Chuck Handle Your Buck." So I had a year of being one of four officers who organized pep rallies and set the agenda for Student Council meetings. That spring before our senior year, Marie Collins and I were running as a ticket. Tom Garden and Susan Chambers were our tough competition. I remember the week that would end in a Friday election. Hambone (Rawson Gordon) had been nominated to run but declined. He agreed to be my campaign manager. I remember heading with Hambone to somebody's house Sunday afternoon for a poster party. I was driving our new black Oldsmobile, and we were planning the remaining campaign events for the week—poster parties with the big campaign party on Thursday night. I remember thinking to myself (I hope I didn't say it out loud to Hambone), "I feel as if I'm barnstorming the state running for governor. One day I'll do that. I feel comfortable asking people to vote for me. This is fun, like being caught up in something big."

We used the strategy of wooing the younger classes, appointing class campaign managers, even courting the eighth-grade vote because their votes counted as much as did those of the juniors and seniors. We had our Thursday

Chuck — North Fulton senior year

night campaign party at an underclassman's home on Lenox Road, with a student band to provide live music. I remember a picture in the *Northside News* of me feeding a made-for-the-party *petit four* to Marie. We edged out Tom Garden and Susan Chambers in a squeaker. They won the majority of the eleventh and twelfth grade votes; we won by the greater numbers of the eighth, ninth, and tenth graders.

Riding the Coattails of My Big Brothers

The only college I applied to was Vanderbilt, so when I went for my admission interview with the venerable Dean of Admissions, he set me on edge with his opening assessment of my chances of getting in. Here's what I remember of our conversation, starting with the dean's sobering opening:

"Well, your grades and scores are not that of your two older brothers; at best you're borderline by our usual measures."

To which I mustered my best defense: "I haven't applied myself the way I know I can. I got caught up in student government and sports. I had too many activities. I spread myself too thin. Here I'll buckle down and focus if you'll give me the chance. Vanderbilt is the only place that I've applied to. I have a great desire to be here."

And following were the words I had hoped to hear: "If it weren't for how well your two older brothers have done, we wouldn't admit you. But because of them, we'll give you a shot. Now, make me proud of my decision."

I then made what would prove to be a tough pledge to keep: "I won't let you down. I promise. Thank you, sir!"

Thus was my conversation with the dean in the winter of 1958. It felt like one of my efforts at passing under a limbo bar—inch by inch, never being sure I would make it. Now I would join Tom Garden and Dillon (both on the football team), with Dick nearby in medical school.

Summer-Before-College Escapades

Come summer of '58, Tom and I met up with Terry Parker, Kimbrough Davis, and John Hatcher, Grady High School graduates who were also heading to Vanderbilt. We formed the Brigitte Bardot Club; the sole purpose was to attend as many Brigitte Bardot films that summer as we could manage—*And God Created Woman* and *Love Is My Profession*, to name two. As far as I can remember, we ended those evenings feeling that we had had a wonderful night together of film and fun. "Let's meet up again." I'm sure we all thought, "I really like being a college student."

Thinking I Was Pretty Cool in My Humble Way, I Headed to Join Dick and Dillon at Vanderbilt

I was excited about finally heading off to college—excitement mixed with some fear as I loaded my relatively few things into Marie Collins' dad's car. I think I did have a small trunk, come to think of it, but Marie had easily three times as much.

My eye caught the dogwood tree with Gram's, Aunt Maggie Belle's, and Mrs. Harvey's chairs under its shade. I could hear their high-pitched giggles and cackles as the three sat together in the shade every summer day at dusk. I could smell the loamy moss under the giant beech tree where Dillon and I would have spent summer hour upon summer hour cutting out slabs of the carpet-like moss with our trusty pocket knives, erecting building frames out of sticks, and applying the moss as roof and sides. I teared up to think of those years with Dillon, who had gone off days ahead to pre-season Vanderbilt football. And Dick, who justly had ruled the roost at home, was entering his second year of med school. Dad was out of town.

Warren was standing there next to our dog, Captain, both looking sad. I went for one last run of my hand through Captain's soft white Spitz fur. I hugged thirteen-year-old Warren and we both tried not to cry. He would be home alone for another five years. Without all three brothers? Worse than that, without even one brother.

As we pulled down the long driveway, I looked back at Mom and Big Gram, daughter and mother, standing together waving. Would they be all right? Would they both still be here when I came back? Even at age seventeen, I knew that my life would never be the same.

Something of Defeat

I learned something of defeat as a freshman at Vanderbilt. I tried to reengage in campus clubs and politics just as I had at North Fulton. I was one of two elected to represent the freshman class on the Student Christian Association Council. I was rushed by and committed to Phi Delta Theta, Dick and Dillon's fraternity. And I joined the cross-country team, coached by Herc Alley. I was on the first floor of Vanderbilt Hall with Tom, so some of early college life centered there.

After our pledge class of thirty or so really sharp guys was set, it came time to elect a president of the class: The two tied with the most votes were Tom Garden and me. I thought afterwards how remarkable that the two of us were the nominees. Our class of thirty was made up of strong contingencies from Memphis, Nashville, and Chattanooga, as well as Atlanta. I hope I didn't think, "I'm happy for Tom that he is out waiting in the hall with me," as if I would be the one expected to be out there, but I might have thought that. We went back in, and I tried as usual to act humble when it was announced that Tom was the president of our Pledge Class, except this time *humble* was turned into *humbled.* I may have thought in my embarrassed self, "This is my first defeat since the voting for second grade officers." I'm sure that was not true, but it may have been.

I didn't make my grades to be pledged into my class at the end of the first semester. I must have had all C's except a D in French. One had to have a 2.0, a C average, before initiation. It wasn't until the second semester of my sophomore year that I became "a brother in the bond."

In that February of my freshman year, just when I was picking up steam in conditioning for the spring track season, in the Nashville cold of early February, I caught the flu. Nashville had had a total snow accumulation of forty-eight inches during that winter cross-country season, yet we ran on. While I was beautifully served during my five days in the infirmary, I was missing out on classes, and I was losing the edge I had worked for in track. "This kind of thing is not supposed to happen to me," I thought.

Running Track

Track turned out to be a bright spot. Every afternoon at 3 o'clock a group of us would traipse down to the track; I'd finish a hard workout just in time to hustle back for 6 o'clock dinner at the Phi House. It was fun to be with Dillon in this. My freshman year, Fred Abington was a senior and the best miler and two-miler in the SEC. I remember with pride his winning both of his events at that year's SEC Meet at LSU. In that meet Billy Cannon, later an LSU All-American, won both the shot put and the 100-yard dash. I always thought that was an interesting combination. (As an aside, for several weeks Dillon, in his senior year, led the SEC in kick returns, ahead of Billy Cannon.)

We had a senior sprinter, first name Lynn, a year ahead of Dillon and comparable to Dillon in speed. They were good workout partners and the nucleus of good relay teams. Teddy Burkhardt and I pushed each other in our events. Lamar Alexander was another of the freshman runners with whom I created a bond by running together for four years.

Here is the best advice I have given to others who are heading off to college:

"I would not have had nearly the college experience I had were it not for track. What was I going to do from 3 to 6 each afternoon without it? I can't see me going to the library; my brain was too fried after getting out of a 2 o'clock class. The go-beyond-what-you-think-you-can workouts blew the cobwebs out of my brain. After the welcomed supper hour both to quench the hunger and as a social outlet, I would go to the library and study for a couple of good hours. Here's one thing to remember: When you put your head down on your arm to take a five-minute power nap, don't drool on the library table."

Vandy's spring 1962 track meet versus Kentucky—second-place mile, time 4:35.6

Chapter 7: Mom

Was Mom Sacrificed for Us?

I wondered years later if Mom was really a strikingly beautiful woman with deep literary interests and talents who was sacrificed to raise four boys. I was told that my mother was pretty and my father handsome, but I have found that it's impossible for a family member to be objective about the appearance of a close family member. Also, a child can only guess at the relationship between his mother and father.

While Mom would remember me from my Day One, I only remember her in Boston and Chicago by way of photographs. (Boston and Chicago were my home cities for the first three years of life.) And the clothing styles she wore in the photos were so different that I didn't think she was particularly pretty. I mean, what pretty girl wears a hat with a wisp of veil over her forehead?

I think I remember Mom at Emory Hospital when my little brother Warren (soon to be nicknamed Binkie) was born. That would be her fourth delivery of a boy. To add to the "tough life" story line, we must have been moving into our newly built house on Piedmont Road while Mom was in the hospital, because I remember sitting on the new kitchen floor stacking cans of Carnation Baby Formula onto lower cabinet shelves. That kept me out of the way, and it was somebody's good sense to know that a five-and-a-half-year-old child can accomplish something that is so much like stacking blocks. I felt important being up so much later than my bedtime, but I also remember fighting a severe drowsiness that must have left me supine on the floor putting out the sweet

Mom as a bride, June 6, 1933

breathing sound that can come from a little boy small enough to be carried still-sleeping off to bed.

I remember Mom in the kitchen of our new house, the room that held the kitchen table that was so central to our lives growing up. Grandpa lived next door and would deliver to the landing at the top of our back steps in the early morning whatever was in season in his garden. There would be eggs from his formidable hens, as well. Mom didn't want any of us to lack the sophistication that she grew up with, part of which is to have eaten and enjoyed every vegetable and meat served in developed countries. Since we were four hungry boys, it didn't take much persuasion to get us to devour whatever she put in front of us. If we lingered long over our food, then it would be the other brothers who gobbled up the second helpings.

I wasn't crazy about collard greens (the kale of my childhood) or turnips, but I could eat them. I enjoyed sweet potatoes by using the fork to flatten them, then making furrows with the prongs of the fork, adding salt as if that were the seeds being planted, and topping it off with butter, the fertilizer. "Don't play with your food" was a familiar instruction from Mom, but somehow this seed-time-and-harvest analogy was acceptable. I could eat tongue and brains, gizzards, and livers, but I could not stomach eggplant. It was purple, almost black, with a texture not that different from acorn squash, which I liked; so it must have been the taste that repelled me. I'm not kidding—it made me gag. But somehow that was not sufficient excuse for Mom to free me from eating it. I was to sit at the table until I ate at least a "no-thank-you" portion. I just couldn't do it. I wasn't trying to be rebellious (or maybe I was), but I sat alone until all but one light in the kitchen was turned out. No matter what I write subsequently, know that Mom was no push-over. I don't remember the outcome, honestly. But it must have been what years later Stephen Covey invented as the "Win/Win." I knew not to take Mom's directives jokingly, and she knew not to serve eggplant to me again.

While the four of us ate our first and second helpings of dinner, Mom and Dad would sit with us and have their highballs (or two). After having the mandatory dessert—butterscotch, lemon or chocolate pudding, ice cream, apple or other pies, and occasionally crackers with cream cheese topped with strawberry jam—we would be excused to wash the dishes (which in about 1950 became rinsing and putting the dishes in a dishwasher, which Dad justified purchasing because it cut down on spreading germs). While we finished cleaning up and went to play or to do homework, Mom and Dad would have their dinner while talking over the day and laughing a lot.

I mentioned earlier that Grandpa would deliver part of that day's garden and henhouse yield to our back steps in the cool of each morning. I should have said "orchard yield," as well. Two of my favorite items were apples made into applesauce and figs peeled, sugared, and put in the icebox to turn cold. Mom would cut up the apples and boil them until they were almost mushy. She would then put them in the cone-shaped colander. Then, with a wooden spindle she would go round and round pressing against the apples that were being pressed against the holes of the colander. The early stages of applesauce would come oozing out and then would cascade down into the bowl beneath. It wasn't finished yet. She then added sugar and cinnamon, both in abundance. The then greenish applesauce would turn brownish with the addition of cinnamon. As with the figs, once chilled either the applesauce or the figs could be eaten straight or put on cereal or ice cream. I appreciate gourmet dishes, but nothing I've eaten since makes my mouth water as does thinking of those heaping bowls of cold figs and apple sauce.

If Mom was gone on a summer's morning, it would be assumed that she was at the A&P or at the beauty parlor. Both were important parts of her life. She would wake up in the middle of the night frequently with the nightmare that we had run out of food. Apparently it took enormous quantities of everything to keep us fed. I think the term used for us four boys was that we had "insatiable appetites." There may have even been a competitive aspect of our eating. Also, we had to eat "for the hunger to come" because eating between meals was strictly verboten. We had no chips or Cokes in the house, and cookies were only to be eaten at the end of a meal, when we had cleaned our plates.

But back to Mom being gone on a summer morn: We had a maid in our home on weekdays all through my growing up, so when we were young, there was

Mom with Dick, Dillon, and Chuck, early 1940s

always at least one adult at home with us. Martha is the maid I remember from my single-digit years. My mom worked hard, but so did Martha. It took both of them a full day to clean the house, make up the beds, and wash and iron all the clothes that four boy-kids wear. We were playing "cowboys and Indians" one morning when we incorporated small crab apples into our game, using them as projectiles. Somehow we grew tired of throwing these small, harmless apples at each other so we decided we would sneak up the back steps where Martha would be in the kitchen. She would represent the Indians. So, setting upon her with whoops and hollers and crab apples, we scared her half-to-death and broke her glasses, which she needed to see. She broke down crying while expressing untypical anger towards us. Our plan was a bad idea gone awry.

When Mom returned from the beauty parlor or the A&P, she was faced with Martha about to walk out—Mom's essential partner in taking care of four boys. There was no village available to help Mom raise four boys, and she certainly couldn't do it without Martha. I remember her saying to us, to me, "What were you thinking?" But she said it in a way that really stung. We were bowled over by what had just happened to Martha, whom we loved. We were angry that anyone would do such a thing to Martha, much less us. So all we could say in deep-seated sincerity was, "Mom, we just weren't thinking. The last thing we would want to do is to hurt Martha."

The silence and Mom's disappointment hung heavy in the air. Mom patched things up between us and Martha. She got Martha's glasses replaced (not cheap, as I remember Mom saying) and Martha stayed on, never again to be treated so thoughtlessly.

Mom carried an extra burden because of Dad's business travel; many weeks he would be gone Monday through Thursday or Friday evening. (Mom said that measles or the like would always run through the four of us on weeks when Dad was out of town.) Back then there was no "expressway" through town, and certainly not all the way out to the airport. (William Hartsfield was a long-term mayor during my youth, so I don't know if the airport yet bore his name.) My dad and others would come in from the airport on a bus to the Biltmore Hotel, and there we would pick him up. I loved riding along to go pick him up. My first memory of Mom's drinking was noticing how close she was coming to cars parked to our right as we drove down Peachtree. Once I would swear that she hit some car's side-view mirror; but Mom was totally unaware. I had a bad feeling.

Mom As a Scholar

I went to a nursery school taught at somebody's home on Peachtree, just across Mathison Drive from our church, Peachtree Road Presbyterian. Ms. Bell Scott was our teacher and Mom assisted her. This was during WWII so gasoline was rationed and fewer people owned cars. We owned a used Packard (later sold to the Buckhead Taxi Company) so Mom drove a carpool of nursery school kids who would pay something for the rides. One spring day after dropping the last child a mile or two east of Peachtree Road on Lenox Road, Mom and I stopped and got out of our car at the railroad tracks behind the Ottley estate and stood with a few others along the tracks. My mother then told me that President Roosevelt's funeral train was to pass by there soon (April 13, 1945). I remember the train itself being black and with nothing that would denote that it was carrying a President. I was four and a half, and I guess even at that young age I was expecting a little bunting, even if there was no music. Mom explained later that the train was intentionally unmarked for fear of espionage. She said that from Warm Springs, Georgia, to Hyde Park, New York, stunned people of many walks of life, black and white, lined nearly shoulder to shoulder all the way, stood by the tracks at attention as the train slowly passed by just to pay their respects to a beloved Depression and wartime president. Even then I was proud that Mom and I were a part of that.

I wonder now if Mom was a daddy's girl; they had a sweet rapport with each other, as exemplified by a postcard from the early 1930s sent from Rome, Italy, just to her dad:

Dear Papa, Have seen lots of wonderful things in the ancient capital of the world. Wouldn't give anything for this marvelous trip. Love, Jane. [Simple address: Mr. W.S. Dillon, Hurt Bldg., Atlanta, Georgia, USA]

She got her love of poetry and literature from her dad. Mom's favorite poets were Vachel Lindsay, Carl Sandburg, and Robert Frost. I'd like to be able to ask her now why this Frost poem, "The Pasture," meant so much to her:

I'm going out to clean the pasture spring;
I'll only stop to rake the leaves away
(And wait to watch the water clear, I may):
I sha'n't be gone long.—You come too.
I'm going out to fetch the little calf
That's standing by the mother. It's so young,
It totters when she licks it with her tongue.
I sha'n't be gone long.—You come too.

Did she secretly write poetry but feared our reaction if she shared it with us? I wonder if there were a sheaf of Mom's poetry hidden somewhere. I remember only one poem; that was about Queen Elizabeth II on the occasion of the queen's inauguration. (I was in the seventh grade then.) I only remember that there were four lines per stanza, it rhymed, and it took two notebook-paper pages.

Mom would go out to the Agnes Scott campus once a year to hear Robert Frost read his poetry. As I remember, Frost had a close friend on that school's faculty; that was the draw for him to return annually. Even though I was a single-digit kid, I was proud of Mom for her almost-intimate relationship with a renowned American poet.

I was glad that Mom was a member of the Evergreen Garden Club that had as its members a lot of the ladies who lived on the two blocks of Piedmont Road between Peachtree and Roswell Roads. The nurseryman Frank Smith would come to speak to the garden club once a year; I had a mild interest in hearing about this and some of the other programs. But what I loved was the annual garden club picnic, always held in the Gordys' back yard. Frank Gordy owned the Varsity Drive-in, so we would have huge 25-gallon reservoirs of Varsity Orange, ice cold. Even as a small child all you had to do was approach the dispenser with a cup, pull down on the handle, and *voila*—heaven. I would drink it slowly so I wouldn't hurt my teeth by the cold, or was it the 50 percent sugar? We could have as many cups full as we could hold.

I loved the fried chicken and the potato salad, but the deviled eggs were what I craved the most. The homemade pies and cakes and ice cream were a good way to cap off a feast that left me happily groaning. You might think that we were undernourished at home by the way I looked forward to this meal. We weren't, but at the same time with four growing boys, we were never able to have all the deviled eggs we could eat; and being both nutrition- and cost-conscious, when we did go occasionally to the Varsity, we were never able to have more than one cup of Varsity Orange.

The Touch of a Mother's Hand

What is it about the touch of a mother's hand on your forehead when you feel sick? Mom was masterful at tending us when we were sick. She had to be; with four boys all living life pretty close together, if one got sick, eventually we all caught the bug. When I was really sick, I got to spend the day downstairs in Mom's bed. That in itself made me feel better. If I felt like eating, Mom would bring me a dish of "milk toast"—warm milk with a piece of bread covered with sugar, cinnamon and butter. It was very soothing, easy on the stomach, and the last few spoons full of the milk were the best. If I was really sick, I would sleep. Mom was frequently putting a thermometer in my mouth, "under my tongue." When I was tired of sleeping, I would listen to the radio. If my fever didn't disappear, then Mom would call Dr. Willingham and he would drop by our house on his way home. He was a kind man, and I liked the feel of his cold stethoscope on my fever-warmed chest. If a prescription was required, Dr. Willingham would call Wender & Roberts Drug Store, and they would deliver the needed drug (along with a jug of milk, if we were out).

Once when I was terribly ill—I must have been just six or seven, because I had a special decoder ring that I had ordered from one of the radio kids shows—as I was bent over the toilet throwing up profusely, I dropped my decoder ring into the toilet, down through the foulest smelling vomit. I started crying hysterically, which made my feverish head hurt, because I surely did love that decoder ring. My mom, who was holding my head while I threw up, knew how much I loved the ring. She rolled up her sleeve, reached into the vomit, and retrieved my ring before it was flushed down the toilet. Heroism? Love? What empowered an act by my mother that I would remember vividly some seventy years later?

If I remember it, should I write it down? Yes, I determined, I should tell this aspect of my childhood: even as a child I used to get headaches so severe that I would feel as if my head were splitting open. Then my face would turn red and I'd be sweating. Mom would sit by her bed, that I now occupied, and pat me gently on my chest until the hysteria would subside, and I would try to maintain composure in hopes that the cessation of crying would also end the headache. The only common thread to these periodic headaches would be that it would finally surface that I was constipated. When that was determined, the only remedy was the dreaded enema. Mom would take me to the bathroom and lovingly give me an enema. I don't need to go on, but I bring this up only because of what it says about Mom. I would lie back down, and in an hour my headache would have gone away, and I would be robust again.

The Beach

St. Simons Island was our beach of choice in the summer. We would rent for two weeks one floor of the two-story green duplex named Riggins, right on the beach. We were not deprived. Mom had to not only pack herself for the two-week stay, she had to coax and coach us in our packing. We traveled six in the car—Little Binkie in the front seat between our parents; Dick, Dillon, and Chuck in the back seat. Cars didn't have air conditioning during my early growing-up years, so the premier seats in the back were by the windows where the hot air coming through the windows was slightly better than no air at all. Fairness was a big consideration when growing up with all brothers, so Mom or Dad established that every 50 miles, the three in the back seat would rotate so each took his rightful turn sitting in the middle.

Even as a single-digit child I was slightly aware that Mom had to keep on clothes and be off the beach a lot because every day she had to go to the grocery store to bring home enough food to tide us over for the 24 hours that followed. Then she would have to spend time preparing all the meals. We boys were good at making PB&J sandwiches, but that was the extent of our culinary skills. Beach fare that she might have to make would include, but was not limited to, potato salad, coleslaw, deviled eggs and always a plate of fresh sliced tomatoes.

Meanwhile, we were out on the beach from after breakfast until being called in for lunch, a break from the sun after lunch for summer reading, and then back out until probably 7 p.m. when we were called in for supper. Mom would occasionally don her bathing suit late in the afternoon and go in the water, bathing cap and all. But what I mostly remember was that every late-afternoon Mom and Dad would go for a long walk on the beach. They would walk so far that they would go out of sight, and it would be some time before they would reappear way down the beach, tiny figures barely perceptible that would only gradually become full sized as they got much closer. I was amazed at their daily feat. I would often run a short distance to meet them, probably shutting down the last of their walking conversation in this one time of the day to be alone together.

We had the beach house for two weeks, as I noted. Well, the first week Big Gram and Grandpa would join us. The second week Little Gram and Uncle Charlie would drive down and spend the week with us. So there was never a day in our stay when Mom wasn't caring for eight instead of the six of us. I am only now sixty-some years later thinking about what she was giving up of herself to give a week at the beach to this older generation.

Our Home

I was always proud of our home. We were not allowed to play in the living or dining rooms, so they were always lovely and outfitted with nice pieces of furniture. One was a dining room sideboard with doors on each side that when

Johnston family's home at 3349 Piedmont Road

opened, revealed intriguing special-use drawers. The most of-olden-days feature were the two-foot-tall urns made of the same walnut as the piece on which they stood—sitting on raised platforms on each side of this five-foot-wide massive piece of furniture. When the tops of the urns were lifted, resting in specially designed slots were the pieces of Mom's extensive silver service. This was a piece of furniture that had sat in Big Gram and Grandpa's home before the home was subdivided into apartments.

I've already established that we had a well-stocked kitchen. We also never went without clean clothes to wear, thanks to Mom's management. I remember that we initially (June '46) didn't have a washer and dryer in our new home (just as we didn't have a dishwasher, air conditioning or television). There were side-by-side deep laundry sinks in the basement, one for washing and the other for rinsing. There was a washboard for pressing boys' clothes to get as much of the soil out of them as possible. Then there was a wringer attached to the rinsing sink to get as much as possible of the water out of the clothes, sheets, and towels. Then one carried a heavy basket of damp clothes and such out to the back yard to the line (strung between trees in the sunny part of the yard) and stretched and hung to dry each item held by clothespins.

While Mom tended to shopping and food preparation, Martha would tend to the almost daily laundry routine. She would iron items for Mom and Dad and put them in their chest of drawers; and she would iron a few of our collared shirts. The rest of our clothes—underwear, socks, t-shirts—were dumped on the cedar chest in the upstairs hall, and we were assigned to take our own things to our chest of drawers. In practice, we would just go each morning to the pile in the hallway and select what we needed for that day. Eventually an electric washer and dryer replaced the most arduous part of the routine (around 1950) but the handling of the finished product by the upstairs residents maintained the time-tested practice of selecting each day's apparel from the pile. As no-nonsense as Mom was, she was not able to perfect this tail end of the laundry routine.

Social Life

Mom had several friends she would get with ever so occasionally. One was Margaret Keiley, an unmarried elementary school teacher. She and Mom had gone to North Avenue Presbyterian School (NAPS) together. Either Mom enjoyed her company a couple of times a year, or else Mom kept up with her out of kindness. Here is part of a note we received from her upon Mom's death:

Dear Dick, Dick Jr., Dillon, Chuck, Warren, I want you to know that friendship with Jane has been one of my life's sweet experiences. Along with you, I have loved her dearly.... Jane called me often to keep me in touch with news about her family ....

Knoxie Roberts was a more robust friend of Mom's that I did look forward to seeing. Even as a kid, I knew she dressed well. By her style I pictured her getting ready to go to a horse race or a fox hunt. She was one of two Scott sisters from a prominent family that had a substantial house on Peachtree, closer to Brookhaven than Buckhead. (The other sister, Bell, ran the nursery school where Mom assisted during my pre-kindergarten years.) Knoxie married Bill Roberts, and they had two sons. (Bill, the older son, had a redheaded brother, Roy, my contemporary, who played basketball at Kentucky.) We saw the sons rarely, but we liked them. One of Knoxie's grandsons, Billy Roberts, is my daughter Jane's friend and contemporary and a most likeable fellow.

There was also a Mrs. Williams (aka Stuart), who would come down from up North. She had a husky voice that somehow I knew as a single-digit kid was from smoking and drinking too much. I didn't know a lot of divorced people back then, but she was one. I remember a dinner in our lovely dining room when Mrs. Williams and her daughter had joined us. When it came time for dessert, somehow the daughter got a much larger serving of ice cream than did we. That was aggravating enough, but what really got me and my three brothers was that she didn't eat it all. Honestly, we had never witnessed anyone who could leave ice cream uneaten in the bowl, but, there again, we didn't often have a girl eating with us.

For adult company on a Saturday night, the go-to couple for Mom and Dad was Uncle Bill and Aunt Marianne. Occasionally, Uncle Charlie would join them. On maybe only one occasion, I heard Mom say, "Why don't they ever prepare the meal and have us over to their house?" I was always proud of Mom for the dishes she would prepare for these good-china-in-the-dining-room occasions.

The Foreign Language of Sports

Sports were a big part of our growing up. Mom, having grown up as one of two sisters, before the days of Title IX, knew very little about the rich array of sports that we followed. She talked some about field hockey at NAPS, but we couldn't relate to that. The players wore skirts. Her father had grown up on a farm, "too far from town to play baseball." During the years that I knew him, he worked hard in his garden and hen houses for his exercise. We five Johnstons loved an array of sports—high school and college football, basketball, baseball, track, golf, boxing, and swimming. We knew nothing of sports that hadn't yet made it to the South such as lacrosse, soccer, and prep school wrestling.

Once Mom came to the dinner table quoting statistics—maybe it was Ted Williams' latest batting average. While we were impressed, we "smoked out" pretty quickly that she had just memorized part of the sports page so she could be a part of our conversation. Poor Mom, she couldn't get away with a thing, nor could she enter into our sports conversations.

She never gave up trying to join the men in her life in those things of greatest interest to them. Here is her postcard account of accompanying Dad to a 1969 Falcons game:

> *The Falcons game yesterday was very exciting, a great looking bunch of birds, and to add to the entertainment, an unwanted guest invaded the stadium. A great big rat was running all around under people's feet, and they were standing on the seats screaming, until somebody clobbered him, and a great big fat policeman bore him out by the tail. Everybody cheered the policeman as if he'd made a touchdown. I hope you get to go to the last game with Dad.*

A Tragic Victim of Alcohol

During the seventeen years that Mom lived beyond her father's death, she devoted herself to looking after her mother—but she could never do quite enough to please her. Big Gram pecked away at Mom by little criticisms about everything from how she dressed to how she was raising her children to how she "kept house." Mom's younger sister, Virginia—who lived in Boston, and then in Tiverton, Rhode Island—could do no wrong. She was the fair-haired daughter who would come down on the Southern Crescent for a month's stay each summer. Having one son instead of four, Virginia was thin and youthful. Meanwhile, it was Mom who took care of Big Gram. Only now, some fifty years later, do I fully realize the psychological grind of having one's mother return kindness and service with continuous belittlement.

In the close of a letter to Mom dated June 21, 1965, lies a hint of a love Gram never showed in person: "I pray each day and night for you, Darling, that God will take care of you. A big kiss from Mama."

We lived next door to the elementary school so Mom made a point of knowing all the teachers. When the teachers would return to work the week before Labor Day to prepare for the school's traditional day-after-Labor-Day opening, Mom would have all of them over to our house for tea and finger sandwiches. Mom must have been using alcohol as a mild sedative at that point, because I remember worrying that she might not be at her best when the teachers would come over, but I don't remember her not rising to the occasion. This would have been in the late '40s to early '50s.

During my high school years, sadly I only remember Mom in reference to her drinking. So much of my life was consumed by sports, studies, school politics, and friends. Mom was there to have supper waiting for us (or not) when we returned home at dusk from sports, to manage the household routines of clean clothes appearing on the upstairs cedar chest, as well as sheets changed, towels replaced, and bathroom cleaned.

The following I wrote as a third-person story as Exercise One in Tristine Rainer's *Your Life As Story*:

Once upon a time there was a boy who returned home at dusk to find his home without lights—dark and quiet. With some trepidation the boy breathed out, held his breath, turned the front door knob, and entered as quietly as he could. He knew undoubtedly that his mother was sleeping, overcome by the stresses of her life and by the alcohol taken as medication for that stress. The two older brothers were away at college, and the boy wasn't sure of his younger brother's whereabouts. His dad was away on business, as was frequently the case during the week. The outcome of the evening was up to him.

As he entered the front hall, he took off his shoes so as to move into the house with stealth, much as he might imagine an Indian slipping up on his prey. His hope of an evening to fix his own supper and do his homework was shattered when he heard his mother break the silence from her bed.

"Chuck, is that you?" she said in a slurring voice.

"Why does my body tighten up and my head begin to throb," thought the boy. The difference between his mom waking up and not was that vast expanse between having a restful and productive evening after a hard day at school and football, and having a night of turmoil and angst.

Turmoil and angst were on as the bedroom door knob turned and out into the gray light stumbled his mom. He probably said for the millionth time something like, "Why do you always have to be drinking when I come home?"

That's all it took to set her off—she challenging him on his holier-than-thou personhood. "If you're such a Christian, why is it you don't take [the neighbor kid], just three doors down the street, to your Student Christian Fellowship? Are you afraid he might not be up to your social standards? Are you afraid of looking bad in the eyes of your friends? What kind of Christian are you?"

He who had always had a volatile temper could feel the blood rushing to his head and his stomach tightening. He knew an eruption on his part would only turn a bad night into a nightmare. He stuffed it and stuffed it and stuffed it some more, tried to make soothing sounds as he resumed breathing. Don't say anything! Don't say anything! Don't say anything! As his mom grew quiet, she walked, she wobbled from front to back; then, as if thinking about each muscle action, found her way back down the hall, and into her bedroom, and in a few more steps plopped into her bed, fully dressed. He pulled the covers up over her, retreated, and quietly closed her door.

"Where do we get our expressions, like 'tied in knots'?"—From my Mom, he thought. And "tied in knots" he was. He could eat; he could always eat, and there were always good leftovers in the icebox. Among his mom's great attributes, she made sure her boys never went hungry. She used to tell us when we (and she) were younger that she would frequently wake up in fright from a bad dream that we had exhausted all the food she had prepared for us and we were still hungry. She was a wonderful health-conscious cook.

He satiated his hunger, though he couldn't say if he had tasted it or digested it. He felt a dreaded headache coming on. He tried to focus on his homework, but his mind would not stop rolling from one frame or one thought to the next. He wanted to cry, sensing that that might relieve the tightness in his throat; but he had trained himself to harden his heart. Stuff it—and move on!

He turned on "Perry Mason" at low volume, watched an episode, and then went to bed. "Tomorrow I will come in quieter. I can't get further and further behind in my homework."

Why 'Holier Than Thou' Was My Vulnerable Spot

A real "hot button" for me was when Mom would throw up at me that I acted "holier than thou." It would really get under my skin. I would have that rush of blood to the head that is like the fight instinct that we have in common with animals. Knowing that any response, any pushback—verbally or physically—with Mom in a drunken state could not end well. Her wild tirade against me would only escalate.

I think I know what the preliminary state of a cerebral hemorrhage must feel like. My head rush was simply all the blood in my body (or so it seemed) rushing to my head. Often I would wake up the next morning with the edge of a migraine that would grow as the day went on. But the question for me today is, "Why was that the accusation that most landed like a knife thrust to the gut?"

Perhaps it hurt because it was, in large part, true. I took my Christian discipleship seriously, and subconsciously looked down on those who didn't share my convictions. Mom would have had to feel the dagger thrusts of things I would say to her about her drinking. So when drunk she was going to fight back if someone looked down on her, especially if it were one of her sons into whom she had poured her very life.

Holier than thou means "I am better than you; I keep the moral code better than you; I am a person after God's own heart, and you're not." I was a rules follower, but I was not about to be a nerd. I courted the "cool" classification. I was, I suspect, however, no deeper into the "cools" than a peripheral member.

A boy about my age had moved into the Logans' old yellow brick house down the street. He was the kind of kid who wore a pocket protector to hold all of his pens. Mom, when sober, would encourage me to do something to welcome him into North Fulton. We would be starting our junior year of high school, a hard point to break into friendships in a new city and a new school. I think the family had moved to Atlanta from somewhere like Valdosta or Thomasville in south Georgia.

It was possible to be Baptist and still be a socially acceptable teenager, but being Baptist was not a plus. My new neighbor was a nerd, he was a Baptist, he was from south Georgia, and he was on the scrawny side—certainly not an athlete. Mom wanted me to take this kid to the North Fulton Student Christian Fellowship, an organization that met every Monday night with a few hundred attendees. I told him about the organization that met Monday nights, and he did begin to come. But I'm now ashamed to say, he wasn't coming with me. It would cost me too much of my precious popularity to be seen as his friend. I was going into the eleventh grade as treasurer of the student body, on track possibly to be president my senior year. He did make friends, but with boys in our class who were his own kind.

Mom rightly resented my superior attitude, and she would call me on it when she was drunk. And she was right to do so. Isn't it too bad that I couldn't have heard her words, even if spoken out of anger and a drunken stupor, and would have begun to correct my attitude? Instead, I was just tied up in knots, knowing that she was right, but unwilling to trade popularity for "putting the needs of another ahead of my own."

I just couldn't do it. And that's why being found out by Mom as being "holier than thou" was such a trigger for my volatile temper. No one likes to face his or her own dark side.

Sad, Sad Memories

Here are some journal entries that, sad to say, shed light on Mom's late-stage disease:

This one from Sunday, August 11, 1963: *Disgusted with myself for sleeping until 11 a.m. Read. Had fun touch game at North Fulton with Dillon, Tom, Woody Woodall and some others. Mom was repulsive as usual, Sunday being no exception. She certainly can make things like a nightmare around here at night. Tomorrow Dillon, Tom, and I head for an overnight trip up North Chickamauga Creek. I hope no mishaps mar our comradeship.*

And another from December 15, 1963: *The other day I turned twenty-three. It saddens me to pass from my years of extreme youth. No longer am I too young to be teaching school. On Wednesday I received these words from Mom:* "When you get this it will probably be your birthday, and though I suppose it will be a routine for you, I will be thinking about what a thrill I had when they brought you in the first time to see me in the Phillips House, Boston. You were a beautiful baby, and since then I have been so happy that you were beautiful, inside and out. You have been a joy to many people, and always to your own family."

Chuck in lederhosen bathing suit of the 1940s

It seems vain to record such words fifty-some years later, but it is the idea that in one's eyes I am remembered as a newborn that struck me. It is so rare that we get an objective glimpse of our own family, especially Mom and Dad. It is refreshing to think of them as fellow humans with emotions not unlike my own.

Something must have happened involving Mom's drinking at the close of my 1969 Christmas holiday stay at home. On her light blue "Mrs. Jane Dillon Johnston" stationery, Mom wrote this line, along with a few others: *We have been missing you more than ever after your sunny presence during the holidays. I'm sorry I had to spoil our last outing together, but hope I can make it up some way in the future.*

Mom wrote this King and Prince postcard six days before she died on Mother's Day in 1970: *The weather is lovely, and we are sipping our coffee on the balcony and enjoying the beautiful view. We have rented a three-bedroom, 2 bath house for the first two weeks of August. We couldn't see the inside because they are occupied. Had a nice Mothers' Day with you. Love, Mom*

This is painful for me since I had celebrated Mothers' Day with Mom the Sunday before the real Mothers' Day. I accepted an invitation from a Columbus/Brookstone family to go to the lake for a party before I realized the invitation was for Mothers' Day. I knew Mom would be hurt so I pretended that

I thought May 4 was Mothers' Day, and we celebrated accordingly. (I had several years before given Mom a dwarf maple tree for the front corner of our front yard. I told Mom that as long as she kept it watered and it prospered, she'd always celebrate Mothers' Day with at least one son. This planting a commemorative tree was something that Grandpa did for my six-year-old birthday—he planted an apple tree in the orchard that was henceforth my tree—and I did not forget it.)

"Whatever we were living through ... seemed to have its roots in 'this too shall pass.'" — Barbara Holmes, Joy Unspeakable

Even though Mom was comforted by a saying that folks latched onto during WWII, "This too shall pass," for her, sad to say, the scourges of life never passed.

She Died Alone

She, Dad, and Uncle Charlie had dinner together in the dining room on the real Mother's Day, May 10, 1970. Mom excused herself at the close of the meal to go to the bathroom. When she didn't return after a while, Dad and Uncle Charlie assumed she had just gone on to bed. Uncle Charlie went home after what had presumably been a pleasant supper.

When Dad went back to the bedroom to check on Mom, she was not in the bed and the bathroom door was locked. She would not respond to his knocking and calls, so he went outside, found a ladder, and climbed to the window and looked in. He saw Mom lying motionless on the floor and knew he had to get to her. I can't even picture how he wriggled through that smallish opening and kept from cracking his head. (I have always pictured him going in the window head first, but maybe he went in feet first.) I cringe even now thinking how close he must have come to rupturing his delicate heart.

At what point did it hit him that she was dead? Maybe not until he got to her body and felt its coldness did that word *dead* enter his cognition.

He called Sterling Claiborne to come over. Sterling came and pronounced her dead. The police might have come to confirm that there was no foul play. The undertakers came from Patterson's and took Mom away from the family land that she first occupied as a pre-teen. Now at the young age of 61 she was leaving that place for the last time—the place of her beloved father, the place where she supported a faithful husband and raised four boys.

The Aftermath of Mom's Death

Sterling Claiborne called and, without a whole lot of emotion, told me that my mother was dead. I had been at the lake that Sunday at a gathering hosted by a Brookstone family, so, just from the sun and skiing and such, I'm sure I was dead to the world when his call woke me up—probably near midnight.

My immediate thoughts were not about Mom, but about Dad. Has ever a man tried to live out the "in sickness and in health" commitment any more than did Dad? He stood by Mom during her most painful drunkenness. His sweetheart of his twenties was now gone, and any chance of her redemption and their enjoying "elder years together" were now gone.

"I've got to get to Atlanta as quickly as possible to be with Dad" was all I could think about.

It's not hard to experience the welling up of tears when I think about Mom. In fact, I find myself some fifty years after her death tearing up when I think about her sweetness, about how much she loved her sons, about the deaths of her father, Walter, and her beloved sister, Virginia, about her love of poetry and of literature in general, and about the emotional beating she took from her mother, Agnes.

A case could be made that Mom was a victim or one who sacrificed herself for the five men who made up her world. But as I sped through the deserted night on Highway 80, through dark, expansive farmland, and going too fast through small towns where not a soul was stirring, I thought of Mom's death as a blessed relief from a terminal illness. Thinking of the toll alcohol must have taken on her internal organs, including her heart and brain, it was a wonder to me that she had lived this long—sixty-one years. It was warm; even at 1 a.m. I had my window down so the wind would keep me awake. Maybe because vision was limited mainly to what was in the headlights, my sense of smell was heightened, and the air was sweet. I supposed it was the scent of honeysuckle.

Dad was alone when I got to our home. He was lost, lonely, glad to see me when I arrived at 2:30 a.m. or so. He chafed a bit that Sterling had asked him if he and Mom had had a fight, as if Sterling thought Dad might have had a hand in Mom's death. But we both knew that, were Sterling to sign the death certificate, which he did, he was legally bound to ask such questions.

I waited until daylight to go down to the little house behind Gram's to tell Warren of Mom's death. These had been tough years for Warren, the only one of four sons close by to bear the brunt of Mom's mean alcoholic moments. He and Dad were close, occasionally sharing a late-night beer together. Now in the weeks and months after his three brothers returned to their lives away from Atlanta, he would be there for Dad.

Maybe Warren and I went together to tell Big Gram; I don't remember. Her husband and younger daughter had already left her via death, and now her only other child was gone—the one whose love-in-action Gram had failed to recognize or appreciate. I'm certain Mom never said, "You'll miss me when I'm gone;" but it would have been true.

Warren and I—one or both of us—spoke by phone to Dick and Dillon and told them that Mom had died. We then went and sat at the kitchen table with Dad, drank coffee, and knew that later that morning the three of us would have to go to Patterson's Funeral Home to "make arrangements."

'You Are Someone I Want to Grow Old With'

After Mom and Dad were engaged, as an affirmation of the decision they had made together, Mom said to Dad—the two of them then being twenty-three and twenty-five respectively—"You are someone I want to grow old with." "Their song," when dating and at their wedding, was Hoagie Carmichael's "Stardust." This song became a Big Band standard, with just about every prominent bandleader and singer of the '30s and '40s performing it,

Putting Mom's statement of love to Dad together with the lyrics of "their song," I weep for the grief and memories that Dad must have felt at this time and for Mom's wish that was never to come true.

Sometimes I wonder why I spend
The lonely night dreaming of a song
The melody haunts my reverie
And I am once again with you.

When our love was new
And each kiss an inspiration
Oh, but that was long ago
And now my consolation
Is in the stardust of a song.

And beside a garden wall
When stars are bright
You were in my arms
The nightingale tells its fairytale
Of paradise where roses grew.

Though I dream in vain
In my heart it always will remain
My stardust melody
The memory of love's refrain.

PART TWO

The Decade of My 20s (1962-1970)

Chapter 1: The Summer of 1962

It's hard to say what were my life's major milestones. Leaving home for college was certainly one. Now only four years later, graduating from Vanderbilt constituted another major change of life. While Aunt Virginia's death in the Orly Airfield crash turned celebrating into grieving, Dillon had put too many plans in place for my post-graduation trip to New York City for me not to carry through with that trip. So off I went for great brother-bonding and to have my eyes opened to cultural experiences that were to shape my life.

Upon returning from New York, I made a brief stop in Atlanta to share the grief with Mom and Big Gram over the then-week-ago death of Aunt Virginia and to repack for my leader role at McCallie School's Academic Enrichment Camp. I headed off to Chattanooga and the first of my fifty years in education, 1962 to 2012.

It's only now, more than fifty years later, that I realize what must have been the depth of Mom's grief; this was her precious little sister. What difference might it have made for Mom if her sister had moved in next door as planned? I was not with Mom in Nashville or later in Atlanta long enough to even see her cry. I did reflect as I pulled out of the driveway how much I loved this home place—our white, two-story brick house next to Big Gram and Grandpa's massive three-story granite and stucco house on five acres—a mimosa and a pecan tree in our yard, three gigantic fir trees, a beech tree, and a dogwood next door.

Houston Patterson, head of the camp, greeted me and quickly got me moved into the student dorm room where I'd be staying for the next six weeks, to be closer to the campers. Unknown to me before arriving, Houston was a gifted math teacher who was most in his element in the deep, dark forests of the Tennessee and North Carolina mountains. In a day or two of my arriving, Houston took the student and faculty camp staff into the Linville Gorge for a three-day hike down the river. I learned a lot about backpacking, keeping my feet dry, and eating from a pillow-sized loaf of dark brown pumpernickel bread, one of which each camper had strapped to the outside of his pack.

I was my usual gregarious self, yet hanging on every word that Houston said and enjoying the testosterone of the specially chosen high school leaders. Towards the end of the second of our three days, I was moving with the speed and agility of a runner when my foot hit a previously unseen wet spot, and I was on my back in the water being swept under a low-hanging rock and down an eight- or ten-foot drop before the river continued on to its succeeding drops. I grabbed onto a boulder and pulled myself out of the water. I had dropped out of sight of Houston and the others, so they were relieved to see me alive and unbloodied when they scampered around the edges of this fall.

The only way out of the gorge was to go another day's hike downstream or retrace one's way back up from where we started, now closer to two days' hike uphill. Linville Gorge is North Carolina's "Grand Canyon"; one couldn't exit up the sides. My wooden backpack frame protected my head; its upper corner was smashed. If I had hit my head on the overhang or had landed on anything other than the pool of water that, by God's providence, I did hit, they would have had to abandon my body to be picked up in a couple of days by a helicopter drop (a helicopter couldn't land here); or if I survived but was too injured to make the remaining descending journey out, they would have had to leave me with brown bread and a water cup until the same helicopter drop could carry me for significant medical help. The group could not have carried me out. And this was a good twenty years before cell phones so that option was not there.

We hiked on. I was sober and uncharacteristically quiet as we ate our supper and crawled into our sleeping bags. I was contemplating life and death, the nano-second speed in which I went from upright and hiking to standing or sitting beside a big boulder in a pool of water with the falls cascading over me. I felt God's intimacy. This truly felt like a near-death experience.

Camp ended. I went home for a stint and then returned to Chattanooga and to my McCallie apartment in Maclellan Hall.

Chapter 2: My Life As Teacher and Coach Begins

McCallie, a boys' school, was established in 1905 and quickly became one of the premier prep schools in the South, known for its academics and its character building. I signed a contract for my first adult job, this in my last Vanderbilt winter. I was headed to McCallie for that 1962-63 school year. The co-headmaster responsible for hiring, Dr. Bob McCallie, was father of my fraternity "big brother," which may have helped me get that job. The other half of the leadership team, Dr. Spence McCallie, was Dr. Bob's cousin.

I taught five English sections of 10th grade boys, coached ninth grade football and basketball, and varsity track. (Funny how a random compliment will stick with you: One of my football team players told his mother that he had never seen such muscular legs as Coach Johnston has.) I pulled dorm duty every three nights, and I took my turn on dining hall and study hall duties. I took boys camping and hiking on the weekends. One favorite Sunday afternoon hike was from Castle in the Clouds (now Covenant College) on the back side of Lookout Mountain down to Point Park, which looks out over the Tennessee River.

One early-March "spring" holidays, I took four or five boys on an overnight hike on the Appalachian Trail where we began at Newfound Gap (5,000 feet) in Tennessee and climbed to the top of Clingman's Dome (6,643 feet) on the Tennessee-North Carolina border. I remember being surprised to find two feet of fluffy new-fallen snow as we climbed to this, the highest elevation on the Appalachian Trail. I was just as surprised to spot a birch tree that to my knowledge then only grew in the more northern clime of New England. I only recognized it by pictures I had seen of the American Indian birch-bark canoes.

We were having so much fun hiking when I said to the students, "Hey, this could be one of Robert Frost's birch trees. I'm going to see if I can climb to the top and swing out, letting it carry me gently to the ground." So up I went, branch by branch, until to my amazement the boys gathered at the base of the tree seemed to grow smaller. I moved by tiny increments, fearful of a premature descent. My heart was beating as if I were on a roller-coaster when it inches to the pinnacle before it starts its mad rush to the bottom.

Nearly panicked about what to do next, I shouted down to the boys, "Grab the Frost book—front flap of my backpack. Quick, quick—read what I do next." Curtis Baggett was the first to *The Poems of Robert Frost* and started reading frantically: "When I see birches bend to left and right / Across the line of straighter, darker trees ..."

"No, no. Skip down. What do I do next?"

So on Curtis read: "He always kept his poise, / To the top branches, climbing carefully / With the same pains you use to fill a cup / Up to the brim, and even above the brim, / Then he flung outward, feet first, with a swish, / Kicking his way down to the ground."

So, with heart in throat, I flung myself kicking into outer space for my memorable ride to the ground—only to hear a crack that echoed off the side of the hill and to find myself hanging helplessly at about the second floor of a three-story tree. As the boys helped me down, it occurred to me that Frost wrote his poem of a summer pastime when sap was running in the trees; here in the highest reaches of the Smokies, in two feet of snow, there was clearly no sap running.

I came away with only scratches and bruises; the boys came away with a great memory. To this day I will still say with Frost, "One could do worse than be a swinger of birches."

It was a full life with lots of bonding with an all-male student body. I worked hard; I earned $312 per month. There was no pampering of teachers, but neither did I hear teachers complaining. Every job hereafter I compared to my initial two years (and three summers) at the outset of my fifty years in education. I was imprinted with the sheer joy of how school is done well. I can't imagine a better place for an eager young man to start his teaching career than McCallie School.

I had some marvelous men to mentor and befriend me. Wrestling coach Jim Morgan and I shared an apartment in Maclellan Hall. Gordon Bondurant befriended me upon my arrival and throughout our careers. Major Burns, Sack Milligan, Jim Lyle, Bill Eskerige, Joe Campbell, and legions more encouraged me at every step. And let me not forget Becky McCallie, who had me and others over for coffee and dessert after Sunday lunch, and Betsy McCallie—the two headmaster wives gave me my first experience of calling an older lady by her first name; they were adamant that I do so.

"Yes, but you only made $312 a month," a critic might assert.

"Well, along with that I got an apartment, all my meals, my laundry done on campus, and my hair cut by the school barber. I maybe only had two or three dates the whole two years—not for lack of desire but for lack of opportunity; so, I didn't spend money there. I saved more money during those two years than I have ever been able to since."

(See **Part Eight: Reflections** for a student's remembrance some fifty-two years later of my teaching.)

Chapter 3: Adventures with Warren

Warren and I worked together at McCallie School's academic enrichment camp two out of the three summers that I did it, in the summers of '63 and '64. We were both blessed to work under Houston Patterson and engage with him on the weekends in sophisticated camping/hiking experiences. Some caving was thrown in there, as well. (Two that we ventured into were Bat Cave and Nickajack Cave, the latter now under the water of Nickajack Dam.) We practiced safety precautions that Houston knew from years of running the outdoor program at Camp Mondamin (North Carolina).

We had a dance once in the McCallie gym with the camp counselors at Girls Preparatory School's camp across town in Chattanooga. The counselors—like Warren, high school students—pulled out clothes they had been saving for just such an occasion. Cologne was "in," so douse themselves they did. This part caught me by surprise: just before the girls came, the boys all traipsed down to the weight room to do bench presses so they would be as buff as possible for the girls. Although just five or six years their senior, I was already of another generation.

As fellow twenty-something bachelors, Warren and I did see each other a good bit. I went over to Athens a time or two while he was there. Then when he graduated, he lived in the little house behind Big Gram's. He built a deck at the back of the house so he could entertain without Big Gram's supervision.

We bought a farm together in Georgia, but near the North Carolina border. It was in Fannin County. I believe it was Blue Ridge where we would go for building supplies. We spent a lot of weekends exhausting ourselves with hammer and saw or by mowing the beautiful big field with the ancient tractor that we bought from Roy Moore, our nearest neighbor and mentor. Existing on the property when we bought it was the shell of a small house with a good roof, sides, windows, and a door. It could have been built to store hay; but we opted to turn it into a really nice vacation cabin. We ran water to our self-installed plumbing system. Before we finished we did have a stainless-steel sink with running cold water. We had an outdoor shower. Plumbing for a toilet was beyond our skill level; besides, our greatest asset was the forest bordering our property and our unquestionable privacy. Except for Roy Moore's residence that we passed coming into this property, we were way far from civilization of any kind. Chief Moore, of Cherokee descent, served as our gatekeeper. We lost the farm in an economic downturn in the early '70s.

I'll always be glad that once Warren asked if I would like to try marijuana. This I did at Warren's little house behind Gram's. I'm not trying to minimize the extent of my smoking, but I couldn't have taken more than three or four drags off of the cigarette. It smelled sweet and felt sweet as the effects entered my body. That was it. And again, that's the kind of brother Warren was. He was not trying to corrupt me, but he was very considerately giving me the option of experiencing something that was at the time sweeping the nation. To this day I could have remained ignorant of this practice or I could say henceforth, "I appreciate what that experience is like."

Chapter 4: The Indelible Year in France

Memory, speak to me about that year in Europe. OK, well, I would not have gone were it not for Anne and Dillon, who were going to live in Paris for a year, Dillon to study the language at the Sorbonne and Anne to do the same at The Alliance Française.

They said, "Why don't you come with us?"

To which I said, "I can't do that. I'm already accepted back at Vanderbilt for my master's."

To which they said, "Come. Vanderbilt will defer your admission for a year."

To which I said, "OK!"

I did decide that I would live in a smaller French

Anne Coggan Johnston

city, which would, I thought, enhance my ease of having French friends. A senior at McCallie had a sister who had lived in Grenoble, in the French Alps, and had made friends. Through her, I had a contact with a young French banker named Claude. In correspondence with Claude, I gained the opportunity to live with a young couple with two little children. They spoke no English, which was exactly what I was seeking.

Dillon, Anne, and I flew over together in early September 1964 via Icelandic Airlines. We landed in Iceland for refueling, so we were in a minority of Americans who had set foot in Iceland at that time. From there we flew to our embarkation in the Principality of Luxembourg. After overnighting there, we boarded a train together heading south into France. In Metz, little more than an hour's ride, I said goodbye to Anne and Dillon as they changed trains for Paris. I cried as I continued south to Grenoble. I cried again (fatigue, you understand) sitting in front of the bank where I was to meet Claude, only to find the bank closed at 4 in the afternoon.

Soon enough the bankers returned, the bank opened up from its afternoon break, and I met Claude Gauthier. He explained that the apartment where I was to live was not yet ready, classes at Grenoble Universités didn't commence for another three weeks. I should take advantage of this time to travel to the Cote d'Azure. So, I did just that—to Arles, Nimes, Avignon, Montpellier, Aix-en-Provence, Marseille, Cannes, Nice, and, loveliest of all, Monaco.

I enrolled in the special program for foreign students, I loved living with Marcel and Geneviève Giroud and their two little ones, and in time I went skiing every weekend with Claude and ate occasional meals with his family. I treated Dick and Mary Anne to a Jacque Brel concert, and they treated me, Dillon, and Anne to a family Christmas in Bad Cannstatt (outside of Stuttgart).

Then, when March came, I sprained my ankle and broke my ski in the slushy spring snow, classes ended, and I headed to Paris and lived with Dillon and Anne in their fifth-story walk-up apartment at Place de Vouge. The three of us had a memorable trip to Andorra and Spain, seeing the legendary El Cordoba dispatch a bull with the star power of a Mohammed Ali or a Michael Jackson.

When we got back to Paris, Anne had to return to Atlanta because her mom was gravely ill. Dillon was finishing his rugby season with the Paris Racing Club; I attended with him his last game in the stunningly picturesque Loire Valley. He and I traveled together to Italy where we were scammed out of what was for us a lot of money. We said little about it at the time because we were so embarrassed at being taken in. We traveled very frugally, using *Europe on $5 a Day*, the student travel bible of the day, so money being wasted was painful indeed.

Anne returned. Warren came over, Dick, Mary Anne and sons met us, and we traveled in Belgium and the Netherlands—two married brothers and two bachelor brothers. We slept in tents in very nice campgrounds and we ate C-rations packed in small cardboard boxes. (I promise I will not bring up the incident of Dick throwing a most delectable French pastry into the river running peacefully beside our picnic site.)

Dick and Mary Anne returned to Bad Cannstatt for another year of Army Medical Corps service; Dillon and Anne departed for Charlottesville via a month's active Coast Guard duty in London, and Lynn Weigel joined Warren and me for continuing European travels. Lynn, who I had last known as a McCallie sophomore, was now a rising senior and a surprisingly mature travel companion. Lynn departed to join a friend's family in Italy, and Warren and I boarded a student ship at Le Havre for our eight-day journey across the Atlantic where we were met in New York harbor by Mom. (After not seeing Mom for a year, I was startled and saddened by her early-morning inebriated state and how bloated she appeared, obviously the ravages of alcoholism over the intervening twelve months.)

Note on Lynn Weigel: I corresponded with Lynn sporadically after our travels together in the summer of '65, but we did not lay eyes on each other again until the summer of 2016, some fifty-one years later. He came to Atlanta and spent an extra day here for our visit before traveling on to Knoxville. Bob Card joined us for a good part of our day. He drove down from Cleveland, Tennessee, and drove back the same day. Bob, Lynn's best friend, was one of my 10th grade English students and a cross-country and track runner.

(See **Appendix 4** for my postcard travel log of this time in Europe.)

Chapter 5: Back at Vanderbilt for a Master's

I found myself back on the Vanderbilt campus, enrolled in a Master's in Teaching English program wherein you took half your hours at Vanderbilt in English and half at Peabody in teaching. I felt a bit like a duck out of water. There were some underclassmen and women who had been younger students at North Fulton. Gretchen Flaherty comes to my mind. I may have also known her from Peachtree Road Presbyterian Church. But I wasn't a part of undergraduate life, and there was no social life among the graduate students.

I lived a short walk off campus in a small apartment in a widow's home. Her late husband had been in the Vanderbilt history department. One residual from her husband's career was a strong friendship she had with Dr. Marchant, a history professor with a disease called elephantiasis. His face was grotesque with oversized nose, ears, and lips. The problem was that the two of them seemed to be always trying to draw me into their social life, which mainly consisted of having suppers together. I was uncomfortable around Dr. Marchant. I was forever squirming out of invitations or just trying to avoid them altogether.

The second semester I spent in a DeKalb high school (Gordon High) as a teacher intern. Wow! North Fulton was nothing like this. I did a poor job; I didn't know how to discipline in such a setting. If it wasn't all white, it was close to it. I can vaguely remember the principal, Mr. Lucky, but he was not much better as a disciplinarian than I was. Anyhow, I got paid and I got half the hours I needed for my MAT. And, during this spring semester, I was a volunteer track coach at Georgia Tech, assisting Buddy Fowlkes by coaching the middle-distance runners.

Chapter 6: Westminster Teacher and Coach

I had my heart set on teaching English at Episcopal High School in Alexandria, Virginia, because the head of the Episcopal English Department was legendary William B. Ravenel, who had written the writing text we taught from at McCallie. I made a campus visit in the dead of winter when the snow was banked on each side of the campus roadways. I felt that it was a good interview, that I was a good fit for the school and the position. I waited and waited for an offer that would not come.

In the meantime, Dave Ulrey was teaching at Westminster and insisted that that's where I should be. So, with nothing to lose, I applied to teach high school English at Westminster. Dave talked to founding headmaster Dr. Bill Pressly about me. Dr. Pressly got it in his head that Dr. Spence was vying for me to come back to McCallie. Being the competitor that he was and seeing the opportunity to beat his brother-in-law to a good teacher, Dr. Pressly created a position that didn't exist—assistant high school English teacher and a position in the boys' dorm. The offer came and I accepted. Then, out of the blue a week or two later came an offer from Episcopal High that I had to decline because I had committed to Westminster.

This was all happening while I was at Vanderbilt pursuing my MAT degree. I was in Nashville that summer of 1966 as a part of the twelve-month master's program. I honestly don't remember failing a course, but at the end of that summer before my beginning at Westminster, I was one English course shy. So, the summer between my first and second years at Westminster I spent at Emory taking the final course I needed. Hence the date on my MAT is 1967.

Working with Westminster senior teachers Pat Rudolph and Dave Lauderdale, legendary teachers of junior and senior English respectively in the Boys School, was comparable in itself to an English degree. *Sound and Sense* was our poetry text, we studied *Moby Dick* line by line under Rudolph and *King Lear* in dramatic fashion under Lauderdale, a book of plays that included *Cyrano Bergerac*, and Ibsen's *A Doll's House*, and a writing program the likes of which I have never seen since. *Strunk and White* was the English usage text. Their teaching has made me a lifetime fan of the well-written one-page three-paragraph paper.

I loved living and working in the dorm—with Jim Bunnell and Charlie Brake the first two years, then with Charlie and Ester Brake and Tom and Cade Garden the third year, the year in which I replaced Bunnell as head of Tull Hall. I was so much in and out of the Gardens' apartment that some of the newer boys were confused about which one of us Cade was married to, Tom or me. Once again, I learned a lot from a respected senior teacher, Jim Bunnell. I was, I think, a good proctor under him, and I was prepared to head it up in that third year.

The dorm gave me some great lasting friendships:

✓ Forrest Simmons, who later served on the Atlanta Youth Academy Board, was my link to hiring Rock Curlee at AYA. Forrest was my link to his brother Greg who, with his wife, Christie, brought son McKittrick and sisters to Trinity, where Greg and Christie befriended JoElyn and me, including introducing us to Tom Key (Theatrical Outfit).

Chuck as dorm master in Westminster's Tull Hall, 1966–1969

- ✓ Jess Sasser, who hitchhiked from Brantley, Alabama, to Greenville, for JoElyn's and my wedding.
- ✓ Sam Dimon, whose parents took me under wing when I moved to Columbus, including finding a cool garage apartment for me, and when JoElyn came the next year, giving her some art studio space in their basement. Years later, the senior Dimons, with Sam and his young family, visited us in Pebble Beach. Sam supported AYA, and he created Grove Park Renewal with his initial $2 million fund.

Track Power and a State Championship

I was excited to be a varsity track coach together with head coach Paul Koshewa and with the other assistant coach, Ken Kiesler. Leroy Buskirk coached shot and discus, but he was mostly focused on heading the Boys Junior High track program. (In the 1960s there was no track program at Westminster for girls.) Paul was a master organizer. He was in the highest realm of respect from other coaches when it came to putting on a meet. The early-season Westminster Relays event was the Masters of high school track in Georgia.

Westminster had historically had some outstanding track and field individuals, but typically they had not been a threat as a team. With my energy in the last half of my twenties and my nonstop running since about age twelve, I brought to the track practices enthusiasm and fun through hard workouts. I ran with the team in our unified warm-up laps and stretches. In the second year of my Westminster coaching we got buy-in to "when the going gets tough, the tough get going." We coined the term "Track Power" to make us feel like we were a new force in the track world.

Paul Koshewa had always had a quality program. Back in 1958, Westminster's quarter-miler Ted Mealor won the 440 in Class A (smaller schools) and then won the All-Class Meet 440 the next week by nipping the Class AAA (bigger schools) 440 champion (me) at the finish line. Another indicator of a quality high school track program is that Paul would take his teams each year to the Florida Relays and the Knoxville Relays. Undetected by the boys, Kosh, Kiesler, and I would slip out after the competitors were abed and have a beer or two, always in the heavy clay mugs then in vogue—quite a treat. How undetected were we? At the award assembly in Pressly Hall, after the boys had gotten their full recognition, they graciously wanted to give us a gift: On stage they presented to each of us three coaches our own six-pack of beer.

In my second year, we matched our bravado with outstanding performances—David Eldridge in the sprints and relays, Larry Jamison in the hurdles and relays, Andy Currie and one or two others in the relays, and Bland Byrne in the distances. In dual meets we were sometimes defeated by teams having greater numbers of boys—boys scoring in the multitude of events where we were weak. But when it came to the state, quality trumped quantity. We probably had three or four blue ribbons and one or two relay firsts, enough to win Westminster's first state championship in track—that in 1968. To give you a sense of the magnitude of this achievement, it was not until 1999, thirty-one years later, that Westminster won its second state championship in track, which shows how talent and close finishes have to come together just right to win a state championship. Since 1999, they've won that ultimate prize again in 2009 and 2013.

Chapter 7: My Aborted Appalachian Trail Hike

I needed an adventure in my life. Thus far every summer when I was teaching for nine months, I was working in the summer camp or going back to graduate school. The summer of '68 was ahead of me with no obligations. How would I use that precious time? My three McCallie summers had entailed a lot of major, heart-thumping hiking under the tutelage of Houston Patterson. I was ready to get back out on the trail (the AT, of course), except this time I wanted to stay out in the wild all summer by myself, growing sinewy and swarthy.

I must have talked about how I was going to hike from Maine to Georgia enough that John McIvaine's five-year-old son all summer played "Chuck Johnston." That's what his game was about—the romance of hiking. I bought good equipment—a little fuel-burning stove, the right sturdy backpack and frame, and some high-top boots made of lightweight kangaroo hide. How little I knew about what I was doing. The only reason I chose to go from north to south is that I thought it would be harder to quit up there if I got homesick.

I knew nothing about the swampiness of the Maine trail this soon after snow melt; and the mosquitos and black flies were big and looking for someone to drive nuts. Once when I lost my sense of where the trail lay in the midst of fallen trees, it seemed that the mosquitos smelled my fear and dive-bombed for me, to buzz so loud in my ears that it made me think I was going crazy (like Meursault fighting the horrendously bright midday beach reflection in the opening pages of *L'Etrange*, by Albert Camus). I fumbled almost blindly in my pack to pull out the tiny tent with mosquito netting, and I climbed inside without trying to put the tent up. The mosquitos still made their horrible concert, but now they couldn't get to me. My sanity slowly returned. I found my insect repellant and applied it generously. Once I regained my senses, I found what was the Appalachian Trail under the debris left by loggers. I continued on. I hate to think what might have happened if I had not been able to recover my bearings and get back on the trail.

At one point in my hike in Maine I spotted a strange animal standing at the edge of the water: "Oh, my gosh! It's a porcupine!" This is one almost mythical creature that I had heretofore only seen in books. Then, on another day, I came upon a mule standing in what down South we would call a deer pasture—an opening with only grass and, therefore, bright with sunshine. "Why would a mule be way out here in the wild? Is there an ancient farmland nearby?" I knew that mules were bred from horses and donkeys, bred to pull a plow or to take adventurers to the floor of the Grand Canyon. They are not out in the wild that I knew of. "Wait a minute. Could this be a moose, maybe a female one?" They don't have moose in the zoo for some reason. I had never seen one. How much fun, for me like stumbling upon an almost-extinct species rarely seen by human eyes. (Instead, I should have said, "Rarely seen by Georgians' eyes.")

What happened to my resolve to hike all summer and toughen up? For one thing, the solitude was getting to me. Having spent the last two years in a boys' dorm where essentially, I was always "on duty," eating and sleeping with fifty boys and two families, I wanted to experience solitude—to get away from people for a while. However, the hiking alone in the true wilderness was stressful. The unknown was always right in front of me. Also, the kangaroo boots established a crease from bending in the back, pressing upon my Achilles tendons. The pain was becoming crippling. Eight days into my 90-day hike all the way to Georgia, I called it quits. I had come out of the dark and ancient woods into the little town of Branson, Maine; and I was not going any further.

Back in the world of people, I caught a bus to Montreal for a few days. I then took another bus down to Boston and stayed with Dick, Mary Anne, Richard, and Clay for maybe ten days. I think it was a stressful time in their family life, so I was welcomed company for Mary Anne and the boys, who were missing Dick in his long work hours. (He was in an advanced research fellowship with a world-class pediatric research doctor, Fred Rosen, at Boston Children's Hospital.) One memorable evening Dick, Mary Anne and I went to the Boston Gardens to a casual symphony program wherein the patrons sat at little tables with drinks and food, something unheard of at the time by me. It was the Boston Pops Orchestra conducted by the renowned Arthur Fiedler. It was symphony for those of us who don't turn to symphony on the radio, and I loved it. Fiedler punctuated each selection with lots of great humor. Memory, help me: was Victor Borge on the program?

From Boston, I bused it down to Charlottesville and stayed several weeks with Dillon and Anne. They lived on one of the Carter family's estates called Redlands in what had been a tenant farmer's house. Even though Anne was great with child, they welcomed me into their little home. Dillon had a bountiful vegetable garden right alongside the house. When he dug up a hill of potatoes and we harvested the little new potatoes from its roots, we steamed them tender, salt and buttered them; and they were as great a taste treat as ice cream. It was for me the greatest memory in my "adult" life of the premium taste of a vegetable right off the vine or out of the ground over one that has been sitting in the grocery store, if only for a day.

There was a tenant farmer on the estate, living with his sister, who had become too old to farm; his name was John. In fact, he was ill with old age and was not expected to live through the summer. Together with either Dillon or Anne, I visited with John and his sister at least a couple of times as we came in and out of the Redlands estate. Soon the time came for Anne to deliver a child. No girl had been born among the four baby boys birthed by Little Gram nor among the four birthed by Mom, nor among the first two birthed by Mary Anne. Dillon and Anne headed into the UVA Medical Center Hospital around midnight.

As very early dawn was putting a faint gray into the pitch-black night, John's sister was awakened by John talking in his sleep: "I see an angel coming down, a pretty baby angel. An angel …. an angel."

And John breathed his last. It was later established that it was at that same dawn's-early-light moment that a Charlottesville doctor announced, "Anne and Dillon, you have a healthy baby girl." Upon reflection by the parents of this long-awaited baby girl, it seemed that John, whom they had grown to love, had announced a new soul into this world as the chariot was coming for to carry John home. The child shall be called Kathleen, and just maybe she carries within her some of John's sweet spirit. This all took place on the ninth day of August, 1968.

Dillon, Anne and baby Kathleen

Chapter 8: The Adventure of Starting a School

Jim McCallie cleared with his uncle, Dr. Pressly, his visit with me, and arranged for us to meet in Westminster's Carlyle Fraser Library after hours. "Chuck, I've been hired to start a new school and I want you to come and help me."

"Wow, that's exciting for you, Jimmy. So, you'll be a headmaster. Congratulations! I don't know about me, but I'm excited for you."

"Thank you. But I want you to come and help me. It will be hard work, and I need you to do it with me. I can't pay you much, but you can be the assistant headmaster."

I knew I'd miss the seventh grade English teaching that I had begun that year. The coaching was exhilarating. (At that point I was in the middle of a basketball season with a ninth-grade team that included Comer Yates, Doug Hertz, Scootie Dimon and others.) I had not aspired to be an administrator. I had always said, "If I wanted an office job, I would have gone into business."

Jim went on: "It's in Columbus, a sophisticated city with no independent school. There's plenty of money in Columbus to build a school, with Ivy League graduates making up the board. Here, let me show you the plans."

At that he spread out a big roll of architectural drawings. He treated the plans with as much excitement as he would have had if he were showing me finished buildings with lush landscaping in place. I couldn't see it, but Jim surely could.

Finally, without being coy, I said, "I can't resist, Jim. I like the idea of helping start something, and I'd love nothing better than to work with you. I guess I'm a sucker for adventure."

The school-to-be, located close to Lake Harding, formed out of the Chattahoochee River, was to be named Brookstone School. The school would start with kindergarten to grade nine and grow to K-12.

Note: When I made my first visit to Columbus, a weekend or two after this late-night library meeting, the fifteen- or twenty-acre campus was hard, cracked red clay, not a tree on the land, with concrete foundations sticking maybe a foot above the ground. It looked more like an archeological dig site than a future ivy-covered prep school on the order of what I had experienced thus far (i.e., McCallie and Westminster). And by now it was probably March, with school to open in five months.

The Flavor of My Brookstone Years

"Before meeting you I didn't like you. Jim told us that you had two degrees from Vanderbilt, that you've lived in France and speak French fluently, that you were captain of your college track team, and you've taught at McCallie and Westminster. And I immediately said to myself, 'This guy's going to be a pain in the rear.'" This was Barbara Hugenberg's confession to me shortly after my summer of '69 arrival in hot Columbus. She was the dean of the faculty coming into Brookstone from the predecessor school, Trinity. She was the dean, not by title, but by right of her sophistication, her scholarship as an English teacher, her warmth, and her sense of humor. She became my biggest cheerleader, and I hers.

JoElyn and I loved both Barbara and her irreverent husband John (who worked with Gunby Jordan at the Green Island Company). She would tell revealing stories on herself such as the day when she got as far as getting the dirty laundry from a household of five into the laundry room, starting the first load, sitting down on the floor on top of the pile of dirty clothes with a compelling novel, and not budging from that position until John came home in the late afternoon to find her there, turning pages. The dirty laundry would just have to wait until another day.

Historic Westville, close by, to the south of Columbus in Lumpkin, Georgia, became an education asset that we drew upon heavily. Brookstone clearly believed that all learning shouldn't occur in the confines of four walls. Historic Westville took preserved buildings from the 1850s and created "living history" including four major interpretive areas: Town Center, Rural, Frontier Settlement, and Creek Indian Settlement. Our students got to see things that I was exposed to as a child such as a blacksmith banging out farm implements, a mule plowing, and the sweet smell of gingerbread men baking. What I didn't have as a child were Indigenous People explaining the advanced life of pre-1836 Muskogee Creeks. I had only had cowboy-and-Indian movies.

Koinonia Farm, another educational asset in the vicinity, impacted me personally more than it impacted Brookstone School. Music teacher and choral director Jerry Jordan was related to its founder, Clarence Jordan (as was Hamilton Jordan, President Carter's chief of staff). My initial visits there were on the weekends and in that one Columbus year I had before meeting JoElyn. I liked using "The Cotton Patch Gospels" as my text in teaching New Testament ideas to students at church (which was in that first couple of years at St. Thomas Episcopal Church). Koinonia Farm consisted of black and white farmers from this south Georgia area working together to improve farming methods, learning together from Bible scholar Clarence Jordan, and, in some cases, living together on the farm. This was an anathema to most of the residents of southwest Georgia in 1942 when the farm began. The intent was to live out the example set by the early church in the Book of Acts. Hostility towards the farm was often expressed physically by shootings and fire bombings. It was only slightly better perceived by the surrounding community in 1969, the year when Clarence Jordan died and the year I first visited the farm. Plains, Georgia, is only thirty miles or less from the Koinonia Farm, and Jimmy Carter was greatly influenced by what was going on there. Habitat for Humanity began at Koinonia, hence Jimmy and Rosalynn's long-term partnership with Habitat.

Again, in that first year in Columbus, I spent many Saturdays sailing with Dr. Danny Franco, a Brookstone parent, on Eufaula Lake. His boat was in the Lightning class, a good size for two or three people. Having not gone away to boarding camp, this was my one-year sailing school, and it was exhilarating. I don't remember ever turning the boat over.

Chapter 9: JoElyn Appears and I Am Smitten

"She is too pretty to have much to her." This I thought as I sat in the Brookstone library one summer day in Columbus, where every day it was so hot

JoElyn Jones in 1970

you could see the heat rising off the pavement. You didn't go out except to scurry from one air-conditioned building to another or to go to or from your air-conditioned car. This comment about beauties being dumb was in response to an art-teaching candidate to whom Jim McCallie briefly introduced me when the two of them passed through the school library where I was working on class schedules.

Later Jim said during our afternoon tennis match, "Chuck, this is the hire I am most excited about. Come on, give me some credit for having discernment about people. I hired you, didn't I?"

"I'm sorry, Jim. Of course I trust you. I just thought maybe you were swayed because she had been 'Miss Alabama,' or something like that. I should give you more credit."

"No, she wasn't 'Miss Alabama,' but I see what you mean. It's probably only because she didn't enter the competition. So, Chuck, you only had brothers growing up, right? So, you don't know much about women, do you? You've judged wrong on this one."

"Convince me I'm wrong."

"Well, she may be the best art teacher around. She was an art major at Auburn. She worked as a commercial artist on a Coke account in Atlanta, she's taught middle school English, and she worked for WQXI Television. [Later she disclosed that she worked with Judy Woodruff.] She's certified in art; she's a great find. And, I forgot to tell you. I think she was the Alabama Women's Amateur Golf champ."

"OK, big brother, I'll give her a chance."

Such was my introduction to JoElyn Jones, in the hot summer of 1970. Little did I appreciate that as pleased as Jim was to hire a really qualified middle school art teacher, he was more excited that he might just have found a wife for his little brother, for whom he felt quite responsible. (Jim, you will remember, was my big brother from Phi Delta Theta.)

When pre-planning faculty meetings began in late August, I lost my aversion to the new art teacher. I couldn't avoid some conversation and I at least found that she had far more to her than I had first thought. At first she called me Mr. Johnston (and I found out later that she assumed I was married).

A few weeks into the school year, this being the second in the school's short history, Jim Smith, principal of Brookstone's middle school, threw a party out on an island in the middle of Lake Harding where he lived. He asked JoElyn to be his date for the party. He picked her up, picked up some bags of ice on the way, and arrived on the lake's bank, maybe seventy-five yards from the island and his cabin.

"We have to do what to get to your cabin, row?" So stammered JoElyn. (Note: JoElyn is not a camper.)

"Yep, that's it. I'll put the bags of ice in the boat and we'll head over." So said Jim Smith.

Later I arrived with my date, Ein Watson, and we were paddled over by some of Jim's friends that he had commandeered to provide the transportation—a form of valet parking forty years ahead of its time. The party was fun, among work colleagues. The ribs smothered in barbecue sauce sent an aroma out across the lake from Jim's island home. The potato salad had enough mayonnaise and hard-boiled eggs to make it special. The beer was cold. We had a lovely meal and good visiting,

I was myself—I have always prided myself on being the same person in my work environment as I am in my "private life"—yet I was conscious of not going over my limit on the beer or the ribs. The sun was going down over the lake and it was beginning to get dark so I suggested to Ein that maybe we should be heading out.

As we made our rounds of goodbyes, JoElyn asked if she could get a ride into the city with Ein and me. So that was established. It seems that she had expressed to her date, the host Jim Smith, that she was ready to go home. Knowing that he could hardly leave the party at that point, he asked her to see if she could get a ride with me since I had already thanked Jim and said goodbye, and he knew I was getting ready to paddle off the island.

I'll never know what Ein thought of this arrangement, but the three of us took the ferry/paddle transport back to the mainland and got in my car. Early in my Columbus stay, I had a date with Steve Butler's sister, a beauty who was making her debut. It was to one of the debutante parties, and I picked her up in my Plymouth that had been a used car when I bought it upon graduating from Vanderbilt six years earlier. She didn't say a word about the car, but there is a chance she had never ridden in a car that old. I was embarrassed, and I determined then that if I were going to date Columbus girls, I was going to have to buy an acceptable car. That's when I bought my new two-door burnt-gold Mustang with bucket seats.

JoElyn climbed quietly into the back seat, that didn't have all that much room. Ein and I were in the front bucket seats. Soon JoElyn dropped her silence, leaned forward between the two front seats, and joined in the conversation—delightfully so. We got to the townhouse that JoElyn shared with Kathy Haygood, Brookstone's French teacher. Kathy was peering out from behind the blinds to see what was going on as I escorted JoElyn to the door. A spark was lit that night. (I have wondered since if there were somehow a connection between Mom's death in May '70 and the freedom I felt when I got to know JoElyn four months later.)

Two weeks later, when I knew Jim Smith was out of town and wouldn't be dating her, I called JoElyn from New York where I was attending an SSAT Conference. I thought she would be impressed by my calling from New York. In the '60s, all phones were "land lines" and you made special arrangements and paid extra fees for long-distance calls. We had a conversation full of laughs at the end of which I asked her if she would like to go out with me that coming weekend. She readily said "yes." This was unlike any interaction with a girl I had ever had, particularly one so pretty. I grew up being self-conscious about asking girls out. I was turned down enough times in high school that just dialing the phone terrorized me. This was different. It was as easy as having a conversation with a boy. This was a most natural beginning relationship, especially for one that, for me, was already tinged with romance.

For our first date, we went to the Springer Opera House (est. 1871) for a play, and to a bar for drinks and food afterwards. For our second date, we went to a wide-screen movie/documentary, *Woodstock*. Since we both enjoyed the movie with a smidgen of nudity and chock-full of the likes of Arlo Guthrie, Joan Baez, Grateful Dead, Credence Clearwater Revival, and the other music groups of 1969, we sort of thought of ourselves as hippies. We were professional in our daylight hours, and, at least in spirit, we were hippies in the evenings when we were together. Hippie maybe; but we were not into the so-called "sexual revolution." I was told in junior high that I would maintain my "good boy" status as long as I didn't touch a girl anywhere on her body that would be covered by a bikini. Here, some fifteen years later, that was still my guideline.

We enjoyed the same things. Our togetherness that fall was marked by laughter and nonstop conversation. We laughed about a billboard promoting movies on TV: "Talked out? Try our movies." We couldn't imagine ever being "talked out."

We did a lot together secretly in October and November. Of course, Kathy and Jim and Nancy McCallie knew, but no one else—or so we thought. We had an easy and relaxed relationship that I early on recognized as courtship (as opposed to run-of-the-mill dating).

Just before the Thanksgiving break, I asked JoElyn to marry me. Without skipping a beat, she said, "You don't know me well enough yet." How about that for a simple and forthright response! Of course, what she really meant was, "Look, buster, I don't know you well enough to say 'yes' to marriage." No stiffness entered our relationship. We went right on with our hilarious verbal fun.

We had a special table partially behind a partition in the Pizza Hut where we would go on an occasional weeknight for a beer and catching up. We were clever, we two. At this point, by the Thanksgiving holiday, JoElyn and I had been to Atlanta multiple times; she had met and liked Dad (and the feeling was mutual); and she and Warren hit it off. Warren was impressed by JoElyn's beer-drinking ability, and when he heard that she downed a whole boot of beer at Emmy's Schnitzel House in Columbus, he nicknamed her "Fish."

As we approached separating for the four-day Thanksgiving weekend, it passed through my mind that JoElyn had never suggested that I go with her to Greenville. Neither one of us spoke of it. Then over Christmas I went with Dad to Spain. This would be Dad's first Christmas and New Year's in roughly forty years that he would not spend with Mom—so we arranged to take this trip that would take us both away from familiar holiday traditions and surroundings. I wondered what this much time apart would do to JoElyn's and my high-spirited relationship.

Chapter 10: In Spain with Dad

"I don't know how one adjusts to the deadly silence of no one in the adjoining bed, or no one across the dinner table to have an end-of-the-day drink with, or no one with whom to discuss taking a trip to St. Simons for a couple of nights at the King and Prince." Such are my thoughts some forty-eight years after Dad became a widower. I must have thought some of these thoughts at Mom's death when I was twenty-nine, though I hadn't experienced having a soulmate at that point in my life, so, I couldn't fully put myself in Dad's shoes. Be that as it may, I did propose to Dad at some point in that first summer after Mom's death that we take a trip over the Christmas holidays. He agreed, and we settled on an American Express itinerary for Spain.

Let me here share my journal entry for the last full day of our fifteen-day trip:

12-31-70 — We walked the New Year's Eve streets of Madrid and felt the excitement of one of the world's great cities. We had 4 p.m. lunch in a café/restaurant combination where many locals were spending their siesta. On our walk we went to the huge national post office, we explored inside the plush European Ritz Hotel, and we examined the Prado from the outside. When we passed through the Puerto del Sol at 6:30 p.m., excitement was already building towards midnight. It is in this square that thousands pack and on each stroke of the clock, a grape is consumed—so that the corresponding month will be lucky.

George and Aileen Blinco, Ron Van Buskirk, Dad and I arrived at Al Mounia Restaurant at 10 p.m. It is built in a Moorish palace. All is North African: the walls and floors and ceilings are beautifully tiled, the waiters wear Moorish clothes, and the food is Algerian, Moroccan, etc. I had brick (meat-filled pastry) and lamb couscous. We drank Champagne. At midnight we tried to eat 12 grapes. The few people left in the restaurant (the others having gone to the Puerto del Sol) were jovial. An owner came and shook all of our hands. We had pastry and minted tea and departed, having paid $10 each for the finest of food and service plus five bottles of Spanish Champagne.

We walked the couple of miles back which got us into the spirit of the occasion by laughing and hollering with others on the streets. One Spaniard, when jovially passing by, offered me a swig from his brandy bottle. Biting cold or not, this was a beautiful gesture that warmed my insides. We returned to the hotel and drank more Champagne from silver goblets that Ron had bought.

But the gesture of the brandy had fired me up for the street people. Dad had caught my cold and felt the need to climb in bed. He was glad for me to further explore the night. So, Ron, George, Aileen and I headed for the Puerto del Sol.

We laughed and sang. I walked on my hands (which they later kidded me about). A group formed around us on the street. Their tambourine made such good music (Aileen danced) that I bought a tambourine for 100 pesetas. As we went into the café, my tambourine made me acceptable. Spaniards would take turns using it and the music and merry-making was wonderful. We left, but I found I couldn't retire. George and Aileen bid us adieu, and Ron and I went back in the café. The music makers were glad to see us. I ordered a bottle of beer which it seemed natural to pass around. Out of two bottles I had no more than three or four sips. One Spanish boy insisted on offering me a cigarette. I explained in beautiful Spanish that I didn't smoke. That didn't matter to him. He was adamant. When I had smoked one, passing it to my beer-drinking friends, he gave me a second.

As the café closed, it caused a refugee problem. Where will all of these displaced people go? Jesus and Joseph emerged from our music group as the ones who would help Ron and me find another bar. Ron was skeptical and finally fell by the wayside at 4 a.m. Joseph, Jesus and I found a large basement room where, from big pots, steaming chocolate was being poured. We had some together with a greasy pastry—all of which seems to be a part of the tradition.

Joseph bought some cigarettes with my money, and we then went to a café for coffee. After exchanging addresses, we three parted ways.

I checked the plaque on the building, saw that I was still in the Puerto del Sol, and I headed out towards the hotel. I walked and walked until I saw familiar lights and a familiar Christmas tree ahead—I was back at the Puerto del Sol. I had gone out the wrong side of the square. My second attempt at escape was more successful. I climbed beneath the sheets at 6 a.m., just as America was seeing the New Year in.

When I recounted this story from memory, before finding my next-day journal account, I remembered parting company with one soulmate, not three, and this is how I remembered it: *I would like to have held the sun in check and have this evening extend another three or four hours, but it was time to part company with my cherished companion. How did we pull away? It wasn't easy. It was sorrowful but had to happen. We probably hugged one another; he may have kissed me on the cheek, as Europeans are wont to do.*

I fell asleep, only to awaken shortly thereafter to a pleasant last day with Dad in Madrid, at the end of which we were on the plane back to Atlanta, and for me, on to Columbus.

(Journals from the trip to Spain are in **Appendix 6**.)

PART THREE

The Decade of My 30s (1970-1980)

Chapter 1: A Beautiful, Intelligent, and Unselfish Girl

Dad and I returned from Spain, and JoElyn returned from Greenville, Alabama, just in time for Brookstone to resume classes in January. In the past two months I had turned thirty and JoElyn had turned twenty-five. Our delight in being together after two weeks apart picked right back up, which was an encouraging sign.

JoElyn has told me much later that it had been those two weeks without seeing me and alone with her parents (even on New Year's Eve) that had convinced her that, even with our differences, she would like to marry me. Back when we had had the earlier ever-so-short conversation about marriage, I had said to myself, "I will patiently wait three months without even thinking about marriage, but when February comes, I'm going to ask her again."

Finally February arrived: "JoElyn, let's just spend this Saturday night together, no one else. I'm house-sitting for Mr. Shorter again. We can cook supper together and not go anywhere."

"Great, I'm for it. We both have been going too hard."

I laid a fire in Mr. Shorter's mahogany-paneled library, ready to be set ablaze. I prepared oyster stew in advance, that by a recipe from Buddy Dimon. While together we prepared a New Orleans shrimp dish and a salad, we sipped Old Fashioneds, the recipe for which I had gotten out of Dad's *Playboy Cookbook*. Yes, and we also got our shrimp dish recipe from there. We had good white wine with our dinner in the dining room.

Oyster stew, salad, wine, and main course. It may have been the best meal ever. We were critical of public display of affection, but here we were alone. We exchanged a meaningful kiss, said a blessing, and began slowly to enjoy a meal that would be punctuated by lots of laughter and talk, as usual. It was a long leisurely meal; we were alone and there was nothing to hurry us, and I had a touch of nervousness about what was to come.

"I guess we can't stay at the table all night." Reluctantly we pulled away from the grand dining room table and the even grander meal.

"How about this: we have some coffee ice cream we can enjoy later. But first, I've bought your favorite, Drambuie. Let's take a glass by the fire in the den."

We sat quietly, close together, and just listened to the crackling of the fire. I could feel the Drambuie burn as it went down my throat. Finally, I broke the silence by asking JoElyn if she would marry me.

"I should like to fall in love. I lead such a fun life but I am sure these pleasures would be amplified if they could be shared. I should like to meet a beautiful, intelligent, and unselfish girl." — Journal aboard the M.S. Aurelia, somewhere in the Atlantic, 8/17/1965

Her simple response: "WHEN?"

I may have given a speech, attesting to all of my passions and my promises for the future, but I doubt it. I think I just broke the profound silence by saying, "JoElyn, will you marry me."

It was February 6, 1971. Richard Nixon was president; Spiro Agnew, vice president. *All In the Family* debuted that year, and Simon and Garfunkel's "Bridge Over Troubled Waters," still one of my favorites, was song of the year. And on June 12 of that year, Chuck and JoElyn were married.

Chapter 2: Large in My Life — Armine and Buddy Dimon

I never tell somebody about my Brookstone years without beginning with Armine and Buddy Dimon:

"I knew the Dimons because of their son Sam living in Tull Hall for the last two of my Westminster years. I got to know them when they would come to bring him back or forth from their home in the Columbus neighborhood of Peacock Woods. When I knew I was going to Columbus, I talked to them before I talked to anyone at the dorm about my plan to leave. They were my confidants. I asked them to find for me, if they could, a guest house or a garage apartment." And thus begins every account when I tell others of going to Columbus.

"I ran with pleasure after returning home this evening. When I passed by the Dimons, they invited me to join them in a bowl of oyster stew, which was delicious. We had good conversation for an hour or so. When I went to pick up JoElyn, she was afraid I'd think her a floozy because the frosting of her hair turned out light. I think it looks great; she does a good job of keeping it looking natural, and it can't get too light to suit me." — Journal 3/9/71

I could not have dreamed up a more ideal living place than the one they found for me. It was a garage behind widow Becky Gilbert's big red-brick home in Peacock Woods. Bachelor John Swift lived next door; I had a bird's-eye view of his tennis court where I was occasionally invited to play. I was also invited to one Gatsby party in his home, but that's another story. Becky had a high school daughter, Gina, a middle school son, Kervin, and an elementary school son, Pierce. We weren't too much into each other's lives, but we had a cordial relationship. During my secret dating of JoElyn the next year, I have a feeling that they knew my every move.

When I was "a lonely bachelor," the Dimons would invite me for supper. Buddy would frequently prepare an oyster stew that I just loved. I asked him for his recipe, and I began to make it myself. Frequently, a year later, when JoElyn would come over, I would prepare Buddy's oyster stew. I observed that JoElyn never offered to cook.

I wrote that off to the fact that she didn't know how to cook, so I didn't press it. After we were married and I discovered that she was a talented cook, she told me she had humored me with my Buddy Dimon oyster stew and my creamed eggs on toast. She had not wished to come across as one of the girls she disdained who were trying to win a husband by their cooking. She was certainly not set on getting married any time soon, and she certainly didn't want to come across as if she were.

The Dimons' home is one of the oldest homes in Columbus. Built in a Greek Revival style, it bears an imposing name: The Cedars. At one time much of the land around it was a part of the estate. It had a large basement where, in our first year of marriage, JoElyn took up the Dimons' invitation for her to create a studio. It became a nice retreat for JoElyn in her limited spare time. She, too, benefited by our occasional meals with Armine and Buddy.

The Cedars had been passed down in Buddy's family. He was a bachelor for a number of years, active in his church as a Sunday School teacher, and a VP for Sales with Centennial Cotton Gin Company. One of the products they were making when I knew Buddy was truck bodies for hauling cases of soft drinks. He fell in love with and married a younger Armine Davis of Savannah. He was forty-five; she was thirty-three. Armine was a deaconess in the Methodist Church, which she had to give up to marry Buddy.

Armine was an active volunteer at the Open Door Community, where she tutored poor white children during the years that her sons, Jimmy and Sam, were young. She interacted with Columbus's black leaders, often hosting meetings in her home. (Her son Sam remembers driving with her to Atlanta and meeting

Buddy and Armine Dimon with son Sam and his family on a visit
with us years later in California.

Benjamin Mays.) Because her sense of social justice did not match that of the close-knit Columbus society, Armine was denounced on Johnny Reb Radio as a "nigger lover," and a cross was burned on the front lawn of The Cedars. She was finally declared "beyond the pale" with this group when in a meeting where participants were taking turns railing against integrating the public schools, this frail and soft-spoken woman rose and said, "It's time that we did this (integrating the schools). It's the right thing to do." Armine made her simple statement at a hearing of the Sibley Commission; through these hearings John Sibley was credited with keeping Georgia's public schools open.

At that point Armine was a public school elementary teacher; when volunteers were sought among the white teachers to go teach in a historically black school, only Armine and two others stepped forward.

She didn't count the cost. In the face of fiercely negative community emotions, Armine Dimon stood up.

Chapter 3: Jim's Magic Touch — How Brookstone Grew

Jim McCallie moved to Columbus with wife Nancy in early June 1969, and I was only a few days behind him. We had a lot of work to do to get a brand-new prep school underway the day after Labor Day (the day that all schools in the South started in this era). Jim was not afraid of hard work, and he prepared us both for the heavy lifting ahead.

"We've got to spend a lot of time with students this summer, because we don't have anyone for our inaugural freshman class. Chuck, you're going to be sick of Snuffy's Shanty, but that's where we need to do our selling."—Snuffy's Shanty being a hamburger/milkshake place that was "in" for teenagers.

We began by selling to Patti Smithson, whose mother, Pat Smithson, was our first grade teacher. Once she was sold, she would recommend students she knew who might be persuaded to help start a new private prep school, something that was not a part of the Columbus culture. However, some of the most respected city and societal leaders made up the Brookstone Board. We ended up initially with five students, two girls (Patti Smithson, Margaret Serrato) and three boys (Steve Bland, Larry Brocato, Curtis Shoemaker) for the class that would begin as ninth graders and progress through the senior year. When the two girls, Patti and

Margaret, were out of sorts with each other, which seemed to be the case often, then it became impossible to have a meaningful class discussion. You might think that having a class of five would be ideal; but, no, there was not the critical mass needed to spark lively and sustainable discussion. When Laura Holladay and Jim Mitchell entered mid-year, it helped the dynamics considerably.

Prior to Jim signing on as founding headmaster, trustee Mary Schley came up with the name *Brookstone*, taking it out of these lines in Sidney Lanier's poem "Song of the Chattahoochee":

And oft in the hills of Habersham,
And oft in the valleys of Hall,
The white quartz shone, and the smooth brook-stone
Did bar me of passage with friendly brawl ....

Bill Turner, truly a prince of a man—and, at the time, one of the five wealthiest Georgians—had given the land to build the new school. He gave significant seed money as well, as did his sisters, Betty Corn and Weezie Butler. There was a lot of money in Columbus. Gunby Jordan, Kent School and Yale graduate, was among the early major trustee donors, as was Edward Shorter. Combined with the wise choice of Jim McCallie as its first headmaster, the caliber of the board was the major factor in a true prep school being birthed in a city so provincial that it was for years the largest city in the United States not included on the Eisenhower Interstate System. This was because of the efforts of some in political power to save their beloved town from the corruption of the outside world that would come from such a highway link to the rest of the world.

It was instructive to me to see first-hand how a healthy board of trustees functions. I benefitted from my board relationships, especially with Jack Passailaigue (first chairman), Tom Black (second chairman), Jimmy Blanchard, Pat Franco, John Illges, Gunby Jordan, Ella Kirven, Red Pound (contractor for campus), Edward Shorter, Henry Swift, Mr. Taliaferro (organizing administrator), and Bill Turner. They trusted Jim and allowed him freedom from their interference in the day-to-day running of the school. (I had a nice visit with Gunby Jordan some twenty years later when he was attending an Atlanta Ballet production and I was the Ballet's executive director. I saw Bill Turner even later than that, sometime in the first decade of this century, in the concession area at Bobby Dodd Stadium; we had a most enjoyable conversation.)

It was not a part of the strategic planning that the revered Columbus public schools would integrate that next year, Brookstone's second; but it happened. The white-flight schools beginning to spring up across south Georgia were an anathema to Jim and me. These schools, falsely claiming "excellence in education," were mediocre at best, at least in the minds of two dyed-in-the-wool prep school guys. We wanted no part of that, and yet here we were accepting students coming to us in droves from Columbus High and Hardaway High. We flexed the growth plan and added the planned tenth grade, but then went ahead and added an eleventh grade as well. Several employees of Callaway Gardens, together with a West Point (Georgia) family or two, created their own bus to bring maybe a dozen students from 40 miles north of Columbus. The best we could do to stand on the virtuous side of justice was to go over to St. Mary's Catholic School across the river in Phenix City, Alabama, and recruit with scholarships two terrific black students, Angela Jordan and Mike Mathis.

JoElyn and I moved into a new duplex built by a Columbus acquaintance from church. He and his wife built it to live on one side and rent out the other side. It may have had just one bathroom, but it was perfect for us. After a couple of years there, we bought a Flowers & Gillam home on Ray Drive. We bought it for $28,000 and sold it for $30,000 two years later when we moved to Berry.

Note: In this house in Columbus, our first, we lived rent-free for two years and made $2,000. There would be in the future a condo at Cross Creek where we lived rent-free for eight months and made $3,000 on the sale. There would be our home on Wieuca Terrace that we bought for $80,000 and sold for $325,000 eighteen years later (net $245,000). So, is it any wonder that we expected the same rent-free-and-profit when we moved from our second Cross Creek residence where we had lived for thirteen years? We bought it for $206,000 and sold to Larry and Jane Vickers for $165,000. Our string of real estate successes came to an abrupt end. One doesn't always make money from home ownership, we learned.

Chapter 4: The Breathtaking Launch of Apollo 16

Within the first year of our marriage, JoElyn and I were invited to view the launch of Apollo 16 as family guests of one of the astronauts, Charlie Duke. The launch was midday on Sunday, April 16, 1972. Charlie is married to Dottie (nee Claiborne) and is my brother Dick's brother-in-law via Dick's marriage to Dottie's older sister, Mary Anne.

The sound and heat from the blast that moved the rocket off the launch pad and the suspenseful few seconds that it took for movement to occur following the initial blast were heart-stoppers. The family was there to support Dottie. Imagine having the one you most love trapped in a small capsule and having that person's ongoing life dependent on every detail of the liftoff going perfectly. Then there is the matter of reaching outer space, of piloting the lunar module onto the moon's surface. So far, so good! The only thing remaining now is to navigate a flawless return from off the moon's surface back to splashdown and then safely to shore.

During the televised walks on the moon's surface, narrated by Walter Cronkite over CBS-TV, Charlie was a star for his Southern accent and for his great sense of humor.

Charlie, together with John Young and Thomas Mattingly, returned safely on April 27, eleven days later. As you can imagine, it was difficult for Charlie to find purpose in his life upon returning from such a "mountaintop experience." Charlie and Dottie went through some really hard times in their marriage until ten years or so later when Dottie turned in desperation to the Lord. It was some time later before Charlie noticed how profoundly Dottie was changed, but eventually "he came to himself" and gave over his success-driven life to Jesus and His manifestation of the Father.

Even though Dottie and I knew each other as friends and as in-laws in high school, it was through our mutual embrace of Christianity that our two couples related as adults. When the Dukes would come into town once or twice a year to visit Dottie's aging mother, Dorothy Claiborne, the four of us would often meet at Church of the Apostles for Sunday morning worship together.

One of only twelve humans to ever walk on the moon, Charlie (born in 1935) travels the world with Dottie as a much sought-after speaker and evangelist. About those nearly forty years of sharing Duke Ministries with Dottie, Charlie has said: "I have never known such an exciting life—a life filled with the love, peace, joy and power of God. You might not be able to walk on the moon with me, but we can all walk together with Jesus, and that walk lasts forever."

Chapter 5: The Enormous Milestone of Having a Child — 1974

I don't remember conversations that JoElyn and I had about children and numbers of children, but we talked about everything, so I'm sure there was no serious divide between us on that issue. JoElyn was an only child; I was one of a posse of four.

We might have had two or three children close together in age were it not for the grave "morning sickness" that was a part of JoElyn's pregnancy with our first child, Jane. It was with JoElyn in all parts of the day and on every day of the week. She was sick.

Common knowledge on morning sickness is that the glory of having a baby brings about mother amnesia—forgetting all the travail of pregnancy. Not so with JoElyn. Her travail was so severe that she knew herself well enough to know she would never forget. Without any prodding from JoElyn, I knew I would never ask her to go through pregnancy a second time. I had a vasectomy, and we were content to be a one-child family.

I knew I would love being a dad. I've told all expecting fathers that of all the hats I've worn (e.g., coach, teacher, headmaster), that that of "Dad" was my favorite. I think having a baby brother and two older brothers made me value the fun things one does as a child. By being a dad, you get to reenter that realm of childhood, to some degree, with your children.

JoElyn and I, marrying at ages twenty-five and thirty respectively, knew that we would be wise not to rush into having children. There was a lot we didn't know about each other, so we knew we wanted time to settle in as a married couple. On advice from doctors, JoElyn started on the birth control pill several months before our wedding so that her system would have time to adjust to it. (The birth control pill was still new in 1970, only ten years after it first came on the market.) I was squeamish about gynecological issues, all the more reason we needed to be married awhile before we had children. I didn't know that there was a medical specialty called gynecology.

When other people's babies began to look especially cute to us, we sensed that we were ready to enter parenthood. Marcia Johnson, Brookstone teacher, and Fort Benning officer Andy, her husband, one of the couples at the time that we enjoyed being with, had a child. Part of the pleasure of being with them was to get to hold their baby. JoElyn went off the pill, and in the second December of our marriage, the telltale sign of pregnancy appeared—severe nausea for JoElyn.

We had driven over to Greenville (Alabama), arriving with just enough time to freshen up before guests began to arrive for Ed and Evelyn's Christmas party. All of their close friends, who had been a part of our wedding, were to be there. Showing no signs of nausea on our drive over, immediately after putting on her Christmas party dress, JoElyn rushed to the bathroom to throw up (what my dad used to call "upchuck"). I'm not sure JoElyn ever made an appearance at the party. Evelyn was unhappy because she was wanting to feature her daughter-returned-home among their close circle of friends. It would be early January '74, upon our return to Columbus, that we would learn that our baby was on the way.

Chapter 6: Transition to Berry Academy in 1974

Every new work position I have obtained has been because of connections, someone who championed my candidacy. Following is a prime example of that when Gordon Bondurant, then president of Darlington School, spoke with Dr. John Bertrand, then president of Berry College and Academy:

"John, I think I know the man you need to head up the academy. He's young, in his mid to early thirties, but he is already a savvy school man. I taught him everything he knows about school work when he came out of Vanderbilt—just kidding about that. But we did teach together at McCallie School and we've been friends ever since. He's got the boarding school experience from McCallie and Westminster and administration from five years with Jim McCallie in Columbus. You should call him."

In February of 1974, Dr. Bertrand invited me and JoElyn up to the Berry campus, on the outskirts of Rome, Georgia. We stayed in one of the 1930s guest cottages on campus. We were treated royally with meals and interviews with multiple college and academy leaders. We accepted an offered contract to move to this 30,000-acre campus (twice the size of Manhattan Island) and to be headmaster of the middle and upper schools that formed Berry Academy. Our prescribed portion of the campus was at the end of a four-mile stretch of road leading from the front college campus back to the Mountain Campus, the picturesque campus now leased by Chick-fil-A as Camp Winshape.

"Is life as random, pointless, and absurd as it seems? Or is it ordained, purposeful, and meaningful? ... The search for that meaning is given structure by honesty, desire, and risk." — Dan Allender, To Be Told: Know Your Story, Shape Your Future

I relished the lore of Martha Berry. She was the most alive historic figure I have ever known. I probably learned more about fund raising from her than from anyone else, before or since. *Miracle in the Mountains*, the film about her starting the school, thrilled me every time I watched it. In one scene she was talking to the mountain folks who would come themselves and bring their children every Sunday afternoon for "Sunday school." Out of this grew the Berry Schools. But in the film was this exchange between Martha Berry and one of the mountain men who spoke slowly with heavy mountain accent:

"Now, folks, you know we have a leak in the roof of this little Sunday School building. So, this coming Saturday I want some volunteers to come and help repair the roof." First spoke Martha to those sitting in the little Sunday School building with clapboard sides and a shingled roof.

Then one of the kindly mountain men spoke up: "Miss Martheee, iffen it don't rain, we won't need to repair the roof. And iffen it do rain, we can't fix it."

Even today JoElyn and I will bring up this exchange in the film as relates to some mangling of logic in something going on around us.

Chapter 7: My Experience of Fatherhood

Initially upon Jane's birth, I was more adept at changing diapers than JoElyn. The experience of having had a baby brother came back to me. Of course, JoElyn caught up and surpassed me, but I was from the start intricately involved in all matters of parenting except nursing. Here are some things that did surprise me:

- ✓ It's easy to clean up even diapers filled by an explosion when it is your own child.
- ✓ Sigmund Freud was closer to the mark with his theory of cross-gender attraction (i.e., boy to mother, daughter to father) than I had credited him with while a student at Vanderbilt. When Jane would toddle to the back door of our Berry Academy cottage to beat her mom at greeting me in the evening, it finally dawned on me that she was competing with JoElyn for my attention and affection. Henceforth, I made a point to establish that her mom was my first love.
- ✓ Why did it tickle me so to take Jane or Evelyn Anne as babies on my Saturday rounds of the hardware store or wherever? I loved bathing them at night. I loved telling them stories while they were in the bubble bath tub, and then reading them stories as we prepared for prayers and lights-out. *Go, Dog, Go!* was my absolute favorite, which doesn't say much for my literary tastes. But *Madeleine*, a bit more highbrow, was a close second. We wrestled on the living room floor at certain intermediate ages. We passed the football, coaching them away from the usual female side-arm throw to the one that comes zipping past one's ear in a spiraling fashion.

Pregnant JoElyn and I moved into the Berry Academy headmaster's cottage in late June 1974. Jane was born August 5th and spent the first six years of her life thinking it natural to have horses she could go pet at any time, fields and lakes and waterwheels, and a swan named Marble in the imagination of her bath-time stories from her dad.

"Jane, Jane, come quick. See the deer passing through our front yard!!"

"Daddy, Daddy, I've seen deer. I'm busy." Imagine having grown up in the center of a deer preserve and, at age four or five, being blasé about seeing deer. To give her credit as a toddler and beyond, she was a girl of nature, loving every aspect of this 30,000-acre nature preserve. Who's to blame her if she thought this was everybody's childhood environment?

I was not as surprised at my joy of taking her up to the nearby stables to pet the horses. Our favorite was Star, owned by a Berry college student whose father was president of Gainesville Junior College. When the student owner was there, she would let Jane sit up on the back of this monster horse.

Chapter 8: An Act of Rebellion

While we tried to be selective in our admissions (Ed Laird, Mike Knighton, admission directors), we were more of a last resort for students and parents who were running out of options. The discipline committee, headed first by Bill Thornton and then Bill Boy, met nearly every Monday because of rules infractions over the weekend. One such case fit the pattern in some ways, but in other ways the infraction had never occurred before and it would be unlikely that it would ever happen again. And I was the precipitating factor in this horrific incident.

"Wait, Jane. Step back. Something's not right." It was a Sunday afternoon, a beautiful spring afternoon on Martha Berry's fairytale-like campus. I was coming to my nice office in Hamrick Hall to spend maybe thirty minutes, to look over something for the next day. Jane, maybe four at the time, came with me—to give her mom a break and because Jane liked to play with little toys I kept in a basket beside my desk.

"Holy mackerel! What is all this glass all over the floor? Oh, my gosh, Jane. Stay back! Somebody has smashed this huge plate glass window."

We carefully stepped in. "Look, here's a monster rock that someone threw through the window. Ooooh, my gosh!"

"Dad, how could anybody be so mean?" Flash forward a few years, and Jane had the same reaction when we awoke the morning after Halloween to find our front-porch pumpkin had been smashed. "How could anybody be so mean?" (We later learned that the pumpkin culprit was a high-school kid, David Turpin, that we liked from across the street—just having "Halloween fun" with his friends.)

By Monday morning, Dean of Students Bill Boy had uncovered the culprit. He was one of the youngest students in the dorms. From Connecticut, he had been admitted on his own merits, and also his grandmother and Martha Berry had been friends. He had never been in trouble of any kind—a cooperative kid. "Son, why did you do it—destroy that huge window and trash Mr. Johnston's office with glass everywhere?" the dean asked.

"I just couldn't stand it any longer. I was boiling with rage. Mr. Johnston is such a phony," said the youngster.

"Phony? That's the last adjective I would expect to hear about Mr. Johnston," the dean said.

"Phony, phony, phony! Nobody could be as happy as he is—and all the time! I just couldn't stand it."

He got the "maximum sentence"—expulsion. He had had it "up to here" with my cheerfulness, and he's the one who had to pack and leave.

Now, some forty years later, I wonder what that kid is doing. He's probably not a kid anymore. I hope he's a counselor in some capacity, a truth teller, as he was as a fifteen-year-old. Though at the time I took his attack as a testimony to my great character—always smiling, always keeping a happy face. It was a product of years and years of practicing "the power of positive thinking" or PMA, Positive Mental Attitude—now I see it as poor mental health. I couldn't have told you how I felt about anything. The communications line from my brain to my heart had been severed ever since I was a kid. I had dealt with emotional trauma (mostly Mom's alcoholism) by asserting that "everything is fine" when it wasn't. I learned to wear a mask, and at some point it was affixed so tightly to my face that I couldn't take it off, not that I would have wanted to.

Chapter 9: Last Visit with Dad

In late December 1976, JoElyn, Jane, and I met Dad and Uncle Bill at the Busy Bee Café in downtown Rome at noon. Bill was in his usual good humor, which tickled Jane (age two years, four months). Jane sat next to her granddaddy, and seemed to find that special. Dad seemed a little tired, but his warmth at seeing us came through. When Granddaddy said he was paying, and when Jane heard the choices on the kids' menu, she immediately piped up:

"Granddaddy, please, please. I want chocolate milk, a hot dog, and fence fies?" (Choices she would never have at home.)

The rest of us ordered from the "meat and three" menu because the vegetables were the reason for coming here, at least for the adults—squash casserole, both turnip and collard greens, coleslaw, baked apples, okra and tomatoes, sliced tomatoes, corn on the cob, and more; all grown in the Busy Bee's own garden. The three men had the meat loaf; JoElyn had trout. Catsup on meat loaf is the best.

From the cheerful downtown café and across the Coosa River, we drove out to our headmaster's cottage on the Berry Academy campus, passing the Ford Buildings and lawns of the college campus, passing nothing but dense forests on the four-mile "stretch" road. Then, when the trees parted, we arrived at the beauty of "the mountain campus." Multiple deer were grazing in the middle of the soccer field. As we drove around the campus and out to the waterwheel and back, Uncle Bill shared, "I've heard of Martha Berry and the Berry Schools for years, but I never imagined it to be this stunning, and here it is December." It was that week between Christmas and New Year's with hardly a soul on campus. You could hear the breeze blowing through the trees on this sunny winter day in the low 50s.

"Yeah, Uncle Bill, she put together 30,000 acres for the college, the academy, and the farming project so the students could earn some of their tuition."

"Thirty thousand acres. I wonder how many football fields that is," Uncle Bill mused.

"Ha, I don't know in terms of football fields, but I do know that it's twice the size of Manhattan Island."

Dad chimed in, "I've enjoyed coming up here since you three have been here. I feel that you're in this idyllic fantasy land."

We went in our cottage to show it to Bill and to rest a bit before the two brothers, both now closer to seventy than sixty-five, left.

"Granddaddy, pweeez, come see the horses." Jane was hard to turn down, even if the men were a bit tired. So the five of us sauntered up to the Gunby Stables about a football field up the hill behind our home. To go and pet the horses was a special treat for Jane. Jane was not quite ready to see the visitors depart. These two brothers, born well before World War I, and this almost-newborn had a sweet rapport.

As we had taken a few steps on our way back to our home and their car, Jane looked up into her granddaddy's eyes with her arms stretched up towards him and said, "Granddaddy, I'm tired. Pweez carry me."

Dad reached down; she jumped up. She was tightly affixed to his chest. After covering about a quarter of the football-field distance back down the hill, Dad said,

"Jane,"—and I think I heard a tear in his voice, for this had been the name he had called for over forty years as he had held another to his chest—"Granddaddy is not supposed to carry heavy things, and you're getting to be such a big girl. I'm going to let you hold my hand and lead the way."

That would be the last time we would see my dad, a man truly beloved by all three of us,. He dropped to his death three days later carrying a case of whiskey into the Cross Creek home that he and Harriet shared together. He was preparing for a sweet New Year's Eve. (Dad had married Harriet Wilcox, a widow, five years earlier—in the fall of the same year in which JoElyn and I had been married, 1971.)

The graveside service was New Year's Eve, December 31, 1976. It was freezing cold. We gathered that evening at Harriet's for lively conversation. I remember few particulars except that either Dillon or Warren brought to our minds a man in black standing right in our sight line as we would look over the flower-draped casket to several yards behind. It connected for whoever was bringing this up because of a dream they had had or one that Dad had had. In the dream the man represented death. As it turns out, this man was one of the somber members of the Patterson Funeral Home team.

Chapter 10: The Transformation of a Bigger-Than-Life Family

For me the love story of Anne and Dillon began when Dillon took me with him on one of his first dates with her—to her apartment to play Monopoly. This was Anne Coggan whom I have adored from that game of Monopoly on to this day.

Let me admit here that, at age seventeen and for quite a while afterwards, I had a negative impression of girls. I felt awkward around them. Growing up in a practically all-male household, I saw girls as not as good in sports as boys, and sports ability was a big ingredient in my evaluation of people. They liked "girlie" things; they were superficial. One of the worst things that could be said about a Johnston boy would be, "You're acting like a girl."

But Anne! She was totally different. She may not see this as a compliment, but I found her as much fun as my brothers and as easy to be with as any boy I had known. After this evening of Monopoly with Anne, I found her to be someone I wanted to spend time with, just for play and good conversation. Whether it was that night or later in that summer, but I began to see her as the ideal. I knew what a girl could be, and I knew I could never date for long any girl that didn't measure up to Anne. She was my standard. I have her to thank for my not "settling" in the decade of my twenties. It would take me maybe thirteen more years of futile dating before I found someone who could hold a candle to Anne.

Dillon and Anne had a storybook wedding on a friend's estate in Westchester County north of New York City. Out of doors, under giant elder trees, on a picture-perfect summer Saturday, they were married by none other than the same priest whose midnight service I had attended with Dillon the year before—Sidney Lanier, a charismatic Episcopal priest and grandson of Sidney Lanier, the Georgia poet. (Anne tells me that the priest was also a distant relative of Tennessee Williams.)

As a young professor of English at Wake Forest University, Dillon started the Wake Forest Press to publish exclusively Irish poets, poets who were early in their careers in Ireland and virtually unknown and unpublished in the United States. I envied this aspect of Dillon's job since the only place to draw up a contract with an Irish poet is in an Irish pub. Dillon was required to travel to Ireland once or twice a year. Sometimes he would take a select group of students for a month to study abroad for the month of January.

The plane bound for Ireland was in motion, taxiing for takeoff, when Dillon got word that Dad had dropped dead. The plane turned around and brought Dillon back to the terminal (which I find remarkable) so that he could join his family in mourning for the death of our father and to be a part of the funeral process. JoElyn and I came down from Rome. Dick and Mary Anne came from New York City, Anne from Winston-Salem, and Warren from British Columbia where he was traveling during the holidays.

The spring following Dad's death, the spring of '77, Dillon and Anne, along with Kathleen and Devin, came to visit JoElyn, Jane (age two and a half), and me at Berry Academy. We had a wonderful time together. The kind of marriage they had was what I worked for in my marriage. JoElyn and I agreed that how they raised Kathleen and Devin was a model we wanted to emulate. Anne put a high priority on getting the four of us brothers and our families together each summer at the beach. As I remember, she did a lot of the reservation work for this to happen. Our family and our closeness gave Anne great joy. It was as if she had grown up with us. By that I mean that we were all just that close to Anne. It was here at the beach that we learned of something that we could never have imagined—Dillon and Anne's marriage was coming to an end.

Now that I'm reflecting back on my life, I see so many incidents that speak of Dillon's love for his brother two years younger. That he chose a one-on-one walk as the means of delivering to me, who had always idolized him, news of the ending of his marriage to Anne, is a prime example. Dillon, Anne, and I were so close that I wasn't accepting the rupture in Dillon and Anne's marriage as a *fait accompli.* I set about to try to bring comfort to Anne while, at the same time, bring Dillon to his rightful responsibility expressed in his wedding vow: "till death do us part."

I remember Al Davis telling me years later, "Your dad was a straight shooter." I knew that what he was trying to tell me was that Dad was faithful to Mom. There was Mom, in later years often unpleasant with her drinking, who had said to Dad during their engagement, "You're someone I want to grow old with." That would not happen, but Dad was faithful. I must have felt motivated by that notion of being a straight shooter to fight for something that I wasn't ready or willing to lose: the Camelot of my older brother's marriage.

As further testimony to Dillon's and my closeness, he asked me to quit writing to him my guilt-enhancing letters of appeal. I was—in heavy-handed fashion, I'm sure—imploring him to choose to restore his relationship with Anne and his commitment to his family unit. I don't remember his exact words, but the gist was that he would understand if I turned my attention from him to "being there" for Anne. Sad as it was, that's what I did.

My family was for me an idol, to use a Biblical term. Dad had succeeded in instilling in us loyalty to one another as "the Johnston Boys," every bit as legendary as "the James Brothers" (i.e., Jesse and Co.). I truly believed the hype that we were set apart for special things, much like the Kennedy boys who in the early '60s were pictured playing touch football together on their Hyannis Port front lawn. "Exceptionalism" is the word used to describe the U.S. by patriots who think that we as a nation can do no wrong. Well, I had grown up taking delight in and taking advantage of "the Johnston Boys being exceptional." At a certain age that may have been healthy, but, as Scripture says, "When I became an adult I put away childish things." It would not have been healthy for me to worship family over God and all His manifestations of healthy spirituality.

Dillon showed me that we as the Johnston boys are not perfect. Years later I came to realize that my shortcomings were every bit as egregious as were his, just manifest in less public ways. In my spiritual walk, I learned about forgiveness, that it was as important for my health, if not more so, as it was for those towards whom I held a grudge. It has taken time, but today I love Dillon's second wife, Guinn, genuinely and deeply, and have the wisdom and maturity to know that this does not diminish my deep affection for and lifelong love for my sister Anne.

As for Guinn, I love her for the encouragement she has given to both Jane and Evelyn Anne. Her assessment of where Jane's heart is and how she might best pursue her sense of purpose was profound, I thought—this in Jane's forty-third year of life. And, when Evelyn Anne was single and in her mid-twenties, Guinn and Dillon hosted her in St. Louis and showed her the graduate writing program.

She has become a good friend and encourager to JoElyn and me. We love her, and she loves us.

I might not have felt as close to a sister born amongst "the Johnston boys" as I have felt to Anne. Evelyn Anne is named in part for our sister Anne. Anne and I have been involved in demanding school administration and the demands of our children (even in their adult years); likewise, JoElyn has been a conscientious teacher and mother/grandmother. So while we would like to have gotten together with Anne much more often than we have, we've relied a lot on telephone conversations and email exchanges. We have spent time in each other's homes. I love being in her house on West End Boulevard. Now we are committed to a trip together once a year. As I noted to Anne recently, "I couldn't write anything significant about my life and those whom I most have loved without you being right in the center."

I continue to probe my behavior and attitude toward the dissolution of Dillon and Anne's marriage and how I have navigated, often quite poorly but hopefully with increasing health, my relationship to each of them separately since. As a son of a poet and a lover of well-crafted stories, I know that the best characters are complex, each struggling to do what they think is best within the limitations of their own experiences, perspective, passions, fears, needs, hopes, dreams and present need to simply survive.

People write about someone being closer than a brother, and I could say that about my being "joined at the hip" to Dillon. Yes, an idol was shattered, but a richer character emerged both in my view of Dillon and our relationship. A truer, more loving relationship has taken the place of the ideal I had imposed, because it allows for the complicated realities of being human the best we can and choosing to love rather than grade one another in that process. I feel the love from Dillon when we call each other, much in the way Dad used to call us on Thursday nights (when Harriet was away at her bridge night). I'd rather have a dear flesh-and-blood brother than a superhero.

Chapter 11: The Emory EMBA Experience

At the Berry Schools, which included the college and the academy, Joe Walton was the Vice President for Business, so the financial side of running the academy was not my direct responsibility. Nevertheless, I felt that if I were to go on to other headmasterships in the future, I couldn't continue to be clueless about spreadsheets and flow charts. While chairing a SACS visiting committee at Pace Academy, the dean of Emory University, a member of the Pace Board, spoke of a new Emory Business School program that was at that time building its inaugural class of mid- to upper-level business leaders for its first Executive Master's in Business Administration Program (EMBA). It would begin in January '79 and conclude eighteen months later. I applied with no normal business prerequisites for an MBA program, and I was accepted. I laughed in telling people that Emory was just trying to prove in accepting me that they could work magic with non-traditional students. Berry agreed to pay $8,000 and I would pay $4,000 for the full tuition of $12,000. This was in 1979-80; the tuition for the same program in 2019 was $115,324.

This was a bit like having paid weekends at a luxury hotel. I had a card that got me into the parking deck. A continental breakfast was waiting for us when we arrived in the early morning, and lunch was provided. There was a Friday night lecture series that came with drinks and dinner at the Crown Plaza Hotel. Unless we had a Thursday evening project meeting, I would leave the Berry campus in the dark of Friday morning and arrive in time for the 8:30 a.m. start of class. I stayed Friday nights in a little independent motel just off the Emory campus. We would then finish up classes by 5 o'clock Saturday afternoon, and I would drive home for a slightly later supper with JoElyn and Jane.

My memory of staying alone in a motel room far from home and family is a memory of a time when I felt particularly close to God. There was so much math content in the various classes that I often would resort to prayer. "Lord, I don't understand how this equation works. I'm totally lost, and we have a test tomorrow. Please, ease my racing heart and my sense of panic." On most such nights I slept better than I had any reason to expect. I remember once taking one of those heavily math-saturated tests and getting it back with a 92. It was truly as if my mind were taken over and that I came forth with answers that I didn't know.

The entire class went to London for a week. We enrolled in the London Business School for a condensed semester of International Business, the last course we would take to complete our degree requirements. JoElyn and Jane, just a month or so shy of her sixth birthday, traveled with me. We MBA students had one afternoon of field trips. The mistake was to have our first stop at the Guinness Brewery to study their business practices and to sample their products, together with a nice buffet lunch. Our stop after that, maybe at 3 o'clock, was at Barclays Bank. Part of the class dropped by the wayside; the rest of us had trouble staying awake during the bank's talking session.

Meanwhile, Jane was going around London with her mom on double-decker buses and in black old-fashioned taxis. Once Jane got a taste for these vehicles, she had very little interest in walking. They saw a lot and did a lot that I missed as I sat in classes. Jane made friends with people all over the city. At our closing luncheon, our final time to be together as a class, as it were, Jane was back in the kitchen talking away with the serving staff and kitchen staff. They were thoroughly entertained by her. As we were leaving we got lavish compliments on Jane, and several said that she had invited them to her birthday party and they just might show up.

"I have no illusions of being God's gift to IBM, but at least now I am comfortable asking questions in finance committee meetings. I'm glad to have the MBA. It gives me confidence in the business side of running a school." So I would report of my Emory experience.

For my independent study project, I created a business plan for the concept that a network of for-profit schools could be created that would deliver a better learning experience for elementary and junior high students because our very survival would depend on pleasing families and seeing academic results superior to what the student might achieve elsewhere. Also, these schools would accommodate working parents by holding school for 220 days instead of the customary 180 days in U.S. schools. Also, school would extend through the afternoon with lighter learning experiences such as cooking and chess clubs and the like. "We'll call this corporation Family Schools, Int'l, because eventually we will stretch to major centers where Americans work overseas."

Chapter 12: Farm Lady She Is Not

JoElyn was twenty-eight years old when we moved to the Berry Campus. When the wind blew in one direction, from the headmaster's cottage we could smell the horse stables; when it blew from another direction, we could smell the cow manure in the barns built in the style of homes for cows in Normandy, France. We joined with others on the Academy campus in the planting, weeding, and harvesting of a communal garden so vast that every spare moment you could feel the pressure to be in that garden, either weeding or picking.

"JoElyn, we women are gathering this next Saturday to cream corn, and you're included," she was told. "Bring your electric skillet and gloves—10 a.m. in the space outside Avis' apartment."

Later: "Chuck, I've just gone through the remarkable ancient rural ritual of creaming corn. Oh, my gosh. It was unlike anything I had ever experienced; it was a taste of what farm life must be about. The conversation was energized and fun to be a part of."

"Were the other ladies nice to you?"

"Oh, yeah. They were sweet. They showed me how to strip the husk and all those clingy yellow silk tassels: 'Then take your sharp, sharp knife and cut the kernels away from the cob without cutting yourself, put the kernels in the electric frying pan and let them stew. And, Honey,' they would say, 'you've got some good food on a cold winter day.'"

After three or four years of this rural life, with Jane having a "die-for" childhood, and me loving the long dirt roads for running and the rusticity of the setting and its people, JoElyn was secretly praying that God would take us away from there and send us to the city, any city. She loved Berry and its people, but city life was too deep in her blood. Then, on All Saints Day, 1980, after reading of Corrie Ten Boom's sister, who convinced Corrie to give thanks for everything, even the fleas in the prison cell, JoElyn went into town to our church, St. Peter's Episcopal, and knelt and poured her heart out to God: "Lord, if this is where you want me to be, then I will gladly obey you. I will embrace this rural life that has been so hard for me."

It was as if a weight had been lifted off of her. I didn't see her at that point in the day, but she later told me with delight of the lighthearted feeling of being filled with the Holy Spirit.

As I came in the back door of the Headmaster's Cottage a little after six, Jane nearly tackled me, as usual; JoElyn was ready with supper and past-ready for some adult conversation. Just then the phone rang, and I answered. I seldom let the phone interfere with family and dinner, but this time I said, "JoElyn, this is important. Sorry to delay supper, but I need to take this call upstairs."

I emerged forty-five minutes later with a big grin on my face: "JoElyn, that was Howell Adams, chairman of Trinity School's search committee. He wants me to interview to be headmaster of Trinity School and for us to move to Atlanta." Joy burst out all around.

Jane had no experience of moving, but she was soon to find a true "best friend" and soccer mate in Catherine Carson. JoElyn told me of her strong spiritual experience of letting go before God of her heart's desire to once again be a city girl. It was truly a *not my will, but Thine be done* experience in her life, one that she has experienced multiple times since. "When we are willing to give up a desire of our heart, that's when God gives it to us," so has said JoElyn more than once.

PART FOUR

The Decade of My 40s (1980-1990)

Chapter 1: Transition from Berry Academy to Trinity School

As is recorded above, JoElyn, five-year-old Jane, and I traveled to London in June '80 for a week-long course to wrap up my EMBA program. So, when we moved to Atlanta right at the end of June 1980, I was not up to my usual running condition that enabled me to run like a deer and sluff off a 10K race as not worthy of a lot of consideration. Howell Adams, the Trinity trustee who had hired me into my new headmaster role, encountered me at the start and invite me to join him for the race, which I did. Lo and behold, he took off "like a bat out of hell," and I had no choice but to stick with him. By the base of "Heartbreak Hill" in front of Piedmont Hospital, I bid adieu to Howell and slackened my pace. Even so, I ended up in the medical tent with heat stroke and a temperature of 106. They packed me in ice, hydrated me, and sent me off an hour later recovered but chastened. Such was my transition from the rural life to city life.

I worked hard in July and August to prepare this highly respected two-year-old-through-grade-six school for its twenty-eighth school year. Professionally I was entering the beginning range of a child's years in school, so to some Trinity might not seem as challenging or prestigious as the school that provides the gateway into college, i.e., middle and high school.

Yet Trinity was known throughout Southeastern prep school circles for the stand that its founder Pastor Allison Williams had taken some seventeen years before I arrived on the scene. Trinity School accepted Andrew and Jean Young's daughter Lisa into the first grade for the fall of '63—the first non-public school, along with the Peabody's Demonstration School, Nashville, to integrate. (Sixty-one students withdrew over that summer; the church lost 250 of its 1,800 members.) Williams' response was simple: "Our church and our school gained integrity as an institution that was more interested in standing for something than in gaining new members." I was proud to be a part of such a legacy of courage, and it helped shape my life to come.

Jane and I were both starting a new school together.

It's hard for men to devote as much time and attentions to the family as most of us yearn to do. I had the perfect answer to that. My children came to work with

JoElyn, Jane and Chuck, starting their first year at Trinity, summer 1980

me. My first of eight opening days at Trinity School, Jane rode with me and shared in the experience. She was beginning first grade and I was beginning my first year as headmaster.

Obviously nervous, heading to a new school, heading to a real school, Jane asked, "What will this be like, Dad? I've never been to the first grade before."

"Are you feeling a little scared? Guess what? I am, too. This will be my first school day at a new school, too. I'm going to wear a smile, be determined to enjoy it, and just see what happens. Try that, and then we can compare notes at the end of the day. I'll tell you how it went for me, and you can tell me how it went for you. OK?"

Though we were nearly the first ones there on a sultry day-after-Labor-Day morning, Jane was off to find her classroom. That was her approach to Trinity School for her six years there as a student, six years when we rode together to school every morning of those years.

Chapter 2: Our House on Wieuca Terrace

"We can't afford the house Anne Carson is recommending on Dean Drive, and there don't seem to be any houses anywhere around Trinity being offered for less," I said. "We know Cross Creek from our time in Harriett's condo. Let's buy there." Even though JoElyn had her heart set on a house with its own yard, she agreed. We bought a two-bedroom one-bath condo on Elysian Way for $30,000. It was a family gathering place in August 1980, in our second month in Atlanta after we had buried Big Gram next to Grandpa in Westview Cemetery, this the Saturday after we had all been at Pawley's Island together. We liked the glass porch that looked out on some green space and the golf course beyond. Jane and I had adventures in and around the creek that her oldest two children would experience some eighteen years later when JoElyn and I returned to again live at Cross Creek.

Jane had a friend from her pre-school Rome years who would come to visit her grandparents on Wieuca Terrace. These were the Hollingsworths, whom I had known growing up in Peachtree Road Presbyterian Church. On one of these visits Mrs. Hollingsworth, knowing that JoElyn had not given up finding a house, said to us, "You should look into a house just up the street from us. The nephews and nieces of their recently deceased aunt inherited the house. Since they know nothing of the history of its upkeep, they want to sell it as is."

JoElyn loved the street but not the house. She would say, "It's like the house that Jack built. It's not the layout I would choose, but the street is nice and the yard is nice. Let's do it."

JoElyn worked so hard painting in her colors in the dead of winter (with no heat) that she caught serious flu and was in bed for a week. As soon as she could get out of bed she was back at it. As late Sunday afternoon was turning to dark and we three were reentering our Cross Creek condo from working on the house, we found a note from our real estate agent taped to the door saying, "Call. I have a buyer." We were happy to net $3,000 on a property we had owned for less than eight months.

We bought the Wieuca Terrace house for $80,000 in the dead of winter. It had an ancient gravity-flow furnace and no central air.

A big part of our $10,000 in essential upgrades was to put in central air conditioning and heat. The other significant improvement was to replace the small back porch (one that appeared more like a potting room for plants) with an aluminum and glass structure that would for eighteen years serve as our breakfast room and sitting area. We opened up the wall between the kitchen and this new space by taking out the wall above the sink, counter, and dishwasher and all of what had been a doorway. And herein lies a story:

Anne Carson recommended a talented handyman, whom we'll call Rod, to come and take out the wall and install the proper trim. JoElyn and I were watching as Rod used his chain saw to cut perfectly around the periphery of the wall that was to come down. He and we were startled when unexpectedly the entire circumscribed area came crashing down, bouncing off the sink and counter and falling to the floor. JoElyn let out a real scream, not because the wall fell but because easily a thousand roaches came pouring out of the plaster, lath, and wire of the wall. This had been very much like a beehive with a major city full of roaches living in this wall, by night looting the kitchen for food and water. Undoubtedly there were generations of roaches dating back to pre-WWII and, before that, back to the era when prehistoric creatures roamed the earth. While JoElyn and Rod stood with wide eyes and gaping mouths, I managed to get to the roach spray under the sink and douse the unlucky ones that did not scamper quickly enough to the corners of the kitchen and the hallways beyond.

This was a psychologically chilling experience, the scars of which JoElyn carries with her even today.

It wasn't until the spring that we realized the rich heritage we had in the yard. The couple who had occupied the house since the '40s had no children, so they had devoted themselves to planting and maintaining the yard. Around an almost hidden patio with porch swing were camellias, gardenias, day lilies, irises, crocuses, and I don't know what all. In the center of all of this we played whiffle ball and croquet, built playhouses and had sleep-outs. We had a memorable party in the back yard complete with jukebox—this to celebrate JoElyn's and Phil Humann's fortieth birthdays, November 10, 1985. I waited nervously, hoping that a first frost would not kill back the gorgeous impatiens, and it didn't. The back yard we inherited was enchantingly beautiful that night.

It's the house wherein Evelyn Anne read copiously at age four. It's the house where two dogs had short-term stays—one running away and one darting out the front door directly into the wheels of a passing car, and where two other dogs, Pumpkin and Ginger (shih tzus) remained long-term family fixtures. It's the house where Jane didn't come to spend the night the eve of her wedding for fear it would make her so sad for her wedding day. (When Jane learned that we were moving from Wieuca Terrace to Cross Creek, she famously said, "That's well and good for you that you are moving to Cross Creek, but I'm never coming to visit you there.")

Chapter 3: No Two Pregnancies Are Alike

God shapes our lives in the way that is best for us, I do believe. As I said after JoElyn's monster pregnancy and Jane's birth, I was willing to set aside my desire to experience again the delight of being a part of a robust dinner table, a crowded car on the long annual trip to the beach, and a part of a sports-centered family, all of which was a part of my growing up.

Six or seven years after Jane's birth, JoElyn and I began to wonder if the pleasure we had in family life would be enhanced if we became a family of four instead of a family of three. I heard that there was now experimentation in microscopic surgery that would re-attach the vas that connect the testicles to the birthing channel. JoElyn and I began to discuss the pros and cons of having a second child. The common wisdom was that a mother soon forgets the negative side of being pregnant and giving birth. JoElyn declared that she remembered every painful day of being pregnant, but even so we both mulled over the other common wisdom—no two pregnancies are ever alike.

I use in my morning journaling the Ron Blue call to awareness of "don't miss the miracles," but both the birth of Jane and that of Evelyn Anne were major miracles that we couldn't miss.

Was there not still the issue of JoElyn's severe sickness when pregnant with Jane? Again, common knowledge was that no two pregnancies were alike. Who's to say that JoElyn would even be sick the second time around? I saw a respected Atlanta fertility surgeon, and the process towards my becoming fertile again began. I submitted to two expensive surgeries (two, because the first one didn't take), and in due time JoElyn was pregnant again—this brought to our awareness in November '82, nearly nine years since we learned that Jane's arrival was in progress. JoElyn spent that New Year's Eve and Day in Piedmont Hospital under the watchful eye of our friend and doctor, Steve Moreland.

"I remember having faith (shaky) that God would lead me to a wife, and that I would have children. How magnificently He has answered my prayer." — Journal, 9/3/84

JoElyn spent a lot of the next eight months in bed, or close to it. Our grandmotherly next-door neighbor, Dookie Adams, knew how sick JoElyn was; and, being a Catholic, when she saw our Episcopal priest, Bruce Shortel, approaching the house in floor-length black coat with hood from having officiated a cold burial at Arlington Cemetery, she sensed that he was there to administer the last rites and that it was all but over for JoElyn. There were days when JoElyn would like to have died, but she hung on courageously, and she blessedly gave birth to Evelyn Anne on July 22, 1983.

Dr. Moreland's care for JoElyn included strong medications as well as a week at his in-laws' house in Highlands, North Carolina. His idea there was that maybe just getting out of familiar surroundings might jolt JoElyn out of her nausea. Her sickness held steady, but Ed, Evelyn, Jane, and I had a marvelous time in a lovely vacation home and garden up in the mountains.

Were there any surprises I learned that I had not known by Jane's birth and childhood? Yes, and these come to mind:

- ✓ The sages were right, no two pregnancies are alike. This second one was much worse than the first.

- ✓ Two children out of the same gene pool, both raised by the advice of Dr. James Dobson (before he entered into the political arena), can, nevertheless, be distinctly their own persons. Jane, gregarious and high energy, had to have an activity involving other people. She was constantly on the move. Her favorite saying was, "What's next?" Evelyn Anne, on the other hand, did not mind being alone for stints. She found great pleasure in reading. For Jane, reading was a chore indulged in only because of the pressure of the "summer reading" program.

✓ Prayer really does impact a yet-unborn child, and there was a lot of family and community prayer poured upward for Evelyn Anne before her name was known, this primarily because of JoElyn's severe illness. Evelyn Anne had angelic qualities about her, more noticeable as she grew into her two's and upward.

I've lived a charmed life in many ways. I've had privileges and opportunities given to me based on no merit of my own. I've received more public credit than I have in any way deserved. I've been part of starting institutions that will long outlive me. Yet I would give it all up, if I had to, to be "Dad" to Jane and Evelyn Anne.

They say you can tell your true identity by where your passion lies. The best part of my life rests in fatherhood and the family life I have enjoyed together with JoElyn.

What Was Behind Evelyn Anne's Birth?

In October '82, JoElyn and I had attended a marriage-enrichment conference sponsored by St. Philip's Cathedral, held at the Dillard House in the north Georgia mountains. It began on a Friday evening and extended through Sunday morning. Charlie and Dottie Duke led the weekend retreat, together with David and Ginny Collins (the dean of the Cathedral and his wife). During this weekend we disclosed that we had for some time wanted to have another child. David, Ginny, Dottie, and Charlie prayed over JoElyn and me that God would give us another child.

Two months later, this is what I wrote on December 3 to my brothers and sisters:

Dear Support System:

Can you get "revved up" to be uncle and aunt one more time? JoElyn is expecting to give birth in August; Jane will have a little brother or sister; and at my age, I will need all of the help that you can give me.

We are all "beside ourselves" with excitement. Jane has not been able to get to sleep for the last two nights. She lies in her bed laughing and singing, thinking about having a brother or sister. JoElyn and I are equally excited.

This may knock us out of a reunion at the beach this summer, but it increases our incentive to want to be at the beach together in the summers to follow. This newest Johnston will deserve to have the magnificent influence of his or her cousins—and his or her uncles and aunts.

Well, thanks for being interested. The enclosed marathon information seems quite secondary, though the running of it was quite a rewarding experience. [*This was in reference to my first of nine marathons, the Atlanta Marathon run on Thanksgiving 1982.*]

Love, *Chuck*

And here is a less joyful journal entry exactly a month later: *Monday, January 3, 1983 – JoElyn has been as sick as if she were dying of cancer. Saturday night she went to the emergency room at Piedmont; and a shot in the hip put her out of her misery. God seems to be providing for us. Jane has spent several nights at other people's houses; and she is becoming more self-reliant. That's what a second child is supposed to accomplish.*

Birth of an Angel

Jane was, in the summer before her fourth-grade year, enrolled in a drama camp she hated at Northside High School, when her little sister Evelyn Anne was born. We had called Steve Moreland in the middle of the night to let him know that JoElyn's water had broken. He said, "Rest until daybreak, and then I'll meet you at Piedmont Hospital."

I woke Jane up a little earlier than she was accustomed, but she was amiable when I told her we would stop at McDonald's and get the two of us breakfast; and, secondarily, I told her that her little brother or sister was coming that day. Even though JoElyn was hurting, she supported getting some breakfast for the other two of us. Maybe she foresaw the adjustments Jane was going to have to make after nine years as an Only Child. "Please, Mommy, let me have pancakes," dared Jane to say. "OK, Jane, as long as you also eat a scrambled egg." A McDonald's breakfast in the flat cardboard containers was a real luxury for us because we rarely partook of "fast food," due to JoElyn's careful and loving attention to what Jane and I ate.

Jane got to see JoElyn received into Piedmont's maternity department, and hooked up to monitors and IVs by people all dressed in white. It was then time for Jane to say goodbye and be off to "You're a Good Man, Charlie Brown" camp. My administrative assistant, Weesie Carter, who lived in Brookwood Hills, came by the hospital and took Jane to Northside High. Jane would return in the afternoon to find that her family of three was now a family of four.

It was probably more the nine years of intervening medical history rather than a comparison of Floyd County Medical Center and Piedmont Hospital. But the 1974 experience of Jane's birthing and Evelyn Anne's 1983 birthing were significantly different. In Rome, JoElyn was totally unconscious and struggled to wake up enough to see a little red baby that couldn't possibly be hers because it was red and had slicked-down black hair. Meanwhile I was off with Chaplain Larry Green having supper at Shoney's (where a roach crawled out of my salad), only to discover upon returning to the hospital that I was father to a baby girl.

In Evelyn Anne's birthing, JoElyn, having had an epidural, was wide awake. I was there to help her in the deep breathing. JoElyn was so alert that, upon Steve Moreland announcing a baby girl and saying to me, "Well, Chuck, we did it," she said through a strong but cracked voice, "What do you mean "we"?

Evelyn Anne
and Jane in
1987

We provided the name *Evelyn Anne* for the birth certificate. (If she had been a boy, he would have been *Joel Edward*.)

One aspect common to both births was that we didn't know the gender until each was born. We had a choice in 1983; I'm not sure we did in 1974. Though I knew nothing about little girls, having not been one and not having grown up with sisters, I was delighted to have girls. I didn't think of gender, my saying of which might be a bit like one who today says, "I don't see color when it comes to race." Be that as it may, I am certain that I didn't think gender when we wrestled on the living room rug, or learned to correctly pass a football, or when we were constantly moving from one father/child adventure to another, from tree houses to climbing mountains (e.g., Stone Mountain, Kennesaw Mountain, Blood Mountain).

You've read that Evelyn Anne's was the birth that shouldn't have happened. We saw it as an answer to prayers, which was no different than our experience of Jane coming into the world, only in that it was a bit more of a stretch for God to grant our prayers for this second child. Not only did she have the October '82 prayers on the St. Philip's Cathedral couples retreat, she had copious prayers from the church and school communities over both JoElyn and the yet-unnamed baby she bore.

And as she grew in wisdom and stature, Evelyn Anne had an uncanny fondness for the Bible and its stories. She seemed to have an innate spiritual thirst. Roy Jones, her second-grade Sunday School teacher at Church of the Apostles, said on several occasions that he learned as much from her in class as he was able to teach her.

Chapter 4: Thanksgiving Feast and Confusion of Identity

Perhaps it was Anne Carson who decided I should dress as a Pilgrim for Trinity's Thanksgiving Feast. I went to Trinity in its twenty-ninth year; I suspect that the Thanksgiving Feast, prepared by students, was an annually anticipated tradition extending over most of those years. One class made the butter in an old-fashioned churn. Another made the applesauce by baking the apples and then squeezing them through a cone-shaped colander. A third class made bread, and the aroma of fresh bread baking filled the entire school.

The Tuesday before Thanksgiving came, and parents and grandparents filled the amphitheater to hear their students sing Thanksgiving songs. I was the convener and master of ceremonies. The rest was done by students; leadership was a big focus of the school, and among the sixth graders was leadership well demonstrated.

The young students—some as young as two years old—were initially afraid of me until they learned that the Pilgrim was simply Mr. Johnston dressed up. I got enough accolades for my transforming myself into a Pilgrim to encourage me to do it for the next seven Thanksgiving Feasts. I was identified so strongly by some as a Pilgrim that I got a couple of invitations back to reunions, but the invitations came with the proviso that I wear my Pilgrim costume. After a couple of years coming just as Mr. Johnston, I was soon no longer invited to reunions.

Thanksgiving '85, I persuaded JoElyn to dress as a female Pilgrim. Reluctantly she agreed when I promised her that no one would see her dressed like that except the Trinity folks. When I was delivering the welcome and JoElyn was standing beside me, I held two-year-old Evelyn Anne in my arms. She knew I was talking, but I was not looking directly at her; rather, I was making eye contact with the audience. She sweetly and tenderly reached up, put her little hand on my chin, and attempted to turn my face to her. At that exact moment an *Atlanta Journal-*

Constitution photographer snapped our picture, and that was the paper's big front-page picture on Thanksgiving morning. Needless to say, JoElyn's cover was blown, and I've not gotten her in a costume since.

GREETING A PILGRIM FATHER: 2-year-old Evelyn Anne Johnston takes a look at her black-clad dad, Trinity School headmaster Chuck Johnston, during Thanksgiving festivities Tuesday at the school. Johnston's wife, JoElyn, is at right.

"Chuck, we need somebody to wear the Bee A Buckler bee costume Friday at carpool, and we think you'd be the perfect one." I may have shown some initial reluctance, but that was fake. I loved the idea and Friday at 2 o'clock, there I was, dressed in my yellow running tights, wings, a mask, and little antennae sticking out the top of my head. When Evelyn Anne came out to get in her carpool, I picked her up and she screamed bloody murder, for she truly thought she was being carried away by a giant bee.

One last Trinity identity story: I made a practice on the first day of each new school year of going class by class to greet the students. I found myself downstairs in a class of three-year-olds who I knew from the two days a week that they had come to Trinity the previous year. "Boys and girls, do you know who this is?" So said "Miss" Anne McCullough to her students.

"I know you, I know you," said one precious little girl as she looked deep into my face. Oh, I was so pleased that even with the lapse of the summer this bright student remembered me. "I know you—you're Mr. Rogers."

"Oh, sweetheart," I said as I picked her up and hugged her. "No, I'm not Mr. Rogers, I'm Mr. Johnston. But you have paid me a huge compliment. Thank you, thank you!"

Chapter 5: Rumblings Against Me in 1986-87, My Seventh Year as Trinity's Head

Here is the charge that Trinity Board Chair Jim Carson had given me in the halcyon summer days of '79 before I first either met faculty or began my first pre-planning faculty meetings:

"The faculty of 'old Trinity' has become stale, stuck in the ways we have always done it. School in the Woods has scholarly research behind it, starting with the years that Carol and Darla were teaching colleagues at the Speech School. If you find yourself having to decide between a School in the Woods way or an Old Trinity way, favor the thinking of School in the Woods. That's one of the primary reasons we acquired them, to help us become more progressive."

While the two former heads of School in the Woods were headstrong, their energy, enthusiasm, creativity, and imagination brought life into this new working space. I tried to work with two of the long-term former Old Trinity administrators. My effort lasted three years with one whose buy-in I gave up on and asked to leave.

My working relationship with the other lasted longer, maybe because her unwillingness to grow was not couched in negativity. In fact, she was quite pleasant.

Parents didn't like to hear that their three- or four-year-old child had a learning disability. More often than not, the parents were grateful after they processed the information, especially those who chose to do something about it by applying to the Speech School or to Schenck School for remediation. Research was clear: the earlier a child gets help, the easier is mitigation achieved. And, in the process, the child avoids the stigma of being labeled as slow. With their frankness, the two former heads of School in the Woods offended some parents, just as I earned negative dots from Old Trinity trustees who thought the long-term pre-existing administrators hung the moon.

We had held a $3 million campaign in the first year I was at Trinity (1979-1980) to pay for renovations of what had been Birney Public School (APS) on Northside Parkway. We launched a $5 million campaign in the 1986-1987 school year to pay for the Larry-Lord-designed Kinder Gothic renovations and additions to the campus that can now be seen as the Atlanta Girls School campus. In any campaign of this size, the last dollars are the hardest to raise. What remained for the chairman of the campaign to reach the campaign goal were those parents who hadn't yet given. They were frequently parents who had a "bone to pick" with the two former heads of School in the Woods, or me. I contend that they were non-givers just manufacturing a reason not to do their part.

Be that as it may, my friend who was a trustee and chairman of this larger campaign got it in his head that I needed to go. "Chuck, you remember when you told me that you probably wouldn't stay at Trinity forever? Well, this might be a good time for you to exercise that departure option." I was rocked back, as much by his using against me something I had shared with him as a friend when a year or two earlier we had ridden together to south Georgia for a quail shoot.

He recruited two other strong trustees to his persuasion, and they took it to a board meeting. Jim Carson, who had been the board chair when I was hired, knew my value to the school and he effectively squelched the uprising. He told me afterwards that I had the job as long as I wanted it.

I had the assurance from Jim Carson that I would not be fired, yet I questioned whether or not I wanted to remain even with just a few unhappy trustees. Hence this journal entry in the summer before what turned out to be my last year at Trinity:

8/29/87 — My very career path is directed by God. The conclusion of the 16th Psalm says, "Thou wilt make known to me the path of life; in Thy presence is fullness of joy; in Thy right hand are pleasures forever." I can rest assured as I begin my eighth Trinity School year that my exciting and loving Father will direct me to remain at Trinity permanently, to go to a school in NYC or London, or to develop a book import business.

Chapter 6: Amid Career Drama, the Childhoods of Jane and Evelyn Anne Bring Richness

When siblings are nine years apart in age, perhaps it's easier to see their similarities and differences. Here are a few of my journal entries that hopefully will be meaningful to Jane and Evelyn Anne as adults:

- ✓ *2/15/1983* – Happy, our dog, ran away yesterday. The ring from her collar hung at the end of her leash, and she was gone. We drove and looked for her but we had no luck. Jane wondered why she would want to leave. Jane fed her faithfully, and she played with Happy at every opportunity. My only comment to Jane was that maybe Happy was born to be a great runner, for she certainly had extraordinary speed and strength. Maybe she was born to roam the country and have high adventures.

- ✓ *3/11/84* - We are in our room at Disney World's Golf Resort at 8 a.m. on Sunday morning. Evelyn Anne is crawling on the floor, making the sounds of a cooing dove and playing with rattles, her rubber bear, and two sides of a L'Eggs package. Jane is putting pressure on us to be first in line at Space Mountain. JoElyn is drying her hair. Jane babysat E.A. while JoElyn and I went on a two-mile run at 6:30 a.m. We will have a devotional in our room to mark Sunday before we head out for the Magic Kingdom.

✓ *2/14/85* - It's God through me Who comforts E.A. in the middle of the night when she stands in her crib holding her blanket and crying. She needs to be patted while standing and then to have her forehead stroked, and then she's back to sleep. It's God through me Who, at the same time, responds to Jane's need "to be checked on" and brought a small glass of lemonade for her sore throat. "Now it's better. I love you."

✓ *6/10/87* - Jane was reading on top of her bed, presumably from 10 to 11:20 p.m. She and I had a comfortable discussion. She accepts a bedtime, even though she says it's like being on "the good ship lollipop."

✓ *6/18/87* - Thursday, Seagrove Beach: Last evening, around 7:15 p.m., Evelyn Anne went down on the beach alone looking for Jane and Heather (our upstairs beach neighbor). I had gone to get milk, and no one realized that Evelyn Anne had left. Even though her flipflops were on the boardwalk, I found it hard to believe she had gone walking because she had walked to Seaside and back (two miles) earlier, in the late afternoon. Neighbors began to stream out to help in the search. I drove back down to the grocery and called the Sheriff's Department. They were sending two units to help when Ed intercepted me, and we called back to report the good news—Evelyn Anne was found on the beach. In her mind she never was lost; she knew where she was and what she was doing. It was only the rest of us who didn't know. Heather reached her first, though a Jewish man and his son, whom we had spoken with several times on the beach, had suggested that she might want to turn back towards home. She said, "No, I'm looking for my sister." But upon seeing that it was getting dark, she did, in fact, turn to re-trace her steps when Heather "hurt her feelings" (to the point of sobs) by saying that everyone was looking for her and that I had called the police. "NO, he hasn't called the police," EA insisted. We had all prayed individually for EA's safe return, so, after thanking neighbors, we went as a family with Papa and Grandma and each offered together a prayer of thanks. EA has now asked us not to speak of her "being lost" since she herself was never lost. We will abide by her request since we respect her clear wishes even at her age of 3 years, 11 months. She does understand that she is not to ever go off without clearing it with us.

✓ *9/28/87* - While swinging in the back yard, able to pump herself and swing for thirty minutes at a time, Evelyn Anne exclaimed, "I love being four!"

Chapter 7: Eight Years at Trinity End on a Sad Note Just Ahead of California Move

On Sunday, June 12, 1988, JoElyn's and my seventeenth wedding anniversary, family friend Greg Simmons, forty-two years old and father of five children, fell to his death while leading his children on a hike up around a waterfall at their Highlands, N.C., farm—ironically named Sweetwater Farm.

I had first connected to Greg and his Chattanooga family when his brother Forrest was in the boys' dorm at Westminster. Some ten-plus years later, Greg and his wife, Christy, became parents at Trinity while I was headmaster, eventually enrolling all five of their children. At the time of Greg's death, the oldest child and only son, McKittrick, had just graduated from Trinity and was heading to Pace Academy as a seventh grader.

He was twelve years old. Jane was two years ahead of McKittrick, but our family and theirs were close friends. Greg had a short stint in education as a teacher at Westminster before going into a lucrative key-employee insurance business with Hank McCamish; so he knew that school leadership could be a lonely job. Greg and Christy had realized that we needed friends, so they frequently took JoElyn and me to dinner and then to a Tom Key play. Greg had been a key friend and financial supporter of Tom Key and his Theatrical Outfit.

I bring Greg into my memoirs that are mostly about family, because his death at age forty-two, leaving behind a wife and five children who needed him, has challenged my sense of God's goodness ever since. Greg was a charismatic Christian business and family man and a leader of men—neither arrogant nor self-focused.

His death came just days before my last Trinity day and our five-day trek across country to Pebble Beach / Carmel, California.

Chapter 8: Family Schools, Int'l / RLS

I first knew John Shank when he courted and then married Diane Hensley, whom I had hired early on as business manager for Trinity School. John was a frequent presenter at NAIS conferences and had a quasi-official relationship as

NAIS advisor to member schools on business matters. At one conference—perhaps it was GAIS at St. Simons in the fall of '86—I had sat down with John and shared my Emory EMBA final paper on establishing a network of schools for profit. "I like what I see, Chuck," he said. "I'd be happy to take a copy of your paper, look it over, and then look for opportunities to test it. I like your creative thinking."

A year after the '86 conversation with John Shank, long enough after this conversation for me to think that he had just been being polite, John contacted me to say that he had a school willing to give us the opportunity to test our theory. JoElyn was willing to consider this prospect even though it would take us to the coast of California. The school that would hire me was Robert Louis Stevenson (RLS) in Pebble Beach; the school that I would be in charge of equipping with a more progressive curriculum and year-round program was Briarcliff School, next door in Carmel. It was RLS's headmaster, Joe Wandke, who was open to this progressive thinking and to our family.

In January '86, two years before we flew out to see the California possibility firsthand, I had written in my journal, "God wants me to build schools. He wants me to plan, to build, and then to launch out." Seeing this as that God-ordained opportunity, I agreed to consider becoming principal of Stevenson's recent acquisition, a lower and middle school being gifted to RLS by one of its trustees.

The process of my being hired took longer than I would have wished. It was after the New Year of 1988 when we as a family were invited out for a visit. Being far from satiated on travel, I was snowed by the five-hour flight out to San

First Christmas in Pebble Beach, 1988

Francisco and then the connector flight down to the Monterey Peninsula. After being on a plane maybe fourteen seats across and boarding the commuter plane that had a total of ten passenger seats, four-year-old Evelyn Anne exclaimed, "This is a skinny plane." Describing a plane as skinny seemed funny at the time.

I was offered and accepted a generous contract from RLS—$60,000 with car, housing, and meals provided. The problem was having to tell Trinity I was departing, and it was already into February. I told the board on a Monday afternoon regular meeting, and then I announced it to the faculty at our Tuesday morning faculty meeting. I was bolstered by a strong sense of God's presence. Here's what I recorded at the time:

God acts in our lives daily, hourly. … Clearly He triggered the events that had John Shank call me on October 8. Clearly He laid the Briarcliff Academy opportunity before me. Clearly He laid the 12th chapter of Genesis before me this past Tuesday when I was feeling shaky in my resolve. Clearly He prevented rumors from circulating about my departure and enabled me to tell Trinity's Board and Faculty in my own words and way. — Journal, 2/6/88

A month later I got a surprise additional job offer from Child Care Inc., the owner of which I had met through John Shank. He was offering me the presidency of the company with some ownership, good pay, and a move to Boston. I stuck by my commitment to RLS, dismissing the thought that I might be passing up a huge opportunity.

In late summer '88, we moved into a brand-new apartment in Silverado Hall—three bedrooms upstairs, living room, dining room, and kitchen downstairs. The perks were nice: the sunroof in the furnished car, dining hall meals, the temperatures always in the 70s, and the freedom for Jane and Evelyn Anne of living on a campus with other children always around, or, in Jane's case, the dorm students.

In the fall, a couple of months after school was underway in Carmel, Joe Wandke and I flew to Boston and met John Shank; the three of us then flew to John's place on Martha's Vineyard for an intense two-day planning session as to how Little Stevie (aka Briarcliff) would be set up—the year-long calendar, the full day program with cooking clubs and such through the afternoon. When I went before the assembled parents a couple of weeks later to sell the new concept, I was figuratively booed off the stage. When one or two in the audience played the bully, I wasn't prepared to handle them. I was caught by surprise; but, let's be honest, my toolbox is empty when it comes to standing down a power

"Progress is a nice word, but change is its motivator, and change has its enemies." — Robert Kennedy

player. I believe some of the parents had come to believe that they owned the school.

I've already said that I don't have all the tools, but I do have dogged determination—so, soldier on I did. Local attorney Hugo Gerstl, who had initially embraced me, assumed the role of "leader of the opposition." His wife, Lorraine, was our sweet and highly professional first-grade teacher. She managed to stay neutral. I wonder what price I would have had to pay to have had Hugo on my side? When we held a Saturday admissions open house, the opposition put derogatory flyers on the car windshields of those attending. The local CBS channel broadcasted film of the opposition airing their grievances. Hugo put together a lawsuit aimed at me, Joe, and RLS. (It never came to court.)

Typical of the kindness and love that my daughters have showered upon me over the years, is this incident in the first of our two California springs:

"Dad, give me your folders and sit down on the couch." Jane may have gently pushed me so that the back of my legs hit the sofa, and I went down, like it or not. Then she had primed to start on the tape player, reggae music and the words that came flowing over me, "Don't worry, be happy." For you see, Jane had heard from her mother that I had had another bad day at Little Stevie. Maybe it was the day that Hugo Gerstl served notice of a lawsuit against me and all responsible for trying to change their comfortable little school. Before I had come along, it had gotten along happily in Carmel for nearly a decade.

Here are some of Bobby McFerrin's words that eased my tension and brought a big smile to my face:

> "Here's a little song I wrote.
> You might want to sing it note for note.
> Don't worry, be happy.
> In every life we have some trouble,
> But when you worry you make it double.
> Don't worry, be happy.
> Don't worry, be happy now."

At the end of that first year for us in California, in June at a faculty end-of-the-year party, RLS surprised us with an all-expense-paid vacation trip to Hawaii. "We don't want you to think that the way you've been treated this past year is what we do out here in California." So said Joe Wandke as he handed us plane tickets, car rental and hotel reservations in Maui.

Our second California school year began well. I was particularly proud of how the teachers jumped in to make the afternoon clubs fun for the kids: Walking /Jogging Club, Cooking/Gardening Club, Outdoor Games, Bicycle Club, Social Dance (Middle School), Community Service, and Spanish. Patsy Wester's ballet continued on as a great draw to the school.

Evelyn Anne had great fun in ballet school, with lots of practice, performances, and costumes.

Jane and Evelyn Anne in Hawaii, summer 1989.

Chapter 9: The World Series 7.1 Earthquake

I was driving back from a Little Stevie soccer game in Monterey, bringing one of our seventh grade players to his Pebble Beach home not far from the RLS campus. This was October 17, 1989. I had stopped at an intersection in Monterey, when all of a sudden I noticed the stop sign vibrating back and forth like crazy; the plate glass bank window was vibrating as if it were about to pop out; and our car was vibrating.

"That's some burst of wind, isn't it," I said to my 12-year-old passenger.

"That was an earthquake," he said without hesitation. How did he know? Had there been earthquakes in his lifetime on the Monterey Peninsula?

We drove on to his home as if nothing too major had happened. (We were wrong.) We weren't aware of electricity being out since it was broad daylight. I dropped my young friend at his home and made it to the RLS campus at the center of Pebble Beach. Gradually the magnitude of what had happened began to dawn on me and others who began to come out of the faculty apartments and the student dorms.

Some had heard early news reports that a 7.1-strength earthquake, with its epicenter in the Santa Cruz mountains, had wreaked havoc on San Francisco and Oakland, just sixty miles north of the epicenter.

JoElyn arrived back at the campus with fifteen-year-old Jane and six-year-old Evelyn Anne. They were returning from Evelyn Anne's soccer practice; Jane was the coach. As they were exiting up a steep hill from the soccer field at the end of practice, the ground began to shake and they couldn't keep their balance and fell. They made it funny in the retelling. In fact, for the first couple of days afterwards, Evelyn Anne loved operating by candlelight in the evenings. Later she moaned, "I want the lights back on." We may have been four days without electricity and out of school. All the buildings had to be checked to make sure there were no ruptured gas lines underneath.

Our apartment was filled with RLS boarding students from the San Francisco Bay area trying to reach their families to make sure they were not victims. We had one of the few operative phones on campus. (Remember life before cell phones?) We did feel that we were being useful and were providing some comfort to worried and scared students.

RLS's water polo team was playing a match in a pool near Santa Cruz when the quake struck. The water rolled up out of the pool to one side of the pool, then came roaring back to slap against the other side and up above the side. Students could have been crushed. I still don't know how both teams got out of the pool unhurt.

"Why weren't Monterey, Pebble Beach, and Carmel flattened as much as San Francisco? You were just as close to the epicenter as San Francisco, if not closer?" one might ask. [The epicenter was sixty miles from San Francisco/Oakland and forty-something miles from Monterey.]

Well, the Monterey Peninsula rests on rock; for the most part, San Francisco rests on sand. We had three or four books to topple to the floor from a top shelf, and no one else reported more effect than that. The aftershocks were unnerving and tended to come at night to wake us up. These lasted for three or four days.

Did I say that the '89 World Series between the cross-the-bay rivals Oakland and San Francisco was halted before game three got started? It could have been even more of a disaster had not Candlestick Park held up under the impact of the quake. The stadium did suffer some minor damage that required repair, so it was ten days later before the games resumed: halted October 17, resumed October 27. Oakland swept the Giants 4–0.

Chapter 10: The Final Straw That Broke the Back of Our Glorious Effort

A lot came crashing down when science teacher Garth Gilchrist went rogue. I was attending a lovely Board lunch hosted by Marilee Wandke at their home when I got a call, "Come back to the Carmel campus; all hell has broken loose." It was March 16, 1990. The eighth grade students had the teacher that they had most loved and trusted cornered, having learned that he had sexually molested their classmate, Philip.

I, too, felt betrayed. I had hired Garth, and I had trusted him with these precious students and with the success of the Family Schools, Int'l, trial balloon. Evelyn Anne loved Garth's use of storytelling to teach young students about science. For years afterwards she played a tape about "George the Water Molecule," the molecule that traveled from the food someone ate to the stream and eventually out into the ocean.

Garth was arrested and spent six years in a California prison. In hindsight it was this felonious misstep by Garth that put the ultimate squash on our proving the effectiveness and appeal of the Family Schools, Int'l, model.

When the school break came in June, I sat down with Joe Wandke, who told me that as well as I had handled two rocky school years, it was felt that I was too much of the lightning rod on whom the dissenting parents focused their anger. He needed to put someone in as principal who didn't carry the baggage that I did. Gari Ann Truscott, assistant admissions director at the Upper School, was tapped for the job.

Joe offered me the opportunity to work in some capacity (perhaps admissions) on the high school campus; or, if I preferred, RLS would pay for a move back to Atlanta and would pay my full salary up to a year or when I commenced a new job. I conferred with JoElyn, and we took the Atlanta option. Joe and I maintained our solid professional friendship. In fact, RLS was incredible in how they supported and treated us, from the first exploratory trip out in January '88 to the backup of a full year's compensation after only two years in their employ.

Don Covington became a Christian friend as well as an excellent and respected PE teacher. He stood by me through all of the turmoil, sacrificing friendships of dissenting parents to remain loyal to Little Stevie and to me personally. When he learned that I was "pulling out" and returning with the family to Atlanta, he expressed genuine anger towards me: "Chuck, I have banked my personal credibility, my family's security, and my professional future on your commitment in Christ to weather the storm and to stick with the mission. I feel that you have betrayed my trust in you as a man of his word just to hide tail and run."

Since I had pledged to Joe that I would not disclose the choice he had given me that led to our leaving, I could only stand accused with no defense. I have ever since felt sad about this ruptured relationship.

I was rightly humbled by this experience, but because of the clarity I had upon embarking on this adventure, clarity that I was being called by God to do this, I never felt our having left Trinity and having come to the Monterey Peninsula was a mistake. My confession to God at this point was to say that I could henceforth be content without orchestrating some nationally-significant educational breakthrough; and I was giving back to Him my long-held dream of tailoring and heading a major school, starting something significant as did Dr. Pressly, and as did Jim McCallie. Let me just continue to try to follow His lead.

PART FIVE

The Decade of My 50s (1990-2000)

Chapter 1: Transition to Atlanta Ballet

There has been enough failure in my life to see God's hand, all the while grasping for the next gold ring that will fulfill my dreams of success. In July of 1990 I returned from two years in California with "my head bloody but unbowed." I had full compensation from RLS School for up to twelve months or until I found a job. This was recognizing that there would be no suitable independent school jobs available in July.

After nearly three months of job searching, in late September of 1990, Lynda Courts approached me about considering the Atlanta Ballet's Executive Director position. As I am quick to say, the position of Artistic Director was admirably filled by Bobby Barnett, former principal with Balanchine's New York City Ballet, and married to Ginger Rich Barnett, daughter of Atlanta icon Dick Rich (Rich's Department Store).

Things began poorly for me, I thought; we were gathered in Bobby Barnett's office for an announcement interview with Helen Smith, *Atlanta Journal-Constitution* Arts writer/critic. She hammered away to know my salary. When I expressed great reluctance to disclose what I felt was personal information, she said it was a matter of public record (something not applicable in the independent school world) and she could get it anyway; Lynda gave her the figure—$85K. This set off a bit of a firestorm in that Bobby was not making that much. For his long Atlanta Ballet career, I suspect that the Ballet Board had not paid Bobby what he was worth because he was married to the heiress, Ginger Rich.

I would not have even talked to Lynda about the position had I not been deeply impacted by Patsy Wester, teacher of ballet extraordinary at "Little Stevie." All of the lower and middle school students of Stevenson School, boys as well as girls, took ballet throughout their years up through the eighth grade. Patsy had raised an athlete son, now a professional water skier, so she knew boy athletes. Such were her boy students. I learned to extol the athleticism of ballet.

When I assumed my role as Executive Director, Evelyn Anne was already well underway as a student in the Atlanta Ballet School. When she was in class or production at the downtown studios, I loved our rides home together in the dark of the late afternoon.

Beyond that, I was a fish out of water. Politics existed through the organization that I had not experienced in schools. The director of finance, Greg Williamson, had wanted the job I had. It became clear that he was working to undermine me, and I terminated him, thus alienating Bill Swartz, head of the board's finance committee. He proceeded to make my life miserable and to eventually have me terminated.

In my second year at the Atlanta Ballet, we held open auditions for *The Nutcracker's* children's roles instead of

Evelyn Anne as a toy soldier in *The Nutcracker,* Christmas 1990 all of those children coming from Bobby and Ginger's Atlanta Ballet School. The line of children waiting to try out went out the front and around the corner and down the side street. Children came from all the counties surrounding Atlanta as well as from other Atlanta ballet schools. Because each child in one of three casts brought tons of family and friends to buy tickets, the revenue from *The Nutcracker* that year exceeded $1 million, bettering the intake of around $600,000 in other recent years.

Evelyn Anne's five roles began as a toy soldier, then littlest party child (with its built-in laugh), to "party boy," then to a major role as bad-boy Fritz, and culminating as a candy cane for her last of five years in *The Nutcracker*, this in Christmas '94. During my three Atlanta Ballet years, I viewed twenty-six *Nutcracker* productions each of those years. As much as I enjoyed my frequent post behind stage, to this day I fail to relish, as others seem to do, the *Nutcracker* music when it is piped through the malls and over the radio.

The production manager was congenial enough, but he finally told me to stay quiet during the negotiations with the music union. It seems that I was too friendly with the opposition, when he knew a sterner countenance was required. Things really blew up when the production manager had put himself out to negotiate for a lead tenant space in the newly and funky retrofitting of the old King Plow factory into an arts center. He was pretty far along when Richard Courts declared that financial backers would see this move as too "far out" and would not support it. (This in 1992.) We put a squash on pursuing King Plow further. I let our marketing director at the time take the heat on this one.

I worked closely with Lynda Courts to retire the $900,000 debt that was tying Bobby Barnett's hands and causing the strike by the Ballet Orchestra. I brought very little money that was "new" to the ballet, though I am confident that I was a positive influence on the "old money." But for that reason, and because I couldn't keep up with Bill Swartz and Michael Acquino's fast-moving and acrimonious financial discussions, I was let go after three intense years of service.

> "The pain of something old falling apart … invites and sometimes forces the soul to go to a new place … Otherwise, most of us would never go to new places. The mystics use many words to describe this chaos … Whatever it is, it does not feel good and it does not feel like God. You will do anything to keep the old thing from falling apart."— Richard Rohr

Chapter 2: Children's Education Foundation

Michael Youssef and his wife, Elizabeth, were family friends from our days at St. Philips Cathedral and into the early years of Church of the Apostles. The cement to our relationship was the friendship between Jane Johnston and Sarah Youssef. At least a couple of times, Jane traveled with the Youssefs on family ski trips, having the opportunity to see Michael at his most relaxed and most humorous.

He was one of the people I confided in when my Atlanta Ballet job was coming to an end. While I was in a four-month severance package from the Ballet, Michael approached me about a job opening: "Hank McCamish is looking for someone who knows fundraising and education to run the Children's Education Foundation [CEF]. It's providing small stipends to inner-city kids to enable them to attend Christian schools. Would you be interested in talking with him?"

"That sounds like something I'd be interested in, yes. Thank you for looking out for me, Michael."

In the fall of 1994, I interviewed with Hank and his stepson, Gordon Beckham, over lunch at Chop's. They offered me the job with a salary of $90,000. Plus, I had my own office in his nineteenth-floor suite. The suite was the entire floor of Buckhead's One Buckhead Plaza. It had a kitchen stocked with lunch options so that employees would not have to leave that floor for lunch and waste time waiting in restaurants. I loved it, and I never took for granted being able to step from the kitchen onto the open terrace and gaze upon the cityscape of downtown Atlanta. Hank had put on that nineteenth floor a full gym with free weights and machines.

I had administrative help and my own laptop, something a bit more novel back in 1994. "But, wait, I've never learned to type."

"We'll install Marva Collins' Typing Tutor into our central system; you can work on it when you have the time," replied Hank.

I learned later that the dozen or so employees of McCamish & Associates were amused when they saw Typing Tutor in a technology system which, for its time, was at the top of the sophistication charts. I didn't care that they chuckled. In college I had paid other students and some office employees to type my papers for twenty-five cents a page. That was the cost-effective path then; now I was enjoying typing, and some twenty-five years later I still enjoy it. Without being able to type, I couldn't pursue my memoir project. (The fee for someone else's typing is now $15/hour. I still use help [Karen Cone] to transcribe handwritten material into my Evernote system.)

I made friends with school heads around the city; most of the schools we served were small and struggling. Bobby Scott, then head of the Perimeter School and now advisor to Danny Werhful at Desire Street Ministries, and Kevin Bratcher, then head of Intown School and now head of Whitefield Academy, are two with whom I still connect.

I worked with perhaps fifteen or twenty schools helping identify worthy kids who could escape the "government educational system" for a Christian school that would give them spiritual, intellectual, and behavioral gifts. Hank McCamish was anti-government and anti-tax—a strong advocate for vouchers, the concept of which was that a student could take the tax money being spent on him or her in the government school and apply it to the cost of a Christian school.

I could skirt all of the right-wing leanings of those who Hank supported with his philanthropy. I did attend the monthly meetings of the Georgia Public Policy Foundation that Hank underwrote. "Right wing" was not as combative then as it is now, and I met some interesting people. One was Tom Perdue, who, since I knew him in the mid-1990s, has gone on to manage campaigns for conservative candidates statewide and regionally.

I enjoyed working with two favorite urban schools in seeking to reach marginalized students and families—Our Lady of Lourdes (Auburn Avenue) and Saint Anthony's (West End); $2,000 or $3,000 went a long way in enabling some ambitious students to attend these Catholic schools. Ebonics was a current interest of the African-American community in some of the schools where CEF provided scholarships. Their perspective on history was that Egyptians were Africans; this gave the African-American perspective many more math and science heroes to claim. And I, being a proponent of "Black Is Beautiful," could not fault them, though at the time I thought their linkage to Egyptian history a bit spurious.

I got to know Louise Whatley, one who ruled the Carver Homes projects with an iron fist. If a politician or public service person wanted to do anything in Carver Homes, they had to go through Ms. Whatley. Fortunately for me, Hank, or someone helping him set up CEF, made peace with her; in fact, her two grandchildren were recipients of CEF scholarships.

Chapter 3: An Exchange with Ed and Evelyn

I have introduced Ed and Evelyn Jones earlier in my memoir. Ed was JoElyn's uncle, who later became her stepfather. He had become a widower when his wife,

Anne, died of cancer. Later, Evelyn, JoElyn's mother, became a widow when her husband, Joel, Ed's younger brother and JoElyn's father, died of heart failure. Ed and Evelyn corresponded, she in Chicago and he in Greenville, Alabama. Three years after Joel's death, Ed and Evelyn were married at the chapel on the Northwestern campus in Chicago, and then settled into life together in Greenville, causing some disruption in JoElyn's later teen years, I might add.

Evelyn and Ed Jones

The following exchange of letters came not too long after a vibrant Ed Jones was struck down by a serious stroke. This was nearly twenty-three years after JoElyn and I were married.

> March 2, 1994
> Dear Ed and Evelyn,
> Perhaps by the time you receive this, Ed will be healed. That is my urgent request each morning before God. I picture God giving you, Ed, your full voice, 20/20 vision, and limber limbs. And, then, I picture you witnessing before those now lifeless members of your church what it's like to stay in a close walk with God, regardless of one's circumstances.
> Ed, I think of your circumstances as if you were being held hostage, as Admiral Stockdale was in Vietnam for eight years, and I pray for your release every day.
> Ed, I remember the day I asked you for JoElyn's hand in marriage twenty-three years ago. Thanks for taking a chance on me. She is as good a wife as is her mother, and that's saying a lot.
> Love to you both,
> *Chuck*

Shortly thereafter:

> Dear Chuck,
> I'm writing this for Ed—but it comes from my heart, too. Your sweet note came at an especially opportune time! We had had a difficult day. I'm sure at times Ed feels completely alone. After reading your note he agreed, not only are you a precious son but also the best male friend he has. Thank you for your compassion and understanding, but most of all for your fervent prayers.
> We love you,
> Ed and Evelyn

Chapter 4: A New Major Prep School Is Launched

Our friend Marian Campbell had, it seems, spent a good bit of the summer of '95 away from her Atlanta home, some of which she spent in Pennsylvania, and the last part in Chattanooga, Tennessee, attending a wedding.

"Let me tell you about the most impressive group of boys I've been with ever," said Marian to me.

"OK?"

"Well, this was at the wedding in Chattanooga. The groom and all the groomsmen had graduated together from Chattanooga Christian School. Now out of college, they are the coolest, cleanest, best-educated young men you'd ever want to meet."

"Sounds like you're talking about typical preppy guys."

"No, these boys are different. It's about how real their faith is. They possess a faith that they live, and they got a pre-college education second to none. Sharp, sharp, sharp!"

Marian's enthusiasm was infectious. "Marian, I'm a sceptic when it comes to Christian schools: one, they are usually mediocre academically; and, two, they do more to kill than to nurture a sustainable faith. But, here, after college and everything else these boys have been into, you say that they are living their lives as believing academics. That's pretty strong!"

"Here's the thing," Marian continued with her characteristic certainty. "Atlanta doesn't have a comparable school. You need to start one."

I assumed she wasn't really thinking we could just up and start a school. All the bona fide prep schools, Christian or not, were either started in the first few years of the 1900s or in the first few years after 1950. Here we were in the 1990s, and the only schools started in the past thirty to forty years had been white-flight schools / segregation academies. And while they claimed "excellence in education," as I had said before, they were academically mediocre at best.

"Marian, do you realize how much acreage and how many millions it takes for a really topnotch school? I don't think so."

It made me mad, I'm ashamed to say now, that Marian was so naïve as to think that one could just up and start a school. Again, the inaccessibility of land and money made it humanly impossible. I didn't show anger to her. I just did what I often would do in my life. I would not tell a person "no" to his or her face, but I would be noncommittal and proceed with no intention of enacting the other person's suggestion.

I tried that ignoring tactic for a week or so until I began to sense that Providence was on the case of my starting something like a Stoney Brook School in Atlanta, a school that was thoroughly Christian and thoroughly academic. I remember as a youth reading a Peter Marshall sermon entitled "A Tap on the Shoulder" about how God sometimes gets our attention quietly, with just a little tap or a quiet whisper. Marian had delivered that tap on the shoulder.

I began to put down on paper some things that would make a new school distinct. It would be at the highest levels possible academically while showing that faith and intellect bolster each other. "Anything that flies under the banner of Christ must be of the highest standards in every aspect of its existence." And Frank Gabelein's quote from The Stoney Brook School, "All truth is Christ's truth," gave me encouragement that a school could be thoroughly Christian and thoroughly academic. There would be no banning of *Catcher in the Rye* for its bad language or *The Old Man and the Sea* because Hemingway was an agnostic reprobate. We would look to the historic linkage of Christianity and science. I began to read about the likes of Kepler, who in trying to show God's perfection by proving that heavenly bodies travel in a perfect circle, found instead that heavenly bodies travel in a perfect oval. And I read of the Jesuits, who were known for their scientific achievements—including Galileo's systematic use of the telescope.

Harvard was founded in 1636 to educate the English and Indian youth in knowledge and godliness.

I was into it now, and I had Marian and her naiveté to thank. The money did come, all $16 million, and the land for a campus came, all fifty-seven acres. Henry Blackaby said, and I paraphrase: "Instead of creating your own plans and goals, and then asking him to bless them, figure out where God is already at work and go join him. It will be a lot easier."

Clearly God was the one initiating this school, and Marian was His faithful instrument. She declined a place on the founding board because she felt it would compromise her husband Glen's youth ministry, Student to Student (STS) at Church of the Apostles, which was reaching students from five or six different schools. She had done her part. She was humble and obedient, and she moved on, never once, to my knowledge, saying or thinking, "Hey, if it were not for me, there might never have been a Whitefield."

The Launching of Whitefield

Jane fed me the latest and best educational concepts from her senior-year studies at Vanderbilt's Peabody College. A lot of the language in our description of this school-in-the-imagination came from Jane, including the vision statement that is still used today: "Whitefield Academy, a Christ-centered college preparatory school, exists to bolster Christian families in rearing young people who go on to college and life with a passion for learning, for others ahead of self, and for the living and active Jesus." Jane shared my disdain for weak academics and memorized faith. I loved the unconventional aspects of her ideas. On paper we had a school about which a comatose person could get excited. (See **Appendix 7** for an early description of The Cranmer School.)

I formed a board, as you will see below, and we chose to use the name of Archbishop William Cranmer, founder of the English reformation and creator of the Anglican Prayer Book. We liked this name because Cranmer was both a scholar and a true believer. (Later, a change was to come when we joined forces with Mount Vernon Christian Academy. Preferring to pick a new name for this combined effort, we settled on Whitefield—as in George Whitefield, a close Oxford classmate of John and Charles Wesley and a leader of a great pre-Revolution revival in the American British Colonies.)

The following conversation was between The Cranmer School's nascent board (Betsy Akers, Gordy Germany, Lorraine Gilman, Joe Hamilton, Matt Hawkins, Chuck LeCraw, Larry Powell, Stacy Quiros, Wade Williams and me) and Bruce Lockerbie, a consultant affiliated with The Stoney Brook School (NY), whom I had invited to come meet with our board. Like so many of the germinating activities of the school's founding, it took place in our living room on Wieuca Terrace.

"Before you think of launching out as a school, you need funds."

"How much money are you talking about, Bruce?"

"I would say a half million. Normally I would say to give yourselves an August do-or-delay-a-year deadline, but since this is the Olympics summer, set October as your deadline for having this money if the school is to start in September '97."

Moxie: Defined As Vigor, Verve, Pep, Courage and Aggressiveness

The Lockerbie conversation took place in late April. Around that same time, I had breakfast one day with David Jones, chairman of the board at Mount Vernon Christian Academy. Since I knew David from working out with him at Australian Body Works three mornings a week, and he had told me about the financial troubles of Mount Vernon, I felt obligated to tell him what we were attempting to start as The Cranmer School.

I didn't want him to think that we were trying to undermine his good efforts. Out of that came David's reaction: "Let's join forces."

So here he was, in July, meeting in our living room with the Cranmer Board to discuss the joining together of equals.

"We are drawn to you because of your fresh ideas and your passion. But it would help me persuade my board that we are truly equals if y'all had some money to bring to the deal." (As Paul Quiros would famously say, "All Cranmer School has to offer is moxie"—which, I found out, is huge.)

"How much money are you talking about, David?"

"I would say that $500,000 would tip our skeptical board to a yes vote."

I was about to proceed with other agenda items upon David's departure when Larry Powell said, "Wait a minute. I suggest that we pray now about this matter of money. Independent of each other, Bruce and David have both named $500,000 as the money we need to start. That's not a coincidence. We need to stop right now and pray about this matter of money." So pray we did.

Betsy Akers said that she might know where some of that money might be found. She had been invited to sit on a charitable board that was to have its inaugural meeting in a couple of days. She thought they might be able to give us as much as $200,000.

The next evening Betsy appeared at our house with a white box tied with a ribbon. I opened it to find an envelope inside. I opened the envelope and read:

> To the Cranmer School Board,
> The Ginny Millner Foundation hereby grants to The Cranmer School board $500,000 to spend as it sees fit in the starting of the school.
> In Christ,
> Ginny Millner

What happened? Betsy's anticipated meeting at Ginny and Guy Millner's home was the next morning after the Cranmer Board had met with David Jones, sooner than Betsy had thought before looking at her calendar. She arrived a little early and found Ginny actually dancing around, beside herself: "Betsy, Betsy, I can't wait for the meeting to tell you. God impressed on me last night [i.e., the night the board was meeting] that, instead of parceling out the available funds in small gifts, we are to give it all where we can really have an impact. That recipient is to be The Cranmer School."

We Are Underway

I went under contract with Whitefield as of September 15 as Founding Headmaster for $100,000 annual salary. A few weeks later, I hired Jane as my administrative assistant, and we moved into adjoining offices in the UFO Building on the Mount Vernon campus. We were a good team. Mount Vernon had one more year of its existence. Jane and I were officed on its campus as Whitefield's advance team. The next year this same campus would be rechristened as Whitefield Academy.

The most important thing I would do at that point would be to put together a top-flight teaching team made up of some Mount Vernon teachers, but also all-stars from Westminster, Darlington, Marist, and elsewhere. I knew we would all have to do some heavy lifting in creating a new reputation for a new school on an old campus.

I made some enemies among those Mount Vernon faculty and staff that I didn't retain, but I contracted some beloved and talented Mount Vernon teachers—history teacher and coach Terrell Gilbert being at the top of that list. He garnered Whitefield's first teacher contract. Robert Spiotta, ace admissions director, was the second to be contracted. Then followed my team of those from schools at the top of the prep school list of excellence: Bob Neu from Westminster, Bert Mobley from Marist, and, from Darlington: Bob Montague, Tara Nix (née Roberts), and Barbara and John Murray. Barney Cochran came from college history teaching at Emory and Georgia State, and David McBride came from Baylor in Chattanooga.

I never left far behind my deep fondness for coaching, when accompanied by classroom teaching. I thought of these men and women, old and new, as my team. I would coach them, I would encourage and inspire them, I would exhort them to dig deeper for the grueling work of starting something new. Together we would hit those times when things looked bleak (as had happened for me when Jim McCallie and I trusted each other, saw the sun appear from behind the dark clouds, and experienced Brookstone School emerging). We would hang tough as professionals. They would have a profound professional growing experience. We would model unity of purpose and shared joy in what we were about.

My standing with other heads of schools around the city, and my rapport with some philanthropists and foundations (e.g., Courts, Campbell, Woodruff) gave the school instant credibility. Probably more important than my standing in the prep school arena was my hiring key faculty members from Westminster, Darlington, Marist, and then in year two, from Lovett. Jane continued to play a key role as junior high Bible and English teacher and as soccer coach to middle-school boys and varsity girls. Evelyn Anne's influence was huge as leader of a strong freshman class. I will always wonder what toll it took on her, feeling responsible for the behavior of Marshall, Chandler, and others.

Hiring Eddie James from Lovett in year two brought Tim Morris, Paul Delaney, and other talented AAU players to Whitefield and catapulted Whitefield to the top ranks of the basketball world. We would follow the credibility path of

Wesleyan—top academics, authentic Christian application, and highly competitive sports.

The Back Story on Launching Whitefield

Most folks with a modicum of ambition probably think at one time or another about starting a better model of whatever work arena they are in. Bernie Marcus and Arthur Blank, both young employees of Handy Dan Home Improvement, said to each other, "We're going to take the best practices of this hardware chain, add a strong dash of our own entrepreneurial ideas, and start something we'll call Home Depot."

My career in education had begun near the pinnacle of first-rate prep schools, McCallie and Westminster. Yet in my combined five years at those two schools, I saw both things I would emulate and things I would avoid if I were starting a school. In working with Jim McCallie in starting Brookstone, I saw the building blocks that go into formulating a fine school. It was only natural for me in my fifth year at Berry Academy to craft my final Executive MBA project around starting a better school, a better brand of the top-notch schools.

I had eight years at Trinity School during which I refined my plan, put it before a Dartmouth Business School professor, John Shank, and through his contact wound up putting the plan into practice in Carmel, California. Fierce opposition to the changes in an existing school brought lawsuits and negative coverage on the local TV news. I was literally sent packing—back to Atlanta with my confused but loving family. Evelyn Anne took leaving Trinity for California hard. She took leaving California to go back to Atlanta even harder. (We told her at a "Family Night Out" dinner at the OK Café that we were leaving Trinity; and we told her at a weekend in San Francisco that we were leaving Carmel and Pebble Beach.)

"Lord, I put my dream of starting a model prep school in Your hands. Henceforth, I'm willing to give that up and follow Your lead and Your plan for my life, wherever that may lead." And I meant it.

Five years later Marian Campbell thrust upon me her conviction that Atlanta needed a Stoney Brook type school that was thoroughly academic and thoroughly Christian. I cringed and fought it, but in the matter of ten days, the idea wouldn't go away, and it felt distinctly like the Master's tap on the shoulder.

This is the greatest experience of my life of "joining God in what He's doing," finding that considerably easier with a more assured outcome than to make one's own plans and then asking God to bless them. We got a $500,000 grant to get us started, paying my salary and that of my administrative assistant, Jane. In short order we raised $16 million and created a new campus on a fifty-seven-acre horse farm. We attracted a super-strong faculty and administration.

I had given up my dream of starting a school. That's when God must have said, "Now he's entirely dependent on Me and not on his own wit and charm. Now I can work with Him." My dream was realized. My assurance that God is real and is everlastingly a miracle worker grew as much as did the Grinch's heart: "Well, in Whoville they say that the Grinch's small heart grew three sizes that day. And then, the true meaning of Christmas came through, and the Grinch found the strength of ten Grinches, plus two!"

Advice From Dr. Pressly

I had taken the position at the outset that I would be open to learning from others as we walked this path of creativity together. I remember visiting with Dr. Bill Pressly, founding president of the Westminster Schools, in his and Alice's apartment at Lenbrook Square. My takeaway from our congenial conversation was, "Chuck, I'm just not sure in this day and age one can create from scratch a truly fine prep school. It takes a lot of land and a heap of money."

As I walked away from my last time to see Dr. Pressly, I chuckled to myself and thought, "What do you want to bet that someone said that very same thing to Dr. Pressly in 1951 when he was about the business of forming The Westminster Schools?"

I was not deterred by Dr. Pressly's remark because I knew from the outset that this would succeed only if God were doing the heavy lifting. There were too many potential land mines and impossibilities for mere man to walk through and survive. This would be hard, hard work.

Jane As My Co-Conspirator in Starting Whitefield

I was learning in this year of working together closely with her that my daughter, my own flesh and blood, had talents that I had never seen, talents that kept informing her work and enabling her to play a key role in our hiring a first-rate faculty and in enrolling enough students to be viable as a first-year new school.

I knew a lot about Jane going into the job interview. Without a title and without Jane knowing how seriously I took her, she fueled me with the things from her Peabody studies that excited her most about education. Together we drew up a description of this new school. She came up with the language that beautifully reflected how we both felt about the Christian aspect of what we then called The Cranmer School. I remember her using an expression something to the effect that we would not use Scripture passages as Band-Aid solutions for life's tough stuff. We insisted on the concept that "all truth is God's truth"—a premise advanced by Stoney Brook School's founding head, Frank Gabelein.

Frank had called Stoney Brook an "experiment" in Christian education and set its mission as being a rigorous college preparatory school thoroughly rooted in the Christian tradition. Education was not merely an emphasis on strong academics for the education of the mind, but more importantly was an emphasis on building character for the education of the heart—a distinction he linked with an adherence to the gospel. Frank's son Don was the longtime head of The Westminster Schools in Atlanta and my professional friend.

I knew that Jane would be the best person to assist me in putting the plan and the founding faculty together. She agreed to come and work with me the first year, with the proviso that she would join the founding faculty in year two. She was young, her ideas were fresh, and the result was that the now Whitefield Academy appealed to students. Some twenty years later, the cutting-edge educational philosophy that she espoused is called Student Centered Education or project-based learning. Jane was there in 1996.

When I hired Jane, I didn't know fully her writing skills or her technology proficiency. I knew she was good with people, but she exceeded my expectations in being both a good listener and an engaging conversationalist. I really rode her acceptance into the Mount Vernon Christian Academy community to my being accepted by the students, though my approval by the students took considerably longer than hers.

Let me back up a bit and look at Jane's senior year at Vanderbilt. She had the exhilarating success of heading a ministry that she and Lee Mitchell started, called Nathanael's Place. Its place was to serve Christians in the Greek community who might feel too cool to engage in "church" during their college years. Nathanael's Place had its up and downs. Jane would describe herself at times as "low as a slug;" then the prayer and singing of praise of a Nathanael's Place gathering would leave Jane and the others "giddy with the Holy Spirit." This leadership experience as much as her four years of college courses prepared Jane as a leader.

The student teaching of her second-semester senior year was anything but "exhilarating." At one point I prayed for Jane, that "God will tame the wild children as Jane teaches in front of the hostile supervisor." Around this time Jane canceled any future interviews for teaching jobs. It was in April of '96 that she randomly said one day, "I want to be the admission director at The Cranmer School."

As summer began and she was feeling the grief of Vanderbilt now being in the past, she and I had a conversation about the horror of not having a purpose. She had felt that lack of purpose in the weeks immediately following graduation. She would fall into that slump occasionally in this season of not knowing. What would be her first job as a college graduate? Sometime in July '96, Jane and I began to talk about her serving as my administrative assistant.

It took maybe a month after I had resigned at The Children's Education Foundation and had begun to draw a salary from the Ginny Millner Foundation seed money before I hired Jane. I had her spend some time with David Jones, Larry Powell, Stacy Quiros, Betsy Akers and others before I announced her in September '96 as the second employee of the new school. The understandable skepticism about nepotism exists and is better headed off before we might subject Jane to criticism. By the time I announced her as my administrative assistant, all were convinced that I could not have found a more perfect fit than Jane to try to brand the school.

Jane and I moved into adjoining offices on the Mount Vernon campus. Betsy Akers found respectable furniture for us. We had everything but telephones, which came a few days later. While 1996 doesn't seem all that long ago to me, it was still pre-cellphones, at least for office use.

Just as Jane won the hearts (also the business minds) of key trustees—David, Larry, Stacy, Betsy—she was a relationship wizard in working with trustees and donors. When she won the Mount Vernon faculty and administration to her side, that was winning men and women who had every reason to be angry with their school entering a merger and their jobs in jeopardy. The two of us could be the target of their angst. Yet, in short order they liked Jane and, therefore, they liked the fresh breeze we were bringing in.

Overnight Jane had become an adult. She was meeting the community and working shoulder to shoulder with the school's trustees. She got to know the Renfroes by "randomly" running into them at a church Wednesday night supper. Just that day Stacy and Betsy had taken Charlie Renfroe to lunch to ask him to join the Whitefield board, so Jane was becoming an influencer. Jane lingered after a meeting so that she, Lorraine Gilman and I could pray for trustee Betsy Akers and her serious parent concern. As I borderline-panicked over some prospective teachers who were turning me down, it was Jane and Betsy who reminded me that God knew exactly who was to make up the founding faculty. "Be not afraid"— coming from my daughter. Early in 1997, anticipating that she was to be the junior-high Bible teacher, Jane traveled to Chattanooga to learn Bible teaching from the best, Jane Henegar at GPS. Here Jane Johnston was drawing on her network, a network embedded in some of the finest prep schools.

Her work wasn't easy. One day she hit a crisis in getting coffee invitations out, but she solved the problem and moved on. She felt pressure, and she handled it. I recorded the following in a journal entry: "Jane loves her work so much that she has withdrawal pains when she comes home in the evening."

She created a recruiting video that we played at our major student-recruitment party at Harrison and Chandler Powell's home. Jane was the master of ceremonies for this event that was so critical for the new school's future. A few committed teachers and students spoke, but Jane's film was the centerpiece. Through the hilarity of the student interviews and clips from *Ferris Bueller's Day Off, Tommy Boy,* and *Billy Madison,* this low-budget, high-comedy film gave more than ninety students the reasons they needed to come that first year to this school. Though separated by the chasm of the major experience of college, she knew exactly what these students wanted in a junior high / high school. This film imprinted on the prospective students' minds that they would be treated with respect should they come to this cool, academically rigorous school.

Jane went on a Mount Vernon student trip to Boston and thus got to know a number of the students and several teachers better (including Mount Vernon history teacher Terrell Gilbert). This level of involvement spoke of Jane's commitment and of her energy. In this regard, she enhanced my position among the Mount Vernon people, and she got better acquainted with her future husband.

Jane brought into the workplace a passion that was unstoppable. When it became known that Jane would be teaching Bible to grades six, seven, and eight, one of the signed-on parents, Mrs. Terrey, said, "I'm excited for my sixth-grade daughter to have Jane as a role model."

Jane may well have been fueled by Scripture such as this: "Be strong and courageous, and do the work. Do not be afraid or discouraged, for the Lord God, my God, is with you. He will not fail you or forsake you until all the work … is finished" (1 Chronicles 28:20). Or was it this: "Life moves pretty fast. If you don't stop and look around once in a while, you could miss it." (Ferris Bueller).

This year of discovering Jane's depth of talent and bigness of heart paved the way for the rich adult friendship that now, more than twenty years later, we enjoy.

Chapter 5: Back to the Drumbeat of the First Couple of Years

There are pressures that I was prepared to take on as a part of the job of headmaster. For instance, Governor Carl Sanders called me from Sea Island to intercede on behalf of his grandson, who was applying for admission. We knew each other slightly from when he was in the Governor's Mansion and his son and daughter were in the dorms at Westminster. This same daughter, Betty, was the mother of the applicant. Governor Sanders' likeable grandson had some issues and would need some special services that we would not be staffed to handle; coming to this new school was his mother's idea, not his. I was able to work with his mother to find a better fit for her son. Perhaps it was St. Francis.

Another example of pressure came from a trustee who expected significant attention for his son, a student in the school. He brought in some guru psychologist who had a theory that seemed to be bringing good things out of this child. To please this trustee, we spent some time with this woman and tried to learn what she had to offer; but, in my opinion, she was off center and was milking these parents for her fees. Better than this woman's theory was the attention the trustee's son received from the Johnston family (Jane, Evelyn Anne, and me) and the fact that his teachers treated him with patience, refusing to be turned off by his antics and negativity. Year One went well.

The unraveling with that trustee came in year two while JoElyn, Jane, Evelyn Anne, I and others from STS were in Sewickley, Pennsylvania, for Gary Wieder's marriage to Julie. Gary was a high-energy and humorous student pastor in the Student to Student program at Church of the Apostles.

One of the Darlington-to-Whitefield founding faculty members, now dean of students, called to report that he had had a confrontation with a 10th grade boy over a web page he was accessing in the Whitefield Library. Whatever it was, he was clearly outside the rules. His father, a Whitefield founding board member, came up to school, challenged the dean's judgement and authority, and took his son home. I met with this father Monday morning after I had talked with the dean. As best I remember, this is the gist of our verbal exchange: I told the board member that he was out of line—one, as a parent; and, two, as a trustee of the school.

"Pulling this kind of power play is unacceptable," I told him. "I will expect you to apologize to the dean."

To this, the adversarial trustee said, "I'll show you a power play."

I had known from the outset that the new school would be very hard work. I wanted people to compare our academics to Westminster, Lovett, and the others, and I think the comparison was favorable because of the veteran prep school teachers who took the leap and came with us. I didn't realize some people would expect that we would immediately look, in structure, like those schools that had been around for fifty years or more.

In year two, we had hired Eddie James from Lovett to work with our basketball program. He had spent years coaching AAU teams and was highly respected in the AAU hotbed of rising stars. With him came Tim Morris, Paul Delaney, and others who immediately put Whitefield on the map as a serious junior high basketball program. These same boys would go on to play in multiple state championship games before they graduated from Whitefield. One year they were coached by Mark Price, the former Georgia Tech and NBA great.

Our academic dean brought onto the faculty a teacher that he had known from Westminster. This teacher was loyal to the dean and didn't care much for me. He saw all the blemishes and he missed the polished programs he had enjoyed at Westminster and that he had expected at Whitefield. His disgruntlement was infectious.

The trustee mentioned above, the one unhappy about the discipline of his son, was immensely successful professionally as one who took private companies public. What initiates this transformation of a company is an Initial Public Offering, or an IPO. Like so many successful undertakings, he had a formulaic approach that seemed to work 90 to 100 percent of the time. To me the most drastic step in this man's approach was to fire the founding team of executives and hire a new team. He apparently felt that "fire starters were not fire tenders." I was a fire starter; that was evident. What was not evident to him was that I could also be a fire tender. If his premise was always true for businesses, I had clear evidence that it did not necessarily hold true in the world of prep schools. My evidence? Bill Pressly, Tom Triol (Savannah Country Day), Elliot Galloway, Zach Young, and others who were my role models. To be like these that I so admired was the crowning career path I felt that God had set before me.

I fought back the first challenge that this trustee initiated among his fellow board members, those who were former Mount Vernon and those who were initial Cranmer. Another trustee whom everyone respected chaired a committee of the board to evaluate how I was doing. I prepared a PowerPoint detailing my administrative style. At the end of a long meeting at the committee chairman's house, the committee came away satisfied that I was doing a good job with the unique and difficult task of starting something brand new. This was in October 1999, and I felt vindicated and affirmed. But the disgruntled parent/trustee as a force of one was determined to have his way.

He wouldn't let go. He was impressed with Woodward Academy for having as its president the former head of a small New England college. He wanted somebody with this level of outside prestige, someone "more presidential." With my consent, he engaged an outside consultant to give me training in being "presidential." This dissatisfied trustee, whom I had brought onto the board, didn't appreciate the personal qualities I brought to this school, nor did he even know of my connectivity and good rapport with Atlanta's donor community.

Jim Adams of SunTrust's nonprofit division told the Whitefield finance committee that he was confident in extending bank credit to Whitefield because of his confidence in me from our Trinity School days of working together.

The frustrated trustee must have figured that he needed the other most influential trustee on his side if he were to make headway in replacing me. He convinced this second trustee that either he, the one who thought I should go, stayed and exerted his substantial fundraising clout and I went—or I would stay, and he would depart. We had all together raised $16 million. Yet, as we were on the verge of moving onto our new fifty-seven-acre campus, the other most influential trustee didn't share my confidence that we could raise all the money we needed, with or without the disgruntled trustee's engagement, so he was vulnerable to this man's pressure.

I had invested a lot in my teamwork with this influential trustee, each of us being among the influencers who brought Whitefield into existence by pulling off the merger of two schools and bringing a ton of good people into the process. In my fifty-nine years up to that point, I didn't know what betrayal would feel like, but it finally dawned on me that that was the cause of the nausea I was beginning to feel.

The disgruntled trustee's drumbeat began to build. I didn't mount a defense campaign. In fact, Michael Youssef, my pastor, couldn't believe I wasn't fighting to save my job since I was the guy that got it all started. Some would say that I took my belief in God's sovereignty too far, but I had seen God's hand so clearly up to this point that I truly believed that if I only had God as my defender, I'd be safe.

In November I had suggested that we work with a National Association of Independent Schools (NAIS) consultant who specialized in bringing boards and heads-of-schools back into alignment. NAIS spends a lot of its energy and resources to bring unity in a school's governance because they see the long-term damage done when schools are in leadership turmoil. The Whitefield Board, however, felt it more prudent to engage Bruce Lockerbie, who already knew the school and its principal leaders. Also, the disgruntled trustee was confident that Bruce would side with him. They voted me down and engaged Bruce. It was in this second engagement of Bruce that I began to see his hidden agenda.

When I learned later that Bruce and our influential trustee had taken my administrative team of four to breakfast at a café and quizzed them about my weaknesses as a leader, I sensed how the person felt who first said, "I feel stabbed in the back." These were the guys who—like in *Braveheart*—I'd hand-picked to stand with me, fight with me—to go down together, if necessary. I was sick, betrayed.

I was most disheartened by one who was probably my most prized addition to the founding faculty—one whom I had groomed into administrative responsibility—because I sensed that he was the most down on me. One of his remarks that I can't shake appeared in a Lockerbie written report: "I drive home at the end of an exhausting day, and I still don't have all my work done."

"Well, sir," I would like to say but never did, "welcome to the real world of independent school administration. Here I am in my twenty-second year of being a head or an assistant; you're in your second year, and you know more about what it's supposed to be like than I do? Here we are creating something from scratch, and you think it's poor leadership on my part that you're not able to start each day fresh with no tasks left from the day before? I hired you in part because of your athletic prowess, and you're not able to translate that into the playing field of independent school administration?"

My ouster began in the December board meeting when, after a positive general meeting, the board went into executive session and I was excused. I learned afterwards that the consensus in that executive session was that I needed to be replaced.

I have to say that Scripture helped me make it through multiple tough times like this in my checkered career—Scripture such as II Chronicles 16: "For the eyes of the Lord run to and fro throughout the whole earth, to give strong support to those whose heart is blameless toward him."

This process of my ouster culminated with the January 4 meeting of the Whitefield Board:

I remember sitting in my office on a cold winter night as the hour got later and later. The board of directors was meeting across a windswept outdoor hallway from my office determining my fate as founding headmaster. The chairman had given me his word that I could speak before deliberations began. Now well into the second hour of their meeting, it was increasingly obvious that I wouldn't have the opportunity to address the board as promised.

On that cold night, I was filling my mind with the words of Jim Cymbala's book, *Fresh Faith*—Cymbala of the Brooklyn Tabernacle. I could not allow myself to contemplate the perfidy that brought us to this hour, so I read and focused. I would not contemplate any of the wrong-headedness and betrayal that led us here:

✓ A trustee with whom I had started the school who, in the face of detractors, had promised that he would stand by me.

✓ A trustee whom I had recruited for the founding board who was convinced that a founding head could not then also be an effective operational head—his experience based on his business of preparing start-up companies for IPOs.

✓ This same trustee persuading other trustees that there is no difference in a business culture and an independent school culture— replace the entrepreneurial CEO.

- ✓ Four administrators whom I had hired to their positions who, without saying anything to me, had sat down with the consultant to catalog my shortcomings. These, remember, were my "assistant coaches"—we were the brain trust that was bringing about something out of the norm.

- ✓ Too many, including some of the professional educators, who thought a start-from-scratch prep school should be as complete as a fifty-year premier school.

- ✓ Trustees who persuaded a consultant to give me lessons in how to become more "presidential."

As the second hour of my isolation crept on and on, the thoughts pushed through that I had been duped, that they never intended to let me state my case. Despite my mind control, I could sense my chest aching and my head tightening such that I was losing brain cells. Here is how I reflected on this in my journal early the following morning:

Wednesday, January 5, 2000 — The Morning After I Finally Feel Fired:

Last night I waited in my office, reading Fresh Faith from 7 until 9:10 for an opportunity to speak to the Board. At that point, the leading trustee came in and told me that a second vote had been taken unanimously confirming the December 5 vote to replace me as leader of Whitefield. He said that he would like for me to consider taking the number two position.... He didn't want me to speak to the board tonight because he was afraid I would resign; and he and all of the board strongly want me to stay. ... When I did appear before the board, God gave me a relaxed and loving spirit. I was truthful, saying that I had no passion for being #2 in the organization. I spoke to some of the things that I was accused of in Bruce's report and elsewhere. A board member whom I had trusted said that he had never heard those negatives, and that most of the discussion had been centered on how incredible a person I am. "How can Chuck Johnston's talents be best put to use for Whitefield?" That's what this trustee said was at the heart of the discussion. At this juncture, it seems to me that the exercise of the board over the last several months has been more one of getting me out rather than of getting at the truth. Why else would I not be permitted to "face my accusers"? Last night was a manipulation, starring the incredibly capable Bruce Lockerbie. Then invite Chuck in and tell him how much we love him.

Here is part of Psalm 12 that appeared in my journaling that morning: "Everyone utters lies to his neighbor; with flattering lips and a double heart they speak. ... The words of the Lord are pure words, like silver refined in a furnace on the ground, purified seven times. You, O Lord, will keep them; you will guard us from this generation forever. On every side the wicked prowl, as vileness is exalted among the children of man" (Psalm 12:2, 6-8).

Why was this more of a blow than a couple of other jobs from which I had been pushed out? This is one in which at its start I was stepping out in faith to respond to what God was clearly commissioning me to do. For years, I had wanted to head a first-class independent school until, in our last days in California, I said to God, "I am finally ready to give up my dream of starting a school. 'Not my will but thy will be done.'" Five years later God had handed my dream back to me. In August 1995, from Marian Campbell's voice I'd heard that Atlanta needed a school that was thoroughly Christian and thoroughly academic. ("All truth is God's truth.") After much hesitation, I had finally been convinced that this was God's tap on the shoulder, a divine appointment.

"Remembrance of things past is not necessarily the remembrance of things that were." — Marcel Proust

At the end, God's story of my life was rougher than I could ever have written it myself. It was the "dark night of the soul" that I had to go through—or "the wall" (described in the chapter "Journey Through the Wall" in Peter Scazzero's *Emotionally Healthy Spirituality*). With God's hand-holding and the help of a lot of His people, I did go through it and come out on the other side.

Who's to say I wouldn't have enjoyed being like Elliot Galloway in the founding and running of a successful school? But I wouldn't be where I am today if I had had my way. My belief that God is sovereign is reaffirmed in the lens of hindsight. If we trust Him, He saves us from our lesser selves.

PART SIX

The Decade of My 60s (2000-2010)

Chapter 1: What Am I Doing in This Job?

In October 2000, while I remained in Whitefield employment in the school year following my removal as head, but in a yet-to-be-defined position under new "president" George Lawrence, I had coffee with Larry Teem. This was in response to a request from Frank and Margaret Ann Briggs, to see if I could give Larry any helpful advice as he found himself leading another newfound Atlanta school with three-headed leadership: himself, Joel Moore, and Leroy Barber. Leroy was involved, together with his wife, Donna, in Tony Campolo's school in Philadelphia, but Joel and Larry claimed no expertise in running a school.

"What would it take for you to come and head Atlanta Youth Academy?" This Larry asked me as we met in the funky environment of Sacred Grounds Coffee Shop in east Atlanta.

So unlikely! Such a foreign environment for me and for my family! Could I see JoElyn taking a vow of poverty to allow me to work among the poor? No, for my sophisticated New York/Chicago wife, as sensitive to the poor as she was, this would not match her artist's dreams.

That evening, in our lovely "Manhattan condo" at Cross Creek, she asked me about my day. I mentioned two or three things, and then, almost as an afterthought, I said, "Oh, yes, I had coffee with Larry Teem and he asked me what it would take for me to come and head Atlanta Youth Academy."

"That sounds exactly where your heart is, Chuck," she said in dead seriousness, and she said it without hesitation.

What was she thinking? Was she so hurt by the still-raw Whitefield experience that she would grasp at anything? No, she truly saw this work as something close to my heart, those students that would be pushed to the back of the educational line by systemic racism. I had sought those kids at Trinity and again at Whitefield. She saw it. She saw something that I didn't fully grasp at first— that this would be a job for which I would jump out of bed in the morning, a job that lined up with my values and the things I enjoyed doing and the things she saw that I was good at. So, if we could figure out the finances, then together we were up for another of God's adventures.

Whitefield agreed to pay my full compensation for eighteen months after a January 1, 2001, move to AYA. The salary part of that package was $110,000. Since that was nearly three times greater than the top teacher pay of $30,000, I felt guilty, and, as teacher salaries rose, I kept my salary at $110K for the first eight of my eleven AYA years. JoElyn didn't have to take a vow of poverty, though it took her sharpest money-management skills to keep us in the black, especially with Evelyn Anne preparing to go to college.

She was right. I loved my job. I loved being accepted by the black community and the start of my journey up the steep learning curve to another culture. I loved

"Chuck's decision to take the reins of Atlanta Youth Academy seemed to go against the flow of cultural expectations or norms. ... All that Chuck had become and experienced was not haphazard. God had spent a lifetime combining education, passion, and experience in order to prepare Chuck for that which He had called him to." — Restoring Hope, Building Futures: A Telling of the Atlanta Youth Academy Story

a high approval rating, whereas in other jobs I always felt as if I were being judged and found wanting. At age sixty, I arrived at that work for which God had been grooming me through all of my other job experiences.

Chapter 2: They Threw Me a Party

As a harbinger of the decade of my sixties, I reached my sixtieth birthday. It was cold and dreary, and yet Jane and Evelyn Anne began weeks before to turn darkness to light, gloom to cheer. They planned a birthday party to gather as many of my friends together as they could, including a plea out to my brothers to fly in and surprise me. Look at a weather map and Denver, St. Louis, and Vermont invariably have the most challenging winter weather. Dick and Dillon made it through their obstacles; Warren was unable to fly at the last minute because of New England weather.

The thinking was, "Don't turn on much heat in this American Legion hut because when the space is packed, we'll all be sweating." Well, there may have been people in the room sweating, but it was certainly not I. All I can remember was my shivering, and some of that could have been from emotion.

The tributes began to feel forced, and I suspect that was in part because my self-regard was at a low ebb. When it had felt to me as if enough had been said, I asked that we end the speeches. (I had been to too many funerals and commendatory events when I knew that some of the remarks were excessive, if not fraudulent. I didn't want to be a party to that for myself.)

"You shouldn't have stopped the toasts, Chuck. I had something I wanted to say. Everybody in the room was your loyal supporter and wanted to make sure you knew that." Thus Robert Spiotta chastised me for not being able to receive good wishes from good friends. I've always felt a little sad that Robert and maybe others didn't get to say what they arrived prepared to say.

But the kindness of my two daughters can't be overstated. JoElyn and I were both at a low point at this juncture, and there came Jane, assisted by Evelyn Anne, to lift us up. Having Dick and Dillon there certainly added to the significance of the event.

Chapter 3: Terrell's Many Hats

My son-in-law Terrell was indispensable to me during the first three and a half years of my Atlanta Youth Academy eleven-and-a-half-year tenure. I was the executive director; he was the administrative director.

In the early go we searched for a new site for AYA since the top class in the last year in the current facility was the fifth grade. If we were to go to sixth, then seventh, and finally to the eighth, then we needed considerably more space. We were maxed out at the Blacksmith Shop, a restored building in an old complex that had once been a debtors' prison on the edge of Grant Park.

At first we thought we would end up in an unoccupied Atlanta Public Schools building. We created a big piece of corkboard with eight or nine pictures of possible buildings, my favorite being the beautifully designed building on English Avenue where Gladys Knight went to elementary school. After pursuing this path for two or three months, Joe Martin (a Vandy Phi with me and past chairman of the APS school board) advised us that while they wouldn't say so, there was no way that the Atlanta Public Schools would sell one of its old buildings to a private school.

So, Terrell teamed up with AYA board member Harold Melton (later, in 2018, to become Chief Justice of the Georgia Supreme Court), and together they found and contracted with East Lake United Methodist for its unused and abandoned Sunday School wing. Terrell then spearheaded the successful effort to get volunteers in to clean and paint. Some were shocked with the bright colors Terrell chose, but the scrub bucket and color shouted, "This is a place for kids."

We purchased a used bus, from where I don't remember, but it was a troubled bus—always breaking down in the least opportune times and places. Felton was the bus driver. He would call Terrell at 6 a.m. or so needing to be rescued because of a bus breakdown. Leaving Jane and Baby Ellie still in the bed, Terrell would go out and rescue Felton. Times when Felton couldn't drive, then Terrell would get behind the wheel. He had a much better sense than I of where our students lived, many of them in the projects that were downtown near the state capitol.

Terrell was the primary operative in creating our budget. During his first three or four months at AYA, we were officed in the stables at the Glencastle complex. One big room, the size of half a football field, was broken into a honeycomb of cubicles inhabited by multiple ministries. Terrell was then beholden to FCS Urban Ministries' Mary Maynard, who did our bookkeeping. Terrell could be right in the middle of a phone conversation, and Mary would come right up to him in animated conversation about some unorthodox financial move Terrell had made. With Mary, manners were secondary when it came to riding herd on the finances. With Terrell, unorthodoxy was required to keep AYA open. Every two weeks Terrell had to make sure that we had enough money to make the Friday payroll. He was a master of making do with little.

He was so respected by our SunTrust partners that one payroll week, Alma, who managed our account in the SunTrust non-profit group, honored our full withdrawal on a Friday because Terrell assured her that we would have the money by Monday. God honored Terrell's faith/bravado, and the money needed to cover the gap came in on Monday.

Terrell also had the trust of the faculty. They liked his personable and easygoing manner. In Terrell's and my second full school year of working together, Derrick Lockwood joined our team as principal, giving us strong, level-headed decision-making moving forward.

I liked Terrell's sense of the need for bonding as a means of having a unified and happy workforce. Each summer, in the week before school started, Terrell would come up with a travel adventure for the faculty and staff. One year it was to his Uncle Dan's White Water Express up on the Ocoee River in north Georgia. That was late summer '01, the year that JoElyn joined the faculty as second-grade teacher. I remember her making it to the top of a climbing wall, and then rappelling down the other side. I can't imagine anything further outside her comfort zone than this, but she did it, and was proud of herself afterwards. This was the whole idea of our "retreat." All teachers, young and old (most were young), in shape and not, made it through these bonding exercises.

But Terrell wasn't through with us yet. After a sack lunch, and a breather, we all donned safety vests and crash helmets and took our positions in two rafts to go down this gurgling whitewater section of the Ocoee River—the same river on which the world's finest kayakers competed in the '96 Atlanta Olympics. Supposedly the guide at the back of each raft would tell us everything we needed to know as we would wind our way down to safety.

On a similar outing for our church leaders, organized by Terrell, JoElyn's experience was even more dramatic. JoElyn described her guide as a mean, muscular woman, sort of scary. Early into the downward journey a bee stung the guide, and she went berserk; she may have even jumped out of the raft. However it happened, they got the raft over to the shore, the guide recovered, and they resumed the trip down, hit one of the roughest patches in the Ocoee, and out popped JoElyn as her team was helpless to come back and get her. JoElyn, not a strong swimmer, managed to climb onto a rock, and the next raft, with a skilled guide, picked her up and brought her the rest of the journey to *terra firma*. That was one "group bonding" experience that she will never forget nor let Terrell forget.

Another year we went to the condo of Mary Elizabeth Teem's mother, Betty, at Destin. There was a tropical storm expected while we would be there, but that didn't deter us. We knew a tropical storm wouldn't dent our fun of being together away from school. Terrell's New York City Marathon prep schedule called on him to run twenty miles the Saturday morning that we were there, so he set out in the dark of the morning to run to a point on the beach road that was ten miles away. There he turned and headed back in the direction he had come. I left running from the condo at a calculated time to enable me to run out to the five-mile mark and meet Terrell on his last quarter of a twenty-mile run and run it back with him. That gave me a ten-mile run.

It had been eerily quiet and still all the while since my awakening and his 5 a.m. start. Just as dark was begrudgingly giving way to light, it felt spooky. I was glad to see Terrell. As I turned to head back and Terrell came alongside me, we felt a few flecks of rain, and then some head wind, and then real drops of rain, and then gusts of wind. A time or two the rain and wind would both abruptly stop, and then they would return stronger than when they had left. Those "intermissions" became a thing of the past when the rain came in sheets rather than drops and the wind tried to rip our shirts off. We ran with boisterous laughter at the absurdity of what we were doing.

"Terrell, can you hear me? This is fun," I shouted.

"Wow, I never would have thought this to be fun, but, yeah, you're right, I'm having fun." So said Terrell, as the pain of the running was forgotten for navigating our way through a tropical storm (winds at sixty mph) back to safety. Actually, it never was an issue of seeking safety back at the condo as it was rewards in this order: a long, hot shower, a big mug of coffee, and breakfast.

As we settled back into the milieu of a faculty/staff working retreat, warm and beaming with inner joy, we looked over at each other and exchanged a big and knowing smile. This was a beautiful bonding adventure that we both treasure having done together.

Terrell recalled the experience in his own words, writing to me a few years later: "… I would run ten miles down the road and then you would meet me and run the five miles back to the hotel with me. … And then the rains came. Without question, that twenty miles in near hurricane conditions was one of the most difficult runs of my life. I'll have to admit that around mile sixteen or seventeen, as the wind and the rain pounded into my face, I had thoughts like, 'Why couldn't I have married into a family with a father-in-law who has a passion for backgammon or woodworking?' and 'I wonder if Chuck is trying to kill me?' At the end, though, the two of us running into the hotel parking lot and conquering the storm together gave birth to a feeling of pride and camaraderie that you just don't get from backgammon."

Chapter 4: JoElyn Taught Herself into a Stroke

"They need so much. Here some of them are in the second grade and they can't read or write. I'm determined to make it happen, if it kills me. They're smart, I know they're smart. What happens to them if they get out of the second grade and still can't read and write? I can't let it happen."

This was JoElyn in the fall of 2001. Still recovering from having to stand by while her husband was under attack, she became AYA's second grade teacher to twelve children, all from low-income households and, for the most part, from parents who themselves were not very educated. This was AYA, holding classes in the long-empty unused educational wing of East Lake United Methodist Church, Jesse Gordon, pastor. The building was so unused that half of the top floor was dubbed "Pigeon World." I'll let your creative mind figure why it bore that name.

"We can't have Jane and Terrell over for Sunday night supper; I've got to get my week better planned. Plus, I've got to create the cover they'll use for this month's folder papers." She was under the Calvert School program. Jane Pehlke would come down two or three times a year to evaluate how well each teacher was doing with the program. JoElyn wanted to be perfect. Even so, in many respects she was enjoying what she was doing. She was demanding, but the students knew she was their advocate. She didn't take excuses. She cared about the children's home conditions, but she didn't let the hardship some of her students faced deter them from doing homework and from focusing and doing their best in class. She adored them and had funny stories to tell about each.

"Oh, Meeze Johnston, too hard." Such were Jose's plaintive words when JoElyn told him he was going to have to copy something over for a third time. This was an assignment that would go in Jose's folder papers that would hang in the hall.

Penmanship—the Calvert script—was deemed important. Even with keyboarding so prevalent, Calvert taught that we would be forever judged by our penmanship. There will always be forms to fill out. "Students, the impression you make when you fill out forms will be your first impression, your first opportunity to show a future admission officer or employer how well educated you are." It was all about giving these students every opportunity to succeed.

In December, we had a Friday Partnership Morning when those patrons who were supporting a particular student would join us for a chapel and then go to the classrooms to see what their Scholarship Students were accomplishing. JoElyn reported feeling "tired to the bone" by the time Friday afternoon rolled around.

To give her a little respite from her 24/7 approach to her job, we went to the Cross Creek Café for a glass of wine and a bite to eat. We were both ready to crash into bed early that night.

Jane met us the next day on a cold December Saturday morning for our accustomed end-of-the-week run, followed by bagels at Einstein's. We waited until 8 a.m. to start, in hopes that a few rays of sun might hit us and warm us on this 30-degree morning. We talked and laughed as we set out. We are a verbal lot, and talk made a run go by quickly. Once on Hanover West, just off of Bohler Road, with Jane and me slightly ahead, JoElyn called out plaintively, "I just can't do it. My legs won't cooperate. I feel all awkward. I've got to turn around."

That was so unlike any of us, including JoElyn. We took our runs seriously: "Neither snow nor rain nor heat nor gloom … stays these Johnstons from their morning runs." Bone-tiredness had hit a new low. We got back to our condo at Cross Creek and were talking when Jane said, "Mom, has your mouth always drooped to one side?"

"No, I don't think so."

The emergency room doctor said, "You didn't get here one minute too soon. You are a 'stroke in progress.'"

Needless to say, our running was over for the day. And for JoElyn, it would be eighteen months before she could fully go back to exercise and life as it was before. Except she didn't go back to "life as before." Never again was she to think solely about her job, no matter how noble the cause. Never again would she exhaust her reserves thinking that going woefully sleep-deprived was an honorable lifestyle. She would become slightly less intense, slightly less of a worrier, slightly less driven—if only slightly.

Chapter 5: God's Manner of Sustaining AYA

What if AYA had been Hershey Academy that has trouble spending all the money that each year pours off the endowment left by chocolate-bar magnate Milton Hershey? I would have taught a class or two and would have imprinted the lives of fantastic, underfunded kids. I could have created professional growth plans with each faculty and staff person, such as I did at Berry Academy. I could have spent time on the campus landscape.

But, alas, God had a different plan for sustaining His beloved Atlanta Youth Academy. His plan is best described as "find people who have money and go ask them for some of it." The Foundation was set up to help identify donor prospects who had a heart for what we were doing. At the $9,000, $10,000, and eventually $12,000 level, the donor was matched with a student as that student's Scholarship Partner.

The first full year I was there, we had to raise $770,000, a budget that before too many years grew to $1.5 million. We set our goal to have the entire current budget raised by the end of February or March so we could begin to raise the next year's budget well before that next year began. Terrell summed up our naiveté about the ride we were in for: "I won't forget thinking, 'I can't wait until we get past these short-term cash flow problems.'"

Remember, we were working with God, and He preferred that we eke out the last dollar we needed in July, often on the last day of July, with the new fiscal year starting the next day. There would be a payroll due at the end of that next two weeks. This plan kept us on our knees and did make the raising of funds a spiritual matter and not a fiscal one. What a bonus in this work to have my longtime friend, Frank Briggs, as board chair and my encourager.

Hudson Taylor (Olympic sprinter, subject of *Chariots of Fire*) had this to say about fundraising for believers: "It is a good comfort to me to know that God ... knows why He placed me here—whether to do, or learn, or suffer. Meanwhile, beware of the haste of the impatient, impetuous flesh, and of its disappointments and weariness. In the greatest difficulties, in the heaviest trials, in the deepest poverty ... God has never failed me: the financial balance for the entire China Inland Mission yesterday was 25 cents. Praise the Lord! 25 cents ... plus all the promises of God."

Another relevant Terrell remembrance: "I won't forget coming to understand at an early stage the intricacies of what I'll refer to as the Great Circular Discussion. It would go something like this. We'd say, 'We need your money in order for AYA to operate.' The prospective donor would respond, 'That's great. I'll give you some of my money just as soon as you can assure me that you're operations are sustainable.' We'd say, 'Great! We're sustained by donations from people just like you.' Then they'd say, 'Great! I can't wait to donate. I'll write the check just as soon as you reach sustainability.' Basically, people like to give you money once they're completely sure that you don't in any way actually need their money. If there ever was a Catch-22, that's it."

Chapter 6: I Was Out of Place — My White Place

It was June '04. The morning dawned bright and on the cool side. The sun was just peeking up, and one by one, others began to join my car parked along the curb outside of East Lake United Methodist Church—some parked further up on 5th Avenue and some along Hosea Williams Drive. It reminded me of the opening scene in *Porgy and Bess* when first one person ventures out on the dimly lighted dawn morning, then a second appears making some rat-a-tat sound, then a third and fourth, and then a crescendo of people pushing carts, carrying flowers, making a melody of these let's-begin-the-day sounds and motions. This was Atlanta Youth Academy's long-anticipated first graduation—those who had started as second graders with the birth of the school were now eighth graders ready to leave the nest.

As the 10:30 starting hour approached, the sanctuary became festooned with flowers on all sides. Ropes were applied to the rows of pews designating the seats for the graduating kindergarteners, for the graduating eighth graders, for the rest of the students behind them, and the pews for parents and other honored guests.

I had watched time-honored prep schools graduate their seniors in appropriate "pomp and circumstance" at McCallie, Westminster, and then with the first graduating class of Brookstone School. I was the primary planner at Berry Academy with the faculty and graduating students winding their way up the serpentine walkway to awe-inspiring Frost Chapel. The chapel bell rang out at the exact moment when the procession was to start. This same bell pealed out five minutes of cascading jubilation at within a minute of the appointed time when the ceremony was to say its benediction. An army general could not have planned a high-moment ceremony with any more precision than could I. I love ceremonies, and I love the planned timing that goes with the best ceremonies.

Back in East Lake, the other students, parents and guests were all in place at 10:30. And the organ sounded the signal that sent the robed and mortar-boarded kindergarteners marching down the aisle to their front-row seats. Then the organ heightened its awe-inspiring sound to launch almost adult-sized eighth graders down the center of the aisle to their seats behind and towering over the kindergarteners, who, by the way, were having a heck of a time keeping their mortar board graduation hats on their heads. We proceeded nicely with a welcome by one of the eighth graders followed by the pledges to the Bible, to the Christian flag, and to the American flag. Then it was time for James Daniel, founding and beloved kindergarten teacher, to conduct the "graduation" of the twelve kindergarten students. Coming out of the white culture, I had thought that kindergarten graduation was in poor taste, but I bowed to the norm in the black culture which was for the graduation of five- and six-year-olds in full robed dress. I entrusted this part of the morning's program to James. I sat back in my up-front pastor's chair and relaxed, more or less.

The program proceeded with appropriate decorum for tiny people until the point when James "dropped the bomb." Without any forewarning to me, he said, "I was praying last night when God impressed upon me that we are to pray for our fathers. So, I'd like all of the fathers in attendance to come down front, and I will ask, then, that pastors, elders, deacons, and others who will, come down and pray for these men individually." It was bedlam for a moment, but that quickly settled into the hum of people praying for people.

I knew that I had lost it—that is, my tight grip on the day's ceremony. I was out of place in a culture that didn't function by clocks and watches. Time was sacred to me, and I'm sure my blood pressure must have felt that it was going to pop at the top of my head. What was I to say or do about James' "word from God"? I had no choice but to appear to be "in the Spirit" and to fume a little in my soul about the program that went nearly an hour longer than my plan had called for.

After former Falcon star Wallace Francis spoke, we concluded in jubilation with the spine-tingling school song, "AYA, you're forever in my heart." I enjoyed the people and saying "goodbye" to students and teachers. My quandary about time began for me the process of confronting my white cultural norm.

Chapter 7: The Start of Life for Ellie

In August 2002, Jane and Terrell invited his parents, Ted and Liza, and JoElyn and me for a post-church Sunday lunch at their recently purchased Chattahoochee condominium. I assumed they were just creating more opportunities for their respective parents to spend time together. In a move that was the farthest thing from any of our imaginations, they presented each couple with a wrapped gift containing a framed announcement: "You are invited to the birth of your grandchild, April 6, 2003."

I wish I could record the inner thoughts of the other three grandparents-to-be, but I'm not given that privilege. Theirs were probably little different from mine: tears welled up in my eyes. I was overcome with emotion. Was *The Lion King's* "circle of life" theme coursing through my body? Probably not, but I was thinking of "Baby Jane" being a mother. As oriented towards young people as were both Jane and Terrell, I couldn't imagine any two young souls better prepared to be the best parents ever. I could never have foreseen the joy, satisfaction, extension of life that I would later receive from the funny "human bean" that would be born less than nine months hence. (And I certainly couldn't imagine the emotional stories and incredible hijinks that would later bring along two more distinctly different grandchildren.)

Jane was almost twenty-eight and very athletic when she became pregnant with Ellie. She ran five miles and more on the road routinely, and she worked out with the weight machines at the Y. In fact, our YMCA "club" adored Jane already and they were so impressed that she didn't let pregnancy slow her down. While only having minimal "morning sickness" was probably a stroke of God's mercy, her lack of other expectant-mother serious problems had to be, at least in part, because of her superb athletic condition.

She continued with our seven-mile Saturday run, from Cross Creek to Peachtree and back, deep into the expected nine months—the run and the reward-bagel to follow at Einstein's. Even with some semblance of routine and normality, the wait must have been nearly intolerable for Jane, as I guess it is for a lot of women in pregnancies. I remember her telling me in September that "being pregnant isn't easy."

In the first few days of March, she and Terrell were predicting an early delivery date, earlier than the original April 6 "due date." The doctor had told Jane that "Baby Gilbert has dropped," and that, I was told, is a good sign. "Baby Gilbert may be arriving right around the corner."

Fast-forward a couple of weeks and here's what I wrote in my journal covering the events of March 22, 2003:

Jane had become so pregnant that she was now resorting to power-walking instead of running, and JoElyn and I were happy to make that adjustment to preserve our practice of a multi-mile Saturday run (now walk) with the reward of an Einstein's bagel afterwards. On this particular Saturday, March 22, Jane called to say she would be delayed because Terrell was just going to run her by Piedmont Hospital briefly to check on something. The idea was that we would just begin our walk a little later.

Telephone rings: "Hey, guess what? I'm staying. They're saying that the birthing process is underway."

(Jane is "something else" in seeing adventure and promise in every experience, like the time she called us from her Ritz-Carlton bathroom on her wedding night, so excited that they had a telephone in the bathroom. She just had to use it.)

At 1 o'clock or so JoElyn and I arrived at Piedmont Hospital; we saw Jane and Terrell, and then we began the vigil with Ted and Liza Gilbert. Terrell would come out periodically and give us updates. We had left Evelyn Anne messages that the birth was occurring. She finally called back; unbeknownst to her mom, she was beginning the drive down from Annapolis, Maryland, to surprise Jane and to greet her new nephew or niece. I was to say nothing.

Finally, around dusk, the four grandparents-to-be went across Peachtree Street to the Black Bear Café and had a nice supper, sitting in the open window on a warmish March evening. ... At 6:15 Ellie (JoElyn Eliza) was born—seven pounds, seven ounces, twenty inches long. The two nurses who had been helping Jane all day came out and said that they just loved our family. Jane said she cried when the two nurses left around 7:15. Lacy and Sarah came. Later Holle and Brian Kennerly came. We departed around 10 p.m. Evelyn Anne arrived around 12:30, getting to be there during one of Ellie's nursing sessions.

The next day after JoElyn, Evelyn Anne and I had gone to Apostles, we went by the hospital to see the new mother, father, and child—all within the first 24 hours of adjusting to their new roles. We took a break to go home in the afternoon, then returned in the evening. Here is my astute observation of my new granddaughter I wrote the next morning in my journal: *The sweet little girl cries when she needs a diaper change or when she has gas; otherwise, she seems to be a child of contentment.*

While Jane was breast-feeding Ellie, JoElyn, Evelyn Anne, and I went across the street to the Black Bear Café, a second evening there in a row for JoElyn and me. When walking back to the stop light to cross back over to the hospital, we encountered Walter Henegar, who was preparing for a Christ Church movie night in an otherwise closed Atlanta Bread Company. We had a delightful short sidewalk visit with him; meanwhile, Anne Henegar was across the street visiting with Ellie and her parents.

Late Monday afternoon Jane and newborn were discharged from the hospital. The four grandparents assisted Terrell in getting them home and settled. We grandparents had been initially invited for an April 6 birthing; and here it was March 24, two days after a March 22 birth. One might say that Ellie arrived fifteen days ahead of schedule. So if there was a bit of setting up work to be done at the Gilbert condo, who should be surprised at that? But finally, with work finished, around 9 p.m., we sat around on the floor of the nursery and ate the herb chicken and cornbread dressing that Margaret Ann Briggs had prepared for just such a homecoming.

With Jane and Terrell at the end of their energy tether, we quietly departed, leaving a new mother teary at being out from under the security of the hospital, an exhausted new father not used to functioning on two hours of sleep, and a totally new person who thought everything was just fine—as long as she remained the center of everyone's universe.

Tuesday through Friday moved along slowly. JoElyn and Liza worked in shifts over at the Gilbert condo holding Ellie so that Jane and Terrell could take naps and showers and have meals. Since I had to be at AYA after missing Monday, I had the light caregiver role. One of those days, I contributed by bringing Jane and Terrell Steak 'n' Shake milkshakes and then staying to eat lasagna with them. (Friends had been good about bringing over food.)

Saturday morning JoElyn and I ran five miles (I was sore later). The phone rang at 9:30 as we were coming into our Cross Creek home. It was Jane who needed help, so I grabbed up my clothes and went over. (Terrell went in to AYA to get work done and to be there for a volunteer work crew from Peachtree Road Methodist Church.) JoElyn followed to the Gilberts a little later. I did things like hold Ellie while Jane took a shower. I entertained Robert and Paul at the river while Virginia and Brant Bousquet visited with Jane and Ellie. I went and bought four concrete planters to put some of their gift plants in—for the deck. I greeted other guests as they came to visit (e.g., Brett and Elizabeth).

One morning that week I read the thirteenth verse of Isaiah 66, "As a mother comforts her child, so will I comfort you." After reading it I wrote: *Wow! Now that I have the living image of Ellie in the hands of her parents, I see what it is to submit and to be truly dependent. Let me be so dependent on my loving Heavenly Father.*

Terrell and one-year-old Ellie, summer 2004

Chapter 8: Ellie in the Six Months Leading to the Birth of Her Brother

When Ellie was in her second year, JoElyn and I realized Jane and Terrell's need to have uninterrupted time together to synchronize their calendars and just to really check in with each other. So we established a Sunday afternoon hour when I would take Ellie on an adventure while JoElyn prepared a meal for us all—this, by the way, something we continued on with Chad and Martha Jane into today, some fifteen years later. (One difference: the young adult children have adventure enough of their own, yet the meal continues on in robust fashion.)

Cross Creek, it turns out, held some pretty cool adventures. Here's what I wrote of March 14, 2005: *Sunday was a particularly good trip down to see the ducks and fish with Ellie. Coming back she took great delight in running, being fast. The ducks and swans and geese were consistently up close and entertaining. It took a while, however, for the fish to warm up to us and eat the crackers that Ellie faithfully brought to them each week.*

Ellie turned two on March 22, 2005. When it came to her birthday, she was not to be upstaged by anticipation of a baby brother. She had a pizza party on the Tuesday night of her birthday at the Chattahoochee Chase condo. The cutest part of the night was when Ellie got a microphone from Liz and was "on stage" (fireplace) performing and Sarah Kennerly got up on stage with her, which clearly threw Ellie off.

This account of two months later, June 5, was a bit different:

I had a delightful time picking up Ellie and taking her to see her great-grandmother Evelyn. From Evelyn's we went to Chastain Park and watched horses and riders work out under the big roof. One white horse was going over some low jumps. Ellie was unafraid of the horses in the ring, even though we were on one side of the rail and the horses were just on the other side. However, when we went into the barn and there was a horse with much less between us and it, Ellie pulled away, saying, "Home, home." From there we went by the playground. With the seat of her pants Ellie dried off a couple of slides that were wet from the rain. We then met Mimi (JoElyn) at home for supper and a bubble bath, reading and prayers. Ellie went to sleep peacefully and without resistance. Jane and Terrell picked her up around 10 pm after having gone to a Gilbert family event at Sarah and Josh's, Terrell's sister and then brother-in-law.

Ellie was a hearty child. We took a road trip to Annapolis at the first of June with the three Gilberts. It was only towards the tail end of an eleven-hour drive that she gave in to a few minutes of sleep. The only concession to her two-year-old age was that when the rest of us rode the train into Washington for a

Braves/Nationals game, Ellie and Terrell stayed back. Otherwise, she was center stage whether it was at a meal at The Rock Fish (where Evelyn Anne worked as hostess) or in this last hour before we headed back to Atlanta.

The mental picture to preserve is that of all of us sitting in the sun at the harbor drinking our City Docks coffee while Ellie talked and played with Alex Haley's statue and those of the children listening to him.

When Jane's thirty-first birthday rolled around, Ellie showed her gracious social skills. At a nice birthday breakfast for Jane at West Egg, Ellie was calm, while entering completely into the spirit of the social occasion. She was a part of the celebration without having to be center stage. That evening, at an ice cream and cake celebration, Ellie loved the Bert and Ernie birthday tape.

So did Ellie play a role in Chad's birth? You bet she did! On a Saturday afternoon swim at the Cross Creek pool, Ellie challenged her oh-so-pregnant mother to jump into the pool. Jane complied, at which point she felt somebody rebelling against such a bump. Ellie's outrageous challenge to her mother and the full moon conspired to bring on Ellie's little brother, Charles Edward Gilbert.

Chapter 9: Jane's Workouts While Pregnant with Chad

I remember with great pleasure the long runs we took for years on Saturday mornings. Even when Jane was pregnant with Chad, she didn't slack off one bit from our run that would take us up to Peachtree Road at E. Rivers and back, a picturesque and pleasant route on quiet early Saturday mornings. JoElyn was fully a part of that as were other guest runners, like maybe Mathias Henry (AWPC) or Chris White, who would often join us.

Jane had been conscious of staying fit up to a point when pregnant with Ellie, but with this second pregnancy she was determined to "show no quarter" when it came to continuing our top level of fitness. It must have been particularly cold in that winter of 2005 because I record one run at 22 degrees and several in the low, low 30s. We got up early and did one seven-miler on a Friday because of anticipated ice for the next morning. Sure enough, the winter world was covered in a sheet of ice that Saturday morning and no one could stir out of the house. It was April of that year before I recorded a sane, good-weather, seven-mile run with Jane on a crisp and sunny 50-degree morning.

My apologies to you, Chad, but it was June and July of '05 before I recorded your presence except as you may have made Jane mildly sick and as you caused her to turn to swimming as an alternative to running in the later stages of pregnancy. Apparently you, Chad, were complaining about the jarring you were getting with the running.

I can't imagine two sets of grandparents working any better together to support their mutual young family than did Liza, Ted, JoElyn and I. Here was Ted in late June taking the master bedroom in the Chattahoochee Chase condo and turning it into two rooms. Granted, the room designated for baby Chad (whose name we didn't know at that point) was tiny, but it was crafted with love. For my part, I signed a home equity check over to Jane so that she could make a $2,800 payment to Piedmont for anticipated hospital costs for the birth of the baby to come (a loan which, if you care to know, was paid back in full).

At one point, Jane asked me to pray that the new little boy would come on August 8. You, Chad, showed early signs of "having a mind of your own" by waiting nearly two weeks later than that, August 21, to make your august appearance. At least you and your sister knew the perils of having a birthday anywhere close to your mom's hallowed annual day of celebration on August 5.

Here's my perspective as recorded in my journal of how things came to landing you, Chad, in the hospital on the 20th of August:

We were returning down Peachtree from a welcome-home party for Jim and Elisabeth Irwin when Jane called to say that she, Terrell, and Ellie were headed to the hospital. While watching a movie, the water broke. Jane was in considerable discomfort. A security guard named Ted prayed over Jane as she was getting out of the car. He pushed her wheelchair to her room. Together with Ellie we went with Jane to check in. We took Ellie back to our house where Liz Olmstead met us. Liz stayed at our house. We joined Ted, Liza, Lacy, and Sarah in a vigil until the birth at 4 am.

No telling when you might have been born had not your young older sister shamed your mother into jumping into the Cross Creek pool late the afternoon before going to the hospital that evening. Your mom clearly felt your complaining about that jolt.

Do you know what loving aunts you have? All were with you on the occasion of your birth, though it took Aunt Evelyn Anne a flat tire and a full day on the road from Annapolis to get to you. She arrived at 1:45 a.m. Monday.

You were born at 4 a.m. Sunday morning (seven pounds, six ounces; nineteen and one-half inches). Here's what I recorded in my journal of your homecoming Tuesday:

Chad came home from the hospital. … (Evelyn Anne) and I picked up the pizza and met the others at Riverbend. JoElyn and Ellie had arrived ahead of Chad and Co. to put balloons at the door.

There for all to see in the next Sunday's Church of the Apostles bulletin was this announcement: "Born to Jane and Terrell Gilbert on August 21st, Charles Edward Gilbert."

Chapter 10: A Glimpse into Evelyn Anne's St. John's Life

Wishing to be more specific about some of Evelyn Anne's St. John's College experience and of her well-being at this time, I refreshed my memory by looking at my journal entries for a random nine-month period. And here is what I came up with in a span leading up to her twenty-second birthday:

First of all, she was gaining confidence and independence through these four years of living on her own, some 670 miles and a ten-hour drive from home. She made a healthy assessment of this season in her life by saying that 80 La Rue was not really her home and Apostles was not her home church. Her home, until she marries, is wherever she may find herself, "be that Annapolis or Dublin or Atlanta." Rather than being a forlorn declaration, JoElyn and I received it as a healthy fulfillment of our prayers for Evelyn Anne since her childhood—that we raise her to stand on her own, to be strong enough to be independent of us.

Over the Christmas holidays '04, JoElyn, Evelyn Anne, and I traveled to Charlotte for the funeral for Dr. Doug Briggs, Frank's brother. He had hanged himself on Christmas afternoon. Evelyn Anne came to tears during the service thinking of the intensity of the pain he, Dr. Briggs, must have been feeling. She could identify with that, though she was quick to say that her faith would never let her take her own life (even though she occasionally heard voices that urged her to do just that).

Back to her growing sense of independence, Evelyn Anne relished eventually leaving the dorms and entering rooming house life in Annapolis. It gave her a feel of what post-college living might be like. When the apartment she had wanted fell through, a spare room opened up at her friend Brumley's. I remember as a kid the term "flophouse," meaning a place that was not really like home but more a place where you could flop down to sleep. That's how Brumley's struck us, but it was an answer to prayer for EA.

We had brought a mattress up from Atlanta for Evelyn Anne's new place, and the only way to get it in this antique building was for Terrell and me to climb up on the roof at the back of the place and hoist the mattress through the kitchen window. Terrell and I carried box after box of Evelyn Anne's things (mostly books) up the staircase from the front that was so narrow and steep that we had not been able to fit the mattress. Interestingly, on the street level under this upstairs set of rooms was a sporting goods store that specialized in equipment for a sport that had not yet made it to the South—lacrosse.

Evelyn Anne had worked in the admissions office since her sophomore year with an admissions director that she enjoyed and admired. Then, in December '04 Evelyn Anne interviewed for a job at a new chef-centered restaurant, The Rock Fish. She was hired as hostess, and her orientation and training kept her in Annapolis within a day or two of Christmas, which she didn't mind. As she moved into that job, she found that she had a knack for sizing up customers and delivering them to just the right table in a frame of mind making the wait person's job more pleasant. The Rock Fish staff loved her and tolerated her occasional bouts of depression that would cause her to call in sick. It was a job for which she was well suited. Mothers' Day 2005 she worked a heavy load of diners, on her feet and hustling from 11 a.m. to 7 p.m.

Somewhere in here I have to give credit to Jane and Jim Pehlke, who always hosted JoElyn and me—and the Gilberts, as well—when we were in Annapolis to see Evelyn Anne. (Jane Pehlke had worked with us as coach on the Calvert Curriculum at AYA.) We shared many meals together, both at their condo and at restaurants. Early in Evelyn Anne's St. John's years, Jim even sat with Evelyn Anne in the hospital ER as she struggled with an onslaught of her illness. The Pehlkes remain our friends to this day.

During our late-July family beach week at Gulf Shores, when Evelyn Anne and I were on a late-night walk to the Beach Club to hear a band, after viewing and discussing the night sky the conversation topic changed. I recorded in my journal that "… she then timidly brought up the topic of finances, which we discussed without tension, I believe. She does say that she gets *mixed messages* about earning her keep versus the age-old assurance that her mom and I want her to focus on her studies while she is in school." It's interesting looking back to see that we did not shield EA from financial concerns that her mom and I wrestled with, be that right or wrong. (Even in 2018 finances remain a sometimes topic of stress between JoElyn and me.)

Between Memorial Day and July 4, 2005, she worked seven days a week, either at the admissions office or at The Rock Fish. So nobody could accuse her of slacking. I will say that instead of creating a savings account for the upcoming school year, she was covering summer living expenses and paying off a credit card debt from the winter. (A bank sent her a card unsolicited and made it seem harmless, much in the way drug dealers hook some unsuspecting souls into drug use.)

That summer I had let Evelyn Anne know by e-mail that Dookie Adams, our wonderful Wieuca Terrace next-door neighbor, had passed away. Evelyn Anne emailed back, reflecting on sadness, that maybe it wasn't all bad. She even said that it was a topic she might like to explore more deeply.

Here we get a snapshot of why it took Evelyn Anne six years to earn her diploma from St. John's. As the onslaught of her manic/depressive disorder came upon her in full bloom in her freshman year, she found it impossible at times to focus on her reading and writing, and at other times she was physically unable to make it to class or seminar. Part of the strength and beauty of St. John's was its emphasis on unflinching attendance at and participation in that which took place around the seminar tables. Here, in a December 2004 journal entry, is an example of her challenges:

She called … in a few minutes on the brink of collapse. She had "writer's block," with two papers due. She couldn't go to that morning's class without a paper. I insisted that she go talk with the tutor and get an extension. She did; he was abrupt and said he would talk with her at don rags later that day. She then encountered a student who said she would let EA dictate to her; she would help EA get beyond her writer's block. My urging, and EA's desire, is to have a paper to turn in when she goes to don rags; which, by the way, she did. (Don rags = the tutors or dons talking in the student's presence of the student's strengths and weaknesses over the past semester. It was always a positive process for Evelyn Anne.)

When Evelyn Anne's health was stabilized, she was as if born to this style of education. Consider my journal entry of May 11, 2005: *Report of don rags: Mr. Russell said, "Miss Johnston has a self-effacing way of making very insightful comments." One of the others said, "Miss Johnston is one of the students who makes discussion fun." Evelyn Anne said (to herself), "I'm now a senior."*

Evelyn Anne had her share of physical ups and downs, many common to all students who find themselves sleep deprived and under pressure. Muscle spasms and headaches might qualify here. We talked one summer morning when she was walking in to work at the admissions office that she had been up all night because of the caffeine content of the Excedrin she took for her migraine. Here is an example from my journal of March 8, 2005, of physical down and up within hours of each other. Here she is on the road trip home for her spring holidays:

Evelyn Anne had an eventful drive home. Near the exit at Potomac, Virginia, her menstrual cramps became so severe that she was beginning to hyperventilate. She called 911 from the side of the street after she had exited. An ambulance picked her up and took her to the hospital, where, with hot towels, the severe pain left her. She took a cab back to her car, and, with a giant bottle of Gatorade and Advil, she proceeded on in joy. At one point in our multiple phone conversations she said that she felt more herself than she had in years. Evelyn Anne arrived home in wonderful spirits at 11:45 pm; and she and JoElyn and I visited spiritedly until after 1 a.m.

The ten-hour drive back and forth between college and home on I-95/I-85 was a big part of the St. John's experience, especially since all of our family enjoyed road trips. On one drive home she blew a tire, and a state trooper beat AAA there and changed Evelyn Anne's tire for her. For $39 she had a new tire and was back on the road, arriving home around 12:30 a.m. When driving down in August to meet her new nephew, Chad, Evelyn Anne again had a flat tire. This time an "Alaskan Christian" changed it for her, and she was home by 1:45 a.m. And here is an August 2005 journal entry that gives some color to the positive role that the drive played in her college years:

I had some nice visiting time with Evelyn Anne, hearing one CD of poetry on the "Seven Stages of Man," another that was "Jars of Clay" with the Blind Boys of Alabama. … She headed out this morning at 6 am. She, JoElyn and I circled up at the ATM machine and each said a prayer for her trip and for her glorious senior year about to start.

While not a "road" trip, Evelyn made an adventure out of flying home for her twenty-second birthday July 22, 2005. She arrived at Reagan Airport in perfect timing for her 4:15 flight to Atlanta, only to find that the plane was to take off from Dulles Airport. After a frantic $65 taxi ride to Dulles, she missed the flight. Delta's only option was a 6 a.m. flight the next morning. Pamela Heard (AYA) found her a flight online on another airline. When she got to that ticket desk, she was rewarded with a half-price ticket ($92) because it was her birthday. She was home with us by 10 p.m. We celebrated as best we could with balloons, pizza, beer, and a chocolate pudding birthday cake. Ahhhh, to be twenty-two.

Chapter 11: Evelyn Anne Defends Her Senior Paper

At the same time that Evelyn Anne was cloistering herself in Annapolis to write her Senior Paper (one that would have to be defended in front of the faculty experts on T.S. Eliot) her maternal grandmother, Evelyn Jones, for whom she was in part named, was slowly running out of energy or the will to fend off impending death.

Regarding the paper, which was on Evelyn Anne's primary focus, *The Love Song of J. Alfred Prufrock*, I loved the opportunity it gave me to relate in small measure to the depth of the schooling in the classics that she was getting at St. John's College. In a letter after a telephone conversation about the opening pages of her paper, I said to her, "Your language is colorful and dense with content. Prufrock's feeling of being an imposter is one shared by people at the head of corporations and in other lofty positions, so I'm told. It's the feeling of being hollow. (That sounds like a harbinger of another poem.)" We also discussed the theme in the poem of "aging exposing Prufrock's flaws."

Grandmother Evelyn died in Hospice Atlanta in the early morning hours of January 30, 2006. At around 7 pm the evening before, we had circled around Evelyn's bed, laid hands on her, and each prayed. We sang "Jesus Loves Me," and then we asked Ellie, age two years, ten months, for a song suggestion. She immediately came up with the "goodbye" song from *The Sound of Music*: "So long, farewell, auf Wiedersehen, good night ... So long, farewell, auf Wiedersehen, adieu ... Adieu, adieu, to you and you and you."

EA turned in her completed Senior Paper Friday night at the end of that week and joined the celebratory party for the seniors completing this milestone. She flew in the dark of the morning to Atlanta where we met her with blankets and pillows at 8:30 a.m. for our three-hour drive to Greenville Saturday, February 4.

We had a meaningful graveside service and then a memorial service for Evelyn in the small sanctuary of Greenville Independent Methodist Church. Latisha Johnson, our friend from AYA, sang "His eye is on the sparrow"; Evelyn Anne and Jane gave meaningful tributes to their grandmother; and JoElyn praised the church for the extraordinary sense in which they had cared for both Ed and Evelyn—that they were truly the Body of Christ. Ted and Liza were there to take care of little Chad and Ellie during the services.

Chapter 12: A Mythical Family Trip to Ireland

It was March of 2007 when our schedules aligned such that we all could take a great trip to Ireland. Terrell was about to graduate from Georgia State Law School. Evelyn Anne was in the year of her faux graduation from St. John's. Terrell and Evelyn Anne had coinciding spring holidays. At times in March it is windy and rainy and cold in Ireland, and so it was when we were there. You remember how it is flying overnight to Europe; you feel pretty tired and grungy when you arrive. That didn't stop Terrell and Evelyn Anne from going to a pub in the airport and having a big 8 a.m. stein of Guinness—because "Guinness is good for you."

Our time was to be spent in Galway and in the Dingle Peninsula, and we were to have taken an easy connecting flight from Dublin to Galway. However, the winds were too treacherous to fly, so

Terrell and Evelyn Anne share a toast.

we boarded a bus for a longer journey to Galway. We were fascinated by the roundabouts that dotted our path—fascinated and jostled a bit as we swung into the curves. With a few miles to go to reach our destination, Ellie (age nearly four) and Chad (age eighteen months) grew quiet until Chad broke the silence with a quiet but distinct up-chuck, all over Terrell, soon to be followed by a responding up-chuck from Ellie. I don't know how they got cleaned up a bit; I do remember that the three of them moved to the back of the bus.

I won't give a travel log here of our trip, but let me say that there were no wimps on this trip. In Galway we walked in wind and sometimes rain and loved it. In the pubs we would huddle near the peat-burning stoves as we had our food and beverage. Ellie and Chad added to our being taken in by the Irish wherever we all went together. Whenever there were musicians, the two of them would sidle up close to the players as possible; and, of course, the musicians loved this attention.

On our way to the Dingle Peninsula, at Evelyn Anne's insistence, we stopped to climb to the top of the Cliffs of Moher. The wind was blowing a steady thirty to forty miles per hour. Evelyn Anne was determined to make the climb, Terrell was game to do it, and JoElyn went along in her yellow rain slicker because she somehow thought that maybe she could keep the other two from being blown off the top of the cliffs into the sea.

The rest of us stayed in the warm car. The three climbers had not gone far when eighteen-month-old Chad unwittingly pulled at the door handle, the wind whipped the door open and slammed the door against the front door. And Chad was pulled out onto the gravel parking area below. When we finally got to him, he was bleeding and crying.

Terrell, sensing trouble, turned back to join us. He comforted Chad and then headed out again into the wind to recover Chad's Crocs that had been ripped off his feet and blown more than the length of a football field to the other side of the parking lot.

The other two made it to the top and back down in one piece, with a great photo to prove that JoElyn had, indeed, made it to the top. JoElyn happened to have a butterfly bandage in her purse that served almost as good as stitches to stop Chad's bleeding and pull the forehead slit together. And on we went to our lovely bed-and-breakfast and to our innkeeper John O'Farrell, who had opened just for us, the only ones adventuresome enough to come in March. Being there in March, absent other tourists and buffeted by wind, rain, and cold, gave this trip a flavor and character that none of us would trade for the world.

Dillon, Evelyn Anne, and her favorite tutor, Gisela Berns, at St. John's College graduation, May 2007

Chapter 13: Atlanta Westside Presbyterian Church Launched

In January 2007, nineteen men and women gathered every Sunday night in the small Henegar living room to embark on a risky venture of starting a church that was to focus its eyes and heart towards the city. Jane, Terrell, JoElyn and I were a part of that nineteen, as were Walter and Anne Henegar.

What were JoElyn and I doing in such a youth movement as was Atlanta Westside Presbyterian Church? I was sixty-seven and JoElyn was sixty-two when we launched. Walter, Terrell, and Anne were thirty-five, and Jane close behind them. That left thirteen others who were in their mid-to-late twenties: Will

Brown, Beverly Easterling (aka Maxwell), Sarah Grizzle, Hannah and Jeff Heck, Kristie and Sean Maddox, Summer and Steven Owens, Hannah Parker (aka Skinner), Aaron Saylor, Sara Scheu (aka Huey) and Rachael Smith (aka Fishman).

We were there because God so directed us and because we wanted to sit under Walter's teaching. We had met Anne Sexton, later Anne Henegar, through Sarah Youssef when Anne had graduated from UNC and was headed to Nashville to join Campus Crusade's Vanderbilt team. We supported Anne modestly, and Jane was nurtured by Anne in Jane's final two years of college. We first knew Walter as a mandolin-playing skilled carpenter who had moved to Nashville to date Anne.

Later, when Walter was graduating from Westminster Seminary (Philadelphia), I spoke about Walter to Al LaCour who was looking to add a pastoral position at Christ Church PCA. Much to our pleasure, Walter and Anne, along with young Abigail and Emily, moved to Atlanta, Walter coming to serve as pastor to young adults at Christ Church. We, along with Jane and Terrell, would skip a Sunday at Church of the Apostles occasionally to go hear Walter preach.

Eventually all four of us individually said to Walter, "If you ever start a church, we want to be a part of it." And that launched us into a glorious season of spiritual growth as part of these young church planners. From January through August 2007, we focused on CDs and books and discussion so rich it made my head swell with a bigger picture of what it means to follow Jesus. The best contemporary theological speakers and writers (or the ones Walter and Anne put before us) spelled out that Biblical communities were to be made up of people who don't all look alike and who are not all in similar income brackets.

So, we were charged up that we could be a multi-racial church, we could be an adopting church. We would be a generously giving church; we would give away twenty-five percent of what we gathered in tithes and offerings because we were putting only rent money into our "facilities."

The people of the Biblical communities were, we imagined, living in close proximity to each other, as did the early Christians we read of in Acts. They lived life together. I imagined it being just short of living in a commune, something that has always intrigued me. Your ministry was to be off of your front porch, starting with continually examining the circumstances around you and God's leading in "what constitutes good neighboring." This was to be a daily focus; consequently, few programs would be planned at the church building with the corporate focus on worshipping together Sunday mornings.

It was said that "often the best Christians make the worst neighbors because they are always jumping in their cars and heading out to the church building." But the gathering Sunday morning was to be where we would all come together and bring neighbors who sensed we possessed something sweet and who were willing to explore what that "something" might be. The pastors and lay people who led from up front were to constantly envision the "empty seat," being careful not to use insider language.

After a trial service in the ministry building of Victoria's Friends (freeing striptease dancers who felt trapped), the church had its opening service Labor Day Sunday, September 2, 2007, at what was to become its ten-year rental home, The Defoor Center. From the get-go, Jim Irwin and I set up the chairs for worship and moved from the storage closet the pulpit, music stands, mikes, and a rolling sound board with its complexity of cables. All this was to transform the central stage-area of The Defoor Center into a sanctuary, albeit a funky one. We ended by setting up the lone Sunday School / nursery room, a distance from the sanctuary. We would save installing the little pop-up tent (a gift from Abigail and Emily) until the end because it was the most fun piece in the room to put together.

What was it in that time of labor for Jim Irwin and me together? It was mysterious, but whatever it was, Jim and I loved it and looked forward to this early-Sunday-morning time together. Jim was the one who placed the first chairs, the ones on which the rest depended for consistency and for the closest possible proximity to the worship team and to Walter. (The fully Spirit-filled worship team did not ascend to the stage in the first few years, to emphasize that this was not a performance on their part. They only moved up on the stage when their floor space was needed for more chairs.)

Jim and I loved each other in the Brotherhood. After a few years, we reluctantly gave way to others who wanted a shot at the joy they saw us having. Laboring together gave us a bond that has been lasting. As a result of that, I have often said that I hope we never go to permanent sanctuary seating.

That Brotherhood was fed when Jim, Michael Vestal, Jeff Heck and I were elected as the church's first elders. First of all, we had to learn a shortened version of the Reformed theology that Jane and others learn in multiple years at RTS or Westminster seminaries. At the end of our study, the four of us were subjected to examination by three elders from Presbytery who grilled us, asking me, for instance, why I almost exclusively referred to God and seldom used the Second Person of the Trinity, Jesus. In one way or another these Presbytery elders cast aspersions on aspects of Walter's and our vision of a "local" and "minimalist" church. (Our founding core values of what we wanted to be as a church were prayerful, contextual, minimalist, serving, local, and missional.) They were so undone by Jeff's assertion that the Genesis account of creation was more likely poetic than literal that they required him to write a paper on the subject. They must have felt that they inflicted enough travail on Jeff that they ultimately confirmed him as a Ruling Elder.

(See later iteration of the brothers in **Appendix 8**.)

PART SEVEN

The Decade of My 70s (2010-2020)

Chapter 1: We Move to Grove Park

After seeing how miserable assisted living life was for her grandmother (Evelyn), Jane was dead-set against JoElyn and me ever ending up with such a lonely and demeaning life in our old age. "When you get older, we'll build a guest house or garage apartment behind our house and you can live there. That way your grandchildren can come check on you, make sure you're still alive."

Then one of us said, "Why do we have to wait until we're 'old' old? Let's do it while we can enjoy it."

We looked at some land on Cambria Avenue, on the Collier Road side of Underwood Hills. Next we became enamored with Howell Station. We were serious enough to ask Chuck LeCraw to come and give us his opinion about two side-by-side lots abutting the fence around the Rice Street Fulton County Jail. We felt virtuous and brave in saying, "No prison escapee is going to stop at the first houses just outside the fence. They're going to want to get further than that."

One problem Chuck LeCraw saw? "The street all the way down to these lots, while shown on the map, does not exist. The cost of road and sewer would be prohibitive."

It was a little bit of a stretch, but with Mary Stuart Iverson's encouragement, we began to explore Grove Park. This began in early 2008 after a full year under the drum-beat encouragement of our new church (AWPC) to spread out into the full expanse of our parish.

Evelyn Anne made the first move—to what may arguably have been one of the most abandoned and neglected streets in the neighborhood, Markone, which we first pronounced *mar-cone* until we saw Marktwo and Marktrey. Her house cost $71,000. (The seller, who had renovated the house to flip it, paid off a $108,000 mortgage at the October '08 closing.) Evelyn Anne added a privacy fence in the back yard, burglar bars, an alarm system, and a lovable Great Pyrenees dog named Sweeney.

"Your body is not an isolated, separate entity. We are our truest selves only in community—with our ancestors (carrying their stories and DNA), our natural environment, and our neighbors."
— Richard Rohr

I had met Evelyn Anne's next-door neighbor-to-be, Carlton, in the process of our back-and-forths in getting Evelyn Anne moved in. Carlton was reportedly TI's cousin, referred to on the back of TI's CD cover as "Big C." His job was as a bouncer at TI's club on Hollowell. As I had done everything I could to get Evelyn Anne settled, and it was finally time to leave her alone in the house for her first night in Grove Park, I was tearfully trudging across the lawn to my car. I spotted Carlton sitting on his porch in the gloaming.

"Keep an eye on my little girl, Carlton," I said with a break in my voice. Barely audibly, he said, "I will." Later Evelyn Anne reported a bone-chilling knock on the door. (The metal protection door reverberates when given a substantial knocking.) Evelyn Anne pulled up a little stool and looked through the transom. When she saw that it was Carlton, she climbed down off the stool and cracked open the door.

"Here's my business card," he said. "It has my cell phone number on it. Call me if you ever need anything. I work close by when I'm not at home." And that was it! I have since used this as the best example I know of what it is to be a neighbor, especially considering that she was an uninvited white guest in an up-to-then solidly black and close-knit neighborhood.

The second great act of welcome came in May 2012 from a stranger who has now become a lifetime best friend, Mike Allen. I was coming out of the West Lake Market to get two bags of ice from the ice bin when two men stepped in my path, having determined I would be an easy target. Mike, together with my neighbor Alfred, noticed the interaction from where they had been visiting in front of the store. They stepped in to my defense. Mike, a lifetime resident of Grove Park, gave me the blessing of his friendship, giving me protection as if coming from the neighborhood godfather.

The Gilberts moved into their $32,000 Grove Park home (31 Evelyn Way), after charging $30,000 on credit cards for a kitchen upgrade and a *few* other improvements, in November 2010. They had to clean out the scraps of toys and children's books sadly left behind by the squatters who were the previous occupants. The original floors were distressed throughout; they became part of the house's charm, except to Scott Williams who fell though the kitchen floor as the volunteer renovation crew worked to make the house habitable.

JoElyn and I followed to Grove Park in September 2011, moving two doors down from the Gilberts (35 Evelyn Way) into our $30,000 house with $141,000 in renovations. By the way, that we ended up on a street named Evelyn, the same as that of JoElyn's mother and, in part, of our second daughter, Evelyn Anne, was either a coincidence or Providential. We didn't choose properties on that street because of its name.

JoElyn and Chuck at home at 35 Evelyn Way, September 2011

We and the Gilberts were, like Evelyn Anne earlier, well welcomed into our new homes. Vivian walked over to greet us when we first parked to look at the house at 669 South Evelyn Place, right across Evelyn Way from her. This would have been two or three years before we actually moved in. She said that she had recently seen people going in and out from the back of the partially boarded-up house. Abandoned homes were considered public domain for those conducting business in drugs and prostitution. They could also be welcome shelters for the homeless.

Chapter 2: The Much-Celebrated Advent of Martha Jane Gilbert

As a part of the January through August 2007 Westside Church "launch team," we listened to an impactful sermon by Ray Cortese entitled "When the Pastor Gets the Gospel." The Florida Welfare Department came to him desperate, overflowing with children needing foster homes. "We've gone everywhere we can think of seeking homes for these kids. You are our last resort."

"Last resort? The church ought to be your first resort." Pastor Cortese's heart was changed. He and his wife took on foster children and numerous other families in his church did the same. His statement to his congregation was, "The adopted adopt."

There is plenty of Scripture to back up the theme of adoption:

"He predestined us to adoption as sons through Jesus Christ to Himself" (Ephesians 1:5).

"… but you have received the Spirit of adoption as sons, by Whom we cry 'Abba! Father!' … heirs of God and fellow heirs with Christ" (Romans 8:15, 17).

"We know that the whole creation has been groaning as in the pains of childbirth right up to the present time. Not only so, but we ourselves, who have the first fruits of the Spirit, groan inwardly as we wait eagerly for our adoption as sons, the redemption of our bodies" (Romans 8:22-23).

Jane encountered the blog "Kisses from Katie" from Kate Davis Majors in Nashville, who made a strong case for American Christians to adopt from the thousands of Ugandan children orphaned by the AIDS pandemic. She related positive experiences of her own in making more than one such adoption. Jane and

Terrell had considered their family complete with no intention to have any more children, but maybe they were being called by God to adopt. The more they pondered the prospect and prayed about it, the more moved they felt to proceed with the process. This "call" came late in November 2009.

Here is what I recorded on December 5, 2009:

The train is off and running on Jane and Terrell's adoption of a child from Uganda. They had a 45-minute "welcome" telephone conference with an official of Lifeline Children's Services. They have paid an initial $250 fee. They are preparing an appeal letter to ask for supporting funds. In the midst of all of that, they had an offer on their condo, with counteroffers; it finally collapsed.

The adoption agency, Lifeline Children's Services (Tyrone, Georgia), first did a home study of the Gilberts' fitness to adopt when they lived at Chattahoochee Chase. Terrell, Jane, Ellie, and Chad were clear as far as criminal/drug records, and their moral turpitude was "Check." And, somehow, their cramped condo passed as adequate for a third child. So, they had a green light.

Then, in preparation for the move to Grove Park, having found renters for the Chattahoochee condo, they moved to a small two-bedroom unit in the apartments at the rear of Cross Creek. Uh-oh! Now the adoption green light was red again until another home study could be performed here at Collier Ridge. The kindly agent came in due time, and they were again green-lighted.

A third time their progression towards adoption was put on hold as the Gilberts moved to 31 Evelyn Way in Grove Park. When Scott Williams fell through the rotten kitchen floor and other imperfections in the house showed up, some of us quietly questioned the adoption agency's stomach for this as the third Gilbert prospective location. But in due time the kindly agent came, and their approval became locked in. This would have been in November 2010.

I really can't speak for Jane and Terrell, but here is my observation on the tediousness of the adoption process, this on February 15, 2010:

"'Shall a child be born to a man who is a hundred years old? Shall Sarah, who is ninety years old, bear a child?'" — Genesis 17:17

Should we write a book about God's timing? Jane's blog is pretty much about that. Why had God waited so late in their lives to give Abraham and Sarah a child, Isaac? Why does God not free us to move to Grove Park? Why is Jane and Terrell's adoption seemingly held up? God could be much more expedient, but somehow expediency doesn't seem to be his priority. Abraham laughed at the apparent absurdity of God's timing.

Help me not to laugh at God (but with Him maybe) I will laugh with God as He provides the "daily bread" we need at AYA. I will laugh with God when He springs us free to move to Grove Park— may it be in time to be a neighbor to the elderly on our block. I will laugh with God when I hold a grandchild from Africa.

The next solid move towards adoption I recorded after I had said in December '09 that "the train is off and running," came on Evelyn Anne's twenty-seventh birthday, July 22, 2010, at Tybee, when Terrell faxed from the YMCA some updated information that Terrell and Jane had to sign and get back to the agency. They must have gotten an encouraging prompt from Lifeline to do this. Yet, it's February 2011, six months later, that Jane and Terrell are in line to adopt an eight-month-old precious girl who has the HIV virus, and we get this message from Terrell:

"Hey everyone, wanted to follow up with an update.

"I'm not quite sure how these things work, but somehow Jane and I have come together in a pretty cool, unified and peaceful way in the past 24 hours or so. In short, we've decided to go ahead with the adoption, pending a review of her referral packet to make sure that there aren't further issues that we might not be equipped to handle. Assuming that goes well, though, we'll be adding a new little person to our family really soon.

"First of all, her name is Martha and she's pretty cute. We're not sure about how she got the name Martha. If it has significance, we're likely to stick with it. If it is random, we may change. Still figuring this out.

"We'll get her referral packet this week and make an official decision sometime shortly after that. You'll be the first to know, of course, once a final decision is made.

"The HIV positive part of this is obviously the curve ball. It's not completely out of the blue. We have seriously considered the fact that any orphan adopted from Uganda could end up testing positive, given the high rate of HIV in the country. However, it was incredibly strange to be given the opportunity to choose a child with the virus ahead of time.

"In the end, for me, the decision came back to why we were initially moved to adopt in the first place. God has blessed us beyond what we could have imagined or asked for, and we feel Him leading us to share what He's given us and bring another person that He already loves into our family. We knew that an adopted child would have certain heavy issues to deal with as life progresses and while we can't do anything to take away those issues, we feel like a child is far better off facing those issues in the context of a loving family. I came around to see it the same way for a child with a chronic illness ... Martha will still struggle with her sickness, but she'll have Ellie and Chad to root for her along the way.

"We're still learning about what HIV means in the practical, everyday sense and we'll share with everyone what we learn at appropriate times.

"I guess right now, please pray for us that we'll have wisdom and clarity in reviewing the referral packet and that, if Martha is Gilbert #5 (or #6 if we include Cocoa), that we would be united together very soon. (On that note, if we accept the referral this week, our case worker said we might travel at the end of April or sometime in May.)

"Finally, let me say that Jane and I sincerely appreciate each of you and your support, advice and encouragement along the way. We're aware that what we do in our immediate family has a direct impact on each of your lives (and vice versa, of course). Our choosing to adopt, and then to adopt internationally, and now to adopt a child who is sick, is something that everyone will have to process at their own pace (including Jane and me). We're definitely still processing and we respect your need to process at your own speed and on your own terms.

"We really do love each of you and look forward to this next step.
        "Terrell (and Jane)"

You see this matter of timing? In February Terrell is saying, "[that we will be] united together very soon." It will be August 29 before the Gilberts are united with Martha Jane (aka Martha) in Uganda. At one point in all of this I write, "Will I trust God, even in His 'slow as molasses' timing?" The DeBardelebens started the adoption process after Jane and Terrell, yet they had already gone to Loving Hearts Babies Home and come back with Martha Jane's playmate, Charles Tucker, on New Year's Eve 2010.

Melissa and Dee did return with a photo of Martha Jane peering longingly over the top of her crib, the photo that was central to the Gilberts' celebration on June 19 of Martha Jane's first birthday. (Additionally to their party at home, Jane and Terrell sent the means for a birthday party for MJ among her infant friends in Uganda.)

Now we flash forward nearly five months to Jane's initial email report, received August 29, 2011, on first meeting Martha Jane. All five of the traveling party (Jane, Terrell, Ellie, Chad, and Liza) were equal in being the first to see Martha Jane. Liza was a central part of the quintet that first greeted Martha Jane. Jane emailed us:

"After getting dressed, we went downstairs and met Martha Jane! She is more amazing than my wildest imagination. Full of smiles and a beautiful dimple on one cheek. She clung to me all day, but wouldn't let anyone else hold her, except Ellie by the end of the day. Ellie and Chad loved all over her all day and she loved kisses from Terrell as long as he didn't try to hold her. She did fall asleep with him mid-day on a sofa on our balcony. After lunch, she took a nap with me in our big bed and when she awoke, rather than being scared, she looked around, spotted me, and gave the biggest most beautiful smile. We took her to dinner at a Greek restaurant in walking distance of the babies' home and she was wide eyed at the sky above, the trees and all the new sights and sounds. She ate most of my potato salad. (: We

Martha Jane Gilbert at age seven (2017)

brought her back and she eventually had her medicine, a bottle, and went to bed in her own familiar crib with another big smile.

"I love you all! Jane (:"

The "hurry up and wait" and even the (lack of) assurance that the Ugandan government would permit the adoption would end up making this a long and painful month in Africa. They went with young Ellie and Chad and sat in a hot courtroom awaiting their appointment with the judge, an appointment that never came. Back they came the next day, and, by the grace of God, they saw the right judge who showed them favor. Ironically, it may well have been Liza who tipped the scales. Here's how Jane reports it in her September 1st email:

"We were prepared for the accusations he [the judge] supposedly brought to families of harvesting organs that their biological children need, or [his] questioning children about their role in the process, or demanding why we would come here for their children when we were healthy enough to have our own ... etc. We were to call him 'My Lord' and take the insulting questions as reasonable. ...

Instead, he ... praised our recommendations, which people had written with full disclosure, and said he knew that we truly cared for children and that we led lives of genuine service to others (he doesn't really know, but that was awfully nice) and that it was clear we had holy intentions for the best welfare of children. (And he is Muslim and often makes derisive remarks about Christians.) Martha was getting so squirmy, and I was exhausted and sweating like a dirty runner on MARTA after a long run on the 4th of July—all I had left keeping her from screaming even as I was overwhelmed by tears at this man's response to our family. ***Let it not be missed the role that Liza played!!!!*** The judge was so impressed that we had brought a mother along and said nobody with wicked intentions brings their mom along."

(See **Appendix 9** for copies of the emails Jane sent back from Uganda over a month's time.)

Here is my journal account of the September 23, 2011, homecoming of the expanded Gilbert family:

We gathered for an hour at the top of the airport escalator waiting for Martha Jane and family. It was a glorious celebration. When Martha arrived in the arms of her tear-filled mother, she played to the crowd instead of being terrified. Jane & Martha probably visited with everyone there including Sara Chapman, Walter, Carson, Holle, Sean, Caroline, and more. There were easily 50 or 60. ... We loaded the seven large suitcases onto Ted's truck. JoElyn & I walked Jane & Martha to the far end of the parking lot to the Gilbert family (5) car. We ended up eating with them as Martha threw the Cheerios on the floor and spread the applesauce over her face. It was one or two in the morning Uganda time. Chad went from falling asleep in the car to being asleep in his bed at home.

As I had rested in comfort back home getting these reports, I'd written this question: "Lord, what are You doing in Uganda in the lives of Jane, Terrell, Ellie, Chad, Martha Jane, and Liza?" Some of my answer came in the form of Jane's October 12 *Compelling Grace* blog, "Life Through Death":

"What was I shown, or given sight to see, or just on the brink of seeing that pushes my attention back to the place that was so very hard (i.e., our month in Uganda)?

"'But those who suffer he delivers in their suffering; he speaks to them in their affliction.'—Job 36:15

"Ever since Adam and Eve broke their covenant with God, redemption comes through suffering. God delivers every single one of His children in their suffering. He speaks to me in my affliction.

"Over and over there [Uganda], I was shown my weakness in ways I couldn't pretend otherwise. Over and over there I saw my selfishness, my entitlement, my impatience, my critical attitude, my lack of love, my lack of faith and so on. And over and over again there I was shown His kindness, His generosity, His patience,

His compassion and His love in ways I couldn't miss. When I am less, He becomes more to me. Here I am more, and too quickly, He becomes less to me."

The huge positive in Jane's time in Africa, and the reason she has this surprising longing to go back is summed up in these words of hers: "When I am less, He becomes more to me." And, for myself (Chuck) I would add:

"I will give you a new heart, and I will put a new Spirit in you. I will take away your heart of stone and give you a heart of flesh" (Ezekiel 36:26).

Post-Trip Life with Martha Jane

Around the time of Jane's "Life Through Death" blog post, she came, with "squirmy Martha Jane" in her arms, and spoke to an AYA chapel. She followed Pastor Elijah, who had spoken and had shown a film of his Ugandan orphanage. Derrick presented Jane with a gift of diapers—from the sublime to the everyday realities.

Here's a babysitting report for the evening of November 5, 2011:

We babysat for Chad and Martha Jane (Ellie was at Emily's). I changed Martha Jane's diaper when she woke up, and for the first time she clung to my neck. It felt good.

Martha Jane, you're going to feel left out when you read this next one from December 5, 2011, but remember, you were not even a year-and-a-half at this point. If you hadn't gotten this sleep, you wouldn't have grown to be the fine and healthy young lady that you are today:

As Terrell headed out to join in a small group of Walter's closest friends in a celebration of Walter's 40th birthday, Martha Jane slept at the Gilbert house under supervision of the monitor, and JoElyn, Jane, Ellie, and Chad had pizza here. We watched The Grinch movie.

Chapter 3: How I Knew It Was Time to Retire from Education

I'm not used to not being liked. Being well-liked has been a campaign of my life. But AYA's sixth grade class had maybe four or five fairly conscientious kids out of the class of twelve. The rest didn't like much about school; and they saw me as a soft touch when I came in to teach the Values class once a week.

Byron was a master at pushing buttons—emotional buttons, that is. I don't remember what I told him to do, but he point-blank refused to do it. In all my years of working with students, I had never been up against such stout disrespect and quiet intransigence. I could feel my temperature rising, as they say. I don't have an issue with high blood pressure, but I felt my face turn red and my head feeling that it was going to pop. Out of my mouth came I-don't-know-what, but I clearly had lost control of myself for the moment. As Dad used to tell us, when you "lose your temper," you are the same as if you were insane.

Stephanie Simpson, daughter of our kindergarten teacher, almost smirked as this was going on. While the change on her face was barely perceptible, I read it out of my peripheral vision as saying, "Mr. Johnston, now I've lost all respect for you.

"I don't care about the schoolwork in this class or the others. I will put forth a minimum effort. I will only participate in discussion reluctantly. I know I'm smart, but I don't care." This was written all over Stephanie, though never stated. Three older Simpson brothers were leaders and high achievers. One of them, Bryce, who had just graduated from AYA the year before, was at King's Ridge on a full scholarship. She wasn't going to follow.

Stephanie had been my project; I wanted to be that teacher that would ignite her interest in academics, the one she would speak of years later as a teacher that changed her life. Now I had blown that opportunity. Her respect I sought, Byron's not so much.

So I had spent my life curbing my hair-trigger temper by just absorbing whatever might be thrown at me, letting it quickly pass through and out of my mind, and then pushing it down into the part of my body that neither thinks nor feels. This meant that I rarely lost my temper, and it never felt good when I did.

I probably forcefully took Byron out of the classroom and down the hall to Derrick. Whatever precisely happened, I had lost any chance to have a positive impact on his young life, I lost the respect of the rest of the class, and figuratively I lost my mind—if only for a split second.

Chapter 4: The Start of Grove Park Renewal

I retired from AYA in August 2012, and on April 19, 2013, JoElyn and I attended an AYA event at which teachers were awarded a stipend out of the Chuck Johnston Legacy Fund. At the event, Sam Dimon overheard JoElyn saying to Benjamin Wills, "I'm concerned about the buzzard real estate agents floating around Grove Park trying to pick off properties on the cheap for absentee owners. That does nothing to enhance the sense of community that has made Grove Park distinctive."

After a lively luncheon and a meaningful awards ceremony, maybe two hours after JoElyn had made her remark, I was walking Sam and Cheryl back to their rental car to return to the airport and home when Sam said, "I think I can help with that problem in your neighborhood."

"What problem is that, Sam?" I had not heard what Sam had overheard JoElyn say earlier.

"If you would be willing to run it, I could create a fund to try to get out ahead of some of the absentee investors."

I agreed in principle to Sam's proposal. He said he would go home and put on paper details of what he was thinking. I speculated with Terrell and Mary Stuart Iverson (who launched several of us AWPC members into our Grove Park homes) about the size of the fund in Sam's mind. We wouldn't go higher than $200,000 in our wildest dreams. Imagine our gasp when Sam came forward several days later with a $2 million proposal.

Terrell did the paperwork to form a limited liability corporation (LLC). Sam was indifferent whether we formed as a non-profit or for-profit. His intention was the same—to make a Kingdom Investment which he did not intend to recoup. We considered the ramification of several names (e.g., Grove Park Neighborhood Restoration, Grove Park Community) and decided on Grove Park Renewal.

Here, from 2013, is what we set out to accomplish:

"Grove Park is on the cusp of changing. It is too close to the heart of the city not to go through the gentrification that has already occurred in other close-in neighborhoods. If no one intervenes, absentee investors will gain most of the benefit of the change, many by just sitting on often boarded-up property. If those with a social conscience intervene, then the current residents, who have weathered the downturn in the health of Grove Park, will be able to remain in their homes and enjoy the returning sense of community. The aspiration of Grove Park Renewal is 'gentrification with justice.'

"Grove Park was carved out of a farm in the '20s and '30s into a lovely white neighborhood of wide streets shaded by towering oaks and elms. Many of the streets, as they went north and south off of the Bankhead Highway, had wide median parks that enhanced the ambiance for the entire subdivision. 'White flight' occurred in the 1960s, and Grove Park became a middle-class black neighborhood. It remained a lovely family neighborhood until the late '80s. What we wish to restore is the sense of community consisting of folks of all ages, of varied economic groups, singles and families, black and white—folks who contribute to meaningful social interaction in a community defined by care for one another.

"(We will actively market to those who want a community consisting of folks … who contribute to meaningful social interaction in a community defined by care for one another. There are no restrictions based on race, nationality, religion, or sexual preference.)"

Hessel Baker, a fellow AWPC elder at the time, came alongside me to help. Why? Because he was hooked by the GPR vision and its synchronization with what he had been doing for years.

As of January 2016, I passed the reins over to Hessel and returned to an area closer to my skill sets—the writing of my memoirs. Hessel hired Justin Bleeker, with a graduate degree in City Planning and Real Estate, to move into Grove Park from Los Angeles and to be GPR's "man on the ground." I had been able to acquire thirty-nine properties. Acquisitions now stand at more than sixty. GPR has played a role in bringing to our Grove Park footprint the ministries of PAW Kids, Restore Life, Mentor Life, and those of Swift Graham, Taylor Pruitt, and others.

I moved on as administrator; but the true founder, Sam Dimon, has continued on with new vigor and with new on-the-ground partners. And the impact of Grove Park Renewal continuously grows larger.

Chapter 5: Hundred-Mile Wilderness, September 4–13, 2015

In the several months surrounding his seventy-fifth birthday, my friend and role model Elliot Galloway ran three marathons—one in Greece in October, the traditional Atlanta Thanksgiving marathon in November, and the 75th Anniversary Boston Marathon in April. I knew twenty years before I approached my own seventy-fifth birthday that I would not run one marathon, much less three, when I turned seventy-five. (Elliot and I were exactly twenty years apart in age, he born in late November 1920; I, in early December 1940.)

But I needed some means of marking this day. I hit upon the famed Hundred-Mile Wilderness in Maine, which, by the time one climbs to the end of the Appalachian Trail and back down Mt. Katahdin, is actually 120 miles. Three years ahead, I recruited a band of five other "brothers" to make the trek with me. The meals at each stop, the weight of everything going in our backpacks, and the spots for our overnight camping were all meticulously planned months ahead by Richard Pitman and Will Stoll. And off we went.

Following are remembrances I jotted down shortly after arriving back into the security of a world I knew better than I knew the wilderness:

The first day I doubted myself; the next morning I felt restored. The second day I had moments of wondering, "Why am I doing this?"

Realizing along in day three that my slower-than-anticipated pace was throwing off our mileage each day and the arriving at camping sites in time to enjoy some daylight and hang-out time, we used the device of slower group and faster group so that one group could get a head start on setting up camp and supper. It took me two or three days to fully grasp that nobody minded, that the spirit of all getting across the finish line together was the DNA of the group.

Each would take his turn with me. I was always one of the last two or three into camp as supper was started and tarps up. (At the Bangor Airport, Peter said matter-of-factly when discussing headlamp longevity that I spent more headlamp hiking hours than anyone, and my headlamp battery lasted.)

I will long remember sweetness about the attention Richard (M.D.) gave me when I gashed my left elbow when falling against a rock in negotiating a narrow passageway.

I grew to not mind that I was an encumbrance. I saw a teamwork form such as I've never experienced. A most seasoned outdoorsman, going for his fiftieth summit, Will Stoll spent much time walking with me at what must have been painfully slow for him. He blew up my air mattress on occasions and laid out my sleeping bag. Strangely I wasn't embarrassed.

Peter, Will, Justin, and I sat at an oasis, an unexpected restaurant, just as we completed the Hundred-Mile Wilderness. As we drank an afternoon beer (and I had a lobster poor boy), I asked Justin, Peter, and Will if I could go up Mount Katahdin with them; and I asked it sincerely since I could be more than an encumbrance—I could endanger their lives. They instantly responded, "We're doing it!"

Thus unfolded the next day an amazing feat of encouragement on upward walks that made the muscles burn. Then, with one soulmate ahead of me and two behind, we were hand-over-hand rock climbing. We paused often to let people pass. We took pictures. Will took pictures all the way up and at the top.

Peter asked me as we rested at the summit with some water and trail food, "What's the one word that comes to your mind?" My immediate response: FEAR.

It was clearly an emotional moment for Will, to have reached the fiftieth summit, the last of the highest peak in each of the fifty states. He lingered by himself for a few minutes as Justin, Peter, and I began our descent. Will couldn't linger long on his incredible feat. He felt, I sensed, that his job wasn't finished until he got me down the mountain alive.

I tried not to look ahead or do much looking out into the magnificent distance.

As we entered each of two rock-climbing segments, I couldn't see over the edges, and that gave me fear. Will at places would tell me exactly where to put each foot and each hand.

I had felt new energy with food, water, and rest at the top. After about two of the 5.2 miles down, the energy waned and I felt I was depleted of energy. Then I felt I was calling on muscles and will power that might not be there. I guess I've never truly been as close to *empty*.

Towards the end, Richard and Terrell had decided to slow their pace and be more contemplative. Bypassing the summiting of Mount Katahdin, they had arrived in the small Maine town of Millinocket a half-day ahead of us.

After being too late down off the mountain to catch the shuttle and sitting exhausted, wondering how we were going to get to Millinocket, here comes Terrell striding over the bridge to our rescue. He looked bigger and cleaner and more energetic than I had remembered him being. Sitting in the bucket seat of Warren and Sandy's Subaru (much like the feeling I had a short while later when I settled into a soft straw chair at the Appalachian Trail Lodge) I felt so luxurious after having only sat on stones, logs or the ground for eight days.

Here are some of my end-of-the-trail high points:

✓ The feeling of hot water in the shower, and putting on clean clothes.
✓ Walking down the street with Terrell in the picturesque town of Millinocket; how good it felt on the legs to walk free of pack and trekking poles.
✓ Joining Warren and Sandy at our dinner/celebration place, seeing Richard with them and the pleasure the three of them seemed to be having in conversation. Warren and Sandy being there at the finish was a real heart warmer for me, more than I might have thought it would be.
✓ My meal of lobster Newburg and Katahdin Red Ale and the stories from Richard and Terrell about Big Foot and his brand of trail magic / trail justice; his ability to drive at top speed while rolling and smoking a joint.
✓ Sitting with Terrell, Richard, Will, Peter, and Justin at the "pub" in the Bangor airport with beer and food, I remember (even now) emotions of pleasure, weariness, and sadness. I likely will not be as close to five other men as I am with these, my mates (Terrell Gilbert, Justin Hitchcock, Peter Pettit, Richard Pittman, Will Stoll) on this Maine adventure, at this moment. And now we go back and split up. (In fact, four of us boarded and left Richard and Will sitting forsaken in the standby seats.)
✓ I have learned that I have serious limitations; I am not invincible (as maybe I subconsciously thought before the hike).
✓ I will henceforth accept help gladly, maybe even ask for it.

✓ I want to live as I hiked, slowly and purposefully.

Following is Psalm 121, read on our hike on more than one occasion and sung on the trail by Richard. And, as if by chance, it was the Scripture chosen for solace by JoElyn while we were climbing Mt. Katahdin:

"I lift up my eyes to the hills. From where does my help come? My help comes from the Lord, who made heaven and earth.

"He will not let your foot be moved; he who keeps you will not slumber. Behold, he who keeps Israel will neither slumber nor sleep.

"The Lord is your keeper; the Lord is your shade on your right hand. The sun shall not strike you by day, nor the moon by night.

"The Lord will keep you from all evil; he will keep your life. The Lord will keep your going out and your coming in from this time forth and forevermore."

Summer of 2015 Appalachian Trail hike, in prep for the
Hundred-Mile Wilderness to come in September.

Chapter 6: JoElyn and The Goat Farm

JoElyn was an art major at Auburn, she has worked in commercial art on a Coke account and with a TV station (WQXI, now WXIA), she has taught art and art history to elementary and college students and all ages in between, but she had not had her real shot at fulfilling her passion—to paint. You just can't sustain losing yourself in your art when you have no place to spread out your paints and stow your canvases. You can't do it "catch as catch can," particularly if you are entertaining dinner guests as the headmaster's wife or tending to the unpredictable needs of children, or bending to the demands of your husband.

When I finally took my gaze off of perpetuating my own success, I looked at one whose needs all along I have been supposed to put ahead of my own. I saw one who had given up her own ambitions to feed and support mine. She was then in her latter sixties, I in my early seventies. What to do? Well, I kept inviting people over for dinner. In other words, I was slow to acquire a changed heart. If I were going to do for her what she has done for me for over forty years, I had better figure it out and get a move on it.

JoElyn's sacrifice for me reminded me vividly of the story behind Albrecht Durer's pen-and-ink drawing, *The Praying Hands*. Albrecht and his brother Albert made a pact that one would work for four years and support the other in art school. Then they would switch roles. Both brothers had substantial talent at fine drawing. Albrecht won the toss to go first to school. When he returned four years later with a budding art reputation, he raised a toast of profound gratitude to his brother Albert for providing the wherewithal for Albrecht's art training. "It's too late for me," his brother responded with tears in his eyes. He couldn't hold the glass to return the toast. His hands were too crippled from four years of working in the mines. It's said to be those hands that Durer drew to become probably his best-known work.

Was my turn to put JoElyn's inner needs center-stage coming too late? No, I pray not. May it be that this is the exact right time. I contend that her art heritage from her mom (working at the *New Yorker* in the company of James Thurber) and dad (creator of window displays for Montgomery Ward Department Stores in New York and Chicago), her studies at Auburn, her work in commercial art and TV, her teaching at Brookstone, Berry College, Pace Academy, and Atlanta Youth Academy all are a part of who she is as an artist in the twenty-first century. In God's timing, she wouldn't have been seasoned earlier to fully emerge as an artist. It's not that she didn't paint some along the way, but now she has her first studio and has hours set up each week when she's in there painting. She's begun building an inventory, preparing for her own art show that finally occurred in February '19 in collaboration with fashion designer and friend Marian Collier.

The Goat Farm is a set of industrial buildings on Atlanta's Westside dating back to the late 1800s. They have the look of the old cotton mills in New England. The enormous beams in the ceilings and the creaky and steep old stairways give it a charm befitting the artistic bent of painters, photographers, fashion designers, and entrepreneurs who inhabit various studios. JoElyn and I had only visited the Goat Farm once in our lives—for a festival back in May 2011—but we had the impression of it as a happening place. As JoElyn sought studio space to no avail in the spring and early summer of '15, Terrell threw out, "Why don't you try the Goat Farm?" It seemed to us to be a stretch, but JoElyn pursued it.

Here's what I recorded for July 2, 2015:

The big miracle was JoElyn's meeting with Anthony and the realization that joining The Goat Farm is so much more that renting a studio. There is a program called "Bell Jar" that fosters a lot of interaction among the 400+ studio holders, the pursuits of whom range the gamut of creativity—start-up efforts, tech companies, and artists in all fields of art. The program of connectivity is called Bell Jar: "Bell Jar is designed to break patterns and create new thinking. Bell Jar seeks to get different fields of practice interacting and exploring unfamiliar systems of thought and solutions."

While the Bell Jar program initially might not have been as Utopian as described, being at the Goat Farm has been awfully nice for JoElyn and her art. Just being around other producing and art-filled people has been stimulating to her work. Kiki Slaughter is quiet and mostly to herself, yet she has been a nice next-door young friend. Marian Collier is much more extroverted, and she keeps her studio door open. She creates eye-popping clothing designs using African patterns of cloth and designs. Colorful and older Mrs. Kimbrel works alongside Marian two days a week as her seamstress. They are quite a pair, full of life and unbounded creativity.

That leaves the multiple noisy photographers. The studio walls only go ten feet up, leaving space of another twenty feet to the roof, so voices and laughter and music carry throughout. Because Kiki and JoElyn and maybe a few others work solo and out of sight, it would be easy for the photographers and their numerous photo subjects to assume that they are the only ones "at home" on the floor, or so they seem to assume.

The two primary photographers, Mark and M.A., are so friendly and outgoing to her, it would be hard for JoElyn to get too upset about the racket. She just listens to classical music and loses herself in her painting.

I think JoElyn started in her studio maybe August 1, 2015, and a month into it, here is what I recorded: *Hearing JoElyn's report on her day at the Goat Farm is glorious; yesterday she attended a hands-on session there with the blacksmith and spent an hour making one nail (and burned her finger).*

When JoElyn doesn't return home until 6 o'clock or later, I know that it has been a good day painting. She is radiant, even happier than when she's enjoying a dinner and wine in a fine restaurant. This is when I know she was born to paint. God planted deep inside her talent and inspiration that springs forth when she stands before a blank canvas.

Because she taught art and had her students produce a piece in the style of everyone from the Greeks to Monet to Jacob Lawrence, she can't just repeat the same successful creation over and over. She's got to be moving in styles and subject matter from here to there and beyond. She may have some idea of what she wants to paint on a given day, but something she hadn't even imagined may come forth on the canvas by the end of the afternoon. Her "floating lines" pop with color and texture. I wouldn't have imagined that she could paint numerous of these striped paintings and have each so different from the other. On top of that, one can mount the canvas vertically or horizontally. Turn it one way and it might remind me of the trunks of trees; turn it the other and it might bring to my mind a lakeshore with fields and mountains beyond. Or maybe it doesn't have to remind me of anything—just lovely shapes and textures and colors.

As much as anything, it's the bright and happy colors that unify JoElyn's florals, cityscapes, landscapes, stripes and abstracts of all sorts. Was it the Fauves who shocked the art world with their bright colors? It's interesting that while teaching Matisse and Van Gogh to her students, their bold colors must have attached to JoElyn's art soul.

Here's a journal account from March 2016 that exemplifies why the Goat Farm studio was so special:

The way God is working in JoElyn's life is nothing but a miracle, the answer to a lifetime of prayers. It's a demonstration of "never give in, never give in, never give in." (As Winston Churchill said.) We are not smart enough (Well, maybe Terrell was) to plant her in the middle of other fine artists at The Goat Farm—how cool is that. She is being noticed. She is encouraged. God doesn't choose to make her set sales records overnight; but by the slow & steady pace of her emerging, she is finding "her voice" on canvas. Yesterday was the second day of "open studio;" it was a lovely day and the crowd was big. While she had no sales, she was pumped by those who took an interest and entered into conversation with her. To top it off (in the miracle arena), Tyree & Keenan Rush came and enjoyed JoElyn's art, went to other studios and then back; and we ended up going to dinner at Satto's Thai Restaurant with the two of them and Aisha & Matthias. We had 2 hours+ of lively conversation & good food. It was a storybook ending to the day to share life with the four of them, with Tyree & Keenan talking about how much they have retained from JoElyn's art classes.

JoElyn with one of her paintings in her Grove Park studio and gallery, where a percentage of her sales goes to benefit Grove Park Renewal and families of PAW Kids.

JoElyn was invited to apply to participate in an Emerging Artist Exhibit at the Anne Irwin Gallery. She was juried and selected to submit four of her works. How cool was it that at age seventy, JoElyn was designated "an emerging artist"? At the opening of the August 2016 show, JoElyn's impressionistic floral still life was the first painting to be bought.

Let it not be missed that on multiple occasions Evelyn Anne has stepped forward to provide the technology acumen that JoElyn needs and lacks for everything from creating websites to entering paintings in competitions, to creating and getting out invitations to shows and to the twice-a-year open studios at The Goat Farm. Jane and family have been cheerleaders and have gathered their friends to come to various showings of JoElyn's works. Jane, as well as Evelyn Anne, has proven to be a helpful commentator on JoElyn's works-in-progress. As for me, my only comment ever is to beg her "not to overwork" a piece. It may only be half-finished, but I always think it looks great as it is.

To date JoElyn has yet to "be discovered" as an artist. Is God in that timing? We think so, yet once again, He seems to be taking His time. She has sold some paintings, certainly, and she has given others as gifts. She will say, I think, that she will paint whether or not she sells another painting. It's in her; she's got to get it out. Yet some sales would help solve what is becoming a storage problem.

And the encouragement that others like what you've done well enough to buy it would provide further encouragement.

Love Art—A Collaboration Between Painter and Fashion Designer

Jump a few months beyond the above writing and come to February 21, 2019, and the monumental Love Art event at Monday Night Brewing's Garage. This was a collaboration with Marian Collier, fashion designer extraordinaire, and JoElyn, the painter on canvas. The event gained much festivity by the inclusion of Stacy Quiros and the Whitefield Jazz Band.

An invitation to Love Art was sent by Hannah West via Paperless Post to 450 people; and this press release appeared on the calendar for Arts Atlanta, on Facebook, and on other social media outlets:

"On the evening of February 21, 6 to 9, one week after Valentine's Day, at Monday Night Brewing's Beltline location (The Garage, 933 Lee Street), two unlikely artists are collaborating in an invigorating event dubbed Love Art.

"JoElyn, a painter with acrylic on canvas in her early 70s, and Marian, much younger and an eminent clothing designer in African fabrics, have come together to form this unusual collaboration. The proximity of their studios in The Goat Farm has helped forge this friendship.

"In the spirit and excitement of collaboration, JoElyn has for the first time created art on fabric which Marian has turned into coats and skirts and dresses. Some of these striking joint creations will be on display and for sale.

"Music for the event will be provided by Whitefield Academy's Jazz Band led by clarinetist Stacy Quiros. Monday Night Brewing will be selling its many flavors of craft beer."

The morning of February 21st dawned, and thus began a long and glorious day for Love Art. It was a massive undertaking wherein we hosted maybe 200-plus guests. It began about 9:45 a.m. when Anthony and I started loading the PAW Kids' van with JoElyn's 65 canvases. Unloading at The Garage took me, Mike, Anthony, and JoElyn. Setting it up took Jane, EA, Larenzia, Mike, Anthony and Marian's crew. Breaking it down took Taylor, Terrell, Jane, Mike, plus Wesley Wills and Marian's crew. It was after 11 p.m. when we got everything in the house and us to bed.

There were nine coats or gowns created out of fabric on which JoElyn had created colorful art; Marian had arranged to have all nine worn by live models. Initially the models posed near the entrance as motionless manikins. Then later they walked around, posing for photo shoots and conversations with the guests. There were a couple of hats that Marian crafted out of leftover painted fabric.

Larenzia was the greatest help to JoElyn in setting up JoElyn's canvases in an attractive and beguiling fashion. Stacy Quiros and three boys making up the

Whitefield Jazz Band added immensely to the immediate sense that this was a momentous event. While the evening served as exposure for JoElyn's art and for the wearable art that emerged out of the collaboration, there were not that many sales that evening. There was a preliminary sale to Monica Kaufman of a pink and green (AKA sorority colors) floral collaboration jacket for $400. JoElyn earned $2,000 in sales, enough to cover the cost of the Garage ($1,250), the food ($233), and smaller expenses.

As JoElyn moved her studio from The Goat Farm (which was closing in October '19 for renovation) to the Dwell office building at 1566 Hollowell Parkway, a new chapter opened on her budding life as a painter. (This building, incidentally, was one I had a hand in buying for Grove Park Renewal.)

Chapter 7: A Letter to Jonathan

Jonathan Clausen married Evelyn Anne Johnston December 4, 2010. After completing his Air Force service in his very early twenties, Jonathan embarked on a thirty-year career as an air traffic controller. He completed that career with the Federal Aviation Administration with a sixteen-year stint at the World's Busiest Airport, Atlanta's Hartsfield-Jackson.

Evelyn Anne and Jonathan in Germany

   With that sort of background and with many accolades for "keeping America's skies safe" in the face of "near misses," Jonathan was sought after for air traffic control work in numerous foreign capitals, assignments he was eligible for without adversely affecting his retirement. On the July date of the following letter, he was in the midst of an eighteen-month tour that brought him home once or twice and that gave Evelyn Anne the opportunity of meeting Jonathan in Germany when he would have his once-every-two-months ten-day leave:

Friday afternoon, July 29, 2016
Greetings, Jonathan.

   Perhaps it will be Saturday morning when you receive this. I sorta hope so because I like to think that you are getting better sleep there than when you were keeping the crazy schedule that you did here in Atlanta. It may not be so, but I have come to think of your weekly and monthly schedule there being more sane and more predictable.

   I've stayed up a bit longer this past week for trying to catch parts of the Democratic Convention. I couldn't stay up late enough to hear President Obama speak, but I heard a lot of the others: Cory Booker, Joe Biden, Bill Clinton, Chelsea, Hillary, and Michelle Obama. These words spoken by Michelle Obama Monday night were the most moving of any I heard all week:

   "That is the story of this country, the story that has brought me to this stage tonight, the story of generations of people who felt the lash of bondage, the shame of servitude, the sting of segregation, but who kept on striving and hoping and doing what needed to be done so that today, I wake up every morning in a house that was built by slaves—(applause)—and I watch my daughters—two beautiful, intelligent, black young women— playing with their dogs on the White House lawn. (Applause) ... So don't let anyone ever tell you that this country isn't great, that somehow we need to make it great again. Because this, right now, is the greatest country on earth."

   As JoElyn has expressed for both of us, we were moved by your and Evelyn Anne's sacrificial and substantial gift. It is safely ensconced in a travel fund that cannot be touched by watershed-management bills or grocery bills or for JoElyn's weekly wine bill. We will plan a trip for October, perhaps back to Jekyll; and just as has been true for you and Evelyn Anne, our being able to take such a trip and to have time to anticipate it, will be part of its fun and pleasure. Thanks, Jonathan!

   I understand you are developing an addiction—one of those glorious positive addictions—to the gym. You strengthen my resolve to be like you in that respect.

That you told us a few days ago that you had gone 10 days without smoking meant a lot to me—partly because of the health impact of such a self-imposed deprivation, but just as much because you trusted us with such a sensitive disclosure. Your health is important to me because I want for you the absence, as much as possible, of debilitating pains and worse. It's also important to me because you and Evelyn Anne are now living for each other; what affects one affects the other. I want you and Evelyn Anne to grow old together, just as it appears that God is granting to JoElyn and me. As good as our marriage has been all along (forty-five years), it is only getting stronger. This is truly a sweet season of marriage for both of us. I am grateful for these present years that we are sharing together.

You know, I think, how much JoElyn and I love you. That only grows deeper.

Chuck

The Clausens and their dog, Oscar, at their cabin in the Georgia mountains, summer 2020

Chapter 8: Chad's 12th Birthday Celebration in Auburn

Following is the account of our camping weekend, August 18-20, 2017:

Friday: I packed for the Chad birthday trip to Auburn. I had a visit with Herb and Marybeth focused on borrowing camping gear from them. I told Terrell that I would buy the groceries for Friday supper and Saturday breakfast, which I did at Publix with JoElyn. Home at 1:30 or so, I squeezed in a little nap. I was a little nervous about whether I was really up to handling the next thirty hours, both physically and in terms of adult-to-student interaction.

The eight boys going on the trip (Jayden, Jordon, Nigel, Edge, DJ, Reid, Henry, Chad) gathered at the Gilbert/Edgecomb homes to await Terrell's arrival from work, which came around 6. Evelyn Anne, having come down to spend the evening with JoElyn, was there for the send-off. DJ, Edge, and Henry rode with me; the other five with Terrell. Each of my three boys took a turn choosing Spotify songs the whole trip down. It became dark quickly upon our arrival in the Chewacla Camp Grounds, so it was challenging setting up the two tents (one for Terrell and me, the other for the eight boys) and cooking hot dogs. We pulled it all off.

I'm not sure what time it was when we got in the tents to go to sleep—my watch stayed on EDT and my phone was on CDT—but the boys were animated and even getting out of the tents, causing Terrell to have to either get out of our tent (not all that simple to do) or command from our tent instructions to go to sleep; one kid was still out of the tent and some of the others remained animated. I, who had intentionally left instruction-giving to Terrell, volunteered to get out and see what I could do. I got DJ back in the tent, and I stood quietly outside the tent by the mesh window and gave quiet instructions for a while until quiet prevailed. I walked around the tent or stood beside it for another fifteen minutes until I was fairly certain that quiet would prevail. Finally, we all entered into slumber land around 11:30/12:30, depending on which timepiece I was looking at. (The next morning Jayden said to me with a smile, "Granddaddy, you really spooked me out last night.")

Saturday: We all awoke a bit after the triathlon participants began to awake. I went and brushed my teeth and took a nice hot shower. We had cinnamon rolls, breakfast bars, and juice boxes for breakfast. We set out on a morning at Chewacla Lake by hiking maybe five miles total in the beautiful environs of the lake, watching the triathlon participants swim a long loop in the lake, run up the hill, put on bike shoes, and head out into the woods on the bike leg of the competition.

Chad, Terrell, and camping crew at Chewacla Lake

Terrell swam out to the dock in the lake with Jordan and Jayden hanging onto him because of their fear of the lake water. I stood by on the dock at the shore. The boys jumped continuously off of the high dive on the dock and had great fun. From there we took a fairly lengthy hike to the spectacular waterfalls. Chad led the way on rock climbing, which was on a major-league descent in which a fall could have caused death or major injury. By the grace of God, they made it quite a distance down and back up for a photo op beneath the initial falls from the lake. We were then back to the campsite where some helped more than others to pack up.

In Auburn, we parked in the Municipal Building parking lot quite a distance from Stoops Corner and the campus. We walked that long distance to an incredible lunch place, Cheeburger ("Big is Better"), where four of the boys ordered the full-pound hamburger. Three (Chad, Henry, DJ), for good or ill, finished theirs, and won a picture to hang on the restaurant wall of the three victors, pictures with a monster hamburger created like a stack of pillows. Once across the street on one of the multiple Auburn lawns, led by Jayden, our boys challenged a group of college Frisbee players to a game of touch football. Bring it on; let the game begin. Terrell and I died laughing watching. All of the players were laughing and having a truly joyful time. Our guys would break up their passes. We connected on one or two of our long passes. It morphed into tackle, which was much like big brother/little brother antics when five of our guys would jump on and bring down one of theirs. These boys, and three girls, were all a part of the campus Wesley Fellowship. ... We walked and walked and finally got in a long line to enter Auburn football's Fan Day, held in the team's indoor facility. The boys industriously set about gathering autographs and having great fun. The last stop was for a signature from Coach Gus Malzahn. We got to Stoops Corner where Terrell bought us each one of the famous lemonades—a last and needed energy shot. We got gas and drove back to Atlanta in tandem from 7:30 to 9:30 EDT.

Strangely, as Chad and I dropped off first Henry and then Reid, I felt elated. I felt God's hand in every aspect of the entire adventure. I showered and spent a most rewarding forty-five minutes with JoElyn with our drinks and good conversation, then retired a little before midnight.

Sunday morning: I slept for nine hours—from midnight to 9 a.m.—something I rarely do. I weighed in Friday morning at 138; I weighed in this morning at 133, evidence of the amount of exercise we got. My back was fine. I had a feeling of God and family love all about me. I got to touch base with all the Gilberts and, of course, JoElyn, when Terrell and Ellie headed for her soccer practice and the rest to Cornerstone, and I to a morning of the Psalms and of writing this account. I told Terrell I appreciated his care for me on the trip and the good time we had together.

Side notes: (1) While at Chewacla, a man from another campsite approached us to say that one of our boys had taken his little bag with contact stuff in it from the sink shelf in the shower/toilet room and had thrown it in the bushes outside. My first instinct was that this was a racial incident and that he was falsely accusing us. It turned out that one of Chad's guests had in fact done it. He came clean, and Terrell went with him to apologize to the man; the apology was well received. ... (2) The next morning, when we were packing to leave, there was a University of Kentucky football in the Jeep's back seat. I asked whose it was; this same kid said, "It's mine. I'm going to give it to Miss Caitlin." I recognized it as having been lying near the campground's basketball court with some other balls and Frisbees, and back it went. ... (3) Later, when the boys went in and spent time in the in-town Malone & Johnston bookstore, this same student showed Terrell and me two painted stones (orange and blue) that he had gotten in the store. "Did you buy them?" "No, they were free." Terrell went in and found that they were for sale, and the kid returned them. ... (4) Later, when we walked from the Fan Day site back to the car, Chad's same friend reached over a fence on the Auburn campus to grab a canned Sprite from a case that was stacked up there, which I saw and told him, "You don't take things that aren't yours," and he put it back.

Chapter 9: Trip to Vermont, 2017 — Journal Excerpts

Thursday, July 27 — From Atlanta to Boston:

JoElyn and I got everything together nicely, and climbed into Terrell's car for our ride to the airport. It was a nice opportunity to visit with Terrell. We got to the airport by 8, 90 minutes ahead of our 9:35 boarding for a 10 o'clock Jet Blue departure. We couldn't tell any difference between Jet Blue service and Delta. It was a smooth and comfortable flight, probably made more so because we both had books we were into (e.g., *City on the Verge* for me) ... The water taxi from Logan Airport took us to right in front of our Boston lodging, the Battery Wharf Hotel. We have a nice room with a view of the harbor. (Jonathan provided this room for us.) It was drizzly rain so we took a cab to meet Anne at her Hilton Hotel. There we had drinks and a bowl of nuts. Anne had only had one little pack of oatmeal crackers to eat all day. We walked to the Quincy Market. I was fascinated by a drummer playing on paint buckets and small pans. He was terrific, and he never stopped. He drew quite a crowd. When I took out my wallet, he said, "I smell a twenty coming." I said "no," put my three dollars in, and he gave me a high five (which he did to each donor). ... We found Mare Oyster Bar on Hanover Street, the restaurant that Warren had recommended and where we had reservations. We were seated at 7:15 on the porch where, delightfully, the roof was rolled back when the blue sky peeked through what had been clouds and rain all day. JoElyn had salmon; Anne and I had Risotto di Mare (full of shrimp, scallops, calamari, and lobster on top.) We walked back past a statue of Samuel Adams to Anne's hotel, and caught a cab from there back to our hotel. We slept well.

Friday, July 28 — South Royalton, Vermont — Warren and Sandy's thirty-ninth wedding anniversary:

I got up at 5:30, showered, had my quiet time, made some room coffee for JoElyn. We went to the Battery Wharf Hotel restaurant and had oatmeal with raisins and extra fruit and coffee. ... Our doorman called Larry, his friend in a black limo, to take us by to pick up Anne and go to the South Station, where we caught the Dartmouth Coach to Hanover. We had front seats, enjoyed reading, and saw some gorgeous countryside in Massachusetts and into New Hampshire. Warren was waiting for us at a beautiful new bus terminal in Lebanon. We drove around, bought some produce at a garden market, and went into the Cartoon School, started by two graduates of SCAD in Savannah. At this point we were walking around White River Junction. Anne was interested because Clyde loves to draw cartoons.

She bought him a Cartoon School t-shirt. Sandy left work and joined us at a lovely Turkish restaurant. I had lentil soup and six little falafel balls. Sandy went back to work. We went by a wonderful wine store (Norwich Wine Spirits, Burton House, Elm Street, Norwich) where we bought gift wines for Warren and Sandy, as guest gifts combined with 39th anniversary gifts from the three of us.

We then took the scenic route to South Royalton, traveling some on non-paved roads. … After settling in at the invigorating home on the hill, overlooking Warren's garden, Sandy's beautiful flowers, and the mountains beyond, we took a "walk in the woods" with Izzy and Amalda. There is a designated spot known by the dogs where the leashes come off and they are free to run. They know the route, and they come when Warren calls them. The woods are "dark and deep," but the trail is mowed and maintained by neighbor Bob who owns it and mows it. At a point back around and entering again into neighboring houses, the leashes go back on and we find Sandy back home and waiting for us. We had Prosecco on the porch and snap peas dipped in a yogurt sauce. We then each took jobs preparing for supper. Anne and JoElyn peeled the shrimp, I washed the lettuce (Anne made me run it back through the spinner again), while Warren and Sandy prepared the main dish—a spaghetti pasta with the shrimp and all sorts of other herbs and oils. It was so delicious. Before finishing preparation, we went back out on the porch and watched a lovely sunset. After dinner at the table, we retired again to the porch with wine (and my beer). Before retiring, we all had a tiny glass of Ice Wine, a sweet dessert wine.

Saturday, July 29:

After leisure for quiet time, coffee, rich sprout-bread and granola, JoElyn and I dashed over to South Royalton to watch the Old Time Parade. It was a not-to-be-missed small-town event. Tractors and fire engines (from surrounding little towns) dominated; but there were also floats with kids throwing candy. We visited with the chief of police (the only full-time policeman for South Royalton). He actually lives in Randolph, down the road. … We departed for a drive, with a stop for lunch, that lasted all afternoon. We did get to Woodstock in time to hear Paul Muldoon read some of his poetry. He waved me off when I was taping him (to send to Dillon), but at the end we bought a book and made the connection with Dillon. I couldn't hear every line that he read, nor did I understand all of the poems, but I left with a great sense of peace, of timelessness. I chatted briefly with a dapper gentleman (getting in his Mini convertible) who liked Paul Muldoon's part in a podcast he listens to. We both agreed that his long pauses were a part of Muldoon's charm. … We had drinks on the porch, and then had a bountiful shrimp Low Country Boil, also on the deck. Anne introduced the topic of moral dilemmas: does it matter that mankind survives nuclear bombs and climate change? Should Anne overcome her reluctance to have a dog because the dog will probably outlive her? Should Warren and Sandy share with the family ("inter-generational financial planning") their will and their finances? … JoElyn and I were the first to toddle off to bed as midnight approached.

Sunday, July 30 — Last morning in Vermont:

We woke up in South Royalton and went to bed in Atlanta. That's like time travel. … In the morning, we had plenty of time for quiet, for packing, for breakfast, and for sharing love with Anne, Warren, and Sandy. Warren and Sandy drove us to the Dartmouth Coach terminal. We read and rode to Logan Airport, I sitting next to an incoming freshman at Dartmouth whose American family lives in Dubai, and JoElyn next to a black female marketing professor from Dartmouth. Anne got off first at the Delta terminal, and we disembarked at Jet Blue. … It was noon, and we didn't fly until 4:15. As another of God's blessings, we were standby and then on a 1:45 flight that put us in at 4:15 instead of 7:15. Terrell, Chad, and MJ picked us up. They were in a remake-their-back-yard project—creating a path out of rubberized ground cover. It looks beautiful. Ellie's project was to redo her room, which looked beautiful, and Jane had painted furniture for MJ's room. Chad and Jane were painting the driveway with a roller.

Chapter 10: Family Beach Vacation at Tybee Island, 2018 — Journal Excerpts

Saturday, July 21:

We find ourselves in a glorious house at Tybee, right at the point on the south end of the island where the river and the ocean meet. … We got here shortly after 3, picked up the keys, and pulled up to the gate at 1923 Chatham just behind Evelyn Anne and Jonathan, who were just realizing that they needed a gate code. We pulled our cars into the garage and used the elevator to great advantage in unloading luggage and grocery and kitchen items. Having been stopped by the police (90 mph) and stopping for groceries at Kroger, the Gilberts arrived closer to 5.

Sunday, July 22 — Evelyn Anne's thirty-fifth birthday:

The experience for the seven of us at All Saints Episcopal was significant. From all directions, good folks handed us prayer books and hymnals. … In the postlude part of the service, they sang to the seven of us their welcome song. June, the priest, preached on Jesus' washing of feet, as in the stained-glass window just beside where Ellie and Chad were sitting. At the conclusion of her homily, she said all are worthy of having their feet washed—"everyone, everyone, everyone." That resonated with us. ... I spent some time on the beach, and JoElyn and I walked almost to the pier until the crowds of highly diversified people got too thick. This was, after all, Sunday afternoon, the busiest beach day of the week. And it was a beautiful day. ... We had a truly wonderful celebration of EA's birthday. She received iTunes and Chick-fil-A gift cards from us and two vinyls from the Gilberts—Ben Folds Five and a premier punk rock group, Fugazi. Terrell and I introduced EA to our newly invented bottle cap game. Laughter abounded from the three of us while the other seven labored to clean up the kitchen, a task made harder with the dishwasher inoperative.

Monday, July 23:

We went for a run; I have only one gear, and Jane graciously would wait for me to catch up at certain junctures. JoElyn enjoyed coming around the other way and meeting us. Ellie encountered muscle soreness and called her dad to come pick her up. Her condition compels her to drink more water and to take in more calories. ... JoElyn and I went on a 9 a.m. walk—out for 30 minutes and back. ... I had a good time watching Jonathan fly his drone; he enjoyed sharing it with me. He is taking photos from on high. ... Ellie, Chad, and MJ spent a lot of time together in the hot tub up on the crow's nest. ... In much of the 5-to-7 window, we six adults were on the third-floor deck together overlooking the ocean. ... During this delightful time (when Jonathan was fully engaged and fully funny), one of Terrell's beer cans blew off the deck to the lawn below. So, when he finished the next beer, he threw it off the deck in the direction of the other one, much to the delight of all. A third was put at our feet to see what the strong wind would do, and it followed the earlier two. ... Jonathan grilled shrimp that EA had marvelously marinated. EA also produced a wonderful bean salad to go with the shrimp, the feature of which was the avocado.

Tuesday, July 24:

JoElyn and I went on a beach walk all the way to the water tower and back. I stopped in at the pier to go to the bathroom. JoElyn got a little dizzy at one point, but drinking her water that she was carrying seemed to alleviate that. ... I continue to read and enjoy *The Buried Giant* (that Lynn Weigel had recommended). ... We had a lovely supper, with Jonathan, at my request, sharing with us some of his highly successful tennis career as a ranked youth player. ...

Wednesday, July 25:

A joyful Jane came and got me for our run ... While I was no faster, somehow I felt slightly better this run than I had Monday. ... Around noon Jane paddled (on our paddleboard) the two of us over to Little Tybee. It was hard work for her

Gilberts form a pyramid— Chad, MJ, and Ellie, with Terrell and Jane as the foundation, July 2018.

going over—less so coming back. There is a tropical stunning and stark beauty there unmatched yet comparable to the Clausens' deck [in Ellijay] or one of the mountaintops on the Hundred-Mile Wilderness. It was a joy sharing those moments with Jane. … We had a worthy *bocce ball* tournament on the beach around 5. Both grandparents did well enough in the early go that we were accused of practicing at home. Terrell and I made it to the finals, and Terrell prevailed— as did good sportsmanship all around. … We had crab cakes and "poetry night," both highlight events. Evelyn Anne prepared two crab cakes apiece with an avocado and basil sauce on top—that together with her homemade coleslaw. We circled the chairs on the second-floor porch and gathered during a fierce rain to read poetry. Jane led off, followed by Jonathan reading "Casey at the Bat." Martha Jane read a Shel Silverstein poem, and then she would intermittently read another. JoElyn read the poem "in the style of Langston Hughes" about the rent getting paid. Terrell read one from *Joy*, the book of 100 poems he had also given me. It was the beautiful nature poem about frogs on a mountain in Scotland. Jonathan came back later and read "The Road Not Taken"—this from a man who said one thing he didn't do was read poetry. … JoElyn and I cashed in a little after 9.

Thursday, July 26:
Evelyn Anne worked with me to clean up the transition from my previous

Lenovo laptop to this new one. (My laptop was stolen last week.) Just reminding me that I can control the brightness of my screen has greatly enhanced the readability of my screen. She was very patient and seemed to enjoy marking off each item on my "wish list" for computing improvements. … I read some in *The Buried Giant* as I'm probably in the last quarter of the book. I can see why Lynn Weigel was so excited about recommending the book. … Jonathan had a negative reaction to a medicine that the Minute Clinic gave him for his infected finger. It gave him shortness of breath. Needless to say, he stopped taking that medicine. … Supper was a wonderful array of pizzas that Terrell and Chad picked out at IGA. They were delicious. … We played a game wherein your team had to guess what was written on the piece of paper that you drew out of the bowl. It was fun. Unlike Charades, you got to speak out more clues. … And a good day was had by all (with the possible exception of Jonathan who was not feeling great).

(Note: For some reason I didn't journal the last few days of the week, but you get a flavor from what I have recorded of how important to all of us is our beach week.)

Chapter 11: An Adult Adoption

LaTonya Gates-Boston, at age forty-five, became our daughter by adoption as the account below details. After having first met in the fall of 2002, some five years later we were members of the same church, then eventually were playing a role in her starting her Grove Park ministry, and living two streets over from each other in Grove Park. Here is how the adoption came about:

Tuesday, July 31, 2018
Dear Dick, Mary Anne, Dillon, Guinn, Warren, Sandy, and Anne,

JoElyn and I are beginning steps for an adult adoption. This will, then, be your niece and first cousin to Rich, Clay, Kathleen, Kristin, and Devin.

We are in the process of adopting LaTonya Gates-Boston, age 45. We first knew LaTonya when she brought her son Anthony to AYA's 6th grade. He is the AYA graduate who flourished at AYA, went on a full scholarship to Whitefield, and then on to graduate from Morehouse. His

Our three daughters, Jane, LaTonya, and Evelyn Anne, at the Rice Awards
dinner, 2019

sister Larenzia followed him to AYA, then to Piney Woods Boarding
School below Jackson, Mississippi, and then on to graduate from
Mississippi Valley State University. They have both set new educational
highs for the family.

LaTonya has never known her birth father; in fact, the last name of
Gates given her at birth is that of her mother's husband who was not
LaTonya's biological father. LaTonya was born in the prison infirmary in
Rome, Georgia, and rescued from becoming a ward of the state by her
"grandmother" who retrieved her and carried her home to Atlanta in a
cardboard box. LaTonya's first "crib" was the lowest drawer of a chest-of-
drawers lovingly padded with a blanket. LaTonya had to live through
detoxification as a newborn.

LaTonya has never ceased longing for an earthly father. In fact, early
on she has called me "Dad," something until recently that I have taken to
be nothing more than a welcomed compliment imbedded in the black
culture. Apparently LaTonya had mentioned to her husband, Carlos, more
than once that she would love for JoElyn and me to adopt her. Carlos, a
practical man of few words, finally said, "Well, ask them."

When LaTonya did first mention it to us, I still didn't take it as a
serious entertainment of legal adoption as much as just an extension of her

love for us and of her appreciation for the roles we have played in her life and the lives of Anthony and Larenzia. First of all, I assumed it wasn't really legal for adults to adopt another adult. Then it dawned on me that we could possibly do something through the church that would further symbolize that all of God's created men, women, and children are meant to be brothers and sisters.

Here's what I wrote in my journal early on the morning of July 19, 2018:

The … spiritual insight I gained in prayer this morning is that it's approved by God that I place family right below Him in my expenditure of love and emotional energy. And I gained a great peace about adopting LaTonya and her immediate family into our family. It's the completion of 'family' that keeps us from being exclusionary, from being all Privileged White. What did we come to Grove Park seeking? We didn't know, did we? We just know we were called to be here. Now, it's dawning on me what was supposed to happen. We are to be a blended family. Martha Jane is to have aunts and uncles and cousins that look like her. LaTonya and Jane and Evelyn Anne are to be sisters. Ellie, Chad, and MJ are to have Anthony, Larenzia, and King [under LaTonya's guardianship] as cousins …. The Holy Spirit has really worked me over this morning, and I'm super excited. One more time: Praise God, Praise God! We are called to be a blended family—truly.

Terrell found (through the law firm website of Claiborne/Fox/Bradley) that there is a legal process to follow through the courts for adult adoption. This confirmed what LaTonya had already said. We then came for our family week at Tybee to discuss, particularly with the sisters, that this prospective adoption would make us even tighter as a family—an expanded family—than we are now. Thus far in life our experience has been that each addition to the family, capped off by the adoption of Martha Jane, has made us all the more bonded.

We'll have to have one of our next few reunions in Atlanta so that you can all meet your new niece and her family. I can see nothing but delight and laughter when such a gathering occurs.

Much love from JoElyn and me to each of you whom we know are there for us as we are here for you,

Chuck

I had spoken with Walter Henegar in August 2018 about our impending adoption to ask if he would support us in what we were proposing; then, if so, would he spiritually recognize the adoption by our church body as part of a morning worship service. He agreed, and we exchanged notes about a date for such a church blessing, figuring that it would take until November to go through the court process of legal adoption.

Walter established the date of November 25 for the blessing at Atlanta Westside Presbyterian, and he proceeded to ask good questions for our consideration. To one of his notes I responded, "Your questions typify the depth of your engagement in this matter. Keep the questions coming; and raise matters for consideration that we may not have yet considered. We invite you and Anne to be full partners in all of this. And, please, help us keep [the adoption] from being a spectacle instead of the Kingdom-centered following of His lead that we wish."

Here is more of my response back to Walter: "The Gilberts, Bostons, JoElyn and I had Sunday night supper together both last night and the Sunday before with good discussions both nights. Terrell, I think, summed up our Johnston/Gilbert/Clausen perspective by stating how he and Jane view Martha Jane—and it's not as an appendage to their two birth children. She is no different in their minds and hearts than are Ellie and Chad. And we seek that same parity in our family with LaTonya, Carlos, Anthony, Larenzia, and King.

"We acknowledged that an adult coming into the family is different than one coming in at fourteen months of age, as was Martha Jane when she first arrived on Evelyn Way. LaTonya can't go back and experience all of the childhood, teenage, and young-adult experiences and memories that Jane and Evelyn Anne

Chuck and JoElyn with LaTonya's daughter, Larenzia, at her graduation from Mississippi Valley State University in 2017

experienced with each other and with JoElyn and me. At the same time, she henceforth can, together with Carlos, be a part of any Sunday night suppers, birthdays, and family trips to the beach. Having stated that, each of the separate family units has its autonomy and privacy. We try to avoid what we laughingly call forced family fun. Each participates in the together events as they wish to and are available."

Evelyn Anne's Message to Her Sister LaTonya, Read at the Afternoon's Celebration, November 25, 2018

My dad is fond of the phrase "In God's economy, nothing is wasted." It comes from Bill Wilson, the founder of Alcoholics Anonymous, who believed that each moment of our lives, including and maybe especially the difficult ones, has a purpose. He believed the words of Jeremiah, "'For I know the plans I have for you,' declares the LORD, 'plans to prosper you and not to harm you, plans to give you hope and a future,'" and spent most of his life trying to share that message with alcoholics, addicts and their loved ones.

Like Bill Wilson, LaTonya has dedicated herself to spreading the word of God's transformational love to not only her students at PAW Kids, but to everyone she meets, in Buckhead as much as Bankhead.

In God's economy, every life is part of the larger plan. God's plan is bigger than any blood line or DNA pattern and (thankfully) he isn't relying on us to carry it out ourselves. He is giving us hope and a future whether we're aware of it or not.

Our family felt complete when it was my parents, Jane, and me. Then Jane married Terrell and we realized that we'd been missing him all along. When Ellie, Chad, Jonathan and Martha Jane came along, it was the same. We wondered how we'd been a family at all without these vital members.

Now we feel it again, because in God's economy, LaTonya has always been Jane's and my sister. She has always been my parents' daughter. Where we see random chance and circumstance, God sees a family becoming whole.

I wish I could be there with you all to celebrate this momentous occasion but for today, this message will have to suffice:

Welcome to the family, LaTonya. We've been waiting for you.

Evelyn Anne

Chapter 12: A Spiritual Awakening in My Late 70s

In a way, I tried to manufacture a new life for young Anthony Gates. We were in school together at AYA when he entered at twelve years old and I was sixty-two. He stuttered, had a low self-image, had no useful faith, and used incorrect grammar.

As a career educator, I was good at presenting an acceptable image of personhood to which the student should aspire. The academic aspiration that I brought to AYA was that of Trinity School, a Buckhead church-sponsored elementary school serving as a prep school for Atlanta's prestigious private schools. As I had done as headmaster at Trinity, I wanted to prepare as many AYA graduates to fit in and succeed at Pace, Lovett, Westminster and others.

When Principal Derrick Lockwood would effectively teach the students to introduce themselves by clearly enunciating their names, by looking the other person directly into their eyes, and with a firm handshake, I subconsciously thought, "That's great; Derrick is teaching our students good manners out of Gloria Vanderbilt's book." This manner of greeting was universally practiced by our students, and for it they got rave reviews from white middle-class visitors. For years, the common response from whites was, "I wish my child would do that!" It's only now, years after leaving AYA, that I realize the truth:

This was not something that Derrick picked up from white culture. It is a practice embedded in the educated black culture that knew it had to make special effort to relate to the dominant white culture.

More important than appealing to the white culture was the embedded value in the broad black culture of respecting the elders of the community. It began by holding respect for anyone older than oneself.

All teachers at AYA were Mr., Mrs., or Ms. That felt a bit stiff for me. I preferred the practice at white elementary schools of students using teachers' first names with a Mr. or Miss or Ms. in front of it: Miss Sue, Mr. Benjamin, as examples. I quickly insisted with teachers that they call me Chuck, not Mr. Johnston or Mr. Chuck. I would do the same with parents; I would move quickly to call all by first names. It felt warmer, more inviting, more seeing each other as equals—this by my norms. I didn't take the time then to evaluate why the black community seemed so stiff in their addressing of each other. I had hoped that in short order we would all be on a first-name basis. They also would use last names, which I refused to do; it grated on me. Derrick Lockwood by the teachers would become just Lockwood. Why not Derrick?

I carried my concept of humility and human closeness into the overwhelmingly black community of Grove Park, when we moved there in 2011. The longtime resident (since 1963) housed between the Gilberts and us is the sophisticated Mrs. Arian Johnston, a Spelman student, a widow, a mother of three successful adult daughters, all college graduates, and three enjoyable grandkids. She was eighty-four at the time of our moving in; I moved quickly to call her Arian instead of the more formal Mrs. Johnston. I guess in hindsight I wanted to assume the closeness of next-door neighbors, which more often takes years to achieve. "May I call you Arian? Please call me Chuck."

We have become close neighbors, even praying together on occasion. I have persisted in calling her Arian. To this day, she has never called me Chuck. In fact, she avoids using a name at all. And she refers to JoElyn when we are talking as "your lady." How offensive I must have been to assume that my white way was the norm, that my version of friendliness trumped anything that stood in its way. It's another arrogance on my part in assuming that the ways of the privileged white were the right way. "White is right!"

Back to Anthony Gates: he did well in his three years at AYA. I arranged for him to have some speech lessons at the Atlanta Speech School, so he almost eliminated his stuttering and often spoke very well on the stage at assemblies. He learned to use Standard English. And I think the acquisition of a sustaining faith did more than anything to elevate Anthony: "I can do all things through Christ who strengthens me" (Philippians 4:13).

I used my influence with Linda Simpson, admission director at Whitefield Academy, to gain for Anthony a ninth-grade spot at that school. The school gave him a partial scholarship, and Steve McCoy, who had been his Scholarship Partner at AYA, finished out the tuition expense. The McCoys had Anthony stay at their house from Sunday evening until Friday morning. The McCoys' son was a senior at Whitefield. Every evening Steve would get the two boys at the dining room table and have them outline their homework and work there until their homework was finished. Anthony credits Mr. McCoy with teaching him how to study; hence Anthony did well in his studies.

There was a contingency of black basketball boys who hung together and who gave Anthony a hard time for his fraternizing so freely with white students. The basketball boys sat exclusively together at lunch; Anthony sat at tables that had a mixture of Anthony's black and white friends.

As he had gone to kindergarten through the 8th grade with all black schoolmates, I thought Whitefield was the perfect place for Anthony to emerge as a young man adhering to the white standards that would make him successful later in life. But life for Anthony was not all smooth at Whitefield. Unbeknownst to me, he functioned out of fear that he might say or do the wrong thing, particularly being stretched between the expectations put upon him by two different communities.

The low point in Anthony's four years of high school was when, returning to the boys' bathroom after lunch to collect his book bag, he found his books scattered about and the bag and some of the books smeared in human feces. The perpetrator was never found. It could have been the black basketball boys or it could have been a white student, unknown to Anthony, who maybe resented Anthony's friendliness with all students, regardless of color.

In his senior chapel talk, Anthony spoke of the fact that built into the traditions of the families of his white classmates were certain colleges. Maybe parents, uncles and aunts all went to UNC or UGA, so that was the legacy of those families. "The legacy of my family," Anthony said, "was going to prison. From my father to my grandmother to aunts and uncles and cousins, it seems as if they all found a way to prison at one time or another." He went on to say, "My grandfather was a drug addict, my father was a murderer [suicide], and I am a child of God."

The college counselor at Whitefield narrowed Anthony's prospective good-fit colleges down to one—Covenant College atop Lookout Mountain. I went to work with Walter Henegar to see if we could find funds in the Covenant College catalog of scholarships to cover housing, meals and tuition. The more we talked about Anthony's merits to the admission director, the more enthusiastic the director was in helping find applicable scholarships. I feel quite certain that Walter called upon his father, Henry Henegar, to help make Covenant College doable for Anthony. Henry was involved over a great portion of his adult life in raising funds in and around Chattanooga.

Time came for Anthony to come to the Covenant campus for his interview and overnight visit. He entered into the campus visit in good spirits, and then, by the end of his visit, was depressed. That it was a small liberal arts college was part of its appeal. That Anthony only counted nine students of color over the length of his visit caused him to say, "I can't go through this for another four years. I survived Whitefield, but Covenant College is too much like the makeup of Whitefield. I've decided I want to go to Morehouse."

I began to lecture him: "Anthony, you've come a long way—you're now comfortable in both the black urban culture and the white culture. Won't going to Morehouse make you more one-dimensional? You've got a full ride to Covenant."

"I appreciate the work that you and Pastor Walter have done to give me that opportunity, but that's not for me," he said. "After my visit to Covenant, which is where I had thought I wanted to go, I realize I want to go to Morehouse and graduate as a Morehouse Man."

"You are making a mistake," I thought to myself, "and this after so many people have tried to give you what we feel are the best opportunities."

Four years later, JoElyn and I had the beautiful experience of sitting outdoors on a sunny May morning on the Morehouse campus and watching Anthony and 550 other young men graduate and become Morehouse Men. What I came to learn was that the four years among all black classmates gave Anthony and the others a healthy confidence. They knew that they were put on this earth to accomplish great things. No longer was being a black man something to run from, which was a subtle message Anthony had been getting from white mentors, teachers, and classmates, and I paramount among them.

The Morehouse Man prepares himself for leadership and service, not by trying to be a clone of successful white men, but by being proud to be black and, therefore, more confident in working side by side with his white counterparts. Brooks Brothers didn't invent the blue suit and red tie. Since long ago, black ministers have set that example as the black standard for "dressing for success." It's not the white norm for success that Anthony and others should aspire to. That's fine for the white people, but let the black people—like Nikki Jusu and Keenan Rush and Anthony Gates—celebrate the richness of the historic black culture.

Anthony and Chuck

Chapter 13: Ellie's Thorn in the Flesh

In the summer of 2016, Ellie went to a week-long Olympic Development Program soccer camp in Alabama. It was an honor to be chosen to go. The problem is that Ellie experienced such muscle soreness, even with ice baths and all, that she was limited in her full participation. When she got back home, Jane took her for a series of tests that eventually turned up a diagnosis of rhabdomyolysis.

Rhabdomyolysis is the breakdown of damaged skeletal muscle. Muscle breakdown causes the release of myoglobin into the bloodstream. Myoglobin is the protein that stores oxygen in your muscles. If you have too much myoglobin in your blood, it can cause kidney damage. About 26,000 cases of rhabdomyolysis are reported in the United States each year. Most people with rhabdomyolysis are treated with fluids in an intravenous (IV) drip.

In late July/early August of 2018, Ellie had a particularly severe episode and ended up in Scottish Rite Hospital (Children's Healthcare of Atlanta) for five days and was released on the sixth. Since her diagnosis two years earlier, Ellie knew what she needed to do to stay free of the sidelining effect of this disease. Essentially it's to stay hydrated at all times, to consume 3,000 calories a day, and to get enough sleep. Not wanting to jeopardize her soccer career, she has been super-conscientious about these preventative measures. (Well, maybe not so much on the sleep piece.)

But here's what happened to throw her in the hospital for nearly a week: on Monday, July 30, when she had her first soccer practice of the fall season (after having most of the month of July off), she spent the night after practice with one of her teammates. She had eaten very little all day and she didn't take in sufficient fluids. They were up late. At around 3 a.m. she had such severe muscle pain that she called her parents to come pick her up.

Two things to realize here about rhabdomyolysis: it takes intense exercise such as running a marathon to put the muscles under the level of stress that brings on the onslaught, and the pain is severe. I was impressed that the hospital put her on morphine to ease her pain. And, I am further impressed at the physical demands Ellie has been putting herself through to compete as she does at the top level. She is no wimp.

Getting enough fluid into your body is the first and most important treatment. They must start IV fluids quickly. This fluid should contain bicarbonate, which helps flush the myoglobin out of your kidneys. Ellie stayed attached to an IV drip for the entire week. When she entered on Tuesday the count of the enzyme entering her bloodstream from muscle breakdown was 150,000; when they finally let her go on Sunday it was 4,300. It was still well above normal (below 500) but they trusted Ellie to stay super-hydrated to flush out the last of the excess myoglobin.

Ellie was seldom alone in the hospital. Her parents alternated spending the night, letting her finally have Saturday night to herself. Both sets of grandparents made visits. Friends came. JoElyn and I were probably most welcomed the day we brought banana pudding and mac and cheese, gifts from Marybeth Edgecomb for Ellie. She dug into both. (She was still not over-eating, as she was supposed to. The hospital food was not to her liking, and the serving sizes were geared for younger children.)

The U.S. all-star soccer game was played at Mercedes Benz Stadium on that Wednesday night. The Gilberts had planned to go as a family. They proceeded with one down; JoElyn and I watched the game on TV with Ellie. Jane then came after the game to tag us out and to spend the night.

This, the first week of August, was Chad and Martha Jane's first week of school; so Jane and Terrell had to do some jockeying back and forth to take in the wonders of a first week in third and seventh grades respectively for their two younger children while giving maximum attention to First Born. Ellie missed no school since Westminster had not yet started. She did miss all but the first day of her first week of Top Hat practice, but she easily recovered from that. If she had to miss a week, this was the best one.

This is a bit of a side note, but at the time of this writing (October 2018), Ellie has just returned from a Sunday-long visit to Vanderbilt and its soccer coaches. Jane had disclosed in a parent questionnaire, done just a few days earlier, Ellie's CPT2 deficiency. They had already run it through the Vandy Medical School and had gotten back, before Ellie arrived, a full report, including a dietary plan tailored for Ellie. For them, the condition was a non-issue.

Ellie will be playing soccer for the University of Georgia, where she received a scholarship.

Chapter 14: 'Love of Dog' — Jane's 'Compelling Grace' Article

Daughter Jane is a marvelous writer who deals in honesty of thoughts and emotions. It's in her blog, "Compelling Grace," where one will find riveting accounts of life in Grove Park. But the entry below (posted October 13, 2018) is more personal than some in sharing the unexpected depth of grief that comes from the death of a longtime family pet, in this case Cocoa the Labradoodle:

Chad with the beloved Cocoa

"If I speak in the tongues of men or of angels, but do not have love, I am only a resounding gong or a clanging cymbal. If I have the gift of prophecy and can fathom all mysteries and all knowledge, and if I have a faith that can move mountains, but do not have love, I am nothing. If I give all I possess to the poor and give over my body to hardship that I may boast, but do not have love, I gain nothing.

"Love is patient, love is kind. It does not envy, it does not boast, it is not proud. It does not dishonor others, it is not self-seeking, it is not easily angered, it keeps no record of wrongs. Love does not delight in evil but rejoices with the truth. It always protects, always trusts, always hopes, always perseveres.

"Love never fails. But where there are prophecies, they will cease; where there are tongues, they will be stilled; where there is knowledge, it will pass away. For we know in part and we prophesy in part, but when completeness comes, what is in part disappears. When I was a child, I talked like a child, I thought like a child, I reasoned like a child. When I became a man, I put the ways of childhood behind me. For now we see only a reflection as in a mirror; then we shall see face to face. Now I know in part; then I shall know fully, even as I am fully known.

"And now these three remain: faith, hope and love. But the greatest of these is love" (1 Cor. 13:1-13).

Cocoa our beloved dog died in the night, at home, on Tuesday. After surviving parvo as a puppy, then Addison's disease as a chronic assailant, then heart failure a year and a half ago, she finally couldn't overcome her kidneys shutting down.

Those are the medical facts, about an animal, and I am trying to understand why the grief my husband and I have experienced this week seems more appropriate for a human loss than a pet. My best guess, for now, is that she epitomized God's love without the complication of human depravity. It's not that she didn't wreak her fair share of havoc, stealing our food off of momentarily unattended plates or "relieving herself" on bedroom carpets from time to time. She was a big responsibility and not an inexpensive creature.

But she was a constant companion, willing to play catch with a ball or enthusiastically join in on a run, or snuggle on the sofa watching a movie, or rest cozily next to one of us while we read a book. She was a hiker, a paddleboarder, a beachcomber, a squirrel chaser, a cat enthusiast, a house protector, an alert for strangers on the porch, and a sympathetic presence when my kids couldn't sleep or one of us just needed not to be alone. On walks in our neighborhood or with kids alone at home, she always protected. No matter what we did, she always trusted. As far as we know, she was never angry, never kept records of our wrongs, was never envious, boastful or proud.

How can the Gospel be communicated through a pet dog? She delighted in being present with us, whether on our terms or enjoying her own play with us. God has not called us to live isolated, wholly independent lives from Him or one another but to live in community and communion. In the interdependence is the reminder that we share one another's need. We need relational presence and faithfulness but have grown to accept the impossibility of such a desire. Our pets expose a deep loneliness and longing that isn't always even conscious but is no less real.

What if I began to love my immediate family as Cocoa loved each of us? I would be more eager just to be with my people rather than feeling my agenda interrupted by them. I would delight in them rather than being so critical. I would listen far more and talk a whole lot less. (Nobody enjoys a yappy, constantly barking dog.) I would be thrilled by the mundane rituals of dog food clanging into the bowl rather than being picky or unimpressed by the repetition. I would be curious about every new sight, sound, and smell, interested in where they'd been and who they'd met and what delicious thing they might have in their possession. I would be eager to join in their play or dancing or even to just be near on the front porch. I would want to keep an eye on them at all times until they were out of sight of the front room windows or front porch wall. I would always be available.

What if I began to love my immediate family as I loved Cocoa? If they take my food off my plate, so to speak, I would be quick to forgive, not holding a grudge or keeping a list. If they poop on the floor, or some such costly offense, I would appreciate the limitations that caused the mess and clean it up without judgment or raging anger or demands for restitution. I wouldn't expect from them what they were never created to do or be for me, but I would seek to constantly make them feel loved by rubbing that place in front of their ears or giving treats because it made me happy to make them happy. What if I invited them to come with all their weight and sit all over me and my space on the sofa, just glad to be snuggled even if it was sometimes a little crowded?

"But the fruit of the Spirit is love, joy, peace, patience, kindness, goodness, faithfulness, gentleness, self-control; against such things there is no law" (Gal. 5:22-23).

May God's Spirit bear more of His fruit in me that I may be to my family more of what Cocoa was to us all—the love of God demonstrated in the love of our dog.

Chapter 15: The Presence of Jamar 'King' Dorsey in Our Lives

When King was maybe six months old, his mother gave him away for better care to a friend who was in no better position to care for him than King's mother, who was headed for a prison term. This friend gave the baby to LaTonya's sister, who recognized that LaTonya and Carlos were better equipped to care for King. Hence a baby became part of the Boston household.

Larenzia, LaTonya's daughter and Anthony's little sister, was smitten with King and took him for stints to stay with her in Mississippi. There he got lots of love and attention from Larenzia and her friends. Back in the loving Boston home and neighborhood, LaTonya and Carlos came to be known by the child as Mommy and Daddy. Together with the observations of friends around them, LaTonya and Carlos came to recognize that King was still in the midst of drug withdrawal from his months in the womb. They immediately began to build the support and love that enables a toddler to thrive. I love the picture of King and Carlos going off for their Saturday haircuts and shopping adventures.

Those of us who became part of LaTonya and Carlos' extended family through adoption spent time with LaTonya, Carlos, and King at the beach in January 2019, so we have seen the unstinting love and care and attention they have given to King. I accompanied LaTonya and King to the Atlanta Speech School and saw again his extremely limited vocabulary and attention span. The lead speech and language pathologist at the speech school, Meagan Gordon, along with the executive director, Comer Yates, were prepared to come alongside King to make sure he got all of the intervention known to today's behavioral science.

As a kindness to King's birth mom, LaTonya drove with King to south Florida in December '18 so King could see his mom and so that his mom could see him. Unbeknownst to LaTonya, the mom must have seen a preppy and handsome little boy—never mind his inability to speak and, therefore, his tendency to tantrums—and decided she wanted him back. Also, the mom's family members put pressure on her to retrieve King for the government support checks attached to King. She came after him aggressively, accusing LaTonya of kidnapping her baby. Thus began three court appearances and a police raid on LaTonya and Carlos' Elizabeth Place home.

On the night of February 12, 2019, the police came with King's birth mom to the Boston home sometime between nine and ten o'clock to take King away. A call went out through the neighborhood, and soon LaTonya and Carlos's living room was filled with neighbors—men and women, black and white—who stood between the police and King, who was asleep and unaware of what was going on.

That day LaTonya and King's birth mom, Jonesia Rogers (henceforth referred to as Rogers, the name she goes by), had been in court with their attorneys and had heard the judge say that nothing was to change until they convened again a month later, which would be March 12. The mother was here, in the dark of the night, trying to use the police to go around the judge's order. Justin Bleeker gave me every impression that he had gone to law school by how forceful he was in standing between the officer and LaTonya. And LaTonya, to her great credit, remained calm. She only got emotional one time, after she had gone back and seen precious King asleep in his bed.

White attorney Terrell and black attorney Justin Giboney were the lawyers in the room who held out against the forcefulness of the police officer (Brady by name). Swift and Stacy Graham were key players, remaining seated the whole time (for fear that Swift could be arrested), but issuing wisdom periodically, such as that Officer Brady did not think LaTonya was lying; he was just trying to do his job. The officer, Swift noted, was in a tough spot with the mother wanting LaTonya arrested for kidnapping. Oh, it should be noted that Jane physically stood between Officer Brady and his going to fetch/snatch King from his bed. Jane said she was willing to go to jail, though she laughed later (even with Officer Brady) that she wouldn't do well in jail.

It wasn't until Terrell and LaTonya's attorney, by conference call, reached the assistant district attorney, who had authorized the police to retrieve King, that the assistant district attorney reversed himself and told Officer Brady to "cease and desist."

The room was filled, black and white, all in love and support of LaTonya and King: Jane and Terrell, Justin Bleeker, Justin Giboney, Swift and Stacy, JoElyn and me, Larenzia, Anthony, and Carlos. Swift prayed a powerful prayer at the end, thanking God for this beautiful picture of unity in the Body of Christ. LaTonya began to sing, only to be cut short by the police officer returning to the door encouraging us to stay put until the mother had departed—to avoid a scene. We departed all together, close to midnight, with Carlos taking King, LaTonya, and Larenzia to a motel for the night, and the rest of us scattering to our cars. (In his official report of the night, the police officer stated that the Boston home was filled with lawyers, which we learned meant "whites.")

Flash forward a month: here is my journal account the morning following the fateful March 12 Juvenile Court appearance:

Wednesday, March 13, 2019:

The mind of Christ: *Trust in the LORD and do good; dwell in the land and enjoy safe pasture. Take delight in the LORD, and he will give you the desires of your heart. Commit your way to the LORD; trust in him and he will do this: He will make your righteous reward shine like the dawn, your vindication like the noonday sun. Psalm 37.*

Application/Prayers: *Father, apply these words to LaTonya, Carlos, Larenzia, and Anthony as they work through the grief they feel at the abrupt departure of King from their home and perhaps from their lives.*

Don't miss the miracles: *From 8:30 to 3 we spent at Juvenile Court over the case of where King legally should reside during this season in his life—in the home of the Bostons where he has been for the past two years or with Rogers, his birth mother. Judge Juliet Scales decided that King should be returned to his mother. There was nothing, she determined, to substantially prove that he would not be safe and well treated at home in Fort Pierce, Florida. Present to support the Bostons were attorney Ashley Willcott, a child advocate named Paula Myrick, Pastor Moses, Jane Berry, Lacy (a Grove Park neighbor), Justin Bleeker, Auntie Cynthia Hines, JoElyn & I. Rogers doesn't believe the Speech School report of King's developmental delay and thinks LaTonya is "creating" that scenario to strengthen her case for keeping King.*

If LaTonya and Carlos had been white, it would have more clearly appeared to be a case of affluent folks thinking the advantages of a household providing more opportunities from better educated/connected parents is better for a child than being with a birth mom and brothers who live in a project. LaTonya said to the birth mother in a one-on-one meeting with her that morning that she had no intention of taking King away from his mother permanently but only caring for him until the mother was free of drugs, gainfully employed, and in a household free of drug-using men coming and going. This LaTonya reiterated in court—maybe not so explicitly.

LaTonya, Carlos, Larenzia, and Anthony (as well as the rest of us) had to walk past King, playing with Legos, with his mother, grandmother, and aunt, without a hug or a goodbye—this for the sake of King, who was oblivious as to what was happening to drastically change his life.

King at age three, November 2019

Roughly six weeks after the extreme trauma on King and his Atlanta "family," King's mother, Rogers, brought him back to LaTonya, where he now seems to be permanently and lovingly lodged. She said that King had been crying inconsolably since leaving Atlanta. She said she now realizes that King does have developmental problems that LaTonya is better equipped to address. She, Rogers, wants the best for her boy, and King being with LaTonya and her family will give him the best opportunity for success.

As we near publication, King (born March 3, 2016) is close to five years old and is beginning to speak. He's a beautiful little boy, with a precious, friendly spirit.

Postscript for the Decade

As the decade of my seventies draws to a close, and *Don't Miss the Miracles* is soon to go to press, JoElyn has turned a youthful seventy-five (November 10, 2020) and I have turned a less youthful eighty (December 11, 2020). Lord willing, we will celebrate our fiftieth wedding anniversary June 12, 2021.

Meanwhile, we have been in some form of Coronavirus quarantine and partial shutdown from March on. We have attended church every Sunday, but not in person – online, sitting in our kitchen. For ten months we have not been to a movie, nor have we been out of the house for hors d'oeuvres and wine, which we on occasion have loved to do. Joe Biden has been elected our forty-sixth president and Kamala Harris, vice president. The year 2020 has been one to remember.

PART EIGHT

Reflections

Chapter 1: Thoughts Behind Writing This Memoir

Why We Remember Things As We Do

I wonder if I tend in my memory to put myself in the best possible light? While I certainly haven't intentionally changed facts in my accounts of past events, perhaps subconsciously I have softened my rough edges and, like Walter Mitty, have glamorized myself a bit or have made myself manlier than, in fact, I really am. Also, I suspect that I don't place as much blame on myself as is warranted when I have been in dispute with family or friends, or with a group of upset parents, or with a board or boss that makes life harder for me.

When writing from my memories, I want to make sure there is no meanness regarding someone I love, primarily my family members. In my memory, whether conscious or not, I tend to soften what I record about someone. Sometimes my journal accounts of the same occurrences are more factual, with less concern about hurting someone with how I reference him or her. My nature is to "see the best in people"; hence, negative emotions I may have had at the time of an occurrence have mostly melted away by the time I record from memory an encounter I had years earlier.

We Are Only Seeing One Side of a Human Interaction

Occasionally I'm writing about a solo experience—a walk alone in the woods or in a time when I want to be alone—but much more often both in my journals and in my from-memory writing, I'm writing of my engagement with one or more humans. And in those incidents, I don't know what's inside that other person: what unexpressed thoughts, what subconscious triggers, what disposition, what history, what that other person thinks of me. How presumptuous of me to ascribe motives to another person; but often I do.

I have known JoElyn and been married to her for half a century. How much closer could I be if I knew, really knew, what was going on inside her? So anytime I write about JoElyn and me (whether my memory of an earlier time or my morning journaling of yesterday's events), it will not be 100% true. If this is true of the person I know best and with whom I spend the most time, how much further from the truth will I be when I write of others in my memory or in my current life? I am entirely likely to ascribe motives to JoElyn and others that are far from true.

It's well worth the effort to learn of another's primary influences, their fears, their desires. We were created to need others. To be our best selves, we live life in and around other people. I have devoted substantial days, weeks, and months to this memoir undertaking. In part I do it because I feel that writing about my life *vis a vis* others will carry me to a deeper level of understanding of them and me. Isn't that interesting: we learn from writing? I become a deeper person; I throw off some of the masks I didn't even realize I was wearing. I perhaps get a bit closer to knowing and understanding others.

God Has Put Remarkable Influences in My Life

I start with my early and late memories of those who nurtured me because they taught me in words and by how they lived what I wanted to emulate and what I wanted to shun as the person of Chuck Johnston was forming. Some of those lessons are still my North Star and come to my mind from time to time. Mom is my primary influencer, for reasons I hope you now understand from my writing. Dad and Grandpa come right in behind her. And then there is Big Gram, who, in part because she lived for ninety-nine years, impacted me and JoElyn both. Little Gram did not have a great impact on me, in part because I saw her a lot less. But I cannot think of this five-foot-tall paternal grandmother without thinking "soft and sweet." These, my closest childhood elders, may not be more remarkable than another's "people" might be, but they were exactly who I needed to shape me.

Biographies that I read from the R.L. Hope Elementary School library inspired me. They were thin so I could get them read in time for our weekly book reports. They put the notion of "greatness" in my soul. I then wanted to be great—as I would define greatness for myself. I will share sheepishly that my dreams did include being president of the United States.

I was shaped in part by reading these biographies of famous historic people; I was given hope that I, too, might possibly "amount to something." So maybe I, though not a famous person, want to do my part in leaving a little of that hope behind for those I love—in the lives of my children, my grandchildren, and perhaps descendants beyond, that they might better understand their own ups and downs by reading of mine and how I handled them:

- ✓ Hope that "this too shall pass"
- ✓ Hope that I can "make lemonade out of lemons"
- ✓ Hope that I can overcome pain in a physical activity and come out on the other side experiencing the rewards for going through the pain
- ✓ Hope that one day I can find a life mate, a soulmate, and experience true "companionship"
- ✓ Hope that one day I will "catch up on my sleep"
- ✓ Hope that I can transition from seeing life in terms of extremes (hesitant here to say "black and white) to one of nuances and subtleties
- ✓ Hope that a simplistic faith can grow to take into one's soul the complexities of faith, especially the mystery of God's extraordinary love for us, the reality of eternal life, and living with "not knowing"

There is the self-narrative in life's first half that "I can do anything I set my mind to." In the second half of life, our self-narrative begins to take into account that we humans have limitations. Now that I'm in life's fourth quarter, I can better identify some of those limitations, and it might be useful that I acknowledge and point out what some of those realizations have been for me.

Tombs and Monuments

Some of the ancients built pyramids to entomb their greatness into the minds of those that would follow for as long as man exists. For some others, those coming after them erect statues and monuments to remind us that nobility of spirit is achievable (e.g., the monuments on the Mall in Washington).

Is that why I am writing my memoir so I won't be forgotten? Who, me? Wearing my long-accustomed mask of humility, I would have said, "Not on my life! There is nothing distinctive about my life that bears preserving." But trying myself to dig deep and uncover what's under the mask, I might more honestly discover, to my surprise, "I will write my life's story in a way that makes it memorable. Yes, I do want my life to have mattered, even if it's little different than the lives of a million other well-intentioned people." I want to leave flares along the path for those coming behind. I want them to avoid pitfalls; I want them to be encouraged at moments when life slams them. Without trying to dictate how they should live their lives, I would most want my descendants to be adventurers. And, I do want to be remembered.

Let me compare myself to JoElyn in this one respect: When she is in her studio painting, most of the time she has a glow about her. When she returns from a long afternoon behind her easel, I recognize that "that girl is her most radiant self." Like Eric Liddell in *Chariots of Fire* says, "God made me fast, and when I run, I feel His pleasure!" JoElyn would say, "God made me a painter, and when I'm creating something out of my heart, I feel His pleasure (whether or not my paintings are selling)!" I feel some inner delight when I am in and around JoElyn's studio writing. I come alive being in God's pleasure. What is retirement but an opportunity to define "purposefulness" for ourselves and to go after it?

Just as JoElyn loves the tools of her art, and even its aromas, so do I love words, the "oil paints" of my art. When we were boys, Dick used to play an LP record of some memorable speeches (I can hear Roosevelt's voice saying, "The only thing we have to fear is fear itself." Or Churchill saying, "… we shall defend our island, whatever the cost may be, we shall fight on the beaches, we shall fight on the landing grounds, we shall fight on the fields and in the streets ….") Words, words—beautiful words!

I want part of the catalog of my life to include, "He was a writer (and a reader)." I could satisfy my writing yen with something comparable to *The Old Man and the Sea* or *To Kill a Mockingbird*. (Even when younger I knew that my own limitations negated a *Brothers Karamazov* ever coming out of me.)

A lacking I felt I had was the keen sense of humor that seems to me part of the writers that I have most enjoyed. (Brothers Dillon and Warren have it; Dick and I—not so much.) The humor I'm referencing is not "fall-out-of-your-chair laughing," but, rather, playing with words in a way that exposes the inconsistencies.

"Write about what you know best" has always been good advice from writing instructors. Writing about my own life seemed to be something that I could do, something attainable.

Dick, all of his career, has written entertaining presentations of complex pediatric research, and he has written successfully in important pediatric journals. Dillon, while giving over most of his career to helping others publish, leaves acclaimed writing about Irish poetry and a solid body of his own poetry to perhaps be recognized posthumously. And Warren, the brother who honestly bears the title of writer, has years of entertaining and informative columns to be gathered together in volumes. As icing on a lifetime of writing, he is nearing the release of a mystery written painstakingly over many years. In their respective fields, my brothers leave behind significant legacies in writing. I want to join them, as well as Grandpa and Mom, as one of the writers in the family.

Chapter 2: Spiritual Journey: From Moralistic Therapeutic Deism to Being Free

My faith growing up certainly was a strong impediment against a host of behaviors practiced by some of my friends, ranging from cussing to sexual intercourse before marriage. (The moralism in which I lived left me open to fantasies in which I could indulge without recrimination.) I wanted to be thought of as "good" beyond just avoiding the things that bad boys did. It included being kind and helpful and polite and friendly. I was not too sophisticated in my theology to look in the morning mirror and say, "Every day in every way I am getting better and better," this the centerpiece in Clement Stone's PMA teaching—Positive Mental Attitude. The first self-help book I ever read was one on Grandpa's bookshelf, *How to Win Friends and Influence People*, by Norman Vincent Peale (who, incidentally, was President Donald Trump's pastor when Trump was growing up). It was a best seller in the late 1940s / early '50s and beyond. Peale was a pastor—of a large NYC 5th Avenue church—so I took his teaching to be akin to Christian theology.

I shirked my duties at times, I told lies, and was disrespecting to Mom, I'm sure. But I had a conscience to go along with my moral code, and I felt a lot of remorse when I transgressed, which was often enough.

As I got older, the urge to kiss a girl was in me in a strong way. But up against that urge was a real fear of girls—a fear of making the wrong move, of looking stupid, of being laughed at. I'm sure my hyper-moral code figured into this stiffness/awkwardness in some subconscious way. I apparently tried to kiss a girl when we were playing in the sandbox as fellow first graders; she fell back against the rough brick exterior wall of our R.L. Hope classroom and skinned her elbow. I experienced some six-year-old shame and was perhaps more traumatized than I realized. I managed a few more kissing episodes along the way, with few being the optimum word. That I can remember a few moments of kissing our across-the-street neighbor (female) shows how rare it was. As I grew older I began to think of my fear of girls as God's gift to enable me to remain a virgin until my wedding night, a top of the chart item in my moral code. While I did enter my marriage a virgin, would that have changed if as a robust fourteen- or sixteen-year-old I had known that it wouldn't be until I was thirty before that night would come?

Clearly I had the notion that God operated a reward system. I gave the following title to a talk I gave during my high school years: "Is the reward of God worth the work that must go into obtaining this reward?" In that talk I quoted Charles Kingsley as saying, "This is eternal life; a life of everlasting love, showing itself in everlasting good works; and whosoever lives that life, he lives the life of God, and hath eternal life." And, out of context, I'm sure, I quoted Mark 10:29 in that talk: "Mark My words, no one who sacrifices house, brothers, sisters, mother father, children, land because of Me ... will lose out."

Twenty-five years later I was still using God as my therapist, to give me courage to face the day. Here's what I wrote in a 1982 journal: *"I can accomplish all things through Christ who, not only strengthens me, but who gives me peace and quickness of accomplishment, when that is in order."*

And mid-career, I called on God to bless the plans out of my Emory MBA thesis: *"Noah planned the ark, he built it, he gathered the animals, and he gathered his family. God wants me to build schools. He wants me to plan, to build, and then to launch out."* (January 1986 journal)

Just as I stuffed my emotions throughout my so-called productive years, I think I pretty much went through my morning "quiet time" without a lot of emotion towards the Father/Son/Holy Ghost. I accessed the gifts of my kind Heavenly Father, but with little emotion, I'm thinking, as this 1987 journal entry indicates:

I wonder how sane a life I lead. It makes me want to live more deliberately, more thoughtfully. Q: What difference does it make to me that Jesus lived, died, and defeated death? A: I can completely throw myself into God's arms. I can truly be anxious about nothing. I can release all manner of worry, and I'll be the world's greatest fool if I don't do that.

That's pretty much all about me. I'm center stage, where I've been since my childhood. When will I relinquish my role as "star of the movie"?

I latched onto this Scripture one early morning as the antidote for the malaise I'd been experiencing: "May grace and ... undisturbedness be yours" (Ephesians 1:2).

And here is how I reacted in response to it:

My sin of late has been defeatism. The Holy Spirit has opened my eyes to this. ... help me throw off this Satanic crippler—defeatism. I have had days when I have been paralyzed at work, thinking that maybe I should quit. I have been too consumed with my fatigue and with the physical limitations of growing old. … I claim the undisturbedness that Paul writes about above. I also claim the surpassing greatness of His POWER. (February 2002 journal)

I loved that word *power*, and I took delight in usually giving it all caps: POWER! Maybe I was a bit like the exorcists in Acts who tried to use God's power for their own purposes. Here is the somewhat funny story:

"Some itinerant Jewish exorcists who happened to be in town at the time tried their hand at what they assumed to be Paul's 'game.' They pronounced the name of the Master Jesus over victims of evil spirits, saying, 'I command you by the Jesus preached by Paul!'

"… They were trying to do this on a man when the evil spirit talked back: 'I know Jesus and I've heard of Paul, but who are you?'

"Then the possessed man went berserk—jumped the exorcists, beat them up, and tore off their clothes. Naked and bloody, they got away as best they could" (Acts 19:13-16).

God let me off light in my trying to use His divine power for my own glory, my own purposes.

My writing and scrutinizing my journals over the past several years or so has enabled me to see my self-centeredness and self-aggrandizement reflected through my journals. Just my latching onto the following J. Todd Billings quote (from *Union with Christ*) shows some awareness and growth on my part, finally: "Rather than placing our own action at the center of the drama and seeing religion as a decision-making rule book that makes us feel good about ourselves, we find our true identities in Jesus Christ as part of a drama in which the Triune God is the central actor …."

And here is how I applied Billings' statement in a 2015 journal entry:

When I have been saying that I am merely joining God in the work that He has begun in Grove Park long ago, I find that I am theologically sound in that statement. How can I deflect the praises of men and rather reflect the Triune God [Who] is the central actor?

So, my eyes are being opened to what has been dubbed *moralistic therapeutic deism*—a term used by authors Christian Smith and Melinda Lundquist Denton in their book, *Soul Searching: The Religious and Spiritual Lives of American Teenagers.* Maybe like the so-called Rich Young Ruler in the Bible, I was good at keeping rules, realizing that being a good moral person was central to living a happy life. I more often experienced the therapy of just the right Psalm or other Scripture (e.g., "He has told you, O man, what is good; and what does the LORD require of you but to do justice, and to love kindness, and to walk humbly with your God?" Micah 6:8). I desperately needed a therapist—why not one of a cosmic order? The following prayer reflects my more mature current faith-stage to which I have progressed at the end of seven decades of teeny-tiny steps of growth:

"We needed forgiveness for all the ways we failed (and continue to fail) to love, worship, and obey you (as you deserve and as your law decrees). ... We also need righteousness—a perfect righteousness. All of our best efforts and good works, our hottest tears of repentance and our most sacrificial acts of obedience, our commitment to do more and try harder, and our resolve to sin less and be more godly availed us nothing," so wrote Scotty Smith in his November 24, 2016, online prayer.

"I will give you a new heart and put a new spirit in you; I will remove from you your heart of stone and give you a heart of flesh." — Ezekiel 36:26

In the past, Shame whispered into my ears saying, "You don't measure up." Conversely, there were adults in addition to Mom who, intentionally or not, sent me this message: "Chuckie can do anything he sets his mind to. We expect great things from that kid." Which voice would dominate my adult life: "You don't have what it takes" or "You are destined for great things"?

God has graciously allowed me to see that there is a third way that carries with it neither the arrogance on the one hand, nor the defeatism on the other hand. Scripture refers to this third way *as the abundant life.*

Snippets That Reflect My More Abundant Spiritual Life, the Life of "Being Free"

God has allowed me, by His grace, to live long enough to experience this abundant life and to see the beauty of being a cog in a universe so much bigger than myself. I see God in His handiwork which so encompasses me when I'm in Evelyn Anne and Jonathan's Ellijay home (aka Clausen Cabin) high in the mountains.

Here Is a Taste of the Beauty That I See Opening Up Before Me

Something strange and transformative is happening in my spiritual life. And it is a great enhancement in my understanding of Jesus the Christ and not in any way a rejection of Biblical orthodoxy.

All of a sudden, as I was in a meditative/prayerful standing position inside the Clausen Cabin porch, inches away from the steady Hurricane Michael rain (October 2018), what had been pieces in my life came together as a whole. Latonya, Carlos, Anthony, and Larenzia, via legal kinship to all of us, are now connected to

Martha Jane, who for some time has not wanted to be the only family member with dark skin. I remember one day a few years ago when Jane was on a phone call and after hanging up, she reported to me that she had been talking with a physician who was inquiring about adopting a black child. Misunderstanding who was doing the adopting, Martha Jane pumped her hand in the air with an emotion-filled, "*Yeeess*, another dark-skinned person in our family." Jane said, "No, silly, that's another family that wants to adopt." It was affectionately said and received in humor by Martha Jane.

Now, with the addition of our newest family members, these pieces were knit together as essential to each other and to the whole. There is no superior/inferior dichotomy, no privileged/disadvantaged divide. There is (all of a sudden for me) no assumption that one culture gets swallowed up by the other. The fear of assimilation disappears.

For the first time I really feel that we can't exist without each other. I think that all of our respective birth families are coalescing into something more magnificent, more real, more harkening back to our Creator than any one of us has been up to this point. Via my reading of Barbara Holmes' *Joy Unspeakable*, I am enamored with the focus on ancestors/ children/adults/elders. I see JoElyn and me standing in the estimable position of elders, one day to be ancestors. I see Jane, Terrell, LaTonya, Carlos, Evelyn Anne, Jonathan, Anthony, and Larenzia as the adults, Ellie and Chad as young adults, and MJ, while still a child, not far behind the transition to becoming a young adult.

Now, add to this the fact that I don't see Arian, Vivian, Mike, Stanley, Tyler, Pastor Harper, the McRaes, Mr. Cooper (and a half-dozen others) as separate pieces. We have become bound together in a way that is not easily broken apart or sectioned off. We need each other. I have known I was supposed to feel this way, but, quite honestly, up until now I have felt I could walk away from any of these parts. Now walking away can't/won't be done quite so easily. The group that gathers on Sunday nights (plus the Clausens) is still the paramount core; but this second group is way more than just "friends."

I am now relieved of being the archangel; now I can just be one of the angels with the rest of you. I can sit back and watch the "cycle of spiritual seasons" unfold, together with the rest of you. What a sweet season JoElyn and I are in with you. (This a journal entry of October 11, 2018.)

I don't know whether to describe myself on the upper or lower end of the "cycle of spiritual seasons," but there is a wisp of sadness, maybe because I have so enjoyed the vitality and adventure of life up to this point. I sort of cling to what I know and love and am slightly off-put by what I know not. I am confident that God will properly prepare me for the great transition when the time comes, just as He will prepare all of us for marriages and births and deaths to come.

Scotty Smith's Prayer November 21, 2016

"Thank you for your commitment to finish the work you began in us, and in your creation. Thank you that our coming life in the new heaven and new earth isn't a mental opiate or wishful thinking, sentimental spin or spiritualized hype. It's your promise, and by your grace, it's our inheritance. Thank you for über-awesome hope and countless reasons to be grateful."

Theologian Matthew Henry's Comment in his *Complete Commentary*

"Our Lord Jesus is God, to whom we are to seek, and in whom we are to trust and comfort ourselves, living and dying. And if this has been our care while we live, it will be our comfort when we die."

Acts 7:54-56 (Noted in My September 16, 2016, Journal)

"At that point they went wild, a rioting mob of catcalls and whistles and invective. But Stephen, full of the Holy Spirit, hardly noticed—he only had eyes for God, whom he saw in all his glory with Jesus standing at his side. He said, 'Oh! I see heaven wide open and the Son of Man standing at God's side!'"

So where does the "being free" in my title come in? It's summarized by these words from Paul at the end of Galatians:

"For my part, I am going to boast about nothing but the Cross of our Master, Jesus Christ. Because of that Cross, I have been crucified in relation to the world, set free from the stifling atmosphere of pleasing others and fitting into the little patterns that they dictate.

"Can't you see the central issue in all this? It is not what you and I do—submit to circumcision, reject circumcision. It is what God is doing, and he is creating something totally new, a free life!

"All who walk by this standard are the true Israel of God—his chosen people" (Galatians 6: 14–16).

Oh, If Just for a Day, Father, Let Me Walk in This Freedom

Here is a journal entry I made in July 1968 from the Appalachian Trail in Virginia, the summer I spent many weeks with Dillon and Anne at Redlands. Maybe if I had spent more time in "the wilds" in my subsequent years, my faith would not have remained stuck in the moralistic therapeutic deism for so long:

Before arriving at this Priest Mountain Shelter, I went out on some ledges that afforded a splendid view west and north of nothing but wildlife. I had much of the same feeling of some years ago when I sat and watched the sun set from the rock face of Springer Mountain, Georgia. "In the wilderness is the salvation of the world." What a charge to get away, by one's self or in fellowship, and sense so graphically that there is a Spirit that is fresh, and everlasting, and invigorating.

Chapter 3: 'I Will Return to New York City Once a Year for the Rest of My Life'

I had not had much experience visiting museums as a child. While I did go with Cub Scouts to an Emory University museum to see a mummy and a few other relics from Egyptian archeology, I don't remember ever visiting the tiny High Museum to view art. On my first trip to NYC, June '62, Dillon took me to the Metropolitan Museum of Art where I fell in love with some of Rembrandt's paintings, and I had my first awareness of the Impressionists, which drew me in. We went together to the Museum of Modern Art (MOMA) where I fell in love with Picasso. His major work, at the time, *Guernica*, filled a whole wall. The painting, done in 1937, depicted a battle in the Spanish Civil War. Dillon gave me my first lesson about abstract art. While I lingered in the sense that it was bizarre, this MOMA visit was my first "baby step" towards appreciating abstraction in art. [You didn't know that nine years later you would marry an artist, did you?]

We went to the Frick House as the third bastion of rich New York art. It didn't sound as if it would be much of a museum, with the word house in its title, but this is the one place I recommend for friends going to NYC with an appreciation of art. This was the city home of industrialist Henry Clay Frick, so you are entering rooms that were occupied as home by his family and their visitors. Art filled every room; he loved art, and he had the money to buy it. The piece that stunned me soon upon entering was El Greco's painting of St. Jerome. The red of St. Jerome's vestment was unlike any color I had ever seen. His angular face spoke of character and contentment. It is a highly spiritual painting without need for a fake-looking halo over his head. During that first visit, I probably went back three times to gaze again at St. Jerome.

We went to see *The Fantasticks*, an off-Broadway musical with enchanting songs and a heart-touching story line. I learned what "off-Broadway" means, and I began to feel sophisticated. I liked the pace of NYC, the chain of lunch eateries called Chock full o'Nuts, and, while I sensed that I would never live here, I did vow that once a year for the rest of my life, I would return to NYC to be refueled in current culture and to be renewed in sophistication. That was at age twenty-one. I came back at age twenty-two; so that gave me a chain of two years in a row. Never again have I gone two years in a row. The cost of a few days in New York and the welcomed encumbrances of a family have made my vow of a once-each-year return null and void. I have probably been back a half-dozen times in the intervening fifty-plus years since first coming up out of the Holland Tunnel and gasping at the sight of America's cultural capital.

My desire to be on the cutting edge of the arts died when reality butted in; instead, I had to settle for pseudo-sophistication, one of the many masks, worn over my lifetime, that hopefully I am now discarding.

Two museum experiences, one in Cub Scouts and the other just out of college, connect. The Egyptian mummy I saw in the Emory Museum and Picasso's *Guernica* in New York now reside in Egypt and Spain respectively. These two U.S. museums came to the broader twenty-first century worldview that just because these museums had the dollars to buy almost anything they wanted, these prized possessions did not rightfully belong in Atlanta and NYC.

Chapter 4: Reflecting Back over the Compatibility of Family Life and My School Career

Jane approached the locked Trinity School door in the first winter light of morning with me traipsing along behind her thinking about my headmaster to-do list awaiting me in my office.

She let out a scream!

"Dad, come quick. The door is unlocked and there is green slime all over the lock and handle. Oh, Dad, some monsters must have broken in and are wrecking the school!"

Thus began the mystery film that Jane put together for a fifth-grade project. In hindsight, this shows to me that she was happy identifying herself as my daughter and that she had the privilege of being in the school at unusual hours and days. We rode to school nearly every school-day together. She didn't call me "Dad" when we would pass in the hallway; neither was she embarrassed to see me. Her friends, in line with Jane going somewhere in the school, were pleased to see me and would light up when we passed in the hall.

Evelyn Anne rode with me for two years on our early morning commute from Pebble Beach to Carmel back in the late '80s. (Often when I mention our residence and my place of work, friends will ask, "Did you get hardship pay for that?") She was always glad to be the first student on campus each morning. And it gave her added confidence that her dad was the principal of her school, especially in the early days of her arrival from "the backward South" to the West Coast "land of fruits and nuts."

Whether it was Jane on the Berry campus, Jane and Evelyn Anne both at Trinity, our life together on the Robert Louis Stevenson campus, Evelyn Anne's and my joint Atlanta Ballet experiences, or the three of us starting Whitefield together, my profession and what was important to JoElyn and me were intermeshed.

I'm glad that we had two marvelous boarding school experiences—one at Berry in the first six years of Jane's life and the other in California when Jane was in ninth and tenth grades and Evelyn Anne was in kindergarten and first. Evelyn Anne, when the Pace Academy admissions director asked her what her favorite school activity was in her last school, thinking that Pace could match or top whatever it was, said, "Whale watching!" Pace was stumped on that one!

I may be overstating it, but I feel that we had and continue to have a rich family life together. We had beach vacations every year with Ed and Evelyn initially, then with Evelyn alone at Gulf Shores. We continued the beach tradition with Terrell, when everyone set aside "normal routines," including career, to focus solely on family. Family was so important that we said that a major test for anyone Evelyn Anne might consider marrying was that he had to be compatible with Terrell, especially during our joint family week at the beach. Jonathan Clausen, Evelyn Anne's husband, cleared that bar so exceedingly that we celebrate continuously having the family triumvirate of Clausen/Gilbert/Johnston (in alphabetical order). Now add Gates-Johnston to those family names.

Think of the other opportunities we had because of being part of school communities:

- Multiple weekends and weeks at Bud Parker's farm, as well as fun parties we'd be a part of there
- Our trip to Maui, all expenses paid, as a gift from RLS
- A hike and spend-the-night atop Mount Le Conte in North Carolina with the Zimmerman family.
- Multiple weekends in Highlands and Cashiers as guests of David and Vesta or Larry and Betsy

Also, JoElyn and I were invited to dinners at the Chastain Amphitheater and to elegant parties and dinners in people's homes.

Reflecting on JoElyn during all these great years of meshing family togetherness with my career, she is the one who deferred her dream in order to be a stay-at-home mom. She gave of herself unstintingly to the three of us and she gave up the life she might have chosen for herself had she been less self-sacrificing. First of all, if the truth be told, she didn't love the role of "headmaster's wife," although she had the ability and social graces to plan and give parties and enjoy participating in the life of the school.

JoElyn was the more consistent disciplinarian, though we were conscientiously in agreement with each other to fend off a child's inclination, when told "no" by one parent, to go to the other parent to see if she could get a more favorable ruling. This is when JoElyn and I would talk things over. We were in agreement about what we wanted the girls to eat and not eat, though I tended to be the more lenient one in these matters. As an example, I favored the Varsity as a place for dining together as a family. JoElyn—not so much.

I intentionally did our own yardwork. It would have been more cost-effective use of my time if I had hired someone to mow and I used that time to knock out some overhanging school chore. But I wanted to model what Martha Berry would term "the dignity of working with your hands," and, truth be told, I enjoyed yardwork. It was reasonably mindless so it gave my brain a rest, and I could immediately see the results of my labor; whereas, I might never see any fruit from some of my hectic hours of school work. My delight was when either Jane or Evelyn Anne would come out and work with me.

While JoElyn was "in her element" teaching art and art history at AYA, still my career for the first forty-five years of our marriage did not draw out of JoElyn her real passion—painting. Hence, at age seventy, she was juried into an *Emerging Artists Show* at the Anne Irwin Gallery. From this "emerging-artist" status forward, her career is slowly gaining steam. The most relaxed and content I see JoElyn is upon her coming through the front door at dusk after a long and fruitful afternoon painting at her studio. Someone famous has said, "The best thing you can do for your children is to love their mother." It may be a little late to impact our grown children's lives, but at last I am able to serve JoElyn as my recognition of how much she sacrificed over the years for my career.

Also, upon reflection, I'm not sure Evelyn Anne was as well-served by my career as maybe Jane was. Evelyn Anne was happy and well-liked at Trinity School as a two-, three-, and four-year-old. So on the night that the private schools had designated as Family Night Out, we went to the OK Café. I told the girls that we were moving to California, and Evelyn Anne burst out crying (much to my surprise). Happily the move turned out well for her. She loved Pebble Beach and Carmel, especially the freedom of the boarding school campus and the deep friendship of kids and adults on campus. Two years into that, we went to RLS's apartment in San Francisco; there we told her that we were moving back to Atlanta. Again, she was devastated.

While Jane was thriving at Pace Academy and then at Vanderbilt, Evelyn Anne was searching for a school sweet spot, first at Pace, then at Sarah Smith, then at Greater Atlanta Christian School (with her good friends Robert and Ryan Germany), and then at Whitefield, the cruelest years of them all for her.

Let me not end this by declaring myself a Prize-Winning Dad, for while I was chasing my career dreams, at least two of our nuclear family of four were paying a price for my pursuit of noble aims.

Chapter 5: In What Sense Has Mom Been in My Life from Birth Until Present?

Why is it important that I make this search for my mother—who is she; specifically, who is she to me? Thomas Wolfe wrote this to his editor, Max Perkins: "The idea that hangs over the book [*Of Time and the River*] from first to last is that every man is searching for his father." (The quote appears in the book *Max Perkins: Editor of Genius*.) I must be an exception to that in that Dad has had, while living and since, a calming presence and now memory in my life. I think I know him in a way that I don't Mom. She is an enigma overhanging my life; he, a positive model for me in many ways. Not just to be argumentative with Wolfe, but Mom has been much more difficult to figure out, both then and now.

There are a limited number of people alive today who knew Jane Dillon Johnston. Those would be Dick, Mary Anne, Dillon, Anne, Warren and me; and, to a lesser extent, some of our friends like Bobby Stephenson, Vance Rankin, Tom Garden, Tim, Phil, and maybe a few more of our friends. Are Bryant and John Newman still alive?

Wouldn't it be a big help to me if Mom had written a memoir? What do we have? An obituary? Letters and postcards from Mom? Does Warren have a copy of Mom's poem about the inauguration of Queen Elizabeth? Biographies of people who aren't famous barely exist. There are a few diaries of slaves with only a first name, maybe a few from pioneers and mountain people, soldiers in the Civil War and other wars. I dare say a writer today couldn't resurrect the life of someone who left no written footprint. So, if I don't write of Mom's identity, then in twenty or so years, she may only exist as a name in the genealogical records of the

Mormon Church. I have an inkling that if I don't bring out her life on paper, then in twenty years or so, when the folks listed in the paragraph above are gone, the last sweep of the fluxing tide will have washed her footprints aside.

I set out to write a memoir of my life, and Mom comes into that, so that to the extent that my account of her impact on me and my brothers is accurate, then a partially true account of Mom's life will exist. It seems egotistic to gauge her identity/value on what she passed on to the four Johnston Boys. But my memoir would be nonexistent or incredibly different were it not for Mom. I want Mom to live on; I especially want the Sober Mom to live on. And, I want to understand Mom's presence in my life as I try to assess the different streams of influence that have fed me from birth.

Before the Disease Took Her Away, She Was That Wonderful Combination of Tough and Tender

For some reason I had to remain in Phillips House of Boston Children's Hospital for two weeks following my birth, even as Mom was released to go home for Christmas. Dad tells that she was so concerned about me being lonesome without family on Christmas that she insisted that the family drive back into the city on Christmas Day to give me some company. This would mark Mom's conscientiousness as a mother until it finally drove her to a debilitating addiction and death.

The memory of Mom as soft and adoring might be blunted in part because she meted out a painful spanking when she deemed it necessary. She used a brown wooden clothes brush with a flat striking surface and a handle that lent itself to rapid and repetitive strokes. One or two strokes and it startled but didn't really hurt. Rather, it was the fact that one feared she would never stop. We got no less than a dozen (twelve) licks with the brush. As brothers we were honor bound and tactically bound not to emit any sounds of pain or protest. In this way we thought she would finally give up this form of punishment as ineffective. That may have been a tactic; but Mom was not fooled. She kept it up certainly for several more years. Fortunately, by the years when Mom's drinking became pronounced, we had outgrown the spankings.

I Have Blamed Mom for My Stunted Emotional Health

I attribute my aversion to confrontation to the years that I had to dance pretty fast relationally to dodge being sucked into a no-win argument with an intoxicated Mom. If I ever mentioned her drinking when she was hostile-drunk, I might as well anticipate a cutting tirade coming back from her about my shortcomings. Attacking my holier-than-thou attitude was my vulnerable spot, and she knew it.

So, as I felt disgust and revulsion well up inside me, physically manifesting itself in a red face and light-headedness, I would seal off my emotions and stuff, stuff, stuff them. Feelings were not useful in avoiding these kinds of wars. This sealing off of emotions writer Janet Woititz, author of *Adult Children of Alcoholics*, calls "numbing out."

And then, in those morning times, when Mom was sober, I didn't want to bring up her drinking and add the weight of my concerns for her to the unspoken guilt I knew she was surely feeling. Should I have campaigned for steps that might have led to her recovery? As a pre-adult, as I was at the time, I knew of no plans or programs that might give Mom new hope, a new life. Oh, how I now wish that she could have been helped. What sadness I feel about that.

So I entered into my adulthood and career life with every tool I needed except three: First, I eschewed the constructive and healthy use of confrontation; I had spent too many nights dodging confrontation with Mom after she had been drinking to embrace confrontation in any way. Second, I lacked awareness that intense striving has a dark side—basically headaches and a lack of contentment. And third, I lacked an awareness of my own emotions. I would not let myself get upset. I certainly learned by experience that indulging in how I felt about Mom's illness would profit me nothing. Again I quote from *Adult Children of Alcoholics*: "Because you believed you had to keep these feelings to yourself, you learned to keep most of your other feelings to yourself."

In my first two post-college jobs, at McCallie and Westminster, I relied on motivation and, hence, had no need to apply negative discipline in the classroom, on the athletic field, or in the dorm. The demerit/privilege system in the dorms supplanted most confrontation there. And generally those students were wanting to do the right thing, something they learned in their homes. Hence, I had little need for confrontation, which is, I suspect, why I enjoyed those jobs so much.

My third job, working as the #2 person under Jim McCallie at Brookstone School, enabled me to be everybody's friend. Jim took the heat for tough decisions that had to be made. I was the fair-haired boy assistant. One incident when my aversion to confrontation could have been deadly was when I sent Bynum Perkins and his older cousin home twenty-five miles to Waverly Hall when I discovered at a Brookstone dance that the two of them had been drinking. I should have taken the car keys and called their parents to come pick them up. Jim couldn't believe that I hadn't done that. Either I thought the whole matter would go away or that I could just put off talking to upset parents.

Anger was one emotion that I knew was bad from an early age. I had a temper, but more and more I was learning to "count to 10" or in other ways to stuff anger. Dad shared that he had had a temper as a boy that he had had to learn to hold in check. He would tell us that at the point when we lose our temper, we lose control and experience a moment of insanity.

It seems that as father to our first single-digit child, I would be "tied in knots" emotionally when Jane refused to do something I told her to do. I would end up yelling, on the edge of losing my temper, while she remained confident and calm. Out of answers, JoElyn and I went to a child psychologist who told us to frame directives to Jane in the form of choices: "OK, Jane, you can go ahead and finish your homework now and watch 'Family Ties' at 7:30 or you can miss 'Family Ties' and either do your homework before bedtime or not." Because of my ignorance of healthy emotions, I missed the opportunity to have meaningful conversations with an emerging soul about all that is going on inside each of us, otherwise called emotions.

Evelyn Anne reminded me of a time when she came late to the dinner table all in a wad. I said to her, "Either you can be cheerful at the dinner table or you can go back to your room until you can compose yourself. We're not going to have grumpiness at dinner." Once again, my stunted emotional growth hurt another. (Ironically, my nickname among the Brookstone students was Cheerful Chuckie.)

Instead of stuffing anger as the strategy I picked up growing up, I have been taught only in very recent years not to deny anger but to turn anger into motivation for a positive resolution. "Anger shows our yearning for a full life. Desire reawakened is rooted in the feeling of anger." So writes Chip Dodd in *The Voices of the Heart: A Call to Full Living*.

Mike Knighton, who worked with me at Berry Academy as the admission director, remembered years later the time I blew up over something he had done. It was so out of character for me—posing as I did as unflappable—that he didn't hold it against me. He seemed amused as he would re-tell it. So, you see, I had no constructive use of anger for most of my working years. It was either stuff it and maintain a composed exterior or blow my top.

Somehow the dance I learned from Mom did not include the healthy recognition of emotions nor how to process them in a productive way. Growing up in a 95% male environment, I learned that to be strong led to success/achievement. I was hyper-independent. I have since read this: "Although self-sufficiency is admirable, when it hides pain, it chokes the life out of relationships," from the book *How We Love* by Milan and Kay Yerkovich. It is all to JoElyn's credit that she waited forty-something years to see me gain insights that she had had from the beginning of our marriage. When one partner in a marriage has one tune to which he dances and the other partner another tune, the two are going to step on each other's toes.

I brought into our marriage the following coping vocabulary: "get tough," "get over it," "grow up," and the killer of all healthy relationships, "You shouldn't feel that way!" While Mom didn't teach me this vocabulary, this philosophy of pain management did enable me to survive the "drip, drip, drip" of her daily intoxication. I became well practiced in the stuffing of my emotions; so doing the same was the only advice I had to give to JoElyn. I had known nothing of a female monthly period, and I suspected that some sort of shifting emotions accompanying this phenomenon were psychological and could, therefore, be controlled by strength of character. "Just pretend those emotions aren't there." Those were the lyrics of the songs to which I was used to dancing.

In January 2000, I was left alone to wait two cold hours while the Whitefield board decided to fire me as headmaster. When they escorted me into their presence and announced their unanimous decision, I was not permitted to speak; rather, they told me how beloved I was, and they laid hands on and prayed for me.

When I returned that night to our condominium at Cross Creek to an anxiously awaiting JoElyn, I told her what the decision had been. She asked me how I felt. And with all the emotional wisdom I then possessed, I said, "Fine;" and I meant it. When later Bobby Mitchell took me to a Christian counselor to whom I told in excruciating detail the story of clandestine meetings and betrayal, the counselor asked me the same question as had JoElyn, to which I gave the only answer I knew—"fine."

Bobby Mitchell was outraged. He, a mere bystander to this counseling session, couldn't contain himself. "Wait a minute! Something's wrong. You cannot tell the story of pain and intrigue you just did and say you feel fine about it." As relates to emotions, being married to me was like being married to a cardboard cutout.

Even though there were probably no perceptible awakenings in my emotional soul at that point, I mark from that day my awareness that I could no longer hide behind "My Mother was an Alcoholic" or "That's Just the Way I Am."

What Was Mom's Own Emotional Makeup?

In fact, Mom was a melancholy figure. Depression was certainly a part of her profile. It is only in my recent years that I have realized the depth of her connection to her father, Grandpa. He died of cancer when Mom was forty-three years old; to whom did she turn for comfort? The love of literature was a bond between father and daughter. But come to think about it, I don't remember seeing them share a hug; they expressed their bond in other ways. There was seriousness about Grandpa that might have been melancholia. Big Gram, Mom's mother, overshadowed the gentleness of the father-daughter relationship with her forcefulness and command.

Mom and Grandpa had a love of poetry in common, hence Mom's reciting poems, such as those of Robert Frost.

And what of her oft-quoting of the simple line from a Milton poem: "They also serve who only stand and wait"? I understood the saying was in much use during

WWII by the mothers and homemakers who could, for the most part, only stand by as the men served in combat. It wouldn't be hard to imagine that she also felt this statement to express that the life she might have expected to live was flying past her; in its place was the caring for four high-testosterone boys while her husband traveled or was off in the army. As an Atlanta debutante, she had known the finer things growing up—fine clothes, servants, top schools, travel. She was somebody. Now she stood and waited, herself the servant. Here I feel her melancholy.

Mom and Dad's "song" had been "Stardust." It may well have been the tune and the soulful nature of the song that appealed, without a lot of thought to the words. Mom had said to Dad when they were courting, "You are someone I'd like to grow old with." She died at age sixty-one, hardly old age; and we hear the refrain:

> *When our love was new*
> *And each kiss an inspiration*
> *But that was long ago*
> *Now my consolation*
> *Is in the stardust of a song.*

She didn't survive to grow old with Dad.

Mom As a Confidence Builder

Later in life, when I developed close relationships with black men and women who, like me, had grown up in Atlanta, I became critical of their self-promotion. When speaking before an audience, many black speakers will tell you more wonderful things about themselves than you might care to hear. They will drop the names of important people they know. "I'm glad I'm not like that," I would say to myself. "I'm humble."

Then a modicum of wisdom seeped into my soul, and I said to myself, "Wait a minute. You have been bragged on, pumped up, and canonized all your life. There's little danger that someone meeting you for the first time will fail to realize how important and wonderful you are. You can afford to wear the mask of humility because someone else will tell of your credentials to an audience or to an individual who hasn't heretofore known you."

That canonization began with Mom. She bragged on me and my brothers from the time we were little. She exercised "positive reinforcement" before it became part of the psychological lexicon. We took on an air of inoffensive confidence that tended to bring "president of the first grade," captain of the Safety Patrol, and other such honors. She built confidence and ambition in her sons. With me, she may have overdone it.

So in what sense has Mom remained with me? I don't remember Mom teaching me about emotions. It was probably my brother Dick who set the standard for the rest of us that it was OK to cry with sadness (e.g., grief) but not with pain. My family members will invariably look at me during the sad part of a movie or when Bobby Cox waves for the last time before descending into the dugout to see tears running down my cheeks. But somehow I have been cold of heart when I think about Mom. I now look behind the noxious drunkenness; realizing her martyrdom thaws my heart and brings some moisture to my eyes.

Mom Passed on to Me the Legacy of Being Driven, an Aspect of Her Life Where She Was Thwarted

So, you see, I felt important, confident, and independent from an early age. And it was orchestrated by Mom. Even though Dad would frequently say, "I don't care what you boys do for your life's work as long as it is something that you love doing," the aura of the family would have said to Dad, "Yes, we get what you're saying. We also know that we're expected to do something important." I have since learned to take Luke 12:48 in balance, but in my ears of youth and early manhood rang, "Unto whom much is given, much is expected." And I knew that I had certainly been given advantage upon advantage. I lived a substantial portion of my life believing that my good standing with God would be established only after a lifetime of striving to do His will.

Why, after leaving the classroom ranks, did I want so badly to be a headmaster? It must have been that I favored my ambition to reach the higher rung in my career field. I calculated that five years was sufficient time to spend as #2. I had watched Drs. Bob and Spence at McCallie, Dr. Pressly at Westminster, and Jim McCallie at Brookstone. I could do it. I was up to the challenge, and I would enjoy the added perks, both for myself and for JoElyn. I could blow away any negativity by exerting PMA—Positive Mental Attitude. An insurance mogul in Chicago, Clem Stone, dished out the stories of people succeeding merely by thinking that they could; he pounded into me this: "Whatever the mind can conceive and believe, the mind can achieve with PMA." And wonderful Zig Ziegler taught, "You were born to win, but to be a winner you must plan to win, prepare to win, and expect to win." Then he closed every positive message with "I'll see you at the top." These were the writers and speakers that I used to pump myself up.

I told Jim McCallie in the spring of year four at Brookstone that year five would be my last. That was the only time I voluntarily resigned from one job before having a job to go to. My self-confidence was just that high. Certainly I prayed, believing "I can do all things through Christ Who strengthens me." I probably emphasized the first word in that Bible citation—"I."

Since every advancement in my life had come because someone intervened on my behalf, I was not surprised when Gordon Bondurant, then president of Darlington, told John Bertrand, then president of Berry College and Academy, that I would be his best pick to head the academy. The academy was struggling.

I've always said that I like going to situations where the need is great. Then the only way I could take it would be up. I said "yes" to Dr. Bertrand's job offer, and I said "bring it on" as I learned more about the academy's dysfunction.

I forced myself to face discipline issues, or, in the case of faculty, I would "gird up my intestinal loins" and root out the faculty members who didn't subscribe to my "can do" philosophy. Tom Raulerson was probably a decent English teacher, but he treated me with disdain in my first year, and he had to go. When he exploded on me a time or two, I learned that he had had a rotten relationship with his father. I attributed his disrespect for me to a disdain for authority figures, thereby relieving me of any need for introspection as to whether or not I could have dealt with him differently. I didn't re-contract him for my year two; I hired Ted Blain to take his place. In this first year I began to experience severe headaches.

I have pretty much been a black-and-white thinker. I seldom saw gray. Therefore, I favored clear discipline rules. Drinking was our biggest issue, so we felt that it was so bad that we couldn't give second and third chances. That meant I had to dismiss little Jim Wilcox (Dad's step-grandson) when he tagged along with some older boys and drank some miniscule amount of beer. I didn't let Robert Lipscomb walk in the graduation ceremonies because he, a day student, stayed in the dorm that last night of the school year and had some alcohol. His father, John, vice-president of the college, pleaded with me to let him go through the ceremony because of out-of-town relatives who were already sitting in Frost Chapel waiting to see Robert receive honors. Black is black, and white is white, and I didn't budge from the decision that Robert would receive his diploma but he could not be a part of the ceremonies. That decision has haunted me. But I pushed on by stuffing it, stuffing it, stuffing it.

If I had allowed myself to make nuanced discipline decisions, then I would have been thought to be weak. Worse than confusing the faculty would be for the students to take my circumstantial decisions as weakness. I was an athlete and a fearless leader. I was not afraid to stand by my right-and-wrong-and-nothing-in-between discipline system, no matter the personal pain it brought me. "What will they think of me if I am not a strong leader?"

I had experienced headaches before my six Berry Academy years, but that would mostly be when I myself had had one alcoholic beverage over my limit. Now rare would be a Saturday morning that I would awaken without a splitting and debilitating headache. The headache would be connected to my stomach. I attributed this misery to the cost of leadership. I dressed up my inability to be in touch with my feelings as what a strong leader must endure.

Realizing Mom's Lack of Support for Her Dreams, How Was I Then to Treat JoElyn?

When I retired from eleven-plus go-go-go years as executive director of Atlanta Youth Academy, I began to think more and more about JoElyn. Her needs and desires had always taken a back seat to my career and my needs, and a back seat to those of Jane and Evelyn Anne.

Even though I was still "full of myself" as I mixed and mingled with important people in the pursuit of renewing Grove Park, I did determine that I wanted to push our good marriage to a great marriage, if there was, in fact, any way to do that. (This thought was a more personal application of Jim Collins' concept which he conceived for businesses: "If we are content with being *pretty good*, then *good is the enemy of ever becoming great.*") As I heard about all the AWPC people, including the pastors and elders, engaging in counseling, I thought that counseling would be a good place to start.

JoElyn and I went to Tim Lane a half-dozen times, primarily to take the Birkman Behavioral Assessment. From that I learned that "desire to be out among nature" was second to lowest on JoElyn's testing and that the enjoyment of the arts and of a fine meal out were legitimized as real needs of JoElyn's. The tests said she liked organization. And, it said she was most comfortable when those around are interested in feelings as well as logic.

If we were going to move our marriage from good to great, then I reasoned that I was going to have to address this matter of emotions. I joined a Men's Emotions Processing Group led by Justin Hitchcock's friend Jeff Grossman. I referred some to the "feelings wheel" that Anne Henegar has advocated for use initially by the women's four-person quads. It's a slow go, but I'm making some progress towards showing interest in feelings, both JoElyn's and mine.

We added the four-per-year early Friday evening symphony concerts to our calendars and more frequent trips to the High Museum and Botanical Gardens. We made a four-night trip to New York to meet one of JoElyn's (and my) felt needs to breathe in again the energy and creativity of NYC. We have taken some two-night trips to Savannah and Jekyll and Callaway Gardens.

Just as Mom had literature and her own creative writing locked up inside her, JoElyn has an innate need and desire to create. We knew she needed a space dedicated to that. She was happily and productively at The Goat Farm from August 2015 until she established in 2019 her new studio on Hollowell Parkway.

How might things have changed for Mom if someone had encouraged her in her poetry writing? What if she had had a few poems published early on?

Mom grew up attending North Avenue Presbyterian Church. She graduated from North Avenue Presbyterian School. Yet she was not as an adult a "pray-er," Bible reader, or church attender. She did, however, make sure we were in church

(Peachtree Road Presbyterian) every Sunday. She had a high moral standard that she passed on to her boys via quotes from *Poor Richard's Almanac*, and the like:

- A penny saved is a penny earned.
- A stitch in time saves nine.
- Early to bed, early to rise makes a man healthy, wealthy and wise.
- Cleanliness is next to godliness.
- God helps those who help themselves.
- Idleness is the devil's workshop.
- Your eyes are bigger than your stomach.

Mom's aphorisms were backed up by sayings on the locker room walls of the sports world in which we lived:

- When the going gets tough, the tough get going.
- No pain, no gain.
- Football is like life—it requires perseverance, self-denial, hard work, sacrifice, dedication and respect for authority. (Vince Lombardi)
- Fatigue makes cowards of us all. (Vince Lombardi)

If this "work ethic" is what Mom grew up under, and she never outgrew it, this certainly would have added to the emotional weight she was carrying throughout her life. Finally it morphed into boredom, depression, and terminal alcoholism.

Struggling with wanting to "measure up" has been in my life and has robbed me for years of a winsome contentment. I felt myself to be like Alex P. Keaton in *Family Ties* (Michael J. Fox)—i.e., " a tight little guy." I was wound up tight. One outward sign of that has been my hyper-aversion to wasting time. Maybe it is developmentally impossible to know at ages twenty-five or thirty what we learn by ages seventy-five or eighty: God could not love me any more than He already does. Nothing I do is going to gain more favor from Him nor make Him disappointed in me.

Elsewhere in my writing I have wondered if Mom were really a strikingly beautiful woman with deep literary interests and talents who was sacrificed to raise four boys. Assuming this to be the case, what would she say today about her number three son—the one who was the baby of the family for five-plus years? Would she understand "the abundant life" that her number three son now enjoys or would she see that he, by his initiative or that of others, was always moving on to the next great job, never staying long enough to leave his mark?

Whether by her conscious choice or by default, I believe she gave her very life for the four of us, and for Dad.

If she were to be disappointed that I turned out to be a people pleaser, an avoider when it comes to emotions and hard conversation, she might say, "But he married a girl after my own heart. I bequeath to her my love of the arts. Let her paint out of her heart—one canvas for each poem I knew by heart, one canvas for each poem I composed in my mind throughout my sixty-one years."

And she might say, "Oh, my precious Chuckie, you had the daughters that I longed for. How I would love Jane and Evelyn Anne. Your first child loves so deeply the unloved. The piece she wrote about Sylvester, the man down the street that had no blood family, that's right up there with the literature I so love. And the other, the younger one, struggling against the powers of darkness so nobly. What I would have given to have had her strength and support to have fought my demons. I know this is fanciful, but I would love to have been her classmate at St. John's and a part of her treasured cadre of friends. I was two generations too early to have shared the freedom that those two wonderful girls enjoy. And I see in how they care for each other the relationship that would have been my saving grace if I had been able to be that close to my sister, Virginia.

"[If a parent had significant shortcomings as we were growing up] grieve for them on the way to forgiveness and healing." — Jason Kriaski in Atlanta Westside Church sermon, October 2018

"And, sweet Chuckie, write. Write not of the Camelot that was never mine, but write of the Narnia that has been granted to you. And if you include me in your writing, write me not as one who bailed on my family but as one who loved you more than anything, even unto death. And when I look around at you and your brothers, I know I have not lived in vain."

"Write not of the Camelot that was never mine …"

Camelot, the musical, entered the American psyche in December 1960. Mom was fifty-one years old and I was within eight days of turning twenty. The world portrayed in *Camelot* was the world in which Mom grew up—sorta. She went to the best schools—North Avenue Presbyterian School, Sweet Briar, and, for a broader experience in her senior year, University of Illinois. She and her father read poetry together and discussed fine literature. She made her Atlanta debut in the mid-1920s. She lived in a fine home with cooks and maids, and vegetable gardens and chickens and orchards in the back forty.

A line out of the opening song in *Camelot* speaks to Mom's life up to the point when adult life crept in: "By order, summer lingers through September in Camelot." For you see, her birthday was in September, so summer had to linger for Jane (aka Mom).

Why do tears come to my eyes so readily when I picture Mom's reflection on our present life? Because, I think, I would love to share with Mom my present life, rich in love and support, with effective help in fighting mental illness and its accompanying addictions. She could be the reader of poetry in our household, together with Evelyn Anne and me on Fridays or with JoElyn and the Gilbert Five on Sunday evenings on the screened porch.

Why does one generation have to give way to the next? Why couldn't my girls know Mom—Mom at her best? Why do my brothers grow older, and, in some respects, more distant? Why do I no longer enjoy the long runs that Jane, JoElyn, and I used to do on Saturday mornings, and then the races—often with Terrell and Rich added in? I would like to be in Ellie's and Chad's and Martha Jane's lives for a long time to come, but that is unlikely.

As the kingdom is crumbling around them, King Arthur says to the page, Tom, "Run, boy, run." Survive to tell our story: "Yes, Camelot, my boy! Where once it never rained till after sundown, by eight a.m. the morning fog had flown... Don't let it be forgot, that once there was a spot, for one brief shining moment, that was known as Camelot."

Chapter 6: A Letter to Mom

February 15, 2017

Dear Mom,

Since your death on Mother's Day, 1970, I have thought sparingly about you until my recent life as a writer of memoir. And now rich thoughts of you come tumbling back. I find I can't separate the life of Jane Dillon Johnston from my life. My first editor, daughter Evelyn Anne, has led me to see you in my life all along, from the time of your death until today. Can you believe it? Your little Chuckie is now seventy-six. But wait—Dick is eighty-one and Dillon is seventy-eight. Warren will be forever young. He's only seventy.

How the generations interact, one giving way to the next, fascinates me more than ever now that I am in the midst of memoir writing. For instance, is there some hidden secret about the fact that you died in May 1970 and I finally met the girl that I could really get close to three months later? It was as if you said at your departure, "Now, go find the one you can grow old with, a dream of mine that your

The annual "Brothers Reunion," on the coast of Maine, June 2018: Dillon and Guinn, Sandy and Warren, JoElyn and Chuck, Mary Anne and Dick

dad and I were denied." She, like you, is very pretty. She, like you, is an artist—she with paint and canvas, you with pen and paper.

Let me ask you a few questions. Do you remember a season in your life when you moved from social drinking to using alcohol as medication? How old were you then? How old were we, your boys? Were you conscious of a time when you realized that you couldn't do without it? I'll have to tell you—it became pretty awful for the rest of us. I can only imagine how awful it was for you. You would hide bottles of vodka or gin under things in the back of your closet or in the dirty clothes hamper or in the water tank at the back of the toilet, and I and my brothers would try to find the bottles and pour them out before you finished them.

Was there medical or psychological help available and you just couldn't bring yourself to go seek that help? Or was it, as I suspect, such a social stigma that you couldn't bring yourself to expose yourself as an alcoholic? This doesn't help you now, but today there is more openness about mental health. In our church, it's the rare member who doesn't go to counseling. At one time, JoElyn and Evelyn Anne were going to the same counselor, and Jane ran with this same counselor and got her fix. Evelyn Anne has spent a week or more on two occasions at Ridgeview Psychiatric Hospital. And it was a Godsend for Evelyn Anne and for us. We sat in classes and learned more about her chronic disease, manic-depressive disorder, and how we could help Evelyn Anne without doing *too much* for her. She learned coping mechanisms during her residency. When she was discharged from the hospital, she gained a lot of ongoing support from Emotions Anonymous and other such resources. Dr. Michael Lyles is her psychiatrist. She has hardly missed a month of seeing him for the past ten years.

The onset of her illness probably began when she was fifteen or sixteen. It became full-blown when she was a freshman in college, and then the only sustained relief she has experienced, and that has been partial, has come in the spring of 2015, when she was thirty-one years old. My point in all this is that Evelyn Anne's disease may or may not be tougher than what you were going through. But there is help out there now. I wish there could have been when you needed it so badly in your thirties, forties, and fifties. You were alone to fight the demons.

You have two namesakes in our family. One is our daughter Jane, born August 5, 1974, in Rome, Georgia. The other is granddaughter Martha Jane, born June 21, 2010, in Kampala, Uganda, to Brenda and to Martha Jane's possibly Ethiopian or Sudanese father, whose name we don't know. Daughter Jane was born with all of the hallmarks of the leader she has become. From an early age she held strong opinions and had a strong will. We were bolstered in parenting Jane by the pre-political James Dobson through his radio programs and through his books, *Dare to Discipline* and *The Strong-Willed Child*. We also sought outside parental counselling. Were you, Mom, anything like that or were you a compliant child?

I wish you could know Jane now. She would totally get you. To be a fulltime mother, she, like you, has given up a lot of what gets publicly recognized. She loves being with her children, and because of it, they reflect her heart for the "forgotten people." Her fourteen-year-old daughter, Ellie, wrote on her mom's valentine yesterday, "You see people who aren't seen." How's that for recognition from your teenage child?!

She now is back in the world of working outside the home, stemming in part from financial pressure, but also very much from the strong desire for work that gives her joy while fully using her many passions and strengths. Her assistant-teacher work with fourth grade students does not reflect what she really wants to be doing, but it's an entry point back into work outside the home. Eventually she would like to be paid to work in our neighborhood, Grove Park, to identify those who need help, and then to find for them the help they need.

Granddaughter Martha Jane, your other namesake, is thirty-six years younger than Jane the elder. She is now six. Martha Jane has beautiful, rich mahogany skin compared to mother, father, sister, brother, four grandparents plus three aunts and one uncle, who all have lighter skin. She, too, is funny; she loves to read; she memorizes song lyrics in a jiffy and loves to sing. She adores and is adored by her older brother and sister, and she is not afraid to give them push-back when she deems it warranted. At a young age her parents have told her about her adoption and all they know about her mom.

She began to ask if she could meet her birth-mom, Brenda. As Jane and Terrell (Jane's husband, who is a lawyer as was your dad, Grandpa) tried to get more current news about Brenda, they learned that she had returned to the couple that had taken her under wing when she was a child. This time Brenda was deathly sick with what Jane speculates was AIDS. She got better, left this caring couple once again, and died soon after, back out on the street. At Terrell's request, the caring couple sent Terrell the best picture of Brenda that they had. Terrell had it enlarged and mounted on a Styrofoam backing, and gave it to Martha Jane as they told her about Brenda's death. Martha Jane broke into sobs welling up from deep inside. At somewhere in the five-turning-six era of her life, she was distraught that she would never have a chance to ask her mom questions. A year later, just recently now, she wrote the following words to Brenda: January 26, 2017 — *"Dear Brenda, I hope you loved me. I never got to see you."*

As she concluded, she certainly showed no lack of love for her Gilbert family. It was a beautiful glimpse into her sensitive heart.

I don't know what a storybook marriage would look like. It might not be such a healthy thing. I honestly think God intended that there be some friction in a marriage, or else what would the Scripture referring to "iron sharpening iron" mean? The other aspect of God's plan for marriage is that it can be his best instrument for teaching us to be less selfish. "It's all about me" doesn't stand up very well in a healthy marriage.

I know that you and Dad had disputes from time to time. It's hard for me to assess to what extent Dad being out of town so much contributed to this. His traveling seemed in the category of an indisputable necessity, so there was never pressure on him to get another job, as far as I was aware. (You did used to say that it would be the week that Dad was out of town when all four of us boys would come down with measles or mumps or chicken pox.) I know that at one time you may have wanted a really nice rug for the living room while Dad wanted a spaced-brick wall separating our front yard from the side patio. I know that you worked it out so that in time you both got your wish, with maybe the beautiful wall getting a bit of a lead over the beautiful rug. (The wall has long since been gone, but your Shalistan hand-knotted Persian rug graces our living room and is enjoyed by JoElyn and me, the two generations after us, and by special guests we have in our home. It would be interesting to know how many subsequent generations will enjoy your rug. Not that we didn't take great pride in our spaced-brick wall and enjoy many a family gathering cloistered inside it, but, as I said, it is long gone.)

You would like JoElyn. She's a girl, mind you, and she was an only child, but other than that, we are just alike. (Ha ha). She worries about money, that we are going to come to the end of our money before we come to the end of our bills. Yet she is a terrific money manager. She has a couple of funds set aside for the big expenses that aren't in our monthly budget (e.g., medical, home and car insurance; vacation; car repair), but every time she dips into those funds, it grieves her. For some women, I understand, the monthly period is a time of distress—not now for

JoElyn. Her time of distress comes twice a month—the two times she sits down to pay bills. I have to "walk on eggshells" to avoid a dispute on the nights after bill paying, with the possibility of her saying, "We've just got to stop spending so much money," and my saying, "JoElyn, we haven't missed a meal in our 46 years of being married." .... You'll be pleased to know that we are determined to continue inching our marriage closer and closer to *great.* Issues over money are now handled without rising blood pressures.

JoElyn has a studio at The Goat Farm, where three or four afternoons a week she cloisters herself and paints. She is encouraged by some outside recognition of her talent, and she is selling some paintings. I go to that same studio space in the mornings and write. I feel a sense of purpose when I can reflect on my life by way of my memoir writing. Maybe I will have something, like with your Shalistan rug, that can be passed down from one generation to the next. JoElyn's paintings will most assuredly be passed down the avenue of succeeding generations.

Mom, just as I wish I knew more about your life, I want you to know how your legacy has prospered since the last time we were together.

With great love and greater understanding, I am your #3 son,

Chuck

A Final Word on Mom

I wish for her namesakes, Jane and Martha Jane, and for many others that I could end my memories of Mom here—the story of a sheltered yet courageous member of her generation who absorbed a lot of pain and self-sacrifice, and bore up under it.

But since I'm trying to get as close to the truth as I can, I cannot leave it here. Since I seek truth about my own life and Mom's presence in my life, I must tell the whole truth as best I know it.

If a beloved family member spent the last decade of his or her life wearing diapers and not knowing who anyone is, might that prolonged Alzheimer's infect our sweet memories of that family member? Well, I realize that my ability to embrace the sweet and full-of-purpose Mom of my memory is gone, and I'm trying unsuccessfully to bring her back. I know it's there, but try as I will, I can't go back there in my heart and soul. Alcoholism is a more horrific blot on a person's life than an illness should be. Maybe a child's view of it is a bit how we as a child and young person might respond to divorce or suicide in a parent. In our self-focus, we might well say, "How could you not think of me when you did this? If you loved me enough, you would have mustered up your strength and selflessness and would not have gone down this destructive path."

Hopefully my reading descendants will forgive me for not conveying my deep love for my mother, but I can't feel it. I like to think that I felt it then, especially as a toddler, as an elementary student. But as I entered my high school years, my emotions were so frayed by hoping and then having hope turn into inner rage, that gradually I replaced my natural smile for a fake one, my innate optimism for a manufactured *power of positive thinking*. In other words, I stuffed my emotions so successfully that I lost the capacity to feel. It has taken the help of Bobby Mitchell, JoElyn, and Atlanta Westside Church's emphasis on the heart to gradually bring back my ability to feel love and anger, joy and shame, happiness and apprehension, to view all as God-given and therefore good emotions. Along with this new consciousness of emotions is the reawakening of my love for Mom.

"We all know stories that end in failure, but we wouldn't necessarily say that those people were themselves failures. Why does it seem clear to me that your mom's life was not a failure, despite the unpleasantness of her final years, or the fact that she never fully realized the ambitions of her childhood?" — Evelyn Anne Clausen

Chapter 7: 'I Will Stay in the Classroom and Teach'

While at McCallie School in the early 1960s, I settled the issue of using the classroom as a steppingstone to "more prestigious" positions in school administration. "No way," I said to myself firmly. If I wanted a desk job, I'd go into business. I knew I'd make more money as an administrator, but the reason I chose the field of education was because I loved kids, and English, and sports.

There would have been no place in the world better to start my professional life than at McCallie School. I taught five classes of tenth-grade English to boys, I was the head ninth-grade football coach (with Barry Mosher), the assistant ninth-grade basketball coach (with Joe Campbell), and I coached varsity middle-distance runners in track. I lived and worked in the dorm, and I took boys hiking and camping on the weekends. In the summers I worked with Houston Patterson in the Academic Enrichment Camp, which included weekend hiking on the Appalachian Trail.

Here is a gratifying note I got in 2016 from Bob Card of Cleveland, Tennessee, fifty-plus years after I had had him in my McCallie classroom:

August 14, 2016

I want to thank you for having the biggest and best influence on my life of any teacher or coach. I am 53 years late in saying this. My father and my uncle had the most and best influence of all on me, but when I arrived at McCallie I did not know what a noble man was like until I met you. I decided I wanted to grow up to be an honorable and noble man like you. I had not known what idealism was. You also said work hard, play hard, and do the right thing.

I am so glad I got a chance to reconnect with you in May and again in June. You have not changed. At lunch I asked you what saying I remember best from our McCallie days, and you guessed it was when you said "when the going gets tough the tough get going" which was correct; but I remembered the abbreviated version of that best. When I would pass by you while running around the track you almost always said "be strong." You took some of us dorm boys on hikes on Sunday afternoons of which I still cherish the thoughts. When you moved on to teach at Westminster and I came back to McCallie for my third year, I wanted to go home when I learned you were not there. My mother insisted I stay. I wondered how I should proceed. I decided I would "be strong." Since graduating from college, once a month on a rest-and-relax day, in honor of you I get out something you taught me in the best class I ever had—high school sophomore English. What I reread and remember is mostly Shakespeare, Kipling, William Faulkner's Nobel Award acceptance speech, and English literature. Not only do I remember what you said back then but also how you said it.

Most people know you as a headmaster, a founder of schools, and for your ideas on education. It is easy to follow your outstanding successes at these schools. Your reputation is well known. There is nowhere near the amount of information on your short years as a teacher and coach. That is one reason I am writing this letter. Perhaps someday one of your descendants who knows about your headmaster and founder career will wonder how you taught. You taught well and with so much enthusiasm that it has stayed with me my entire life. It was not easy being a 14-year-old boarding student at a military school in the early 1960s, but you made it very worthwhile.

Thank you very much.

Bob

My Reply to Bob Card

August 19, 2016

Bob, I have waited this long to read your message to me to make sure I had the time and serenity to answer you with as much thought and love as you have shown to me.

First of all, I got into education to teach and coach, the perfect combination for an adult of one age to fully get to know another fully-alive student of another age. The hiking and other encounters only added richness of life experiences for me. I was getting as much from you and others as you say I was giving to you. (Funny how that works.) I felt called to the administrative roles, but administration was never as personally gratifying as the one-on-one with students. That's why your note means so much to me.

You and Lynn [Weigel] were, among all the students at McCallie with whom I worked, the two I wanted to keep up with. I would say that I felt a kindred spirit with you. You responded to the things that I liked, that I valued, that I thought added to the richness of life. When Scripture speaks of "the abundant life," I think that means:

- Don't take the easy path, the lazy path.
- Be an adventurer; take risks; learn how to win by sometimes losing.
- Don't ever think we've quit learning or quit sticking your neck out.
- Have a heart for the marginalized; Jesus certainly did.

Your engagement with Catholicism is an example of your searching and growing. If you had been a lifelong Catholic, spiritual refreshment might have come from becoming a Presbyterian. We just need to keep seeking a fresh perspective.

I'm glad you referenced Faulkner's Nobel Acceptance Speech: "He [the young writer] must teach himself that the basest of all things is to be afraid; and, teaching himself that, forget it forever, leaving no room in his workshop for anything but the old verities and truths of the heart, the old universal truths lacking which any story is ephemeral and doomed—love and honor and pity and pride and compassion and sacrifice."

Thank you so much, Bob, for your kind words that lead us to see that over 50 years ago we did have an impact on one another's lives. It's such a joy to revisit that and celebrate that.

In His adventure and love,

Chuck

Chapter 8: Sunday Night Reading of 'O Captain, My Captain' — What Is Behind the Tears?

Exult, O shores, and ring, O bells!
But I, with mournful tread,
Walk the deck my Captain lies,
Fallen cold and dead.

This verse above concludes Walt Whitman's dirge written upon the death of Abraham Lincoln in 1865. Why, when I read this poem recently (February 2017) at a Sunday night family supper, did I get choked up?

First of all, I sensed that I was continuing a tradition begun in my life, in my single-digit years, by my grandfather. He read from *One Hundred and One Famous Poems*, and this little book and the poems that Grandpa read from it had a surprisingly big impact on the person I grew to be. In fact, I introduced my McCallie sophomore boys to this book and its collection of poems. And it is from this book that I am now reading to my grandchildren.

What else triggered my tears when I read this particular poem? For one thing, Lincoln was a favorite of Grandpa's, as he is with many people. So, maybe subconsciously I was thinking of Grandpa. He was the first person to die that I dearly, dearly loved. I was twelve years old. I liked the attention that the bereaved family group gets at the death of a loved one, but I sure did miss Grandpa. I couldn't quite figure out how a person can be so vital in the lives of others and so alive himself and then be totally gone. I was experiencing that burning in the throat and tightness in the chest that often, inexplicably, brought on sobs of tears. So, that was there when I read the poem aloud to my family.

My own mortality must have been mixed in my emotions as I read the poem. While awaiting me is walking with the Father and the Son without distractions, I am too much enjoying the special ones God gave me to love (my family) to run towards the splendid transformation of life that will come. As I go back and ask my memory to speak about Grandpa and the others who poured into my life, I sense more clearly the cavalcade of dear, dear loved ones who preceded me. Now, as my generation mounts the stairs towards ancestry, we bequeath our previous stairway landings to Jane, Evelyn Anne, Terrell, and Jonathan of early adulthood and then the productive middle years. They, in turn, pass on to Ellie, Chad, and Martha Jane youth and then early adulthood.

[*Note:* If the chapter above were written today, it certainly would have included our third daughter, LaTonya, and her family. But, alas, I wrote this in response to an event that occurred in 2017, before God brought to us as family LaTonya, Anthony, and Larenzia.]

It must feel to the four just behind us who are moving from "early adulthood" to "productive years" as if they are being pushed. Maybe so? Hopefully not. Ideally the movement up is embraced as the next great adventure.

JoElyn and I, again by the grace of God, stretched our "productive years" into our early and mid-seventies. Now we have entered the fourth quarter. We'll call it our senior years, our retirement years. What we make of these years is more free for us to choose than any of the earlier stair landings. Why is that? Well, we no longer have to "make a living." We no longer have children to raise. We no longer have to plan for the future. We're there.

We are freer than we've ever been. Our schedule is ours alone to make. Is this a day when I can linger and read the paper with breakfast; or do I save it for lunchtime at home? What we read, what we attend, who we spend time with—there are no more "must do" items and only a few "should do's." We are now in February of 2017 in the early days of *Retirement.* Jane, Evelyn Anne, Terrell, and Jonathan are in their *Productive Years,* and Ellie, Chad, and Martha Jane bring us honor maintaining the *Youth* landing on the stairs.

Why else did I choke up when I read this poem? There is the beauty of the poem itself and the emotion that it draws from the reader. There is the image of cheering, adoring throngs waiting at the port to greet their beloved leader.

Unbeknownst to the cheering crowd, the beloved one lies on the deck, cold and dead.

"Rise up, Captain, it must be a dream. Rise up and hear the bells. It's for you they cheer," says the poet. An incredible victory has been won, a victory the poet can't enjoy. The Captain of this voyage to knit the union back together is not here to exult in the victory.

> O Captain! my Captain! our fearful trip is done,
> The ship has weather'd every rack, the prize we sought is won,
> The port is near, the bells I hear, the people all exulting,
> While follow eyes the steady keel, the vessel grim and daring;
>> But O heart! heart! heart!
>> O the bleeding drops of red,
>> Where on the deck my Captain lies,
>> Fallen cold and dead.

> O Captain! my Captain! rise up and hear the bells;
> Rise up—for you the flag is flung—for you the bugle trills,
> For you bouquets and ribbon'd wreaths—for you the shores a-crowding,
> For you they call, the swaying mass, their eager faces turning;
>> Here Captain! dear father!

This arm beneath your head!
It is some dream that on the deck,
You've fallen cold and dead.

My Captain does not answer, his lips are pale and still,
My father does not feel my arm, he has no pulse nor will,
The ship is anchor'd safe and sound, its voyage closed and done,
From fearful trip the victor ship comes in with object won;
Exult O shores, and ring O bells!
But I with mournful tread,
Walk the deck my Captain lies,
Fallen cold and dead.

Chapter 9: What Defines a Life Well Lived?

I received this writing assignment from Evelyn Anne one day:

What defines a person's life, either in terms of "a life well lived" or some other similar phrase? Maybe figuring out the phrase is part of the question. For example, how would you describe your mother's life in a sentence? Obviously, each life is more complicated than a single adjective, but what is it that we are describing when we talk about "how" a person lived?

How do we go about answering that question? How do we even talk about a life in terms of how it was lived? It is too simplistic to say a person "lived a good life" and too generic to say a person "lived a complicated life." So what is our metric when looking at an individual after they are gone? What does that say to us who are still alive about the kind of life we should seek to live?

Even if you can't directly answer the question of what makes a good or important or worthwhile life, write down whatever train of thought this brings to your mind.

Francis Schaeffer asked a similar question this way: "How should we then live?"

And to that I would say, live your life with some of the qualities of my Top Ten (a Top Ten that could be replaced by several more Top Tens. These are just some folks that came quickly to mind):

- ✓ The priest in *Les Misérables* — In the scene with the silver candelabras, his heart beat more for a person than for "priceless" material goods.

- ✓ Atticus Finch, in *To Kill a Mockingbird*, who lived in the deep South, as we do, but lived with Biblical values that put him at odds with the privileged white culture surrounding him.

- ✓ Jimmy Carter, who refused to slip away in shame. He might have said, "How can I maximize my experiences and my worldwide friendships to make life better for others?"

- ✓ Queen Elizabeth II, who put duty ahead of the life she might have had.

- ✓ Elliot Galloway (founder and longtime head of Galloway School), who had an easygoing manner focused on other people (of all ages). His lack of self-importance in the world of puffed-up headmasters was like a refreshing drink of cold water. He fed his mind with books, his body with marathons. He obviously loved Kitty, his wife.

- ✓ Grandpa — I didn't know him except in his last six and a half years. What I saw was a man who created purpose when the identification of a career was gone. His routine said to me "these things are important enough to me that I do them every day without fail: studying, writing, making things grow and making live things thrive." He sowed into the lives of his grandsons: poetry, public speaking, taking life seriously. (We are not here just to have fun.)

- ✓ Larry Teem — He defies the odds and will follow an inspiration until multiple doors are slammed in his face or until he turns the inspiration into a ministry for the underserved. He has positively impacted untold numbers of kids through sports leagues where sportsmanship is paramount and where prayer with both teams together precedes the competition; through summer camps at God's Farm; and through Atlanta Youth Academy with its vision of a prep-school-type education for low-income urban kids. He has another mysterious quality: he cedes credit and center stage to others, such as me.

- ✓ Henry and Jane Henegar (Walter's parents) — Their modesty preaches. They are the epitome of lifelong educators and learners. They are so easy to be with.

- ✓ Ed Jones (JoElyn's uncle and stepfather) — Was there a self-serving bone in his body? I couldn't find one. He served his first wife, Anne, with her alcoholism and then cancer. He turned down higher leadership positions with Alabama Power because moving would be unsettling to his handicapped son, Carrol. He was so giving to Evelyn and JoElyn.

How I define a life well lived will differ from anyone else's definition. Just looking at this list of characters tells me, "Nobody else could have the same list." What qualities above stand out?

- ✓ People over things (non-materialistic)
- ✓ Living with defeat, without shame
- ✓ Others (duty) over self
- ✓ Absence of self-importance; modesty
- ✓ Living life with *purpose*
- ✓ Generous in giving credit to others
- ✓ Leaving a legacy in other's lives
- ✓ Congeniality
- ✓ Knowing that you are not defined by your job
- ✓ Being bold

I will sometimes end the day by saying to JoElyn, either for myself when we have spent the day apart, or for both of us when we have spent it together, "This has been a well-spent day!" It would be a bonus if at the end of this life I were able to say, "Mine has been a life well spent!"

Having just written that last sentence, I was startled by the arrogant edge to that statement. So, I hastened to say (write?) that I'm not talking about virtue. I'm talking about the right balance of frivolity and seriousness, of routine and adventure, of taking risks and playing it safe, of guarding my time and in giving my time to others. This life that has the right balance between craziness and earnestness, between feasting and kale, of enjoying a crowd and solitude.

Thinking about Evelyn Anne's writing assignment on "a life well lived," the book of Proverbs means more to me because that's what Solomon is writing about. Maybe I could just purloin his saying. "Those who help others are helped" (Proverbs 11:25) is like my saying: "Friendly people nine out of ten times are met with a friendly response when they initiate friendliness. Speak to a person in passing, and, when he or she smiles and/or speaks back, it will light you up."

"I [Lady Wisdom] am both Insight and the Virtue to live it out. ... O, my dear friends, listen carefully; those who embrace these my ways are most blessed. Mark a life of discipline and live wisely; don't squander your precious life. ... Blessed the man, blessed the woman, who listens to me, awake and ready for me each morning, alert and responsive as I start my day's work" (Proverbs 8:14, 32-34).

"... but they that wait upon the LORD shall renew their strength; they shall mount up with wings as eagles; they shall run, and not be weary; they shall walk, and not faint" (Isaiah 40:31).

Proverbs 10:22 reads, "God is solid backing to a well-lived life, but he calls into question a shabby performance." Here, God is not critical of someone who doesn't complete every task in front of him or her. In fact, I think He applauds the one who, at dusk, leaves work and goes to be with loved ones, and, if possible, takes some daily Sabbath time to rest. We were made for work, but we are to couple it with the daily gift of Sabbath rest. For me a well-spent day would be to work diligently, and then to take pleasure in our work and in our cessation of work.

The following are a synthesis of advice I have gotten along the way, so I'll pass it on as if it were my own:

If my heart softens to the needs of others, it means that I am willing to relinquish some of my own perceived needs.

"Getting and spending, we lay waste our powers," wrote William Wordsworth in his poem "The World Is Too Much With Us." In response, let me modify my human desire to have nicer things and experiences.

If I really crave adventure as I say I do, then I've got to learn to live with some humbling experiences (i.e., failures)—and I've had plenty of them.

Carrying into life a sense of duty is not a bad thing. I believe, for those of us who seek it, there is a purpose for our lives. Searching for that purpose and then attempting to live it out gives one enthusiasm for getting out of bed in the morning.

Be grateful for sobering experiences in our lives that show us we are but a tiny speck in the universe. Once truly absorbing that, and being healed of self-importance, we build back our sense of importance, not self-importance, but sweet confidence that we are just what our Creator made us to be.

I have always feasted on words like gusto, zest, passion, abundance, and delight. Words matter. Subdue what Zig Ziegler calls "stinkin' thinkin'." Joy and purpose are joined at the hip in a life well lived.

Your personal sense of accomplishment is enhanced when you are in a habit of giving credit to others.

Live in such a way that another might emulate something they see in you. Don't be overly self-conscious that there is anything in you worth emulating.

Let it be said of you, "He or she is as comfortable to be around as an old shoe," to borrow an expression. You're not trying to be anything but congenial; make those around you pleased to be with you.

See how much you can find out about a new acquaintance without asking, "What do you do?" It's hard for me not to talk about what I have done because, if I'm not mindful, I will become prideful about the various jobs that I've had. Superior it is to be known for your character rather than your occupation.

Earlier, in the chapter on Mom's effect on my life, I envisioned that Mom might say to me, "Write not of the Camelot that was never mine, but write of the Narnia that has been granted to you." For me that means that the path of my life thus far comes not out of my cleverness or talent; rather, the pathway has been laid down by a Supernatural Force, and for me it has been as simple as following that course. He (Our Creator), even, like a caring mother, has waked me up each morning and has set my feet upon that path.

Did Mom not realize that I had stumbling blocks along the way? I wasn't good at football. I had a hard time with my grades my first two years of Vanderbilt. For almost too long, I burned for and prayed for a female with whom I would have as much fun and be as free-flowing with as the relationships I enjoyed with my brothers. At one period in my life, the decade of my fifties, I left four jobs after seeing the writing on the wall or after hearing the words of that writing voiced by another: "Chuck, it's time for you to move on."

Other stumbling blocks? JoElyn's sense that we didn't have enough money and we were in grave danger of running out was hard on us both, but mostly on her; I hated to see her so agonized.

At some point in her high school years, Evelyn Anne had been suffering from manic-depressive disorder involving hearing voices, and I was no help to her. Here I am an educator and I couldn't even see depression in my own sweet daughter. And then as the illness grew, I was able to do little more than to stand by and watch her suffer.

The following exchange from C.S. Lewis's *The Chronicles of Narnia* sheds light on the ups and down of my life: "Ooh!" said Susan, "… Is he—quite safe?" Mrs. Beaver responds, "Who said anything about being safe? 'Course he isn't safe. But he's good. He's the king, I tell you."

The things that I have declared as "stumbling blocks" are an intentional part of the landscape of my life, and, in many cases, of my family's life. Intentional? By whose intent? Just as the pathway has been laid out by a loving Supernatural Force, by the Same Hand have the stumbling blocks been put in my path.

Oh, at times I have asked for safe passage on the highway for our family, or I have asked for strength to overcome. I have asked God to remove a test from me, but I don't remember ever asking God to cease with His provision of adventure. So, just as Aslan gave the children the life-changing and soul-changing experiences of Narnia, He has given to me Adventure.

"Is he—quite safe?" No, and a lot of my fondest dreams, my most inspired adventures, have ended in "shipwreck." But at the end of the day, I have been able to say along with Mrs. Beaver, "God is good."

APPENDIX

Appendix 1

Grandpa's Bio

From *Men of the South* (1922), book by the Southern Biographical Association, New Orleans:

WALTER SOLOMON DILLON.

WALTER SOLOMON DILLON, ATLANTA, GA.

Walter Solomon Dillon, 620 Hurt building, Atlanta, Ga., has reached a position of eminent success in the past eight years, during which he has practiced law, independently, establishing many influential connections. Dividing his practice into departments, with himself as overseeing head, Mr. Dillon's office is in touch with some criminal practice, but he specializes in civil work. Important cases with which he has been intrusted have been handled with signal ability, and owing to his reputation for integrity and learnedness, his business has grown to be one of the largest in the South. He has numerous clients through Northern capitalists doing business in the South.

Mr. Dillon was born in Elnora, Ind., December 14, 1874, son of Wesley T. and Evangeline (Arford) Dillon. He was educated in the public schools of his native State, and entering Westfield College, was graduated from this institution with the degree of B. S. He prepared for the practice of law in the Chicago Law School, graduating with the degree LL.M. Before he came to Atlanta in 1909, he had practiced law a few years in Chicago, Ill. His first four years of practice in Atlanta were with the firm of Anderson, Felder, Rountree and Wilson.

In 1904, Mr. Dillon was married to Miss Agnes Nelson, daughter of George B. Nelson, of Hazlehurst, Miss. Home address: 302 East Fourth street, Atlanta, Ga.

Mr. Dillon's magnetic personality has made him a potent factor in all civic movements in which he takes an interest. He was elected councilman for the fourth ward of Atlanta, serving during the years 1917-18. He is a popular member of the Atlanta Athletic Club, Lions Club and the Y. M. C. A.

Grandpa, the Writer

A founder of the Atlanta Lions' Club, Grandpa wrote regular columns for the newsletter, *Atlanta Lionews*. The following was published on January 9, 1953.

The Passing Years

By Walter Dillon

EDITOR'S NOTE: It is with both pleasure and humility that we give to Lionews readers this brief but revealing autobiography of our beloved charter member, Walter Dillon, who has for so long been a faithful contributor to the Atlanta Lions Club and to this publication. As in the cases of most good men, the background of this man explains his character, and portrays the half-century of preparation and development which has shaped and molded his sincerity of purpose, his warming friendliness, and his whole-hearted typification of Lionism at its best.

I was born in Daviess County, Indiana, in 1874 in a two-room house, one end of logs. My father died when I was ten, of typhoid fever, then a dreaded disease. This left me saddened beyond words to describe.

When I was about 12 we moved into a new house built of lumber sawed on our farm by my father. I can see the old sawmill now with its millpond where I took a dip on Easter with ill consequences. "How dear to this heart are the scenes of my childhood ... The wide spreading pond and the mill that stood by it ... And now, far removed from the loved habitation!"

My education began when I was four years old. I was then sent to our one-room country school. I stayed till I was sixteen, going to a normal school for a term in the fall. In the meantime I received some valuable experience tending crops and looking after sheep, calves, pigs and horses.

Having taught two years in the country, I was off to a small church college in Illinois, where I stayed for nearly four years. After teaching in Illinois for one year, I entered an evening law college in Chicago for a three year course. I worked in a law office part time, and taught in the Chicago public schools the rest.

Admitted to the Illinois bar in 1900, I practiced there, marrying a Mississippi girl in 1904. We followed some of her relatives to Atlanta in 1909.

Atlanta, as now, was a growing city. My business grew, and I would be ungrateful not to say my success was very much appreciated. Making profitable investments was a most difficult task.

The years moved swiftly. I became a Lion in 1920, having been recommended by a friend in Chicago when our Lion's Club was organized.

About 1943 I suffered a stroke. After consultation it was decided best to retire. Results have been satisfactory. My wife and I have improved our investments, we have made many nice trips, and we have always been comfortable.

My writings, which you have had to endure, originated because of an article I had written for Ollie Reeves, first editor. Gus Keiser later pressed me into service. You know the rest of the story.

Many of my articles have been on the serious side. This comes about because I have searched for the bigger values. These are values, such as nature has created, moral values, events that have made their dent on humanity, etc.

These values are sometimes found in religion, in science, in the education of our youth, and in the various phases of life.

So, these are the reasons for my serious compositions which, perhaps, have not been so highly appreciated by many members.

"It is always in season for old men to learn."

Appendix 2

Poems Grandpa Would Read Aloud to Us from *One Hundred and One Famous Poems*

How Did You Die?
Edmund Vance Cook

Did you tackle that trouble that came your way
   with a resolute heart and cheerful?
Or hide your face from the light of day
   with a craven soul and fearful?
Oh, a trouble's a ton, or a trouble's an ounce,
   or a trouble is what you make it.
And it isn't the fact that you're hurt that counts,
   but only how did you take it?

You are beaten to earth? Well, well, what's that?
   Come up with a smiling face.
It's nothing against you to fall down flat,
   but to lie there – that's disgrace.
The harder you're thrown, why the higher you bounce;
   be proud of your blackened eye!
It isn't the fact that you're licked that counts;
   it's how did you fight and why?

If
Rudyard Kipling

If you can talk with crowds and keep your virtue,
   Or walk with Kings – nor lose the common touch,
If neither foes nor loving friends can hurt you,
   If all men count with you, but none too much.
If you can fill the unforgiving minute
   With sixty seconds' worth of distance run,
Yours is the earth and everything that's in it,
   And – which is more – you'll be a man, my son!

A Psalm of Life
Henry Wadsworth Longfellow

Tell me not, in mournful numbers,
    Life is but an empty dream!
For the soul is dead that slumbers
    And things are not what they seem.

Life is real! Life is earnest!
    And the grave is not its goal;
Dust thou art, to dust returnest
    Was not spoken of the soul.

Not enjoyment, and not sorrow
    Is our destined end or way;
But to act, that each tomorrow
    Find us further than today.

Art is long, and Time is fleeting,
    And our hearts, though stout and brave,
Still, like muffled drums, are beating
    Funeral marches to the grave.

In the world's broad field of battle,
    In the bivouac of life,
Be not like dumb, driven cattle!
    Be a hero in the strife!

Trust no Future, howe'er pleasant!
    Let the dead past bury its dead!
Act, – act in the living Present,
    Heart within and God o'erhead!

Lives of great men all remind us
    We can make our lives sublime,
And, departing, leave behind us
    Footprints on the sands of time.

Footprints, that perhaps another,
    Sailing o'er life's solemn main,
A forlorn and shipwrecked brother,
    Seeing, shall take heart again.

Let us then be up and doing,
    With a heart for any fate;
Still achieving, still pursuing,
    Learn to labor and to wait.

Appendix 3

Letter from John Kennedy

JOHN F. KENNEDY
MASSACHUSETTS

COMMITTEES:
FOREIGN RELATIONS
LABOR AND PUBLIC WELFARE
JOINT ECONOMIC COMMITTEE

United States Senate
WASHINGTON, D.C.

December 8, 1959

Mr. Charles L. Johnston
Box 1349
Vanderbilt University
Nashville, Tennessee

Dear Mr. Johnston:

        I have received your letter of November 20
and appreciate very much your willingness to be of
assistance.

        At the present time I have no vacancies
on my staff. However, I would appreciate your sending
a brief resume of your qualifications and experience so that
in the event a suitable vacancy occurs I can contact you.

        With every good wish, I am

                            Sincerely,

                            John F. Kennedy

JFK:jl

Appendix 4

Europe from Journals and Postcards, 1964-65
(All correspondence was to Mom and Dad unless otherwise noted.)

Wednesday, 9-9-64 - *Journal*

I sit now and watch the beautiful French countryside roll by my big train window. I am on – well, I was in the warm sun on the train out of Nancy, but now I am in the station where I purchased this pen for 15 centimes. I have had an hour's layover here in Lyon and it is here that I have had my first real warm feeling toward my year here in France. I sat in the station and drank two local beverages and watched the people. They are wonderful and I feel a lot of love toward all of them.

The train ride began today at 12:28 p.m. in Luxembourg and will end in Grenoble at 10:30 tonight. Dillon, Anne, and I all changed trains at Metz and we parted company there—Dillon and Anne headed to Paris, and I to Grenoble. I cried as I watched them disappear in the crowd. I then passed through Nancy and changed trains at Dijon. The change at Lyon makes for three changes. The sound of the train whistle is different and neat. The farms were immaculate and green. I saw canals and barges with families and dogs on them – a first for me. Four nuns were on the train for a while. They were interesting and so very French.

To back up a bit, Iceland, our only stop on Icelandic Airlines, was barren, cold, and beautiful. There wasn't a single tree in sight on land or from the air. By air we saw much area which was covered by snow. Our arrival in Luxembourg was marked, I'm afraid, by our inability to communicate. I am glad that we are going to have to speak French in order to get along. It was in trying to check our baggage that we had a hard time. Our hotel was very nice ($6 for the three of us) and our dinner was superb. The city was beautiful and like nothing I had ever seen. Europeans certainly know how to garden. All of their homes had beautiful flowers and vegetables.

The train is closing up in Lyon and now moving out. I will disembark at the stop. When I awake in the morning on the way to make my contacts for my room, etc., I will be in Grenoble.

Saturday night (no date, perhaps 9-12) - *Postcard: Grenoble with Alps in background, to Gram and Warren*

This card shows Grenoble exactly as it is. The mountains are amazing. Of course, being the Alps I should have expected it. I have met three or four people who will be real friends, and all in the shops and restaurants are most kind and helpful. Warren, don't let anyone tell you that everyone in Europe speaks English.

It certainly isn't true. Learn each word that you can. After September 28 I will have a nice room for $28/month in a new building with good heat and all the water I want. I am lucky. My meals, at the school cafeteria, will cost perhaps no more than 38 cents per meal. ~ Love, Chuck

Wednesday, 9-16-64 - *Postcard from Nice, to Gram and Warren*

I am here in Nice sitting on a wall. The Med. is a beautiful blue color. The water is deep, cool, and refreshing. The sun is hot and I will be brown again in a day or two. I got here last night and stayed in a hotel for $3.60. Tonight I will stay here on this hill in a Youth Hostel for $1. Tomorrow I will go to Monaco and visit Princess Grace. The next day I will go to Cannes on my way to Marseille. ~ Love, Chuck

Wednesday, 9-16-64 - *Postcard from Nice to East 83rd Street*

Please save the cards and letters which I send during this year. They will serve for me as a record in picture and word of this year of the "Grand Tour." I came to Nice yesterday from Grenoble for $5.50 by bus. It took ten hours and was beautiful on the Route Napoleon through the Alps. I was practically standing on my head in the bus trying to see everything. My, what mountains! They extend almost to the Med. They are very rocky and barren in some parts. The Cote d'Azur (Med.) is beautiful. The water is green and clear. The hotels are much like Miami. I went to an art Museum this morning and am now enjoying swimming and walking on the beach. Tomorrow I will go to Monaco, and perhaps the next day I will head down the coast in the direction of Cannes. Bus travel is pleasant. People are unbelievably nice to me. ~ Love, Chuck

Jeudi, 9-17-64 - *Postcard: Reflets De La Cote D'Azur, Principaute De Monaco*

Last night I stayed in a youth hostel in Nice and this morning I came by foot and train here to Monaco. I have a nice room for $2.40 and had a wonderful lunch of tomato and cheese sandwiches, a family size-sized Coke, and peach — all fixed and enjoyed in my room as I sat and viewed the castle of Grace & Rainier. I had a wonderful swim in the Med. here and a nap in the sun. I swim laps for exercise. I have seen the castle, the changing of the guard, the yachts, the casino (I lost one franc), and all of the beautiful villas. This spot you will really love. I sit now near a magnificent statue of Prince Edward with ship wheel in hand; I look below and see the dark blue-green surf casting white spray high up on the jagged rocks of the coast. What colors! I have been immensely happy all day. I think that I am now acclimated and have some travel confidence. ~ Love, Chuck

Samedi, 9-19-64 - *Postcard: La Cote d'Azur, Cannes*

I rode here from Monaco in one of those neat trains with compartments. It had that shrill European whistle. I stayed in a hotel with hot showers and took my first since I left your apartment. I sit now along the water and watch two large liners discharging passengers out in the harbor. Cannes has nothing more than Nice has except an exciting harbor of yachts. I received a letter here from Dillon. He said he hadn't heard from Dick. I am traveling comfortably and have made a rule not to eat in restaurants while I am here. I think that will be best.

The statuary and the flowers and parks continue to amaze me. I know that I am lucky to be in the south of France. All the people are pleasant and easygoing.

~ Love, Chuck

Dimanche 9-20-64 - *Postcard: Reflets de la Cote d'Azur, Toulon (cable car in mountains overlooking)*

I had a wonderful bus ride from Cannes to St. Raphael (and then on to Toulon by train). I stayed right by the shore and kept getting glimpses of Cannes with the big cruise liners hovering off its coast. This morning I rode this cable car up to a mountain which gave a wonderful view. There were battlements left from the allied invasion of August 15, 1944. In the museum my spine tingled to read an old U.S. poster with the Statue of Liberty on it which said: *Au pays qui nous à donne La Liberté … Nous rendrous la liberté.* (To the country that gave us the liberty, we give it the liberty.) I will go on today to Marseille. How are all of you?

~ Love, Chuck

Monday, 9-21-64 - *Postcard: Marseille – Basilique de Notre Dame de la Garde*

Last night I sat in the Crow's Nest on the right of this big church and watched the sun set over Marseille. I was high above the city and the water. Marseille is very big and has a lot of old, dirty parts. There is not much beach, etc. I have had good luck with hotels this trip. Each, however, costs me at least $2.60. Last night I broke down and had supper in a restaurant. I had a cheese omelet and spaghetti. Today I am going to get a haircut before I leave for Aix. Those winds that Warren warned me about are really blowing here now. So far I have spent $40 on this trip. At this rate I will not travel all next summer. However, France is the most expensive European country. Here I went to a 4th century monastery.

~ Love, Chuck

Mardi, 9-22-64 - *Postcard from Arles*

Aix was pretty with its fountains, but besides the Cathedral St. Sauveur, not that much to see. I enjoyed meeting Anna Baker, a Vanderbilt In France student and daughter of Dr. McCallie's secretary. She showed me around Aix and we ate dinner together in a restaurant. From Aix, I had to hitchhike here to Arles as there were no bus/train connections. This was nice as I walked along beautiful country roads and saw the people at work. It only took 3 hours and 3 rides. It has been sunny & crisp as I have walked among the Roman ruins of Arles today. The arena is in good shape and is used for bull fights today. The country clubs (baths), theaters, cemeteries, and churches are fun to see. I had a nice and filling supper of cheese & tomato sandwiches, am washing out my shirt, and reading my first copy of the European *New York Times*. It makes me feel less far away.

Mercredi, 9-23-64 - *Postcard from Nimes to Warren (UGa, Payne Hall)*

I am really enjoying my travels. I hitchhiked yesterday, and really saw the rural life this way. From Marseille I went to Aix, to Arles, and then here (one day in each city). I will go to Avignon tomorrow and then on back to Grenoble. The arena here and the one at Arles are in good condition and are still used for bull fights. The gardens & parks just bowl me over with their beauty. I am traveling light with only a little duffle-type bag which I wear over my shoulder. I have one of each item of clothing which I wash out at night every 2nd or 3rd day. I keep clean, and I buy my food from the little shops. I know that you are off to a good start. ~ Love, Chuck

Lundi, 9-28-64 - *Letter to Mom and Dad, 8 E. 83rd Street, from Chez M. Giroud, Marcel, 33 Rue Massenet, Grenoble (Isére) France*

I have had a couple of dreams about the two of you, but last night's was the saddest. I embraced Mom and asked her to forgive me for forgetting her birthday. One of these birthdays soon, Mom, we will all be together to celebrate it as it should be done. You gave me a Bon Voyage present which has almost become a part of me, and I have no present for you. Will you let me save up and get to know what the real good buys are and then buy you something really special? Maybe I will make it a combination birthday-Christmas gift.

I am in a friendly little room of the same hotel I was in before my grand voyage. I have been reading French and studying vocabulary at least 5 hours each of the days since my return.

I thought I was going to get into my room tonight, but I learned that the bed has not yet arrived. I do not register until October 7th and it will be ready by then. This will work out fine. Dillon and Anne will arrive in Stuttgart on October 2, and so will I. I will depart Wednesday from here and go by way of Geneva and Bern, Switzerland. It will be a grand reunion. I have so many experiences to laugh about with them and I'm sure they have many more to tell me. It will be a weekend to remember always.

Well, at last I have an address. You can't imagine how nice it will be to hear from you. Just as soon as your letter arrives, I will be permanently living at this address. Please forward any of my other mail which you deem important. (Like a letter from Vanderbilt maybe!)

I finally got a haircut, here in Grenoble Saturday. The barber shop was closed in Marseille where I said I was going to get it cut. I got a fine, Mom-type haircut for 65 cents. Here they call the barber shop the "Coiffure Pour Messieurs," and at first I was afraid to go in.

Wednesday I will start back with the guided picture-tour of Europe with a card from Geneva.

I think about you a lot and have been thinking already about our stay together about the middle of next August in New York. I hope you both are healthy and happy and enjoying this wonderful life – as you usually do.

Dad, did you win your point over the price lowering?

~ Love, Chuck

Mercredi, 9-30-64 - *Postcard from Geneva*

What would you say was the most interesting and beautiful city in Europe? Perhaps Geneva, and it has been raining "to beat the band" since I got off my bus at 11:30 a.m. I have loved the city despite the weather. This "Park of the Reformation" was beautiful and so was the Cathedral of Saint Pierre, a 10th Century church which became the church of John Calvin and followers since 1536. I did not see the League of Nations building & some of the beautiful parks, but since this is only 3 hrs. from Grenoble, I imagine that I will be back. I should have a nice train ride from here to Berne, going part of the way alongside Lake Geneva.

The Swiss countryside is just as picturesque as I had always imagined it to be. I am seeing some beautiful farms and estates from the train. Berne tonight, Zurich tomorrow, & Stuttgart on Friday. ~ Love, Chuck

Jeudi, 10-1-64 - *Postcard from Zurich*

Bern was such a unique & beautiful city that I smiled & chuckled all the morning as I toured its sights. I stayed in a first-class hotel in Bern, but my bed was in the "Salle de Bain." It was wonderful because, after spending all day in the rain, I was able to take a long, hot shower, my second since N.Y. I had my most enjoyable meal in Europe in a cozy, friendly restaurant. I had fondue—a cheese dish which kept bubbling over a burner while you dip chunks of bread into it – and a little "vin blanc." This filling meal cost $1.40. I thoroughly enjoyed a museum in Bern which had some wonderful paintings by Renoir, Degas, Rouault, Picasso, Van Gogh, El Greco & Klee. Bern had a bear park, and the bears walked quite a bit on their hind legs. Switzerland is beautiful. ~ Love, Chuck

Vendredi, 10-2-64 - *Another Zurich postcard*

Zurich has been nice. It is built around a See and has many canals running through it. I rode one of those cable cars from one side of the See to the other. Bern had its bears, and Zurich has its ducks, geese, and swans, and the littler creatures are just as funny as the bears. Here, too, is a fine art museum which I enjoyed. It had a special exposition of Vuillard. There was a wonderful Rodin statue called "Orpheus," and, of course, I enjoyed the Renoir, Van Gogh, Manet, Rouault, etc. I stayed in a nice hotel here with breakfast for $2.60. I slept soundly, then got up at 6 a.m. to catch this train to Stuttgart. The train has these neat compartments with six plush seats in each compartment.

Here and in Bern everything is in German. It makes French seem like my native tongue as here I hope that the people can speak French. It will be great to be with your two sons. ~ Love, Chuck

Friday, 10-2-64 - *Journal*

The conditions under which I have been for the last three and a half weeks have been tremendously stimulating. It would be hard to awake each morning to things so unlike Buckhead and not be totally alert and a tingle. I have cried – once in Place Victor Hugo on the afternoon of my arrival in Grenoble as I wrote home – and I have laughed; and I smile and chuckle to myself all of the time.

I feel so much more love: love for the woman on the bus to Nice who makes sure that I know how long we will be stopped each time and who holds up her grandchild for me to see as she departs at Antibes; love for the great little boy In the park at Nimes who is so alive and laughs and chases pigeons for 1 ½ hours; love for the woman in the shop in Monaco who dumps out all of her money looking for Monacan coins for me, and who enjoys selling me big bottles of Coke; love for Pierre who helps me eat at the university cafeteria and then spends all Sunday afternoon touring me around Grenoble; of course love for Claude who alone is making this a livable situation for me, who has had me twice to his home for dinner, and who has such love for the U.S.; love for America as I watched the 1936 Olympics on French television in a Grenoble café and heard Jesse Owens' name pronounced in French and saw Spec Towns with victor's wreath on his head saluting our blowing flag as the Star Spangled Banner was played; love for the awesome German Customs Official who smiled – oh, a smile from many has made me feel all warm inside.

I have felt the emotion of sadness – which must surely be a manifestation of love: sadness as I heard Gram cry on the phone at JFK Airport; sadness as I saw the bottom part of Mom's dress, bright orange, in the lights of the observation platform and thought of her and Dad standing there waving to their departing children; sadness when, in Metz, Dillon and Anne were off in a flash to catch their train to Paris and I wandered to my train for Grenoble; sadness as I stood in the middle of the great cathedral at Aix-En-Provence, felt the power and the worshipfulness of this magnificent house of God, and thought about the fact that to the French people, this and the other churches were nothing but museums to be visited.

I have been tickled over Monaco and the statue of Prince Albert and the color of this mighty sea; tickled over the poster with a picture of the Statue of Liberty on it, in the Museum to the Resisting Forces at Toulon, on which were the words: *Au pays qui nous à donne 'la Liberté' … Nous rendrous la liberté*; tickled over the sunset from Notre Dame de la Garde at Marseille and over Avignon and over Bern – Bern where I spent the night in the bathtub and ate the wonderful fondue; and tickled over thoughts of the reunion which will take place in Stuttgart later on today.

You see, I am really an outsider here. Why does being an outsider and having difficulty communicating make me feel happy? I guess I am an outsider feeling, nevertheless, the love of those on the inside.

Well, I will certainly appreciate my own language more and will feel great ability to communicate and a greater desire to do so when I return to my own land.

Tuesday, 11 a.m., 11-17-64 - *Letter*

Dear Mary Anne and Dick,

As I have said, I am looking very much forward to our reunion at Christmas. Your two younger brothers are difficult people to do business with, I fear, and I regret that the burden of trying to work out arrangements and reservations has fallen to you. With a young family and an occupation of considerable responsibility, we should make our plans conform to what is agreeable for you, but instead, it seems that it has worked the opposite way.

I am in favor of a plan whereby we can be together for more than three days. Dillon, Anne, and I will cut three days of classes and begin our trip to Bruxelles, Antwerp, Amsterdam, Frankfurt, etc. on Friday, December 18. According to the plan outlined by Dillon, we will spend the night of 23 December at Nancy, where Dillon will have left his car on the 18th, and from there we will drive the 180 miles to Stuttgart on Thursday, arriving not too late in the afternoon, I hope. We will spend a wonderful weekend at the ski resort, and then, since reservations at the ski resort for only part of a week (say through Tue or Wed) are probably not possible to arrange, perhaps we could return to your villa in Stuttgart for 2 or 3 more days together. (We can go out into the neighboring fields and sled.) Dillon, Anne, and I might try to visit Munich before we return to our home bases. If it is possible to stay on at the resort until Tuesday or Wednesday, this would be easier on Mary Anne than having us at your villa. You will know best on this, and also you will know what is possible as far as reservations at the ski station are concerned.

This past weekend I went skiing with Claude on both Saturday and Sunday. I now have all of my own equipment, and I learned an awful lot in those two days. I think it is a new sport that really suits me. As I stood on the crest of a small slope before making one of my practice descents, the snow blew in my face, was frozen to my stocking cap, my pants, and completely covered my big boots, and yet, because of the exercise, I was as warm as toast. It was exhilarating – a rare communion with the elements and Alps. The sport affords wonderful human fellowship too. Claude dates a pretty American girl from Connecticut, and I had a date with a friend of hers, a beautiful Swedish girl who speaks Swedish, English, German, and French, and knows all sports. The picnics which go along with a day of skiing are fun, and the ski group has the feeling of battling the elements together.

Perhaps by Dick's not taking as many days away from work, you will be able to pay a short visit to me here in Grenoble sometime before I depart. I would like that.

I will bring my ski equipment with me at Christmas, and we can take turns using it on the slopes near your house perhaps, as well as at the ski station. I bought skis, ski boots, ski pants, gloves, and Claude and I split the cost of a rack for the car. In all it was a $100 investment for me, but I believe I am wise to take advantage of this rare opportunity which Grenoble affords.

I hope that all goes well for Richard and Clay. I look forward to Richard being one of the gang at Christmas. I hope he will let me use his sled some.

My thoughts are ever with you. ~ Love, Chuck

Wednesday, November 18, 1964 - *Letter to Mom and Dad at East 83rd Street*

Dear Mom & Dad, The both of you certainly do write wonderful letters. I cling to every word. I received your letter last week, Mom, and was really thrilled by the account of the reception which your paper got. Sometimes I almost feel that the class reaction is as important as the professor's. And this evening I received your "precious" letter, Dad. I gained a wonderful insight into how things are going for you both in New York.

Thank you so much, Dad, for the trouble that you went to in order to secure the money for me. I will put $700 in a savings account for next summer and return passage for me and my car, and I will put $800 in a checking account here in

Chuck, age twenty-four, at Chamrousse, French Alps

Grenoble. I will then send Dillon a check for $100. Through one of Mom's next letters, please send me word that you have drawn out part or all of my $300 in the Atlanta Federal to handle interest charges.

I am being careful with my car. My apartment house has a big parking area with few cars in it, and here my car sits most of the week. I am being resolute in my decision to continue my walk to and from school. I feel that my feet, arches, ankles, and knees are in their best condition ever, and I now join the two of you as a staunch supporter of the values of walking. The first weekend after Dill and Anne left, I went on Saturday afternoon in the car with Genevieve, Marcel, Patricia and Eric to a monastery high in the mountains near here. There, at Chartreuse, the monks never leave once they enter the walls. Gen. and Marcel said they had never seen one of these friars before, and we saw two that day. Guess what they do inside those walls? They make liquor! It's called "Grande Chartreuse." It is, I guess, sort of like cognac. The yellow is 40% alcohol and the green is 55%. Maybe I'll bring you some.

Then on Sunday of that weekend I had my first lesson in skiing by Claude. This past weekend we went skiing on both Saturday & Sunday, and I had enough exciting episodes to fill two Hemingway novels. On Sunday we went to a ski station near the borders of Italy & Switzerland in France. Its name is Val d'Isere. There the snow was falling. Once I stood at the top of the small hill on which I was making practice descents, and I took stock of the situation. Snow was blowing in my face, it was frozen to my stocking cap and to my pants, and snow was piled high on tip of my big ski boots. All of this, and yet, because of the exercise, I was warm as toast, and very happy and exhilarated. It is a new world opened up for me — a world which pits one against the elements. It is a communion with the Alps which I would not otherwise have, and it affords good opportunity for human fellowship.

I am still enjoying my class, and I am working hard. Progress is slow still, but I am determined to conquer the language. It will be a fun hobby for the rest of my life.

I haven't heard from Clay or his parents lately, but I will certainly pass on your words, Dad, to Richard the Younger. I'm glad that you sound bright about business. I am sure that your enthusiasm will be catching to some of your colleagues. It is nice to know that even in "cold" New York, there is room in the business world for one whose main reason for being there is his love of people.

If I return earlier than the end of August, it will be either because I have run out of money, or because I can't wait to be together with the two of you for some of our good "kitchen conferences." – OH, I received a wonderful letter from Warren. I know that he is getting an awful lot out of these days at Georgia. It is just the life that Warren has needed for the last year or two. I say, "Needed." What

I mean is that Warren is mature beyond his years and has needed this extension of horizons.

Work hard on your writing, Mom. It's necessary to maintain regular study hours.

Much Love, Chuck

[**November 23, 1964** - *Excerpt from a letter from Mary Anne to Mom and Dad*

Anne and Dillon must be in England or going soon for his exam. I know they will have a grand trip and having a car will greatly facilitate their seeing the whole countryside. We are really looking forward to a wonderful Christmas with them and Chuck. They will probably arrive Christmas Eve, and on the following weekend we are all hoping to go skiing in the Bavarian Alps, with Richard & Clay, too. Richard will love sledding. Chuck, Anne, and Dillon gave him and Dick for their birthdays a large sled, so we'll enjoy using it in our nearby fields and hills.]

Jeudi matin 12-10-64 - *Letter from Les Alps: Le Col du Lautaret (2,058 m) to Warren (UGa, Payne Hall)*

I will miss our hunting together this year.

Tomorrow Genevieve and Marcel are having a fondue supper party to which I am invited. I love fondue. Wednesday I leave for "merry ole England."

Y.I.T.B., Chuck

Monday, 12-14-64 - *Letter to Mom and Dad, E. 83rd Street*

Thank you so much for the birthday greetings and also for the generous present. I'm still chuckling over the card — "a word from the sponsors." There are many things which I would like to get with the money. I'll let you know what I finally decide upon.

Geneviève and Marcel had a fondue party, and by coincidence it fell on my birthday. There were two other couples at the party, and I enjoyed sampling French home entertaining from the inside. We began with an aperitif and tasty tidbits at 8:30 and ate and drank continuously until 12:30. It's a leisurely way of eating. Are you familiar with fondue? It is one of my favorite dishes and now I have the inside information on how to make it. We will have it when I return.

I have changed my pre-Christmas plans and am going to England to attend Jud Harwood's wedding. Dillon and Anne did not seem anxious to spend money at this time, and we will still have time for travel together after Christmas. I will meet everyone in Stuttgart either late the 23rd or early the 24th.

I am rushing this in hopes that it will get to New York before you leave. I will write you a longer letter and send it to Gram's. I received a nice card and note from Aunt Marianne and Uncle Bill and a generous check for a Christmas present. I know that you will have a wonderful vacation in Atlanta. You will be with some very special friends of mine. Now, take Warren for example!

I honestly wish I could write you every day. My experiences here would be pretty empty if I could not share them with you by letter. I certainly think of you all of the time. ~ Love, Chuck

P.S. The skiing goes well!

[**Monday, February 8, 1965** - *Excerpts from Dillon's letter to Gram*

Paris is very gray, now, but the weather is not too cold, and the people become nicer as our French improves. Anne and I are in different classes, but we often walk to school together. This is a long walk, over a mile, down to the Seine, where we cross to the Ile St. Louis and wander through the small streets between the ancient houses. ...

A word about your great-grandsons: Clay is very quiet and much more mature than was Richard at the same age. He was, of course, very tiny when we saw him. Between October and the 1st of January, Richard has changed remarkably. He is much more independent of Mary Anne, now. Sometimes in the night he'll get up and wander around the house. He still cries some, but his disposition is very gentle and kind. He gave us all big kisses. (He doesn't understand how to kiss yet. He makes the 'smack' sound before he reaches you, and he just bounces against you.) He also enjoys a game where he squeezes your nose and you must respond with some sound – like the honking of a horn. He has become a little more responsible, too. When his daddy (that's Dick, Jr.) wants to wash his face, he says "O.K. Daddy," but to hear the tone of his voice you'd think he was saying "Is this really necessary?"]

Samedi, 20 Mars 1965, printemps – Journal

My days in Grenoble are drawing to a close. I am no longer an outsider. I bask in the fellowship of Claude, Jean Patrick, Mme. et M. Gauthier, Genevieve and Marcel. I feel at home in these Alps which have come to mean so much to me. Perhaps it is the time to move on and to enjoy again the thrill of discovery.

There are so many things of my first six months in Europe which I should mention: Jud Harwood's wedding at Callow Hall, Asborne, Derbyshire, England, was a rare experience of being cast back in history a hundred and fifty years. From the time I was ushered in to tea Friday afternoon until I departed twenty-four hours later, the smile of warm fellowship never left my face. I was treated like a visiting dignitary – the epitome of hospitality – and the English sense of humor is something I now relish. The wedding itself was rich with significance: The beautiful cathedral, the full choir, the bells as we walked out, the men in tails and grey top-hats, and the words of the parting hymn, "Will Jerusalem be built on England's great green shores?"

Christmas at Stuttgart was meaningful. Richard grew up so much in the last two months of Clay's presence. He was a true friend to his uncles and aunt. Christmas night we all envisioned ourselves 10 years from then. Dick will be a professor of medicine with three boys. Dillon & Anne will be teaching, somewhere not too removed from New York, like Virginia. They will have a farm where they will spend the weekends and it is here they will keep their works of art and it is here that their children will call home. I will be in Atlanta, living out from the city, and teaching at Westminster. I will have an additional interest such as being an alderman or writing occasionally.

I have learned to relax and take life at a more reasonable and eye-open pace. I feel that my capacity to love is increased. I look forward to being back in the United States and incorporating some of my new values in my life there.

Today is the first day of spring and here in Grenoble it is glorious. After a pleasant and leisurely breakfast with the family, I have passed the morning sitting on my bed finishing *Bonjour Tristesse* ("Vous n'avez besoin de personne, murmura-t-elle, ni vous ni lui.") and writing. My entire bed is bathed in sunshine and the mountains stand before my window. Besides my sprained foot, crutches, and broken ski, "I am leading the life of the chateau."

Sunday night, March 21, 1965

Dear Mom and Dad,

Yesterday, the first day of spring, Grenoble was drenched in sunshine and the encircling mountains stood clear in their snow-capped majesty. Today, the second day of spring, Grenoble is drenched in rain and the encircling mountains have vanished behind the grey blanket of clouds. Both days manifest the presence of spring.

Everything is like happy normal here. Even so it is natural that I am looking forward to meeting Dillon and Anne on April 8th and to our trip to Spain. They are retaining their apartment, so we will have that to return to around April 25th. This is perfect. We will stay there together at least until May 15th and then our plans depend on Dillon's Coast Guard tour of duty. If it is in London the month of June, then naturally we wouldn't have time to go to Italy before. I will keep you posted as plans develop. Of course we have Warren's great arrival constantly in mind.

As I said before, Claude will arrive at JFK around 6 a.m. Wednesday morning, May 5th. I will give him directions on how to catch a taxi into your apartment. He has an invitation to spend the weekend in Philadelphia , so I imagine he will leave you Friday afternoon. In this case, Mom, perhaps you had better not plan all of Wednesday as a "sleep day." Maybe you could get tickets for you and Claude for a Wednesday matinee. Maybe there is a not-too-expensive musical with some songs he would recognize. Please, though, don't feel that you have to plan these two and a half days for Claude. With your advice and good directions, I know Claude will be content to get about and explore New York on his own.

Have you ever eaten artichokes by peeling off the leaves, dipping the tips in a sauce and eating the tender tip? It is a delicious and sociable course with which to begin a meal, and then the heart of the artichoke tastes so much better when you arrive at it. Try it and think of me.

Wasn't that something about Gram's hall getting cleared out! Were the silver urns among the things taken? Isn't that good that you have three guards between you and the outside world.

I enjoy your news-filled letters. Keep them coming. I trust that you both greet each dawn in good health and lively spirits.

[Written on the outside of the envelope: Remember to speak English slowly.]
Much love, Chuck

Wednesday evening, March 31, 1965 - *Letter to Mom and Dad at East 83rd*

Dear Mom and Dad, The letter from Vanderbilt was my acceptance to graduate school next year. I am happy that my plans are now sure. It will be a year of hard work, but it will be well worth it in terms of much needed additional knowledge and future salary and position.

I received a nice letter from Dick and Mary Anne asking me to be Clay's Godfather. I'm sure I was singled out because I am Episcopalian. I do love my two nephews and will naturally always take an interest in the two of them.

At this time a week from now I will have parted Grenoble and will be on the road to Chateauroux (south of Paris) to meet Dillon & Anne, Our ports of call on this trip will be Bordeaux, St. Sebastian, Segovia, Madrid, Toledo, Cordoba, Valencia, Barcelona, Andorra (a little country in the Pyrenees between Spain and France. Do you have a map?) and will then return to Paris around the 25th of April. Your next word from me will be a card from Spain. My address will be 16 Rue St. Gilles for a while now, and you will be able to kill three birds with one stone. Take advantage of this rare opportunity and write us every day. Oh, I did send your wonderful letter on to Dillon & Anne.

You are awfully sweet, Mom, in the plans you are making for Claude. What you have planned for Wednesday is a royal welcome for a "pouvre français." The bus tour, maybe Thursday morning, would give him the total picture. He could then decide what he wanted to explore on his own. If Claude wanted to go out to the fair Thursday afternoon or evening, he could easily do that on his own. The boat trip around the island Friday morning would be a refreshing conclusion to Clause's introduction to America. Have you been on the boat trip? You will enjoy it. It goes right by the Statue of Liberty. You will find that Claude has gotten pretty good in English and I'm sure you will enjoy his company. He was in Paris last week and spent the evening with Dillon and Anne. He is still laughing about the fun they had together.

Let me know if Mr. White is engaged and Dillon, Anne, and I will send him a card of congratulations. Also send his address. How was the dinner party at Larchmont?

Dad, I am toying with the idea of selling my car back to Auto-Europe at the end of my travels this summer. I will have to talk with them and see what kind of price I could get. I love my deluxe car dearly but I just wonder if it would be a reasonable expense during my twelve months of expenses at Vanderbilt. It will cost $200 to transport it transatlantic. I would then have to pay for insurance for the year ($300?). The arguments in favor of keeping it would be my travel expenses in the United States. I can always get rides from Nashville to Atlanta and then there is Gram's car I could use for coming to New York. The depreciation I will suffer will equal or be less than what I would have spent in train and bus fares, especially when you think of Warren and I both using it. Please give me your advice on this matter.

Dick has suggested us all making a trip together into Scandinavia in July. We would go to Northern Germany, Copenhagen, Sweden, Norway, and Denmark. I hope it works out.

I am more than satisfied with my stay here in Grenoble. My course at the university has been enjoyable, and my professor says that I now write like a Frenchman. I do feel that I've learned a lot of grammar. My conversational ability is certainly adequate. I have learned to live at ease in Europe, and it is now time that I move on and broaden my knowledge through travel. Think, for instance, what new interests and information will be mine for having spent two weeks in Spain.

I will stop by and visit an old school friend of Mrs. Lacy's at Lyon as I leave Grenoble. I have written her that I am coming by.

Mom, have you spent your hour this week in the Metropolitan?

I would like hamburgers with all of the trimmings and several thick milkshakes for my first dinner with you, if you'll permit me to place my order this far ahead.   ~ Much love, Chuck

No date, but more than a week before April 18, 1965 (Easter) - *Postcard to Warren: Park in Madrid*

Our travels in Spain have been exciting and enjoyable. Tomorrow, Sunday, we will see the greatest bullfighter in 20 years, El Cordoba. The fight is at Benidorm on the Med. Coast between Alicante and Valencia. We are spending a couple of days at Calpe.

Isn't it glorious that warm weather has returned? I imagine that pledge training is now over and that you are better able to concentrate on your studies. Will you go through formal initiation now? Please let me know how your work is going. What courses do you feel you are getting the most out of? What encouragement or discouragement have you received in the form of grades? (I received nothing but discouragement for two years.) I will write you from Paris on the subject of itinerary. Please let me know where and what day you will arrive.

Also, tell me approximately when you want to return to the U.S. With my acceptance to Vandy, I may need to return earlier. My love and concern, Chuck

Monday (no date / perhaps April 12, 1965) - *Postcard to Mom and Dad: Madrid monument to Christopher Columbus*

Spain is a real experience, so different from our own culture or anything which I've seen in Europe. The people are extremely friendly and give all appearances of being happy. They are very poor. In the country we have seen women gathering sticks to load on the backs of their burros. We have seen shepherds sitting on a lonely hillside, wrapped in blankets, watching their sprawling flock of sheep. The little villages are yellow and black. Warren Leamon and I have been roommates. We are in a beautiful room here in Madrid for 67 cents each. We eat beautifully for 75 cents to a dollar.

We all left Paris Thursday morning, spent that night in Pontiers, France, Friday at San Sabastian, Saturday at Segovia, and arrived here last night. We are seeing an awful lot and yet managing to be leisurely and stay rested and healthy. As always with Dillon & Anne, I laugh most of the day. We will hit the Mediterranean coast and go to a bullfight Sunday afternoon. Write us at Paris.

~ Much love, Chuck

Wednesday (No date / probably April 14, 1965) - *Postcard to Gram: Madrid fountain*

I joined Dillon and Anne exactly a week ago. We have really enjoyed our travels together in Spain. The Spanish people are friendlier than the French and the prices here are extremely low. I am paying 67 cents for a very nice hotel and we eat very inexpensively. The people of Spain are poor.

Thank you for your letter which I received just before leaving Grenoble. Easter will be past when you receive this and spring will be full. Make your great serpentine flower beds the most beautiful.

~ Much love, Chuck

[**Monday (no date / perhaps April 19, 1965)** - *Postcard from Dillon to Mom and Dad: Peniscola, village on peninsula in Med*

Dear Folks, We ate lunch here today on our way from Valencia to Barcelona. We're stuck in a line of traffic of people returning from their holiday.

We spent three days on the beach at Calpe near a huge Gibraltar-type rock. We were awaiting an Easter bullfight at nearby Benidorm. We came to this place after Madrid. The fight was really amazing. Those toreadors killed two bulls each. The star was "El Cordobes," the national idol of Spain. He was gored badly last year, but after being taped up, he returned and killed his bull. We'll spend tonight in Barcelona and tomorrow in, aw! … Andorra (consult your map). We'll be back in Paris Thursday night. ~ Love, Dillon]

Tuesday morning, May 4, 1965 - *Letter hand-carried to Mom and Dad by Claude Gauthier (I wrote on the first half of the page and Dillon on the second half.)*

Dear Mom and Dad, Claude has spent an enjoyable 24 hours with Dillon and me and we now send him on as our personal emissary. We are happy here and looking after one another like good brothers, but we do miss Anne.

Claude has a friend in New York, a girl named Meredith, who will bring him from the airport to your apartment. She works during the day, but perhaps at night they will go out together once or twice. It is with her that Claude will depart Friday for a visit to her home at West Chester, Penn, not far from Philadelphia. I envy Claude the experience of staying with you and of having Mom as his guide to New York. I will write you a longer letter soon, but how is this for fast, personal delivery. ~ Love, Chuck

⎡Dear Mom and Dad,

I was depressed after Anne left, but by studying and sight-seeing with Chuck, I've raised my spirits. The operation was successful, but another, just as serious, will be required when Mrs. Coggan regains her strength.

My decision for Vanderbilt and the fellowship-scholarship ($2,250) had to be made before last Friday. I decided against it, for reasons that I'll explain later. This leaves Tulane and Virginia open.

Gilbert & Sullivan at the Choir School should be very good. Perhaps it's this weekend.

How goes the life there?   ~ Love, Dillon⎤

Monday, May 10, 1965 - *Postcard to Gram: Chateaux de la Loire, Chenonceaux*

Dillon & I found the soul of France this past weekend – the chateau country of the Loire River. It is lush and green, the seat of much history, and the people are kindly. Dillon has a wonderful group of friends through rugby. His team won and Dillon scored. We spent a good bit of time with these other members of the team. Chenonceaux must be the most beautiful home in the world; it is still beautifully furnished. Think of eating breakfast by one of those windows and watching beautiful water flow beneath you.

I have proposed to Warren that we return to the U.S. together on a student ship leaving here August 7th. I think the ship would be a whole lot of fun. We received a lot of pleasure from your last nice letter. Write us again soon as we leave here May 20th for Italy. You are always my happy and strong Gram.

Lundi, mai 24, 1965 - *Postcard to Warren via Gram: Three Michelangelo sculptures in Medici Chapel, Rome*

By not writing, you have made it hard on me to make plans, but I am easy-going and can make plans from day to day. We will not go to Scandinavia this year but will travel with Dick & Mary Anne in N. France for 5 days and then

Dillon will join us for a week's trip to Belgium, Holland, and Luxembourg. The other would have spread us too thin. Now we will feel that we have seen Western Europe. Bring a student I.D. card with you as it will get you in many museums at ½ price. I went ahead and made reservations for you and I [*I can't believe that back in 1965 I would have made this mistake: hideous.*] to sail back together August 9–18. If you wish other arrangements you can cancel these when you arrive and lose only $10. We will have meaningful travels together. ~ Chuck

[**Sunday midnight, May 31, 1965** - *Postcard of Donatello crucifix in Florence Basilica—from Dillon to Mom and Dad*

Dear Folks, Chuck and I left each other at Pisa, and I'm en route by train for Monte Carlo and Nice. Chuck will go to Corsica. Rome was too big for three days, but we gave it a try. We saw the Vatican, St. Peter's, the Catacombs, and Tivoli Garden with the beautiful fountains. I'm happy and healthy and I love you. My train is leaving. ~ Dillon]

Tuesday, June 1, 1965 - *Postcard to Gram: Corsica*

After sadly bidding Dillon farewell and looking around Pisa (the leaning tower), I came by boat last night here to the island of Corsica. It is a part of France; it is nice to be able to speak the language again. This beautiful and natural island is relatively untrampled by "the touristes." As a matter of fact, I am staying with a family here. It is nice as they are able to tell me things about the history (Napoleon was born & raised here). Thursday I will cross back to Italy, go over to see Venice, and then go by Dick and Mary Anne's before meeting Warren. If you get a chance, write me at Stuttgart. Dillon was fine and is looking forward to London. We had a wonderful two months together. ~ Much love, Chuck

Thursday, June 17, 1965 - *Postcard to Gram: Concarneau, Le Betagne, France*

This is a unique land where people wear wooden shoes, many of the women wear headpieces as on the front of this card, and the men go about in their blue sea garb. We have stood on many wind-blown hills and watched the surf break on the rocks below. It is very exciting. Tonight we have wandered around the coastal village of Dinan. We are staying in a very nice hotel for $1 apiece and for $1.50 we ate a meal of onion soup, small lobsters, pork, potatoes, peas, green salade, good bread with real butter, and fresh cherries. We continue up the coast toward the English Channel and London. ~ Love, Chuck

Monday, June 21, 1965 - *Postcard of Saint-Michel (My note: This is a monastery well situated.)*

Our days in Bretagne and Normandy were rich. We saw much of French agricultural life and some beautiful fishing villages. The last two day we have learned much of June 6, 1944, and the events which took place on the coast of

Normandy. There are 9,300 white marble crosses lining the hill above Omaha Beach (American Cemetery) and there is yet wreckage at Arromanches, the spot where the portable harbor, towed across from England, was installed. Last night we saw an exceptional sunset over Rouen and then enjoyed a meal of snails and rabbit. We are now on the Calais-Dover boat and this evening we will be with Dillon and Anne. We have been getting good deals on our nights' lodging.

    ~Love, Chuck

Monday, June 21, 1965 - *Postcard to Gram: Le Mont Saint-Michel*

Our trip in Bretagne and Normandy is now ended and we are on the boat to Dover. We were in the heart of agricultural France, seeing herds of sheep and cattle, fields of brilliantly red poppies, and many farmers harvesting hay by primitive methods. St. Michel (this card) was a well-protected monastery begun in the 800s. When the tide is up, it's an island. Day before yesterday we saw a very moving sight; row upon row of white marble crosses in the American Cemetery on the hill overlooking Omaha Beach. We have learned much of the D-Day invasion in Normandy. During these 10 days in England we are sure to learn much of our great mother country.   ~ Love, Chuck

Thursday, July 1, 1965 - *Postcard to Gram: London – Big Ben from Parliament Square*

England is a beautiful green country rich in history. I feel that I have gained as much from my days here as any I have spent. Yesterday we explored Fleet Street: St. Paul's Cathedral and Dr. Johnson's home built in 1740 or so. Tuesday Warren & I made a trip to Oxford Univ., Stratford-on-Avon (Shakespeare's home), and the Cathedral at Coventry.

We are on our way now back to the Continent. Tonight in Luxembourg and tomorrow Warren will see Clay for the first time and Richard. We begin Saturday on our trip and meet up again with Dillon & Anne July 8 in Amsterdam. Thanks for your nice letter. Our address is now Stuttgart. Oh, we went to Parliament.

    ~ Love, Chuck

Thursday, July 8, 1965 - *Postcard to Gram: Le Grand Place, Bruxelles*

This square was the most interesting part of Brussels. We were here on Monday. Tuesday we saw Rotterdam, the pretty little town of Delft, and then came into The Hague. Yesterday, Wednesday, we really enjoyed exploring this, the capital of Holland. We saw the Knight's Hall where Queen Juliana opens Parliament each year. That afternoon we went north of Amsterdam to a little fishing village where the people still wear the native costumes, wooden shoes and all. We are now waiting in front of Amsterdam's grand art museum to meet Dillon and Anne. We will all be together now for a couple of days. Each night we camp out in beautiful surroundings. We are eating "C" rations. Each person's meal comes in a little box. It is like Christmas to open up and see what each person got. It's good food and our life is happy together.   ~ Love, Chuck

Wednesday, July 14, 1965 - *Azay-Le-Rideau Postcard*

All of your children have been together for the first time since Dillon's wedding, and it took Europe to do it. We were together in Amsterdam, Bruges, Belgium; Paris; and then a nice ½ day at Versailles with picnic on the grounds. We parted there, and the four of us have since seen the cathedral at Chartres, and yesterday many beautiful chateaux of the Loire, Azay-le-Rideau being one of them. If Warren saw no more of Europe than what we have seen these 12 days, it would be worth his trip over. Today is the anniversary of the fall of the Bastille. Last night we saw a torch-light parade, and today we will see much celebrating. Thinking of you.   ~ Love, Chuck

Friday, July 16, 1965 - *Postcard to Gram: Le Corbusier's Chapelle de Notre-Dame du Haut, Ronchamp*

We are now in Stuttgart and spent a fun morning with Richard and Clay while Mary Anne shopped. The chapel on this card was one of the last things we saw in France. It sits high on a hill and is designed to look like a "ship of faith." Tomorrow Warren and I head for Switzerland, Italie, and then to beautiful parts of France: The Cote d'Azur and the Rhone Valley. We will then spend some days here with Dick & Mary Anne before going to Paris and Le Havre. (Warren and Richard made a tent out of blankets and have been playing there happily.) Hope it is warmer in Atlanta than here.   ~ Love, Chuck

Monday night, July 26, 1965 - *Postcard to Gram: Aix-En-Provence square and street*

Aix is your kind of town. The big streets are tree-lined and there are fountains everywhere. We walked around in the sunshine looking at the old homes with wrought-iron railings and beautifully carved doors. We have run into our first real summer weather along the Mediterranean coast of France. We swam on two days. The flowers along here were magnificent: oleander and a rich purple vine that I never had seen. I have never felt healthier or happier. After this year I will always enjoy traveling, like you and Grandpa. Two weeks from tonight we start our voyage.   ~ Love, Chuck

Sunday, August 1, 1965 - *Postcard to Gram: Monastere de La Grande-Chartreuse and mountains*

Coming up through Provence, from Marseille to Grenoble, we passed through many scenes of Roman life. Many ancient buildings are still in excellent conditions (arenas, theatres, etc.) I enjoyed introducing Warren to my family in Grenoble and showing him this city and some of the ski stations. My family had a third child in June, a nice little boy named Bruno. Upon leaving Grenoble we visited the monastery on this card. Its setting is magnificent and a good museum explains the life of the monks within. We saw Geneva, and Berne and are now here in Stuttgart. We will see Germany for five days and then leave for Paris Thursday. Our boat-train leaves from Paris Monday morning and our ship leaves from Le Havre that night. We will be 9 days on the boat before we arrive in New York August 18. Thanks for your nice letter.

Wednesday 8-4-65 - *Letter*

Dear Mom and Dad,

Your letter arrived today, and we have been able to talk of little else but the exciting new move. It is hard to communicate feeling through a letter, but I assume you are both happy with the change. I realize, too, that there is a sadness at leaving an unfulfilled ambition for Fleischman's.

Tonight we ate out and had venison. It was a wonderful party and a farewell for a year or so from Dick, Mary Anne, and our nephews. Richard always says Uncle Chuck now and he loves Uncle Warnie. When Warnie isn't around, Richard calls for him.

We leave for Paris in the morning. Things will be hectic there (that's why I'm writing you now.) I have an appointment to sell my car Friday morning. There is luggage to send to the boat and boat-train tickets to buy. Then we can relax and enjoy Paris.

If Dillon is there, ask him if he has a key to his trunk. Without a key they will have to break it open at U.S. Customs.

Our ship, the M/S Aurelia, docks sometime August 18 at the Holland America Line Pier No. 40, North River (West Houston Street). I guess you obtain the arrival time by checking in the paper.

Could we have supper out in the side yard once or twice before I leave for Nashville? That will be nice, won't it!

~ Love, Chuck

8 aout 1965, dimauche

This has been my last full day in France, and I'm happy I could spend it in Paris. Up at 9 a.m., breakfast (bread, butter, café au lait) in the sunshine in view of the Bastille, to the Louvre at 10:30 where I enjoyed Monet's sailboats basking in the sunshine of the port, Millet's couple pausing at prayer in the field (I joined them in thanksgiving for the joy of my past year), and the majestic beauty of Venus de Milo. We ate a sandwich as we walked through the Tuileries. We walked along the Seine until we reached the Museum of Modern Art. After a pastry and coffee, I enjoyed Vuillard, Dufy, Matisse, Rouault, Picasso, Chagall and Le Corbusier. We once again enjoyed the power of the fountains at the Palais de Chaillot with the

Eiffel Tower behind. We rode out to Cite Universite and enjoyed strolling around seeing the two Corbusier buildings and some tennis players. Back for a last enchanting visit to the Luxembourg Gardens. The flowers were extraordinary, and toy sailboats were on the pond. After resting at a sunny café, we went on to a dinner of snails, goulash, and beer. We walked along by Notre Dame and I thought for the first time about leaving. Notre Dame, in all of her profoundness and splendor, made me sad to leave France. Along Isle de St. Louis, past restaurants where we will stop when we return with money, to the Place de Vosges for a last cool drink in the calm of this spot. I know for me that Paris is a "moveable feast." It will be ever with me.

Tuesday, August 17, 1965 - *Journal - Somewhere in the Atlantic aboard the M.S. Aurelia*

The dark, deep blue of the Atlantic for days has stretched out from us in all directions and yet constancy has not diminished its beauty and enchantment. This morning we see fishing boats in all directions, this afternoon we will haul baggage and in the morning we will see the Statue of Liberty. The spell is broken. An incomparable year is drawing to a close.

America will seem greater for my having been away. I shall be more actively concerned for her problems while, at the same time, enjoying more fully her wonders and charm.

I would like to be a more outgoing person – outgoing in the sense of radiating warmth to those with whom I shake hands. I shall enjoy my two weeks in New York. I must never have an impatient idea toward Mom and Dad. I hope I will neither express nor feel any irritation toward them. A few days in Atlanta, but then I'm anxious to be on to Nashville to put myself in order for a great year at Vanderbilt.

Paris is my favorite single spot in Europe. The Rhone Valley is my favorite area (Provence). Fondue and rabbit stew are my favorite new dishes. Berne and Madrid and London and Monte Carlo are wonderful, especially Monte Carlo. Florence is the richest art center I've seen. The "deux chevaux" and the month's vacation are my favorite French institutions. England and Ireland and Scotland is the area where I will concentrate on my next visit. Sometime, though, I would like to come with my wife to France as a Fulbright visiting professor. Spain certainly deserves a longer visit.

On this voyage I have finished reading *Moby Dick*. I have read *Desire Under the Elms* and really drew from Eugene O'Neill's *Strange Interlude* and *Morning Becomes Electra*. *Intruder in the Dust* is a wonderful statement by Faulkner of the Southerner's responsibility. I am also finishing *The New Reformation* (?) by John Robinson. What is said of the writer is also true of the theologian: "It is a call in the first place not to relevance in any slick sense but to exposure, to compassion, sensitivity, awareness, and integrity. ... It is to be with God in this world."

I am more excited about writing after having written a story during this trip. I should like to do my M.A. thesis in creative writing. I should also like to fall in love. I lead such a fun life but I am sure these pleasures would be amplified if they could be shared. I should like to meet a beautiful, intelligent, and unselfish girl.

Appendix 5

Hundred-Mile Wilderness, Summer of '68 Journal

Monday, June 3, 1968

There is a trail that goes from Maine to Georgia, and, by God, I'm walking it. But my first day out will come without my hitting the Appalachian Trail (the AT). The camp ranger has said that it is too late in the day to make it up and then over to Katahdin Springs Camp. I hate to delay, but perhaps the rest will give me necessary strength. The ranger spoke of the black flies and sold me some black repellent that smells like tar. I now smell like that, but am still holding up in my blessed tent to escape the black flies and mosquitoes. A chipmunk came and carried away my discarded raisin box. A stream spits and blows in the woods behind me. I have sat and looked at Mt. Katahdin (5,267 ft.). No wonder the ranger respects it. I should be forced to wait to climb such a mountain. I will go up the Abol Trail which has provided a way up since 1816. Thoreau went this way in 1846.

At the moment I feel a little out of my element. Being by myself in the woods will take some getting used to. After I pass down from Mt. Katahdin tomorrow, I will go some days without seeing a store. I guess, too, the bugs give me a great sense of insecurity. And I think Maine is rough, perhaps the roughest state in the Union. The ranger said that when I got to that next town, I would know I had been somewhere; that's a great sentiment, and won't even be out of Maine, and I'll know I've been somewhere.

Views today have included logs bounding down a river, patches of snow on top of Katahdin.

Recurrences of masculine feelings come immediately upon hiking the woods. I would like to go naked for the rest of the trip (but the black flies prevent it). I like the smell of the citronella and black tar; I like my coming beard and my increasing muscles.

Tuesday, June 4, 1968: Day #1 of 85 – Hiked 21.7 miles, 18 on AT

Katahdin is incredibly difficult. I saw a great view from the top. It is nippy, and patches of snow remain there the year round, I am told. Flowers and wildlife have highlighted my day. Little white flowers that look like blackberries, scrubby azaleas, blue flowers above the tree line, violets, mosses and ferns in sunless forests. I have seen the protective instincts of mother animals and a beautiful big duck with a red head who neatly marshalled her nine young 'uns across a stream as I passed by on the bank; a ruffled grouse with her one chick on the trail ruffled her neck and came back at me. I backed off two steps and waited so she could help the little one out of the way. She, too, waited. Finally she charged me with hell in her eyes and I hit the swampy woods. I was not about to go back for a third encounter so I circled way around her in the woods, nearly losing the AT on my first day out. I have hiked late today, so I must now sit down to a supper of dehydrated scrambled eggs, dehydrated spinach, and dehydrated potato soup – all lumped together.

Wednesday, June 5, 1968: Day 2/85 – 18.9 miles – 34.9/2025 (total length of AT)

The discomforts of the day were mosquitoes, swamps, and blisters. I understand that it has rained every day here for the past 3 weeks; that helps explain why much of what I went through looked like Louisiana bayou country. Once I had to take off my boots to cross a swollen creek. Because I'm mortal and because my feet were wet, I developed some pretty bad blisters. So I thought as I walked that people who spun a romantic view of "man in nature" did the world a great disservice. The hardships of today's mere 15 miles were real; they were painful. But, also, the exhilaration outweighs the hardship. People are the key. Two women and a man at the Great Northern Paper Company's private sporting camp befriended me. I had the temerity to enter the private grounds and ask if I might purchase a soft drink (These are my greatest craving at the moment); they gave me two cans of ginger ale, compliments of Great Northern. At Nahmakanter Lake I was taken into the kitchen of a sporting camp and given Kool-aide with chocolate chip cookies. I was quizzed by the lady and her three children about what I was doing. Upon leaving I was given three sandwiches to take with me. (Paul & Frances Nevel) From the lady I learned that Robert Kennedy had been shot. This day was spiced by glimpses of two moose, the first of which I thought was a mule.

Thursday, June 6, 1998: Day 3/85 - 11.7 miles - 46.6/2025

There are friendly woods, where one wouldn't mind bedding down, and there are unfriendly woods that are difficult just to pass through. I got lost today in the most unfriendly, swampy, slap-you-down woods I have ever passed. Just at the moment when I could not find the next trail blaze (which was the same moment that I stepped into mud that tried to suck my foot under), hundreds of mosquitos descended upon me. This helped cause me to panic. I was lost, for at least three hours. I used my compass and map; being unable to find the AT after several crisscrosses. I decided to head cross country by compass in the direction that the trail was going. I walked on and on and on. Finally I stopped and ate my emergency cereal bar and had two salt tablets. What Providence that at last I stumbled upon a road with the white blaze on the trees. But it was the road I had already travelled short of getting lost. How my map and compass played that trick on me I'll have to examine at a saner moment.

This is not a sane moment because I am huddled in my mosquito-net tent eating a cold supper and trying to change out of wet clothes. The mosquitos create a den of buzzing as I write.

Earlier in the day I got lost (two miles north) but that was on a road and was easy enough to correct. But this day has hurt my image of myself, which is important if one is to push on for three months. I just hope I make it through this week and arrive in Monson, Maine, and on for three months. I long for the high mountains.

Friday, June 7, 1968: Day 4/85 - 17.2 miles hiked - 63.8/2025

A little hardship is a good thing, but today was so filled with fallen-down trees, stepping in deep mud, and not being able to stop to look at a waterfall because the mosquitos would eat me up – that I have decided not to spend my summer doing this. Tonight, though, has been like being lifted out and being put in ideal surroundings. I am spending the night at York Pond Sporting Camp. I sat around the big dinner table with two Maine fishermen and with the Keith Skillen family. Both the fellowship and the food (steaks, potatoes, salad, milk, biscuits, chocolate cake) were fine. I have washed myself and my clothes, and my clothes are drying before the Franklin stove in my cabin. I am resolved to make it to Monson.

Saturday, June 8, 1968: Day 5/85 - 17.9 miles hiked - 81.7/2025

This has truly been an ideal day in the woods. From Keith Skillen I learned a great deal about foot care. I am actually fired up just about getting my feet in shape. Of course my day that began with orange juice, coffee, pancakes and bacon is bound to go well. The $15 I spent at York Pond camp was essential to building my morale back up. I hit a better pace for 10 miles, stopped, had lunch while I washed my socks and changed them, and then took all afternoon to get up and over White Mountain. These crazy Yanks never heard of switchbacks. I went straight up and straight down a 3,600-foot mountain. Tonight I am at a table before White Creek getting ready to eat as it grows dark. I relaxed today, and enjoyed the wilds immensely. Oh, yes, the mosquitoes eased off. Grouse abounded.

Sunday, June 9, 1968: *(Written Tuesday in Monson)* Day 6/85 - 17.1 miles hiked - 98.8/2025

I started as soon as it was light, after a breakfast of coffee and hard-boiled eggs. Today my treat was to eat my sporting-camp lunch. My hike was over the Chairback Mountains, four mountains between 2,069 and 2,670. I enjoyed a cup of coffee with four men at the Chairback Mountain Camp. At that point I had hiked 10 level miles and felt fine. But the four mountains were ahead of me, and it took me from 11 a.m. until 30 minutes before dark to reach Cloud Pond lean-to.

It made me mad to have to take off my boots to ford a stream because it meant the destruction of my eight or ten blister Band-Aids. This, though, I had to take in stride. For lunch I had my usual Vienna sausage and raisins. It rained lightly on me all afternoon but I was fairly relaxed and enjoying the woods. My legs, though, took on a weariness that was like a disease. I thought I'd never make it to shelter. All the minutes of light there were spent building a fire to dry my socks and boots, putting my mosquito netting and sleeping paraphernalia inside the lean-to, and eating soup and eating the rest of my Sporting Camp lunch. The fire was cheerful and happy and I would have enjoyed sitting before it and thinking, but I had to get to sleep so I could make Monson the next day. The lean-to was beautifully situated with the still pond of water on two sides.

Monday, June 10, 1968: *(Written Tuesday in Monson)* Day 7/85 - 16.7 miles - 115.5/2025

I felt as if I had been drugged. I wanted to put in a big day and get to this mystical place called Monson, but I could hardly move. I arose, had hot coffee and hot instant breakfast. My early climb brought me to open rock ledges on Barren Mountain that displayed much of the mountain lake country through which I had passed. A half-mile later and rock ledges showed me the valley into which I was going. The way down Barren Mountain was so steep that it pounded my legs brutally. As I passed through the flats of Bodfish Farm I was depressed by the thought that I wouldn't make Monson by Monday night. I did push on, though, so I'd make it to a lean-to within 5 miles of Monson. As I sat by a stream to rest and drink (I now love the taste of the icy Maine streams), a strange-looking animal started pushing through the brush on the opposite bank. Its white streak across its back made me fearfully think of a skunk. But then I realized I was watching a clumsy old porcupine try to find an easy passage across the stream. I travelled on, soon entering traces of the "old stage road from Monson to Greenville" over which

I would travel for the remaining 7 miles to Monson. This was a beautiful trail, but again I thought I'd never make shelter. Several deer scurried before my approach. Supper was dehydrated cabbage flakes and flakes of freezer-dried bacon mixed with mashed potatoes. I slept somewhat uneasily on the socks I was trying to dry.

Tuesday, June 11, 1968: Day 8/85 - 5.0 miles - 120.5/2025

When I awoke it was so chilly I didn't want to get up. I did, ate a box of raisins, cleaned up well, and headed for Monson, a town that has grown in magnitude with each passing day. The "old stage road" was not spared of the swamps that have beset me the whole way. I saw something moving on the trail ahead of me that at first I thought was the rear end of a moose (by its brown color). I then realized it was a bear heading for me. He was more startled than I when he saw me; he bounded off into the woods. I trudged on; two deer scampered off into the woods at the fury of my approach.

Somehow even the joy of Monson on yonder hill couldn't quicken my pace. But I made it up the asphalt slant of Maine highway #16 to drink chocolate milk, Pepsi-Cola and eat a sandwich in the general store. There I bought two new pairs of socks and trudged off to explore the town. At the restaurant I had a chocolate milkshake and a hamburger. I then took my clothes to the washateria, as they were in unbelievably wretched condition. I drank a canned Coke and ate an ice cream sandwich. And then the proprietor of the general store brought me out to this fisherman's bunk house to spend the rest of the afternoon and night. A nice old couple ran this camp, and I will have a happy supper with them.

My legs and feet hurt so badly as I sit here writing that I know a week's rest wouldn't bring them around to spry hiking condition. Hardship is good for the soul. And I've had a good taste of it. I have faced swamps and mosquitos enough to last me a lifetime. I have felt my legs and feet hurt worse than ever before. If there were more fellowship in what I am doing, I would continue. But I think I'm more cut out to be a four-, five-, or six-day hiker – and that with good company.

The psychology of these solo trudgings has been interesting. I thought about little that was profound or interesting. It has been as though I am involved in a purely physical endeavor, and there is no room for the mental, little for the spiritual. Nonsense phrases run through my mind. I make some profound observation, and then I keep repeating it until I think I'm batty. For a short while I can talk myself into good feelings and a quickened pace. But then it leaves me as though someone had pulled a plug.

Forty-nine days later in Virginia

Tuesday, July 30, 1968: Day 1 - 14.19 miles - 8 hours (8:30-4:30)

Anne took my picture at Reed's Gap at 8:30 a.m. with a flash bulb, and it has been dark and cool all day. I have hiked steady but leisurely, stopping only twice.

I stopped at a little store at Cripple Creek. Since all I had was a $10 bill, the lady gave me an RC and a 10-Cent cake. Together with two men, we visited. One man said I should look out for bears since the rangers let 5 out somewhere near here. He laughed when I said that I didn't think bears were particularly interested in me. Later I did skirt around a pretty big copperhead sitting coiled on the trail.

The trail has seemed easy compared to Maine. All steep places have been well switch-backed. The trail is well marked and dry. The summer growth is at its height, though, and in several places I walked through grass head-high. The wildflowers have kept me tickled all day. They are so varied, and I've never seen so many weird shapes and exciting colors. The prize goes to an upside-down orange flower that looks like four honeysuckle blooms attached together. But here have been some other dandies: black-eyed Susans, tiger lilies, ragged blue flowers, a demure purple cluster, and a frilly variety of "lilies of the valley."

Before arriving at this Priest Mountain Shelter, I went out on some ledges that afforded a splendid view west and north of nothing but wildlife. I had much of the same feeling of some years ago when I sat and watched the sun set from the rock face of Springer Mountain, Georgia. "In the wilderness is the salvation of the world." What a charge to get away, by one's self or in fellowship, and sense so graphically that there is a Spirit that is fresh, and everlasting, and invigorating.

Wednesday, July 31, 1968: Day 2 – 19.49 miles - 10 hours, 45 minutes (8 a.m. to 6:30 p.m.)

This has been a fun day and not nearly as exhausting as the mileage might make it seem. I was travelling in such a thick cloud all day that I had to be careful not to miss the white trail-blaze ahead. I'm sure this coolness kept me revived. I passed through some meadow-like fields that, according to the word, give splendid views; but the clouds jealously guarded these views from me, as though I were a mortal and was not to see. But the beauty close at hand was more than sufficient for the day, so I hardly miss the panoramic views. The Jacket Ridge and Cole Mountain were the big-name thrills of the day. The open fields on both of these crests contained a never-ending supply of fifty types of flowers; yellow and orange were the colors of the day. As I mounted the crest of Cole Mountain, I had to pass through a healthy herd of Angus. Much to my surprise, they began to nudge one another and start for me in mass. Periodically I had to turn and give them my "football look" to stop them. It suddenly dawned on me that a matador's cloak was not as large or a bright red as my pack [i.e. It was the red backpack that was attracting them.] As I ate chocolate on the top of Cole Mountain, clouds came hurrying from the west to spill over me and on into the valley to the east. The rushing moisture of the clouds was as refreshing as cold French cider.

I had to hike 4.7 miles further than planned because neither Cow Camp Gap nor Bald Knob had the water the AT guide said they did. My night's lodging is

Brown Mountain Creek, and it is doubly sweet because of my lack of water during the afternoon. The first thing I did was strip, bathe with soap, and then replace my two-day clothes. I then set my cooking equipment on a rock in the middle of the stream. The mélange of dehydrated spinach flakes, dehydrated potatoes, and dehydrated eggs seasoned with ground freezer-dried bacon had its usual delicious zip. And Tang is the best drink made. I will soon turn in and sleep contentedly.

Thursday, August 1, 1968: Day 3 - 10.53 miles - 5½ hours (8:30 to 2)

Today's travel was entirely on wooded trails. Though the sun was hot, the forest remains cool. During the morning I paralleled Brown Mountain Creek for two or three enchanting miles; sometimes the trail would get high above the creek, and I would look down at water spilling into a deep spot and I would think of the fun of swimming in such a hole. I traveled for a mile or so around Peddler (?) Lake, the reservoir for Roanoke. Beneath the spillway I met a wonderfully friendly farmer plowing his garden with a mule. He and his wife live there and look after the reservoir. In the winter he frequently is snowed in for 30 days. And his predecessor was once snowed in for 45 days. He has a freezer and lays up provisions for the long winter. He put up 10 quarts of strawberries. I passed through some virgin timber today that made me stop and gaze up. Some of these huge trees were 250 years old. They are a work of beauty and power. I have also passed through laurel and rhododendron, blackberries, and blueberries. The blackberries are sweet and juicy and the blueberries are as plump as any I have seen.

Friday, August 2, 1968: Day 4 - 18.16 miles, 9+ hours (8:00 to 5:15)

I feel as if I have conquered the James River Valley, having climbed down the rocky slopes to the river, crossed it by bridge, and then having scaled the mountains on the southern side to get back out of the valley. Much of the valley was visible from both sides. I got a sense of the Shenandoah Valley as I saw several towns in that direction and then I watched it rain over that way. My day of vista viewing began with the breathtaking 9 a.m. view from the Bluff Mountain fire tower (3,350 feet). I felt proud as I looked back over some of the peaks I had crossed.

I am sure I won't forget these grand views, especially of the wide James River, but I believe I get more genuine pleasure out of the pretty, well-graded trail, maybe even carpeted with pine straw. I love the streams where I stop to drink: Johns Creek, Cashew Creek, Matts Creek, Big Cove Branch, and the water of Marble Springs where I am now camping.

[Lost forever is an account or recall of how this AT hike in Virginia ended. I do recall that I hiked right at 80 miles on this section of the Appalachian Trail, so that would

have left me 17.63 miles on Saturday. I suspect, then, this was a five-day hike that ended late Saturday afternoon with a pick-up by either Anne or Dillon.]

Appendix 6

Trip with Dad to Portugal and Spain
Dec. 20, 1970, to Jan. 3, 1971 – Journal

12-21-70: Lisbon, Portugal, Hotel Don Carlo

7:30 p.m. Our flight from N.Y. took 6½ hours, 9:45 p.m. EST to 10:15 a.m. PST. We had a right to be groggy on arrival, having missed a night's sleep, but the excitement of being in a foreign city buoyed us. The flight was pleasant. I rode with two ladies from Colombia, S.A., who spoke no English. We communicated some. I read 130 pages of Michener's Iberia; Dad finished Sunday Journal-Constitution. We had two meals and beer within a 6-hour flight. Upon arrival I was slightly embarrassed to be part of a "tour," but it did expedite getting through customs and to our hotel. Joana Nalta, a beautiful and dark Portuguese woman, is our hostess.

First impressions: Lisbon is clean and friendly. I saw much minimum-level housing, but so far I haven't seen anyone who isn't making a wage. I have the nice feeling that the place is not overrun with tourists, and so people are pleasant to us. We checked into the Don Carlos; we have a nice room and bath, overlooking a slight descent and the tops of apartments. We stretched our legs some, looking for a café. It was a feat crossing the Marques de Pombal at noon. This is comparable in size to Place d 'Etoile in Paris, and has a six-story statue to the marquis in the center. We climbed a hill and entered the Café Safarque. For $2 we had a splendid lunch with beer. I had a tortilla (omelet with ham & potatoes within) and Dad had a pea-and-ham dish with a good sauce. Beer was 15 cents a bottle.

I am disappointed that it is chilly, but I will just have to wear more clothes. We wandered through the Ritz, a classy hotel atop the highest hill. Dad would have walked all afternoon, but I feared that if we didn't sleep we would feel it adversely for a week.

We have slept from 1:30 to 7:30 and are now ready for an evening on the town. A long and leisurely supper at A Severa: Restaurante Tipico was enjoyable. We had small, sweet shrimp with Madeira. Then I had big sardines, soup, a sour green-pepper salad, crème caramel custard and coffee. The wine was green— something new for me. The entertainment was gypsy—mandolin, guitar, singers and dancers. The woman sounded like Buffy St. Marie. She was good on the loud notes and harsh on the soft. $9 total bill for each seemed a little like tourist prices. We walked around some after we got back to the hotel and retired around 1 a.m.

12-22-70: Lisbon

We arose early and had a continental breakfast in the hotel. A little after 9 a.m. we departed on a morning sightseeing trip all over the city. Our guide, Anna Bella, was charming and full of pep. She was able to give us a good bit of history and information. Sometime within the last 200 years an earthquake practically leveled the city; this destroyed ancient cathedrals, palaces, etc. and it probably has caused Lisbon to be a less rich city. The explorers are commemorated by several monuments. Prince Henry the Navigator seems to be the principal one.

We ate lunch at the Ritz Hotel; even with that name our food was Portuguese. We just barely made it back to the Don Carlos for our nap. The change in time is making both of us feel a little drugged here at the beginning of our trip.

Around 5:30 p.m. we began a long and interesting walk that took us down to Avienda da Liberade to the central area for shops. Fighting pedestrians and cars is really "survival of the fittest" in Lisbon. The cars are particularly wild. There were a few beautiful shops, but not many. And there are far too few cafes, though we finally found one for some espresso. Frankly, the side of Lisbon that I have seen is humdrum, especially in comparison to other European cities that I love.

We ate dinner at the Tavarse Restaurant. The place is filled with mirrors, and ornate gold ceiling, and beautiful silverware and crystal. We were seated first in an outer area in soft velvet chairs where we had two Madeiras apiece. For my main meal I had bouillabaisse soup; Dad had lightly fried white fish. Our white wine was delicious. We enjoyed a walk upon returning to the hotel, and then we retired.

12-23-70: Lisbon

We spent the morning leisurely, reading and napping. We went for a nice walk that took us to the top of St. Jorge's Park. From there we could see the length of Avieda da Liberade and the river that lies at the end of this grand boulevard. At an armory many uniformed men were milling around bags filled with Christmas items, including an apple. Perhaps they were waiting of children to come and claim them. For lunch I had a bowl of potato soup at a bustling café. At 2 p.m. we departed on a bus trip that lasted until 7 p.m. It was a castle tour; we went in three. One, just a little out of Lisbon, was a summer palace built after Versailles. It had a "hall of mirrors" and gardens in the Versailles manner, though not nearly so grand. We arrived in Sintra, a beautiful mountain settlement where Lisbonians go in the summer. The castle on the ground was beautifully furnished—by that I mean it didn't appear musty. The castle high up on the mountain overlooking Sintra was worth the unsettling bus ride up. Around it were a few walls surviving from 7th and 8th century Moorish construction.

As we drove from Sintra to Estoril, a resort on the Atlantic, we saw peasants leading burros with saddle packs on them. There, as well as in Lisbon, we saw women with heavy loads balanced atop their heads. Along the coast were windmills. We passed Cabo da Roca that marks the westernmost point in Europe. Estoril was a strange mixture of luxury resort and weather-beaten fishermen. The fishermen had lowered boats that they were pushing out to sea against the waves. Supper we ate at our hotel, probably our best meal. We had five beautifully served courses for 65 escudos or $2.60. We collapsed early.

12-24-70: Lisbon/Madrid

Our day consisted of eating breakfast, taking a walk, packing, eating lunch, buying some gifts, walking, and then catching the bus to the airport. I bought two large porcelain plates that are copies of 17th century designs. I also bought two brightly painted wooden cocks – the symbol of Portugal. The shop was nice; they treated us to a glass of port. We wandered into a "farmacia" that was built in 1890. It had a "laboratore" and heavy wooden & glass cases. Dad bought Aqua Velva and a Portuguese version of Listerine.

A flight necessitates so much wasted time—getting to the airport and then waiting. Our Iberian Airlines flight to Madrid was fine. They gave us a European Herald Tribune so both Dad and I hungrily read the news, mostly of workers' uprisings in Poland over increased food costs and of rallies in support of Franco in Spain. He is on the "hot seat" in suppressing the Basque separatists.

Madrid is beautifully decked out for Christmas with tiny light bulbs on the trees and several beautiful trees. The city looks prosperous with fountains and beautiful shops. As we walked, Spanish people with noisemakers (and one with a drum) wandered the streets merrymaking over Christmas. It was very cold.

12-25-70: Madrid

This has been a strange Christmas Day, partly because I am in Spain and partly because I have been sick and haven't left the hotel. (I have more cold in my head than I thought humanly possible. It was beginning to affect one eye and give me a headache, but I have taken some medicine that has helped.) Calatrava Hotel is so nice that I gladly spent the day inside. It has reading and writing rooms downstairs as well as big lobby areas. It has a nice bar and a small but attractive dining room. After breakfast I settled in with Michener's Iberia and thoroughly enjoyed his section on the Easter festival at Sevilla, while Dad went on a long walk exploring. I missed going with him, but I loved this time to read.

When he came back we went down for Christmas dinner about 2 p.m. The dining room was so crowded that we were forced to drink sherry and eat olives in the bar until space was available. We began the meal with a hot chicken consommé and then progressed to a shrimp cocktail in delicious homemade mayonnaise sauce. Turkey baked with artichokes and mushrooms was the main course, and topped with the Spanish sauce it made for a memorable Christmas meal. We also had champagne, ice cream, and small cakes. We shared our meal with an attractive blonde woman from Dallas who, though somewhat hardened by the experiences of life, was beautifully sensitive towards the Spanish people and towards foreign travel in general. She was an example of what Michener said: "To be a tourist is to stand gape-eyed with love." (The subject arose because there were "ugly Americans" in our midst—in from other American Express tours, which made me happy that our group is so sane and kind. One fellow in the other group talked loud in the bar and sings. He said he found no good wine in Italy. All he wanted from this bartender was the best red wine … he just wanted the best there was.)

Well, by 4:30 our Christmas feast was ended. I returned to our jolly room with a balcony and read hard for three hours in order to build an appetite for supper. It began snowing lightly around 5 p.m. while Dad was out walking.

12-26-70: Madrid/Torremolinos

We woke to find a thin layer of snow over everything. This day was practically all spent in travel. By the time we packed, met the group to go by bus to the airport, arrive at the airport one hour ahead and then wait for the tardy plane, five or six hours have elapsed. I enjoyed the drive to Madrid's airport. There are beautiful apartment buildings in that city. We saw two or three startling modern structures It is alive, and I look forward to our return there at the end of our journey.

It was raining when we arrived at Spain's Costa de Sol; rain was blowing like a real tropical storm. Before dinner we had two glasses of sherry apiece, Dad's the dry and mine the sweet. We had some delicious olives stuffed with anchovies. At dinner we sat at the table with a one-armed German from Munich. He spoke little English so he and I fell to talking French, which was sort of bad because Dad was left out. This man, William Swiss, lost his arm during the last days of the war at Monte, the monastery in Italy that was destroyed by the Americans. William thinks that only the crazy pursue war. He thinks that they (especially the French) wouldn't raise an arm to resist the Russians. In his eyes the U.S. has lost its credibility as savior of the world; he doesn't see the Europeans rallying around us.

12-27-70: **Torremolinos**

This crystal-clear day was perfect for walking along the Mediterranean, through small streets with seaside cafés and bars and along crowded in-town streets lined with clothing and jewelry shops. One open-fronted café interested both Dad and me, and we will go back; it has fresh seafood stacked up and hot grills right on the counter. You order and watch it being cooked.

Along the cliffs rising from the sea are some enticing apartments with big front terraces and considerable privacy. Their view is nice because the coast curves and gives one a glimpse of Malaga and of some snow-peaked mountains. We also went into a beautiful hotel that has appealing lobby areas and a big dining room overlooking the sea—las Palermas Hotel. Torremolinos surprised me—I thought that because it is all tourist trade and has so many shops luring the tourists that I wouldn't like it. But despite the tourism, the town is very Spanish; the tourists are very international (Sp., Fr., Germ., Scand., Eng., & Am.); and I like it.

In the afternoon we had a beautiful drive to Marbella along the coast. The contrast of mts and sea make the whole coast exciting. Throw in olive trees, bulls grazing, oranges, goats, eucalyptus and cork trees, and a complete assortment of magnificent hotels, and you have a drive that excites. Then throw in a good, clear view of the Rock of Gibraltar rising out of the sea—it is much bigger than I imagined; a whole island with room enough on top for a whole city.

We saw 1½ hours of bullfighting at the Plaza de Toros de Nueva Andalucía, just beyond Marbella. This is a new 22,000 capacity ring. The afternoon was complete with band to play "el Toro" and to trumpet each changing aspect of the fight. The matadors were young upstarts, and none of the six fights were clean and classical. One horse was gored down and its rider knocked out; one toreador was gored, though not hurt badly. And no one killed on first thrust and only one killed on his second thrust – all signs to me of beginners. *[When did 30-year-old Chuck become so knowledgeable about bull fighting?]*

Upon returning we had sherry and olives stuffed with anchovies and then ate dinner. We watched a show that Flamenco dancers (three) accompanied by two young guitar players performed. It was probably just loud and touristic—not the real art of the Flamenco. *[Flamenco expert, too]*

12-28-70: **Torremolinos**

It was rainy & cold today and since I am almost cured of my cold, I didn't venture out. This "day off" was well spent reading Michener's Iberia. He discussed the Spanish Inquisition and tried to show to what extent this contributed to Spain's decline since the 1600s. It became a "purity of blood" matter that stripped Spain of many brilliant minds that happened to have some Jewish or Moorish blood. I re-read about Granada since we are going there tomorrow. Its location enabled the Moors to hold on there the longest, until Isabel and Fernando finally drove them out in the 1500s. Grenada is enough inland to protect it from coastal pirates; it is enough surrounded by mountains to protect it from inland Castilian Spain.

We found a sweeter white wine that we both enjoyed at both meals today. I had the creme caramel (called flan in Spain) for both meals.

12-29-70: Torremolinos

We arose in the dark, ate a breakfast of rolls and fruit while huddled in our room. We boarded the bus at 7:45 for a lengthy but rich trip to Granada. The sun came up beautifully over the Mediterranean and over the cities of Malaga and Torremolinos, for by this time we were in the mountains behind and above the coast. The scenery was spectacular: Cork trees that were red skinned because they had just been debarked; goats grazing; donkeys with saddlebags being led by a peasant; beautiful olive orchards; grand estates down in the valley or on edges of mountains—so steep you wonder how they ever get out to civilization. AND THEN WE SAW GREAT SNOW ON THE EVEN HIGHER MOUNTAINS AHEAD. It was the Sierra Nevadas. We learned the wind had blown the snow so hard across the highway that it was blocked and that we couldn't get through to Granada. (One of the hazards of December travel). This would have been one of the richest days of our stay. As it was, it was nice. The bus, together with all other traffic, turned around. We were back in Torremolinos by noon.

Dad and I enjoyed walking along the beachfront, investigating in little shops. We had a good time wandering in Torremolinos, and I even bought a few gifts, and included a swede seaman's cap for myself. In the evening we had some Spanish sherry and visited with LeRoy Smith. LeRoy is a black from Washington who is a hilarious storyteller. He has had a sports career that has included playing for the Harlem Globe Trotters and playing golf with all of the greats. There are few sports figures that he doesn't know personally. He had a bullfight poster made that lists LeRoy Smith along with El Cordobes as one of the matadors. This he will have great fun with back in Washington as he is going to tell them that he was here fighting bulls. Our dinner was good and included the oft repeated & delicious potato soup.

[*Note: This reads almost as if Dad was not on the trip. Thus far he is barely mentioned. This was a trip supposedly to help Dad in his grief and loneliness following Mom's death. Did I ever talk to him about that? Was I really that out of touch with feelings that I don't record a single smidgen of conversation between me and Dad?*]

12-30-70: Torremolinos

We spent the morning touring Malaga, a seaport international airport city of 300,000. We began by visiting a well-preserved Moorish (Islams from various parts of North Africa) fortress perched above the city on a hill. It was built in the

8th century. It gave one a good view of the older Malaga near the water and the new city that runs between the hills away from the Mediterranean. (There was a big ship sounding her foghorn as she headed into port; a little tug blasted back as it went to "nest" the ship.)

The Malaga Cathedral is spectacular in the height of its vaulted ceiling. Neither stained glass nor outside were particularly attractive. The choir area is a cloister in the middle. The choir stall for each member is a seat surrounded by beautifully carved figures. The seats that line the walls are mahogany and all linked together, forming the walls of this choir area. This dates from the 15th and 16th centuries. The two organs are also that old, as is a huge book with the Gregorian chants in it. I would love to be in that cathedral in the morning when the Gregorian chants are sung.

We went to a leather goods shop where the craftsmanship is performed. There Dad bought a pigskin sport coat that is soft and beautifully lined and tailored. Cost: $40. He had been looking for a soft corduroy coat in the U.S., so this filled this need. We ended our visit at a winery where we tasted several types of muscatel wines. This was fun. I bought a bottle of Crème de Cacao for $1.

We had a leisurely lunch with George and Aileen Blinco. The sangria was good. It was near the end of the serving time (1 – 3 p.m.) so the waiters were more relaxed. Though they speak no English and we no Spanish, we had a fun conversation. One waiter answered my question about comparative merits of bullfighters by listing El Cordobes as #3 and a clown.

We walked in Torremolinos. We had met Ron Van Buskirk, a citizen of Toronto, in the morning, and he spied us and walked with us. We stopped at a fancy hotel for a glass of sherry on the way back. After dinner we wandered up the road with Ron to Los Palamas Hotel and had Cointreau & café in their bar. The dancing crowd seemed mostly German. Styles are fun to observe in Europe, dancing included.

12-31-70: Torremolinos/Madrid

Getting in the air above Malaga afforded a memorable view of high snow-filled Sierra Nevada Mountains juxtaposed to the blue, clear Mediterranean Sea. The snowy terrain between the sea and Madrid (300 miles) made for an interesting flight. It emphasized how mountainous Spain is.

We walked the New Year's Eve streets and felt the excitement of one of the world's great cities. We had 4 p.m. lunch in a café-restaurant combination where many locals were spending their siesta. On our walk we went to the huge national post office, we explored inside the plush European Ritz Hotel, and we examined the Prado from the outside. When we passed through the Puerto del Sol at 6:30 p.m., excitement was already building towards midnight. It is in this square that thousands pack and on each stroke of the clock a grape is consumed—so that the corresponding month will be lucky.

George and Aileen Blinco, Ron Van Buskirk, Dad and I arrived at Al Mounia Restaurant at 10 p.m. It is built in a Moorish palace. All is North African: the walls and floors and ceilings are beautifully tiled, the waiters wear Moorish clothes, and the food is Algerian, Moroccan, etc. I had brick (meat-filled pastry) and lamb couscous. We drank champagne. At midnight we tried to eat 12 grapes. The few left in the restaurant (the others having gone to the Puerto del Sol) were jovial. An owner came and shook all of our hands. We had pastry and minted tea and departed, having paid $10 each for the finest of food and service plus five bottles of Spanish champagne.

We walked the couple of miles back which got us into the spirit of the occasion by laughing and hollering with others on the streets. One Spaniard, in jovially passing by, offered me a swig from his brandy bottle. Biting cold or not, this was a beautiful gesture that warmed my insides. We returned to the hotel and drank more champagne from silver goblets that Ron had bought.

But the gesture of the brandy had fired me up for the street people. Dad had caught my cold and felt the need to climb in bed. He was glad for me to further explore the night. So Ron, George, Aileen and I headed for the Puerto del Sol. We laughed and sang. I walked on my hands (which they later kidded me about). A group formed around us on the street. Their tambourine made such good music (Aileen danced) that I bought a tambourine for 100 pesetas. As we went into the café, my tambourine made me acceptable. Spaniards would take turns using it and the music and merrymaking was wonderful. We left, but I found I couldn't retire. George and Aileen bid us adieu, and Ron and I went back in the café. The music makers were glad to see us. I ordered a bottle of beer which it seemed natural to pass around. Out of two bottles I had no more than three or four sips. One Spanish boy insisted on offering me a cigarette. I explained in beautiful Spanish that I didn't smoke. That didn't matter to him. He was adamant. When I had smoked one, passing it to my beer drinking friends, he gave me a second.

As the café closed, it caused a refugee problem. Where will all of these displaced people go? Jesus and Joseph emerged from out of the music group as the ones who would help Ron and me find another bar. Ron was skeptical and finally fell by the wayside at 4 a.m. Joseph, Jesus and I found a big basement room where chocolate was being poured from steaming pots. We had some together with a greasy pastry—all of which seems to be a part of the tradition.

Joseph bought some cigarettes with my money, and we then went to a café for coffee. After exchanging addresses, we three parted ways. I checked the plaque on the building, saw that I was still in the Puerto del Sol, and I headed out towards the hotel. I walked and walked until I saw familiar lights and a familiar Christmas tree ahead – I was back at the Puerto del Sol. I had gone out the wrong side of the square. My second attempt at escape was more successful. I climbed beneath the sheets at 6 a.m., just as America was seeing the New Year in.

1-1-71: Madrid

We arose at noon, had a soup brunch, and left at 2:30 on a trip to Toledo. The city dates from several centuries B.C. It was the capital of Spain until well after Isabella & Ferdinand. The city is perched on high ground and two-thirds of it is surrounded by river.

We entered a small church of St. Thomas and viewed a large El Greco mural "The Burial of the Count of Orgaz." It showed St. Stephen and St. Augustine holding the body. The top portion was enthroned Christ receiving the soul—a human fetus.

The cathedral is as exciting as any I have been in, short of St. Peter's. They have art treasures in gold and oil and marble and thread that equaled the pleasure I felt the next day in The Prado. A Cellini sculpture plaque, a Titian portrait painted on copper, jewels that Isabella gave this church, and a solid gold shrine that is carried through the streets at Corpus Christi were all stored in one room. The gallery of art had many El Greco portraits of saints and a crucified Christ by Goya. Raphael was there and Titian and Ribera and Murillo were well represented. I guess my favorite was Caravaggio's large canvas showing John the Baptist as a young boy, looking like a healthy Bacchus. Velasquez had several religious portraits there. All of these were in two stone rooms that were very cold—as was the entire cathedral—and lighted in a way that caused much glare on the paintings. All of the monarchs (except Isabella & Ferdinand) were buried here until Felipe II had them moved to Eschorial. Cardinal Mendoza (powerful during Isabella's time) is still buried here to the left of the main altar. Part of the beautifully carved choir section was done by John of Borgonne, a contemporary of Michelangelo's who gets part of his name from his city, between Rome & Florence.

There is considerably more to the cathedral. I have only touched upon 60% of its excitement, and I haven't done it justice. We were so chilled that I enjoyed brandy for the first time in my life. This chill assured Dad of a terrible cold. Ron, George, Aileen, Dad and I had an elegant meal at Puerto de Moro, a beautiful old palace where guests are served in different rooms. Dad and I shared a chicken cooked in a clay pot. The varied hors d'oeuvres were a treat. At 11:50 p.m. a Spanish couple arrived to begin their dinner.

1-2-71: Madrid

The only charge for the breakfast in our room was a nominal tip for the busboy. We spent the morning touring the Palacio Real (Regal) that was built in the 1700s and is beautiful indeed and still seems livable. The carpets, the satin interior walls, and the chandeliers were the highlights. Franco could live here, but he prefers a royal hunting lodge about 5 miles north of town. The palace is used for a ceremony when Franco receives the credentials of a newly appointed ambassador to Spain. Certain state visitors are entertained here. A dinner was given for Nixon this past fall.

Our guide showed us part of the Prado. Dad was feeling bad so he went back to the hotel with the tour. I stayed and enjoyed myself in the museum for about three hours. El Greco rose in my estimation; Goya rose as tops in the Prado for me; Velasquez, Murillo, and Titian held their good positions with me; Rubens rose, though he's still way behind the others in my personal scale of preferences.

I wandered by the Barflor (New Year's Eve spot for music-making at Puerta del Sol) and had a 3 p.m. glass of hot milk and a potato omelet sandwich. I went by the giant figures of Pancho Sanchez and Don Quixote. Here I ran into George & Eileen who were headed to pick up leather coats they had ordered. In waiting for the store to open at 4:30 following siesta, we went into a nice bar and had hot milk and apple strudel. The weather is sunny and cold. We began to talk a little with a Spanish man at the bar. He said he hated to see people drink milk during holiday time. He had the bartender heat some glasses and serve us a glass of Cardinal Mendoza Brandy; only a limited number of bottles are produced each year and each has a number. He then invited us to his leather & fur shop.

The department store where we went for the coats was interesting. Gift giving in Spain takes place on January 6th, the commemoration of the visit of the Wise Men, so now the Spanish stores are jammed with last-minute shoppers. Later we went to the man's store. The store turned out to be very posh. The man turned out to be the son of an earl. He took us to the private salon downstairs and proceeded to sell Aileen a beautiful suede coat lined with an especially fine sheep fur and tipped with fur around the bottom and the edge of the sleeves. She looked glamorous in it. For really the first time I saw the world of fashion design of customizing of clothes to the person. This is the shop of Joan Kennedy, Audrey Hepburn and others.

"The Earl" had recommended a good restaurant for paella and he might possibly meet us there at 11 p.m. We couldn't find the restaurant, but through a strange series of events we landed in a restaurant an awful lot like one that Dillon, Anne, and I heard flamenco singing in six years earlier. It had blankets covering the windows keeping the cold out. Names were carved and written on the walls, ceilings and tables. There were faded paintings on the walls that looked like Goya's supernatural horror scenes. We went through several rooms to the innermost part. It was 11:45 p.m.

A woman who was either a whore or a fool was leading our area in singing and dancing. An excellent and distinguished male singer came in and the soul of his flamenco singing was stirring. A couple of more notable singers packed in before we had finished eating our delicious roast lamb and sangria. The younger Spaniards contributed—a couple of boys (18, 19 perhaps) would dance with the woman, but it seemed to us that she needs age and seasoning to lead the holiday fiestas. Our second and third pitchers of sangria were shared by three of the performers. They were certainly not performing for us but they were graciously conscious of our presence. We had eaten and drunk of the best for $3.50 each, and we had been a part of the people at their festival time. Three of the young men, one with an American girlfriend, invited us to another café for coffee. I hugged the substantial older performer (she danced with a full class of wine on her head; she held the bottle aloft and drank as it dripped) and wished her happy New Year from America; she wished me the same from Spain in a warm way. I paid the bill and hugged the waiter. I spoke French with one boy and English with the other two. I was in bed by 3 a.m.

1-3-71: Madrid / New York/Atlanta/Columbus

From Madrid, we changed planes in New York for Atlanta. From there I drove late at night to Columbus to be ready for Brookstone's resumption the next day, and Dad went home alone.

Appendix 7

The Cranmer School (Later to be Whitefield Academy)

Note: We prepared the following statement of mission and plans on January 23, 1996, for establishing The Cranmer School (later to become Whitefield Academy). What follows is a significantly shortened version of the original.

Mission

We exist to educate the hearts and souls of young people, as well as their minds. To most effectively educate, we maintain both a challenging and a nurturing environment. Since "man's chief end is to glorify God and enjoy Him forever," then that sense of enjoyment should be inherent in this learning and growing environment. We glorify God by expanding the perceived limits of that which a young person is capable. We do all in the name of Jesus and by the power of the Holy Spirit.

Significance of the Cranmer Name

Thomas Cranmer (1489–1556) was the first Protestant Archbishop of Canterbury and was the writer of the Book of Common Prayer—thus combining strong academic skill with a solid Biblical faith.

Scriptural Mandates for The Cranmer School

◆ ... and Jesus increased in wisdom and stature, and in favor with God and men. *Luke 2:52*

◆ From everyone who has been given much, much will be demanded; and to the one who has been entrusted with much, much more will be asked. *Luke 12:48*

◆ ... the Son of Man did not come to be served, but to serve... *Matthew 20:28*

◆ Do nothing out of selfish ambition or vain conceit, but in humility consider others better than yourselves. Each of you should look not only to your own interests, but also to the interests of others. *Philippians 2:3,4*

Unique Aspects

◆ Students look forward to coming to school (i.e., It is a joyful place). Encouragement from adults and peers alike will abound. Positive reinforcement will be the tool of preference for teachers, coaches, and students. An intercom and assemblies will be judiciously used to dispense appropriate humor.

◆ Classroom learning occurs via creative, high-interest methods. Heavy use of educational technology will give students additional discovery activities, such as with the use of the CD-ROM.

◆ All learning does not occur within the four walls of the classroom. Learning also occurs by going and seeing and doing.

We celebrate that our school exists in Atlanta, and we take full advantage of its rich learning opportunities: Auburn Avenue, Atlanta History Museum, battlefields, the state capital, Georgia Tech, Emory, and the CDC are the tip of the iceberg. Each class would take a major trip that would tie into its curriculum for a given year: marshes/beaches, Boston, Philadelphia, New York, Washington, and Williamsburg are examples. Individually and corporately the students would raise the funds for these trips.

◆ Students learn to serve others by doing just that, as age appropriate, within the school and within the community.

Community Involvement Atlanta (CIA) would engage students weekly at such places in need of volunteers as Atlanta Children's Shelter, Charis House, Egleston, and Shepherd's Spinal Center , and at our intown sister school. Helping the elderly and homeless would also be options.

- Cranmer School has a sister/brother inner-city African/American school with which it works closely. This relationship exists to model Christ's mandated racial reconciliation.*

    * *See the stories of* The Good Samaritan *(Luke 10:33-37) and* The Samaritan Woman at the Well *(John 4:3-42).*

We would develop a partnership with a Christian black elementary school in downtown Atlanta. Our students would be paired by grades so that close friendships could develop, even though there would be six or seven years difference in age between their students and ours. Our students would attend programs and special days at the in-town school when their partner grade was involved. The in-town students would reciprocate with visits to The Cranmer School. When not face to face, students would communicate by letter, video, and e-mail.

- Home and school will support one another's scriptural perspective on sex education—abstinence until marriage. The truth on this subject will surface in Bible and biology and English classes, as well as in other school settings, directed by teachers who are Christ-centered in their perspective.

It is not anticipated that sex education will be taught as a class unto itself. Rather, the components of what is often taught in such a class will come up in context throughout the curriculum. Abstinence until marriage will be reinforced consistently.

- The educational programs are established and guided by the professional educators of the school, freeing the parents from any of these worries.

Parents will take responsibility for abundant social events for each grade level throughout the year, as well as for enhancing a strong sense of community among the parents within the school.

* * *

Span: Grades six through twelve

Location: Ideally the school will be located within the Perimeter Highway (I-285).

Faculty: Teachers are chosen for the depth of their commitment to grow in Christ as well as for their general teaching ability and training. These high-energy, high-caliber teachers are paid the best wages possible.

Program: Growing in Christ, physical fitness, positive human relationships, and intellectual development are the four pillars of the school's program.

- **Student Selection:** Students are chosen from among those who themselves want what the school is about. Standardized testing and interviews will be used to determine a prospective student's ability to handle a challenging college preparatory curriculum.

Tuition: Tuition charges reflect the true cost of an education that is educationally rich, while being rigorously cost conscious. The tuition is all-inclusive, eliminating random costs and charges during the year.

Financial Aid: The goal is to make a place in this school available to all qualified young people who desire to be in the school, space permitting. Financial aid is sought vigorously to span the gap between what less-affluent families can reasonably be expected to pay and the full cost of the tuition.

QUESTIONS AND ANSWERS

♦ **In what sense is this a Christian school?**

Both the curriculum and the teachers are focused on the centrality of Jesus Christ, but the greater in importance of these two is the teacher. The teacher loves the Lord and loves young people. The study of the Bible and its accompanying scripture memory program—both ongoing parts of the school's curriculum—come to life for the students by way of the modeling of Divine Wisdom seen in the teachers.

Materials used in the classroom are chosen from among the best available, regardless of whether the source is Christian or secular; but the guidance of the teacher through these materials is always from a strong Christian perspective.

♦ **What is our approach to teaching reading and writing?**

Realizing that so much subsequent learning and fullness of life depends on one's reading and writing, we give these disciplines our highest priority. Our students know the major works of Western literature and its authors as if they were old friends. Students write essays, research papers, fiction, and poetry. They write something every day. Our goal is for our students to become ardent readers and prolific writers.

♦ **What is our approach to teaching mathematics?**

Our students learn to manipulate numbers with great alacrity. But that is only half of the program. The other half constitutes learning to view life through the eyes of a mathematician, providing abundant real-life situations involving numerical relationships.

♦ **What is our approach to teaching science?**

Young people have a normally insatiable curiosity about the world around them. Our science program depends on teachers who are almost eccentric in their passion for science, feeding that student curiosity. So many of the great discoveries of science have occurred when scientists have pursued further evidence of the perfect intricacies of God's creation; and it is that perspective that we try to recreate.

◆ What is our approach to teaching history?

Young people love biographies of people whose lives have made a difference in this world. Great biographies seem to stick in a person's mind for life. We use biographies to teach of other times and places as well as the great possibilities of the human spirit. Yes, students know dates and events, and in a manner not easily forgotten. And, yes, there will be a history text that lays the past out in chronological order.

◆ What is the focus of our physical education program?

Our bodies are the temples of God. We must learn to be stewards of these temples. Therefore, we must discipline ourselves towards fitness, which includes exercise, nutrition and rest. We will teach physical skills that are basic to lifetime recreational pursuits as well as to sports. Competition in team sports is available in the afternoon hours for all students.

◆ Why should art have a place in this school's curriculum?

God's creation is a masterpiece of color, shapes, and textures. A student's sense of wonder and amazement at His creation is magnified through the study of art. God's crowning touch was His creation of man and woman. God blessed man and woman with the ability to see, record, and appreciate His world creatively through the medium of art.

◆ Do music and drama deserve the emphasis we give them?

A student whose youth is surrounded by hearing and making good music can never be a dullard, now or as an adult. Music fuels the spirit and soul as well as the mind. Acting and play production enhance the imagination and one's sense of self. The great camaraderie and confidence gained from performing before an audience make music and drama life-enhancing endeavors.

◆ Why does a middle school / high school student need to labor over a foreign language?

To be able to understand and be understood by someone who knows no English has practical value. Now or later in life this may enable us to make our way more effectively in travel or in business. And the earlier in life one acquires a foreign language, the easier it is to learn and the greater the absence of accent when speaking it. Equally important, one gains a new appreciation for how our brain and tongue work together—the wonder of speech in general—and that there is legitimate life beyond English speakers and beyond our immediate neighborhoods.

◆ Can Bible be taught for seven years as a classroom subject without killing all interest in the Bible?

I John 2:6 says, "Whoever claims to live in Him must walk as Jesus did." So we study the Bible to learn how to "walk as Jesus did,"" to learn how to walk as

Joshua did, and as Queen Esther did. We learn to be a singer of songs as was David, a dreamer of dreams as was Joseph, and a visionary as was John. We internalize and personalize what God has to say to us about excellence, about male/female relationships and marriage, finances, and conflict resolution. We commit scripture to memory, and we know Genesis to Malachi, Matthew to Revelation; more importantly, we grow to know the Author intimately—"to live in Him" and to resemble Him.

Appendix 8

History of Church Memberships Over the Years

Second Ponce de Leon Baptist, Atlanta, Monroe Swilley, 1943-45

Here, I first sang, "Come, Ye Thankful People, Come." (See "Thanksgiving with Champ" in **Part One, Chapter 6**, for my primary memories of this church.)

Peachtree Road Presbyterian, Atlanta, Dr. Gene Wilson, 1946-62

I was active at Salem Camp, Camp Rutledge, and as president of the Presbytery Youth Council that convened at Central Presbyterian: The Directors of Christian Education (DCEs) were my favorite staff people. (Marjorie Potter, Anne Love) One of them had a Volkswagen that we would get into and roll it down the street. She began to lock it. The front windshield cranked open from the bottom to let in air. I could barely slip my hand into the opening, but I did in an effort to open the locked car, and the windshield made a terrible noise and multiple cracks ran from one side of the windshield to the other. *[At various times in my life I would carry my exuberant nature too far—not knowing when to stop.]*

Through high school, I participated in the Sunday night youth program. And, in the summer before my Vanderbilt senior year (1961), I served as the interim youth director.

Downtown Presbyterian, Nashville, Dr. Gray, 1958-1962, 1966-67

Dillon had attended Downtown Presbyterian Church in the two years that he was in Nashville ahead of me. He had met Mrs. Prueher and daughters Betsy and Martha, as well as Mrs. Prueher's mother, Mrs. Farrell. They attended

Downtown Presbyterian. Mrs. Prueher would invite Dillon and others to her home for Sunday lunch. Tom and I were included in the invitation when we arrived at Vanderbilt. The discipline of getting up to go to church was established by Dillon, and we followed him. It became for me another source of Pharisaical pride to head to church on a cold morning when almost everyone else stayed in bed. Dr. Gray was a shy-seeming pastor who had the mannerism of rolling his black robe up in his two arms and then letting it go—this throughout his sermon. I liked what he had to say; and I liked the non-pretentiousness of the church. The inside was painted in an Egyptian motif. There was a story from before I arrived on the scene (1958) when a young black man came to worship one Sunday and was seated down on the front row without anyone near for several rows. As the service was starting, Mrs. Farrell, who would have been one of the oldest members, got up from her seat about in the middle of the pews, and deliberately walked down and sat next to the black stranger and worshipped alongside of him for the rest of the service. One of my failures was to not keep up with Mrs. Prueher in later years in gratitude to her for her kindness to me. While at Vanderbilt, once I had the flu and went and stayed at her house to be nursed back to health.

I prayed a lot, as I remember, during my Vanderbilt years. I often felt out of my depth with my studies, and I would pray for God's wisdom. I didn't make my grades until the second semester of my sophomore year—that is, a C average. I was humbled, and that was good for me. I didn't drink (except a couple of times) until I graduated; and I stayed away from porn (which was not as pervasive in the early '60s as it is now. There were licentious centerfolds in *Playboy* and *Penthouse*, but I managed to stay away from them, for the most part.) I was respectful in my one-on-one with girls, afraid to be too forward. So, you can see that I calculated my spiritual health on the basis of my moral code which I believed was the Biblical code.

Grace Episcopal, Chattanooga, 1962-1964: Here I was confirmed as an Episcopalian, a move I found spiritually energizing, partly because it was a change from my previous twenty-two years as a Presbyterian. Also, I loved the liturgy.

St. Thomas Episcopal, Columbus, Hal Daniel, 1969-71

Greenville (Alabama) **Independent Methodist**, Larry Alsop / Ralph Stacy: Although we were never members of this church in Greenville, here we were married in 1971, and here we worshipped when visiting JoElyn's family. Our involvement extended through Uncle Bud's funeral in 2009.

St. Matthew Lutheran, Columbus, 1971-74

St. Peter's Episcopal, Rome, Bob and Jane Beeland, 1974-1980: Here JoElyn and I experienced a season of substantial spiritual growth.

Cathedral of St. Philip, Atlanta, David and Ginny Collins, 1980-1988: The last two of our years here, I served on the Chapter (Vestry).

All Saints Episcopal, Carmel, 1988-89

Salinas Valley Community Church, California, 1989

Carmel Presbyterian, California, John Sneider, 1989-90: This was a good church for the family.

Church of the Apostles, Atlanta, Michael Youssef, 1990-2006: As a family we were all heavily involved here in the Student-to-Student Program. Jane served on the STS paid staff in the early years of her marriage.

Church of the Redeemer, Atlanta, John Thomas, 2006-2007: This was our transition year from the Anglican worship to the Presbyterian Church of America (PCA).

Atlanta Westside Presbyterian Church, Walter and Anne Henegar, 2007-present: JoElyn, Jane, Terrell, and I were among the nineteen members of the Launch Team.

Atlanta Westside Presbyterian brothers, session of 2015: Jim Irwin, Chris Talley, Chuck, Andrew Crews, Jeff Heck, Dee DeBardeleben, Peter Pettit, Michael Vestal, and Walter Henegar

Appendix 9

Exchanges with Jane During Her Time in Uganda

Report from Uganda, received 4:30 a.m., August 29, 2011

Hello family! Where to begin? We had a great flight, with an unexpected (though after the hassle of correcting it at the gate, I suppose it shouldn't have surprised us) stop in Kigali, Rwanda. Only Chad slept much on the first flight, but then on the second we all zonked for the first couple of hours. We basically ate our way around the globe, being fed constantly. The funniest moment was when, only a couple of hours after dinner, the lights came back on and the flight attendants came merrily down the aisles saying, "Good morning...breakfast!" It was like a spa prison camp...wake up and eat more. So, there we were at about 1 a.m. eating breakfast after we'd just had dinner not long before and only a short nap in between. We landed in Amsterdam in the 7 a.m. hour there, making our earlier breakfast a bit more sensible. We only had about an hour between landing and boarding the next flight in which time we played on a playground, saw a beautiful living room like area where the airport library that I'd heard about on NPR about a year ago was. They even had a café in which you sat in giant teacups to eat! It was like Disneyworld! (:

We landed in Uganda about 10:30 local time and were greeted by three guys from Loving Hearts Babies Home with a sign that read, "Welcome Gilbart Edward Family!" Hee hee. By the time we got to Loving Hearts, all was very dark and quiet and we went upstairs to our "suite" where we each have a room. Ellie and Chad are in a room with twin beds, we're in a king bed room and Liza is in another twin bed room. We took freezing cold "showers" the next morning (showerlike head on hose in bathtub) and requested the hot water be turned on later in the day, which it was. After getting dressed, we went downstairs and met Martha Jane! She is more amazing than my wildest imagination. Full of smiles and a beautiful dimple on one cheek. She clung to me all day, but wouldn't let anyone else hold her, except Ellie by the end of the day. Ellie and Chad loved all over her all day and she loved kisses from Terrell as long as he didn't try to hold her. She did fall asleep with him mid-day on a sofa on our balcony. After lunch, she took a nap with me in our big bed and when she awoke, rather than being scared, she looked around, spotted me, and gave the biggest most beautiful smile. We took her to dinner at a Greek restaurant in walking distance of the babies' home, and she was wide-eyed at the sky above, the trees and all the new sights and sounds. She ate most of my potato salad. (:

We brought her back and she eventually had her medicine, a bottle, and went to bed in her own familiar crib with another big smile. She is now playing peek-a-boo with Ellie and puts one hand over her eyes and then just smiles.

We'll head to town shortly to the U.S. Embassy to get registered, to the grocery store and bank. Martha Jane has to stay here during that but will get to sleep with us tonight. I'll try to check back in soon…and send pictures when I can.

I love you all!

- *Jane (:*

Terrell and I woke up about 2:30 a.m. last night and were wide awake until about 4:30. In that time, I realized it was just when you were having the church planting meeting and I prayed for that while you were meeting. Little hands are grabbing my shirt so I better go. Love love love!

August 30, 2011 - 4:14 a.m.

The internet comes and goes, but just wanted to let you know I love you. I of course have a cold, but it is no wonder with the coughing and runny noses of all these little children. They are precious and I wish you could be here. You are going to adore Martha Jane…it would be hard not to of course.

The Target brand Robeeze I bought for MJ are too big (I bought 18 mo. size and they look like clown shoes on her!) and was wondering if it would be too difficult to grab a smaller pair to send with Laura Hill (Laura McCall who heads over here this weekend?). I was trying to find the closest thing to solid white and ended up with a pair that I think you saw, white with three bright flowers on them. They may have more at Target in the 12 mos. size. She'll survive without shoes, though, if that is too much of a pain. But maybe like camp, you could send a little note in them and it would feel like a bit of you.

I can't wait to hear from you both. I love you.   - *Jane (:*

August 31, 2011 - 12:30 p.m.

Our judge would not see us and could possibly rule against us because he is unpredictable, apparently. He may ask Ellie and Chad questions, and they could be something like, "Your mommy will have a new baby and not love you anymore?" It scared Ellie. Our lawyer is apparently going to the U.S. next week so is passing our case off to his father and another lady in his office. Our phone didn't arrive until yesterday and is not equipped as it was supposed to be and we can't reach Claire at Lifeline. My internet won't work so the email about meeting Martha Jane that I wanted people to see a couple of days ago is stuck in my outbox. (Whine whine whine) But, the gist of all of this is that I am so so exhausted, emotionally and physically, and scared and don't know how I can make it five more weeks when it has only been five days. The beautiful news in all of this is that Martha Jane is extraordinarily attached to me. She won't let anyone else hold her, now including the aunties here who she used to prefer over me. For the first time, tonight, she screamed and cried at being placed back in her familiar crib and being left by me. That was not so helpful for my emotional state. They said she is fine to stay with us in our room, but she has to have a crib, and I keep asking for them to bring a crib in, which they keep not doing and then telling me she can't stay with us. This is really hard. She won't let me put her down when I do have her, which is precious and exhausting.

Besides all that complaining, will you please pray that we **will** meet with the judge tomorrow (about 4 a.m. your time) and that he will miraculously be kind and easy on us? I don't have the emotional strength for interrogation.

On a really cool note, and for a later e-mail, we met the foster father of Martha's mom, who was a Compassion child. We also got to meet the landlady who cared for Martha Jane when her mom would leave her alone in the house to go out at night. We got the foster father's story on video and he is one of the area directors for Compassion, or was, or something. Amazing. He said that we don't give up on Brenda (Martha's mom) because God never gives up on us. But he also said that prayer is all he can do for her at this point. Incredible experience meeting him and all these Godly people who have been in Martha's life. But it is a lot to take in, and especially without yet sleeping through the night, not having a normal shower, not eating any vegetables or fruit yet and not exercising.

OK, I'm sounding far more negative than this all really should be. I'm just tired. I love you all and can't wait to see you when I arrive home WITH Martha Jane...not soon enough!

P.S. Without forwarding this, could you send a prayer request to anyone who seems relevant for our changed court date tomorrow? I know I shouldn't be, but I'm really scared. I know God is with us, but I also know sometimes His good plan involves heartache...and I'd really like this time for it to be something delightful rather than tragic. I'm so in love with this little muffin, it will rip my heart out to leave her here. Oh please God let us get a favorable ruling...and quickly!

Going to bed...yes, it's even early here, but I'm that wiped out. I love you all and am grateful for you! (I'm typing on Liza's computer.)

Aug. 31, 2011

From: Chuck Johnston
To: Jane Johnston Gilbert
Cc: Terrell Gilbert

Sent: Wednesday, August 31, 2011 9:52:37 PM

Subject: The dawn is coming

Your mom relayed the news of your message today, and it sounds like a bad dream. Let's assume that it is and that the new day (which will start seven hours earlier for you than for us) will dawn with a distinct feeling of the presence of the Holy Spirit. Be filled with that Spirit and assume that all of you will find favor before this judge. There is no reason that the judge might not be kind to Ellie & Chad and reasonable in his questions to you & Terrell. Don't assume anything different.

I was in the kitchen washing the last dish when I got tears in my eyes thinking of being at the airport and greeting you, Ellie, Chad, Martha Jane, and Liza when you get off the plane. I miss all of you, and Terrell, so very much.

Will Brown & Daisy are spending the night in our house tonight. The kitchen was delivered today, and the alarm system won't be operable until tomorrow, and there will be Will on his pad and sleeping bag. Mark told Will how worried he was, and Will just volunteered. What a guy!

Sept. 1, 2011 — Jane to me

I cried at this when I read it this morning and am grateful for it now. I forgot to copy myself or Terrell on the report I just sent. Would you forward it to us? Thanks! I love you.

Sept. 1, 2011 — Jane, prior to the events that follow

Subject: still waiting to be seen

If we aren't seen today, Isaac thinks it should definitely be tomorrow. (:
Thanks for your prayers and please keep 'em coming!

Thursday, Sept. 1, 2011 — Received 3:30 EDT / 10:30 p.m. in Uganda

Subject: Praise Jesus! Praise Jesus! Praise Jesus!

(I refer to Martha Jane as Martha as long as we are here in this home and in court, because that is how she is known and it is just simpler. But, Martha Jane she will be as soon as we are on our own.) Mawtha is actually how it is said! (:

I would say this has been one of the most emotional experiences of my life, but we all know that is a lie...moving, trying to sell our condo...and so on. But this sure makes the short list. I reached the end of my strength and stamina last night, worn down by cold showers and little food on top of the emotional toll of bonding with an amazing new family member. I have consistently woken up in the 2 a.m. hour each night (7 p.m. your time) and remained awake as noon time for a couple of hours, which is not helpful for facing the world in any circumstance.

So, we leave for court for the second day today, get stuck in traffic with 20 minutes until our newly scheduled time, at which point they tell us people are often stuck in these jams for an hour. God, I know your good will for making all things new includes missing court and all sorts of worthwhile suffering, but please oh please could you just love me in my weakness right now and get us through this. At that very moment, we moved totally out of it and got to the attorney's office on time. But of course they seemed in no hurry. We got over there to the waiting room where we sat and sat and sat. Around 2, our lawyer told us it did not look good for being seen today but it is better to wait until 7 p.m. and be assured of a spot tomorrow than to go on home and risk being re-scheduled weeks out. So we waited and waited some more. Then we learned the judge was going to lunch and at this point it was close to 5.

Meanwhile, the ladies who came yesterday from the village where Martha was born and who took care of Brenda, her mother, and Martha when she was left in the house alone each night, sat patiently with us for the second day. Martha finally warmed up to one of them and allowed her to hold her while she simultaneously allowed me to get up and get a protein bar from my backpack across the room. Amazing. (; This woman spoke Luganda to Martha who understood perfectly. She then showed pictures of her home, her family, and the "house" where Martha's mother lived with her for her first two months of life. It was one of those board houses you see where the boards don't exactly touch each other and the roof is corrugated tin and the windows are open with rags covering them. No wonder they could get to the screaming baby each night when she was left alone and then to finally find her when her mother left for good.

They then told me that they had come back for her, to take her home with them and care for her. This took me by surprise and my heart sank even as it felt somehow right. But when they learned she had a new family and that she was sick, they went home and prayed about it and believed it was right for her to go with the new family. That alone wrenches my inner everything as I think of the sacrifice they willingly made for one they hunted down and travelled so far to find and clearly love deeply. So, as I took all this in, we continued to wait, and sweat, and Martha who had missed her afternoon nap got quite squirmy.

She finally fell asleep and we finally were led into the judge's chambers with another family having their hearing and two individuals who were there for their ruling. As we all filed in silently and sat in chairs around the edge of the room, having warned our children to ask no questions and be very still, Martha suddenly awoke with a piercing cry and wouldn't be consoled. I rushed her out of the room not knowing protocol and just had to go with it. Another family had lollipops and when I returned, I kept that thing in her mouth as long as it would last. Finally, after everyone else, it was our turn. We were prepared for the accusations he supposedly brought to families of harvesting organs that their biological children need, or questioning children about their role in the process, or demanding why we would come here for their children when we were healthy enough to have our own...etc. We were to call him "My Lord" and take the insulting questions as reasonable.

Instead, and I cry even to think back on it, he gave a long discourse to us about the integrity of the United States, the genuine humanitarian role that is even better at times than his own people demonstrate and the genuine care for children that he has witnessed. He then praised our recommendations, which people had written with full disclosure, and said he knew that we truly cared for children and that we led lives of genuine service to others (he doesn't really know, but that was awfully nice) and that it was clear we had holy intentions for the best welfare of children. (And he is Muslim and often makes derisive remarks about Christians.) Martha was getting so squirmy and I was sweating like a dirty runner on MARTA after a long run on the 4th of July and exhausted all I had left keeping her from screaming even as I was overwhelmed by tears at this man's response to our family. **Let it not be missed the role that Liza played!!!!** He was so impressed that we had brought a mother along and said nobody with wicked intentions brings their mom along. (:

Our social worker from the babies' home and our lawyer were giddy upon departure. He has even given us a ruling date in less than a week...next Wednesday at 2:30! It is possible we could come home earlier than expected, but I won't jump the gun on that.

In Uganda, Terrell, Jane, and Liza celebrate with Ellie, Martha Jane, and Chad

As we walked outside, it was time to say final goodbyes to the ladies who had travelled two days in a row and sat patiently in this court on behalf of little Martha. They began to walk away toward a taxi and I caught them because I felt they needed the chance to say goodbye to their baby. As I reached them, I of course burst into tears and handed Martha to them. They then began to cry and there we stood, hugging and crying on the sidewalk as they said goodbye to the one they rescued and were letting go, likely never to see again. Oh man. I can't stop crying even as I write it out. She is the most loved baby from so many directions and I promise you are going to fall in love with her too.

I'm hoping to sleep through the night tonight and will try to get my "Meeting Martha Jane" e-mail out this weekend if I can finally get the internet to work on my computer. I am typing the e-mails I can quickly find into this one, but please feel free to forward this to anyone you think might be interested. Also, if you are one who gets it forwarded and aren't typed in above, please extend to grace to my tired self who is on someone else's computer. I don't have Karen and Sarah's e-mail, for example, on my phone for some reason...it is in my temporarily defunct computer.

I am so grateful for your prayers and love and support and encouragement. Adoption, as Sassy and Melissa can testify, comes at a huge price. But what a small taste of the adoption earned for us.

Overwhelmed by His mercy,

Jane (:

Sept. 2, 2011 — Dick to Chuck

And I, also, teared up badly at this story. Jane writes so well (and correctly), and her e-mails from Uganda should be preserved for their family archives. Someday Martha Jane will be reminded of how much her parents and siblings wanted her. And how much her native village did to love her and preserve her life.

Sept. 2, 2011 — Dillon to Chuck

The news from Jane was a great relief. Martha sounds wonderful. Thank you as well for sharing with your wider family this adoption of what must seem like an entire continent.

Sept. 6, 2011 — Jane to Jonathan

I am just getting online for the first time since last Thursday and read Dad's e-mail and the news report about your crash. Ellie, Chad, Liza and Terrell were gathered around the computer as I read it all to them. We are more than celebrating your life and grateful that God protected you in such dramatic fashion. We love you so much!!!! Thank you Jesus for sparing Jonathan!!!!!

Sept. 6, 2011 — Jane to Chuck

I miss hearing from you directly...not meaning to be demanding of a personal e-mail of course, but I am spoiled by our daily visits at home that I feel a real void without knowing your thoughts about life there and what we have shared about life here. I got a sweet e-mail from Guinn, which lets me know you forwarded my e-mail. Thanks for keeping us all connected. I love you and miss you!   ~ *Jane* (:

P.S. I had the flu this past weekend, with fever 100-101.5 for three days. Awful. I thought I was going to have to come home...but that was just in my delirium. We spent the weekend in Jinja which was really pretty and a place that might be a better destination than Kampala. We're hoping to move to Bridge Africa this Friday. I'll write more soon.

Sept. 8, 2011 — Jane to JoElyn and Chuck

I need to be asleep because we have an early start to the day tomorrow... leaving at 7 a.m. this time to head to the IOM (international office of medicine...I think) for Martha Jane's physical for her visa. Our appointment is at 9. After that, we're going to the Entebbe Zoo which is supposed to be pretty cool. That might be about an hour away. We'll come back, finishing packing our stuff, and move from the babies' home to Bridge Africa. As challenging as it has been living here, we've also covered a lot of ground in this little three-bedroom, two-bath quarters. It will be sad to leave for that reason, and that all the people here are amazing and love Martha so much and she lights up when they just say her name. After we move, we're supposed to meet the 60 Feet group for dinner when I'll see Laura and get those shoes. That will pretty much wipe us out and I'm sure beds will feel oh so good. Martha Jane's personality is coming out more and more and she is a clown! She is a happy happy baby who knows how to get us to laugh. She is so smart and picks up on things right away. It's like having a foreign exchange student living with you...they don't really know your language but want to please and pick up on little tricks to win the crowd. She does have some good pipes as you get to hear them when she requires a diaper change or you come to the end of the food she is enjoying. But who is to blame her...don't those things bum us all out? (:

I'm not connected to the internet right now, so hopefully I'll be able to get this to you in the morning before we leave. You'll get it sometime tomorrow. Like snail mail, kind of. Let's try to Skype sometime soon. I'll try to get Terrell to set it up on my computer before he goes. It would be fun to talk with real voices and to see you and for you to see Martha Jane and for her to see you before we come home. Oh how I love you and miss you...I haven't exercised in TWO WEEKS. It is a different world here...not like being on vacation and not exercising...more like being on "Survivor" and not exercising. (: Boy, when

I was sick this past weekend, my legs were hardly able to walk. That was not a good time.

Please pray that we'll be able to have our passport to the embassy by Wednesday at 10 a.m. I really want to come home.

Good night.

Dick to Chuck, What a Difference a Day Makes

Another great communiqué. We are learning interesting things from Jane way out here in Colorado. This will be a huge memory for Ellie and Chad. Thanks for sending it, Chuck. Please convey to Jane how much we've enjoyed her beautifully written, highly colorful, and certainly educational memoir.

Friday, Sept. 16, 2011 — Jane to Chuck

I miss knowing about the days in the life of you. It has now been exactly three weeks since my last run, which was pretty lame as I had not been sleeping well and left your parking lot to return home dizzy with fatigue. This might be the slowest week of our time here. But tomorrow afternoon we are going with our housemates to another friend's place for a play date and to order pizza! We had no idea pizza could be ordered in this place, but they have been here for 6 months and have learned a lot.

I'm so so tired and need to go to bed now. But I love you and am anxious to see you and Mom. If you can't get a pass back to the gate, try to shove your way to the top of the escalator so I can give you and Mom a huge hug as soon as possible. I'll probably cry, if I am not too travel weary to feel anything by that point. (: Hee hee. Oh, and I wrote a blog post today for the first time in weeks.

Love you both so much!

Sept. 19, 2011 — From Terrell to family, "A Visa for Our Daughter"

Just keeping everyone in the loop on something that shouldn't mess up the travel plans, but is a current snag. In short, the Embassy still hasn't received our updated fingerprints from August. Jane is working with the Embassy on her end and our adoption agency is working on it from their end. I've also spoken with someone in Senator Isakson's office and you can see my email below for a little more explanation.

I'll keep everyone updated.

Sept. 19, 2011 — From Terrell back to Jane and Liza in Uganda

Jane and Mom (and everybody),

The guy from Isakson's office called back and said that his contact at the immigration office could see on the system that something had been received by the National Visa Center today. It makes sense that it was the fingerprint file. (He couldn't think of anything else it could possibly be.) If it turns out that it was actually the fingerprint file, it should have been uploaded and Freda at the Embassy should have instant access to it. He couldn't confirm anything and said he'd call if he got any further confirmation. However, it looks like the fingerprint file has been received and uploaded, and that Freda should have access. Should be ok for travel. I'll let you know if I hear anything else.

Sept. 20, 2011 — From Jane to family

This gives everyone a taste of each step of this process that we have experienced here. Nothing can be taken for granted, even to the very last step. While I have been at such peace this week, even enjoying the little things here that I realize are special about this time, there is a low-level yet intense stress underlying each meeting, appointment, and task in this checklist. I'm not sure I realize or will fully process the enormity of this process while still running through it, but I know that when I finally get to see you all of you, it will feel like coming to the finish line of a marathon that has taken every reserve to complete. But God gives us more grace, and we feel that strength sustaining us, even through Chad throwing up all over me twice last night and Martha consistently pooping all over like it's her job. (: God also provides humor (the potty humor never fails, right?) and we will look back on these days with warmth even as we hopefully hightail it out of here Thursday.

Sept. 20, 2011 — From Chuck to Jane

While you have been experiencing your ordeal of great magnitude and lifetime-lasting significance, your mom and I have been experiencing a comparatively minor upheaval: we are moving. In the midst of making decisions regarding components of the rebuilt house on Evelyn Way, she has over an extended period of time organized our move. When we finally are sleeping on Evelyn Way, we will have given away about two-thirds of our book collection. We have swamped Goodwill with things that maybe we used early in our marriage, but now had forgotten that we even had these things, whatever they are. Your mom has taken down perhaps 100 framed wall hangings and has patched the nail holes so that our wonderful lease-to-purchase couple (Jane and Larry Vickers) will have a fresh-feeling home to move into.

Here is our timetable: you and your traveling party come in Friday afternoon. Saturday morning the Westside Moving Company comes and moves our boxes—and most of our life is now in boxes. (Hop City has been our godsend on boxes. Every day they put out a fresh supply, and nearly every day I come by and pick them up.) They take two-thirds to Evelyn Way and one-third to the storage unit. Saturday afternoon, Sunday and Monday, JoElyn and I move pictures and lamps, and Tuesday some professional movers (the ex-cons that Jonathan used and recommends highly) move all the furniture. We have this delay in moving the furniture because we have to let the floors dry 100%. From Tuesday night on, we will be two doors down from you and ready to be a daily part of your life. I have set aside books that I want to read to my grandchildren, some for Ellie & Chad, and some for Martha Jane. I'm also going to put out our big chess set so I can play chess with Ellie & Chad. I'm excited about their creating a clubhouse under our house.

Thanks for your good communications. I love you and am proud of you.

Sept. 20, 2011 – Jane to Chuck and JoElyn

We had a very successful goodbye/thank you party at Loving Hearts Babies Home today. We were the hosts and provided a cake, rolexes (not the watch but these delicious chapate egg wraps), soft drinks and juice boxes. Martha looked like a homeless child by the end who would be focused in on and advertised as only requiring a cup of coffee a day to support this pathetic little one. She had bathed in mango juice and given herself a facial with the cake. But then Aisha, our house mate and Ugandan child soon to be an Oregon child, washed Martha's dress for her better than our machine at home ever could. (She is only 3 1/2 but once children can walk they are expected to work in their homes. Ellie and Chad don't get it.)

I haven't heard anything today about the fingerprints, but am just continuing to hope they will be in as they are needed and that we'll get our visa tomorrow.

We FINALLY got the shoes you sent TODAY and the sweet notes to Ellie, Chad and Martha. Martha at first marched in them, looking down to try to understand these new weights on her feet. But she is walking freely and happily in them now. They will be so great on the airplane and in airports on our way HOME.

I'm sorry that your move is taking so long and seems a long way still from being behind you. I remember wanting more than anything just to be living normal life out of our home rather than having all of our hours be about the home itself. That day will come, though. You will be settled soon and hopefully find some time to rest on the other side of all this. Try to remember that this is a huge huge thing that has been anticipated for YEARS and will not have to be repeated a few months after unpacking.

I look so forward to living daily life as neighbors, wandering down to your front porch for just a few minutes or a long evening.

I'm assuming we'll be somewhat in the zombie stage the night we return, but I sure would love it if you could come home with us. You may be in the zombie stage already with all this move stuff, though. I just miss you two so much and want to snuggle in your big bed, sit around your living room and get back to running and bagels and all the precious things of life. I love you.

Appendix 10

Uncle Dick Receives a High Honor Indeed from Vanderbilt

The following article appeared in *Vanderbilt Medicine,* a Vanderbilt University Medical Center magazine, in 2012.

Photo by Daniel Dubois

A Scholar and a Gentleman

Richard Johnston Jr., M.D., MD '61, dedicates life's work to improving the health of children

By Jessica Ennis

When women of childbearing age wake up in the morning and pour their favorite cereal into a bowl, they can thank the efforts of Richard B. "Dick" Johnston Jr., M.D., for helping them have a better chance at delivering a healthy baby.

Research found that consuming folic acid prior to and during the early stages of pregnancy reduced the occurrence of neural tube defects. What better way to do so than by putting it into staple foods like bread and cereal? "It was during Dr. Johnston's tenure as our medical director that the March of Dimes began its national folic acid awareness campaign. His leadership was crucial to bringing the nation's obstetrician-gynecologists, pediatricians and women's nurses together with the March of Dimes to urge all women of childbearing age to [take] folic acid every day beginning before pregnancy," said Jennifer Howes, M.D., president of the March of Dimes.

Johnston went directly to David Kessler, M.D., who served as U.S. Food & Drug Administration (FDA) commissioner from 1990 to 1997, to urge that folic acid be added to the nation's grain supply. Kessler, a pediatrician and lawyer, was best known for taking on "big tobacco" in FDA v. Brown & Williamson Tobacco Corp.

"I remember going to Dr. Kessler's office with letters from the pediatric, obstetrical, and genetic academic and professional societies and the March of Dimes to urge that folic acid be added to fortified grains," Johnston said. "When I rose to give Dr. Kessler the letters, two lawyers jumped in front of me. He waved them aside and said, 'It's OK, I know these people.' After consulting his nutrition experts in the room, he turned back to me and said, 'We'll have this out by December.' He's a hero for me."

Despite much opposition outside the medical community, the FDA ruling was enacted in 1998, since resulting in a one-third reduction of neural tube defects such as spina bifida in the United States. "We consider this a significant victory for America's mothers and babies because it's so rare to get the chance to prevent a major birth defect with such a simple, low-tech solution as food fortification," Howse said. Johnston first encountered the devastation of neural tube defects during his residency at Vanderbilt. "There was an entire ward occupied with children suffering from spina bifida," he said. "The opportunity to try to prevent these defects was spectacular."

Driven from an early age

A deep desire to make the world better has been a driving force in Johnston's life since he was a child.

Born in Atlanta in 1935, he lived there with his three younger brothers, reared by "outstanding parents" in a household filled equally with a love for athletics and literature. "Our father was an athlete. He had a personable, wonderful way about him," Johnston said. "We were fed on athletics. We set out to be the best, particularly in football and track. Our mother was extremely bright and had a particular sense for words. She raised us on Robert Frost and encouraged our reading of poetry."

Johnston came to Vanderbilt University in 1953 as a pre-med student, but instead of immersing himself in his studies, he was drawn to participate in extracurricular activities. "When I got to Vanderbilt, I was not a committed student nor was I an effective student," he said. He played halfback on the freshman football team until he had a career-ending anterior cruciate ligament tear midway through the season. Former teammate and longtime friend, Garrett Adams, M.D., MPH, president of Physicians for a National Health Program, remembers that Johnston became focused on academics after he was unable to play football.

"I remember visiting him in his dorm room," Adams recalled. "It was so neat. His desk was perfect. His books were in a small neat pile. It was the picture of neat academic pursuit and that's the way he's continued." As Johnston ramped up his studies, he also became more involved on campus, eventually being named Bachelor of Ugliness, which recognized the outstanding male undergraduate from his graduating class. "Somehow I accepted leadership roles, and a part of me has always wanted to be in those roles," he said. Johnston met his wife, Mary Anne Claiborne, Ph.D., at Vanderbilt in 1958, and they married in 1960.

"My grades improved dramatically after marriage, a reflection of the irreplaceable support Mary Anne has given me over the past 51 years," he said.

Johnston, Mary Anne and his brothers, Dillon and Chuck, were all philosophy majors at Vanderbilt.

Johnston paid for college and medical school by working summers at a YMCA camp in Atlanta. "When the camp ended at 3, I went to the pool and taught private lessons to kids," he recalled. "It taught me two things: I really loved interacting with kids—it was great fun for me—and it taught me how rewarding teaching is."

"Where my soul is"

When it was time for Johnston to settle on a career, he chose pediatrics and immunology. "Child health is where my soul is," Johnston said. "My professional goals are centered on doing something to improve the lives and health of children." Medical school was a challenging but satisfying time for Johnston. "I felt like I was tolerated and nurtured until I reached a higher level," he said. "I valued so much the sense of community that we had with the faculty, and the way they were devoted to teaching us was remarkable." Johnston appreciated the high expectations he felt throughout medical school and into his two-year pediatric residency.

"I was taught to never fall short of doing what was absolutely optimal for every patient," he said. "Whatever it took, that is what we were taught; anything short of the best possible was unacceptable."

During an immunology fellowship at Children's Hospital, Harvard Medical School, Johnston did immunology studies for the early development of the Haemophilus influenzae type B vaccine. Later at the University of Alabama-Birmingham he investigated why sickle cell patients were so susceptible to pneumococcal infection and found an abnormality in the phagocytosis-promoting complement system. These results were published in the New England Journal of

Medicine in 1973. He has since published 285 scholarly papers. Johnston first came to Colorado, where he and his wife live and work now, in 1977. He served as professor of Pediatrics at National Jewish Hospital and University of Colorado School of Medicine for nine years. He was recruited in 1986 to join the University of Pennsylvania as chair of the Department of Pediatrics and physician-in-chief at Children's Hospital of Philadelphia. He later joined the Yale School of Medicine, then found his way back to University of Colorado School of Medicine and National Jewish Health, where he has remained for the last 12 years. As the associate dean for Research Development, Johnston created and oversees four committees that the school uses to support research and determine its research priorities.

"He's indispensable," said E. Chester "Chip" Ridgway, M.D., executive vice chair of Medicine, Frederic Hamilton Professor of Medicine and senior associate dean for Academic Affairs at University of Colorado School of Medicine. "He approaches everything with grace and never comes to a problem with an agenda. Quite simply, he wants people to give ideas an honest evaluation. His passion is to push process forward and he has done that in spades on this campus."

Johnston has written and given talks on the subject of ethical decision-making in medical policy and practice and has urged other physicians to question authority and focus on evidence. "This belief is essential to the way I function," Johnston said. "I really resist being told that 'this is the truth.'"

Accomplished yet humble

It's that principle that has made his expertise and opinion a sought-after resource at many of the most respected medical organizations in the nation. He has been president of the Society for Pediatric Research, American Pediatric Society, and International Pediatric Research Foundation and is a member of the Institute of Medicine (IOM) of the National Academies of Science. He has chaired vaccine advisory committees for the FDA and the Centers for Disease Control and Prevention and has chaired seven IOM committees. He received the highest award in academic pediatrics, the Howland Medal, in 2008, in the footsteps of his Vanderbilt teachers and earlier Howland awardees, Amos Christie, M.D., and Mildred Stahlman, M.D.

Throughout his career, Johnston has remained a loyal supporter of Vanderbilt. In 2008, he was honored with the Distinguished Alumnus award. Johnston recently joined the Medical Center Advisory Committee for the Vanderbilt University Board of Trust. For his many accomplishments, Adams says Johnston has remained the same warm, unassuming, genuine person he met during their freshman year.

"The gift he brings is the unusual depth of academic research experience at the very highest levels," he said.

Far more important than his career, Johnston said, is being a father to three and a grandfather to seven. His elder son, Richard, a 1989 graduate of VUSM, is an orthopaedic surgeon and has been a physician for the Atlanta Falcons. His younger son, Claiborne, is a professor of Neurology and research leader at University of California-San Francisco.

His daughter, Kristin, is a pediatric clinical psychologist in Boulder, Colo. Johnston may be inspiring a third generation to pursue medicine. When meeting Jeff Balser, M.D., Ph.D., vice chancellor for Health Affairs, during Vanderbilt's 2010 reunion, two of Johnston's young grandchildren told Balser they wanted to go to medical school at Vanderbilt.

"If I've contributed anything to the world, it's being half of the parents of three spectacular children and now grandfather to their children," Johnston said. "That's the most fulfilling part of my life."

* * *

Postscript

After this article appeared, my friend Mark Riley sent Dick a note that his father, who had been Dick's mentor at Vanderbilt Med School, would be proud of him. And, as I passed along Mark's note, I added this:

"I'm proud of you, too, Dick. This article does a good job of capsuling your major professional accomplishments. What it doesn't capture are the med-student lives you have impacted. How many of today's doctors did you impact while they were young in their careers? How many did you lend your credibility to so that they could get research grants?

"Unless you write it, nobody will know how you have always put yourself out for your younger brothers. At first I was thinking of that all centered on Piedmont Road; but clear up to our current ages, you have taken an interest in everything we three have been doing. You've been an encourager to Dillon, Warren and me as well as to your nephews and nieces.

"You set a high standard for your younger brothers, but instead of rebelling against that standard, we all wanted to be like you. Just one small example: You didn't drink in college; so Dillon and I said to ourselves, 'If Dick can pull that off, then so can we.' I call what we had as The Johnston Boys a code of conduct and loyalty to each other—just like Jesse James and his brothers."

To which Dick replied: "Thank you for your kind note, Chuck. Anything I do for any of my brothers is a true joy and very fulfilling for me. That relationship is central to my life and well-being. I confess that I want my brothers to be proud of me; that's something that I've recognized recently. Thus, your taking the time for this note means a lot. I suppose we are like the James brothers, though slightly more reputable."

Appendix 11

Dillon's Poem: 'Lighter Than Air'
From *Hedge*, the privately printed book of Dillon's poems

An October Friday,
Leaves and cars stray by.
Ahead, a dirigible
Floats slowly, dream-
Like in the blue sky,
Lettered red on cream,
Vantage, ferrying to
And from the course,
Old pros. A look, around
Us in their hearse-
Like Oldsmobiles,
Galleries of gray-heads,
The handsome fairways
Of their faces hedged
Round with rough,
Some bearing the handicap
Of two strokes or triple
Bypass. Clapping hands
At the eighteenth green.

God! I hated golf
At twelve, caddying
For my father, half
Minding the score and jokes,
Half the club pool's
Flashing bodies.
My father's golfing pals;
That breath-held silence
Before his back
Swing; head down, a straight
Left arm, the clean thwack;
The balls arced flight, then
Bending for his tee;
His warm hand on my nape,
He'd stroll with me,
Understating, "Well,
I'm not in trouble."
Then years, the slow rise
From scratch to double-
Bogeys. Sure declension
From par to poor.
So, like these, he
Found the dirigible door
To float in this cloud dream
From whose vantage
Their age advances
Toward the cup;
Shadow looms, crowd's hush,
Before the last drop.

Excerpts from *The Shack*

Dillon Johnston spent many years of his notable career at Wake Forest University as a professor of literature. *The Shack: Irish Poets in the Foothills of the Blue Ridge* was published and presented in honor of Dillon by Wake Forest University Press on March 13, 2015.

Following are excerpts from the book:

"The beginnings of Wake Forest University Press are both moving and curious, as Dillon Johnston, the founder—who remains an advising editor—describes them: 'Our press began in 1974 when I met with Edwin Wilson, the provost of Wake Forest University, where I was teaching literature. Before approaching him, I had written an essay on Irish poetry for Shenandoah for which I had had great difficulty finding the poets' books (all three or four people I talked with at Oxford University Press in New York could not find Seamus Heaney on the Oxford list). Provost Wilson, remarkable for his balance of kindness and judgment, recognized the publishing need and agreed that the universities should contribute to, as well as be repositories for, literature.'

"Edwin Wilson also remembers the project: 'I knew that Dillon had good

Dillon,
professor and
poet

judgment and was familiar with the tradition of Irish poetry, and I was impressed by his willingness to devote energy and time to the experiment.'" (Page 9)

~

"From its foundation, the mission of Wake Forest University Press has been to introduce Irish poetry to an American audience." (Page 10)

~

"… these poems and reflections bring with them a transatlantic consciousness that increasingly come to define our lives. Not only did Wake Forest University Press bring the globe to Carolina, but also, in its way, introduced Wake Forest University to the world." (Page 14)

~

"Once we were lost on the way to a neighbour's house. The path seemed to curve endlessly, with slopes rising and falling on all sides. Vines looped, leaves rustled, birds flapped suddenly out of the undergrowth. It was beautiful afternoon, but we were afraid of dogs, shotguns, men in trucks, the perilous-looking gorge with its rush of water. Anything might happen.

"And then we turned a corner, and there they were, Dillon's neighbours, standing on a lawn, laughing, and drinking from tall glasses. And there was Dillon himself, on a swing beneath a venerable tree, flying back and forth, up and down, a scholar and a gentleman, but also like a child." — A Stoot Remembrance, John Montague and Elizabeth Wassell (Page 25)

~

"We live in each other's long shadows." — Ciaran Carson (Page 37)

~

"We did a reading that night, in the conservatory of Reynolda House. I remember leaning on the grand piano, knees knocking with nerves, while Dillon introduced me in terms so flattering as to render me unrecognizable to myself.

"When did I last see Dillon? … Or during a sojourn in rural Missouri, when I became convinced that Dillon and Tony La Russa were twins separated at birth. … I still even chuckle at the thought of him shuffling to the gate of 'the shack,' hands in pockets and eyes shark-dead to ask: 'You boys lookin' for trouble?' I hope he is well wherever he is, still himself, and that our paths cross once more." — Connor O'Callaghan (Pages 48, 50)

~

"Wherever we are—in North Carolina or Missouri, in Belfast or County Mayo—we talked about the inner adventure of poetry. Dillon's shack reminds me of Ciaran Carson's belief that civilization depends on what a few enthusiasts generate in small back rooms. To quote Derek Mahon, the shack was a place 'where a thought might grow.' Who is more thoughtful than Dillon? He is a visionary. Many Irish poets give thanks that he has so resolutely kept his head in the clouds." — Michael Longley (Page 52)

Appendix 12

Warren's Newspaper Column

Warren prepares a Thanksgiving dinner in 2016. (Photo was featured with one of his syndicated "Raise Your Glass" wine columns.)

Warren Johnston began his career in journalism in 1978 after having spent his initial eight post-college/adult years in Atlanta real estate and as an Atlanta restaurateur. Then after a year in UGA's School of Journalism where he met Sandy, he embarked on a forty-year career of newspaper writing and community activism that took him to the Carolinas, Natchez, Tampa, and Las Vegas before capping off his career with the *Valley News* on the New Hampshire/Vermont border. He wrote a regular column in that paper, and the following is one of my favorites.

Pepita

(Valley News, Dec. 24, 2011)

Her early years were a bit dodgy. We're not sure what they called her, or how she earned her keep. We don't know when she arrived in Las Vegas or in the world for that matter, or even how she came to grief, resting on the edge of the chopping block, until my wife Sandy reached in and snatched her back.

There, of course, were rumors and a great deal of speculation. Some said she'd lived with a dancer or stripper, others with an old lady who died, or perhaps a rakish gambler who tossed her aside when times got tough, throwing her down the chute that landed her in the canine equivalent to the Bangkok Hilton.

The Dewey Animal Correctional Facility was a dank, cavernous tomb where we found her cowering in the back of a cage, shaggy white face stained with tears, black eyes pleading. She sat silently, surrounded by brutish pit bulls, German shepherds and Dobermans all vying for our attention, all demanding that we take them home.

Sandy plucked her from her predicament, just as we heard the footsteps of the matron pounding down the darkly lit corridor, the sound coming toward us like the harbinger of the dark angel of death.

"If you want her, and I don't know why," the matron croaked, "you'd better take her now. She's been here three days, and that's all she gets, not a minute more."

So, we rescued Pepita, drank some beer, ate salty roasted pumpkin seeds and discovered that her name really was Pepita — coincidentally the Spanish word for pumpkin seeds — something she knew all along and was quite pleased that it had finally dawned on us.

She and Sandy bonded immediately — well, why wouldn't they? — staying up all of that first night, talking about who knows what, dozing occasionally on the couch. They had so much to catch up on, a future to plan and a past to forget. Their devotion, set that night, never faded.

Pepita was quite an athlete in her youth, a great runner, very fast, even with her short legs. She once challenged me to a 1,200-meter race, out our front door, down Mason Avenue to Charleston Boulevard, where, deterred by the heavy traffic, she turned, heading back the block between us to mock me.

She was the queen of the chicken rodeos, sprinting 100 feet, catching the tossed giant rubber chicken before it hit the ground, grabbing it by its middle, hustling back to the starting line, with its feet flapping against the ground on one side, head on the other. Along with her reputation on the chicken rodeo circuit, her name also grew, becoming Pepita Fajita Lolita Perrita, Reina del Rodeo de Pollo, a name that means little in either Spanish or English but that was often recounted on those euphoric occasions when one lifts a glass to such celebrity.

She also was a herder, making sure our cat Big Walter Horton came in for the night with a gentle nose up his butt, or moving along young toddlers she'd meet on the sidewalk using the same method when they needed a nudge. She once showed her weightlifting skills one hot summer day by boosting a shocked two-year-old girl off the ground with just a cold nose up the back of her dress.

In New England, she took to snow like an otter to an icy stream, diving into the drifts, bursting out with great sprays of enthusiasm. She'd had prior experience during a freak spring 30-incher in Utah, where her long fur became so balled up with the wet snow that Sandy had to carry her stuffed down the back of her jacket like a child riding on a parent's shoulders, all the while balled snow melting down Sandy's back while Pepita relaxed during the three-mile ride home.

During our first Christmas in New Hampshire in 2002, Pepita embraced the freshly fallen three feet of snow by jumping off our front porch and plunging head-first into the drift, leaving only a wagging tail exposed.

She successfully avoided the pain of meeting porcupines, whether by good sense or happenstance, but she rarely missed an opportunity to confront skunks, meetings that invariably left her on the losing end and our house with a fragrant reminder for months afterward.

It's unclear when the conversion happened, perhaps during her early teens — her 70s as you might — but Pepita became a Buddhist, preferring to live and let live, her Tibetan heritage kicking in. She gave up the pursuit of skunks, voles, small mice and rubber chickens, and took to contemplating birds in flight, the beauty of sunsets and the vistas from her spot on Pee Dee Hill — aka our septic mound — and to teaching her younger sister, Imelda, the value of serenity and patience. Oh sure, she still liked a healthy hike, albeit at a thoughtful pace, particularly with friends Ruby, Eleanor, Barney and, of course, her teammate Imelda. She trod a light foot in the forest, but made sure her passing did not go unnoticed, leaving few trails around this part of Vermont that had not been carefully inspected, marked and remarked.

She fought a thyroid condition for years and the bladder cancer for months, until it got to her lungs and finally slowed her.

Pepita taught us a lot, cheered us through rough patches and gave us comfort with her kindness. She had a good run, and now, it's nice to think of Pepita, able to take in a full breath again, cavorting in the snow, digging for voles and scampering after her departed friend, Barney, the unrequited love of her life.

On the snowy, cold Christmas Eve when we buried Pepita out by the apple trees, Imelda sat by her grave, preferring a long vigil to the warmth of the woodstove and a sibling-empty house. We lingered too.

***

Shortly before Valentines Day, Isadora Maebelle arrived at our house, another shaggy, white Tibetan-influenced terrier like Pepita, the same black eyes as Pepita's and the mild manners of Pepita. Oh, there are some noticeable differences. For one, she's less than a year old and her young life has been pretty rough, far from the glamour of Las Vegas, but it doesn't seem to burden her. She's filled with a zest for fun, seemingly unimpaired by her puppyhood that has already had the adult worries of a litter and has not been overflowing with love or appreciation. (Two kindly women passing by rescued her and her brother from the side of a north Georgia country road where they waited for days for the people who had dropped them off to return and take them home, fur matted and heartworm infected.)

We didn't know what Isadora called herself when she arrived, but after a little time and an evening of beer and some roasted pumpkin seeds, it seemed quite clear to be Isadora, the gift of Isis, the Egyptian goddess who looks after puppies abandoned on country roads, although she said she preferred to be called by the less formal nickname of Izzy, or even Izzy Mae when she wanted to be reminded of her Southern heritage.

Now, Imelda, who is a couple years older, and Izzy are working together as a team. They mine our winter-spotted yard like gold prospectors working a vein as they root and dig through the thin snow pack from grass patch to grass patch following the trails of mice and voles, hopping, bouncing and always hopeful of pay dirt. And inside the house, they share toys, watch out the windows and comment frequently on the squirrels or birds that pass their view.

Maybe this spring, we'll see how Izzy does with a rubber chicken. She seems interested.

CPSIA information can be obtained
at www.ICGtesting.com
Printed in the USA
LVHW101258130821
694765LV00007B/2